KA NGARO TE REO

Ka Ngaro Te Reo

Māori language under siege in
the nineteenth century

PAUL MOON

OTAGO

*This work is dedicated to Erima Henare (1953–2015),
who supported this book from the outset.*

Published by Otago University Press
Level 1, 398 Cumberland Street
Dunedin, New Zealand
university.press@otago.ac.nz
www.otago.ac.nz/press

First published 2016
Copyright © Paul Moon

ISBN 978-1-927322-41-3

Editor: Gillian Tewsley
Index: Diane Lowther
Cover photo: Rob Suisted, Nature's Pic Images: www.naturespic.com

Printed in New Zealand by Printing.com Ltd, Wellington

CONTENTS

Introduction

For a few weeks in March 1834, the Austrian botanist Baron Charles von Hügel trudged his way through the tangled undergrowth of Northland's forests collecting botanical specimens for a garden he was planning to establish near Vienna.[1] For men like von Hügel (and they were nearly always men) New Zealand in this era was an ideal place to satisfy their snatch-and-grab curiosity, freely appropriating in this case whatever exotic flora caught their interest. Midway through his expedition, he reached the Anglican mission station at Waimate North,[2] which was no more than a small huddle of settler buildings on a roughly hewn clearing hemmed in on all sides by thick bush.[3] Von Hügel was keen to find out if Māori in the area had any knowledge about the specimens he had amassed, and with the assistance of the mission's head – Reverend William Yate – he approached a nearby Māori on the offchance that he may know the names of some of the plants he had collected. As Yate recorded, the man 'gave the names of all without exception … not one could be introduced, however minute, or whatever might be the hidden situation in which it had thrived, but a name was found for it'. This was an impressive feat, but was it a case of this local bluffing these credulous Europeans? To confirm the accuracy of the names that had been supplied, the following evening Yate called another Māori to share what he knew about the plants' identities. '[W]ith one single exception,' the missionary later wrote with obvious awe, 'out of three hundred specimens, he gave the same name to each, as had been given the night before. It is so likewise with respect to birds, fishes, insects, garments, and every thing else which they possess.'[4]

Yate took this comprehensive Māori vocabulary of the natural world as a cue to elaborate more generally on the expressive breadth of the Māori language (or te reo – literally, the language or speech): 'I never found a native at a loss to express any of the passions, feelings, sensations; any thing connected with joy, sorrow, good, evil … In short, there is scarcely any thing which we can imagine, but they have an expression for it,' to which he added pointedly, in defence of his own vocation, 'except it be some such words as express the Christian graces of hope, gratitude, charity, &c.; which words, and some few similar ones, always require to be New-Zealandized.'[5]

To be in New Zealand in this period would be to witness te reo Māori as the country's sole language. Apart from the small clusters of settlers who spoke English among themselves (approximately 300 in the mid-1830s),[6] te reo prevailed everywhere. And as Yate alluded to, the obligation lay with Europeans to adjust to te reo rather than Māori feeling under any obligation to learn English.

Of course, such a sanguine state could not last. The impact of colonialism on indigenous communities and their cultures during the nineteenth century followed the same broad atrophic arc throughout much of the non-European world. It started with a few probing jabs, and more often than not culminated with a knockout blow to the indigenous body politic and all its cultural and linguistic vestments. 'European colonisation' in the nineteenth century conjures up a generic type of intervention and consequences that usually circumvent the unique character of that colonisation in specific localities.

There were premonitory hints of the colonisation-to-come in the account of von Hügel's visit to Waimate North, with its metaphors of the penetration of the primitive, the collection, classification and compartmentalisation of indigenous knowledge by European interlopers, and their casual disregard for any aspect of Māori culture that was not deemed worthy of retention. This was especially true of the language, in which – unlike the country's plant life – the Austrian showed no interest. However, surely no one in the 1830s could have anticipated either the rapidity or the extent of the decline of te reo as the country's main language over the rest of the century. Yes, there remained stubborn pockets of resistance – linguistic outcrops of te reo where isolation gave the impression of it being impregnable. These increasingly became the exception that proved the rule of the power of English to assert its dominance and to advance into what were sometimes former strongholds of te reo with evident impunity. And as the tide of colonisation rose, Māori found themselves fleeing ever deeper into the cultural hinterland in often desperate efforts to maintain a cultural, linguistic and social space that they could claim as their own.

Any account of te reo in the nineteenth century inevitably becomes the history of two languages. English shadowed Māori, confronting it with challenges that it was ill equipped to handle, and as the century progressed the language of the coloniser began to eclipse that of the indigene. This book charts te reo's history through the century, assessing it against this linguistic intrusion. The basis for this approach is that the identity and history of languages are conjunctural, not essential. A language cannot remain an island entire of itself once it is confronted with another language; from that point onwards, its history is one of intersections with outside cultural and linguistic influences.[7] It becomes part of the continent of all languages – not as a fraternal member so much as an unexpected arrival vying for survival, drawn into a Darwinian-type process of natural selection.

The way in which this struggle is cast is important for the context of any historical analysis of te reo. The language was under siege by the forces of colonisation during this era. But some caution is needed with the notion that Māori linguistic purity in the nineteenth century was somehow violated through its contact with English, and that developments such as changes to the vocabulary and dialects of te reo necessarily had an adverse effect on the language. Such portrayals have long been part of the accompanying narrative of British colonial intervention in New Zealand, but they can end up playing into the hands of those essentialist[8] representations of te reo and Māori culture that depict them as being part of the untainted, exotic Other[9] and thus reinforce Western discourses of the primitive.[10] Changes to the language brought about by encounters with another language and by the diminution of speakers of the language are two separate considerations that overlap in certain points, rather than being a unitary development. English, after all, could never claim any sort of purity for itself, and yet its constant adulteration was a source of strength – a mark of its endless adaptability. It would therefore be illogical to apply a different measure to te reo by equating a decline in its so-called purity with the language becoming endangered.

One of the most common metaphors applied to te reo Māori in the latter half of the nineteenth century was that of extinction.[11] And after all, when looked at from almost any perspective at that time, what alternative was there? The Taranaki settler Thomas Gilbert put to paper the prevailing settler logic of the era regarding te reo's redundancy when he concluded, 'The Maori language sufficed for the requirements of a barbarous race, but it can never be made an instrument of refined spiritual thought, or become adapted to the higher purposes of life.'[12] Increasingly te reo was considered by some Europeans as at best a linguistic antiquity and, more realistically, a worthless anomaly with no place in the colony's progress.

Even as early as the 1860s, te reo's extinction was being seen as inevitable; and as with the ecological process that the notion of extinction is drawn from,[13] the progression that leads to language disappearance is entangled with everything else that is happening around it.[14] In the case of te reo there were wider political, economic, legislative, demographic, cultural and other forces bearing down on the language, putting at threat not just the Māori lexicon but the associated ideas, ways of knowing, perceptions, modes of living and all else that accompanied it.

There is an element of ambivalence that characterises the role of the coloniser in te reo's declining fortunes over the century. On the one hand, many early missionaries became proficient in te reo, preached and conversed with Māori in their own language and were almost exclusively responsible for the initial stages of te reo being converted into a written language. On the other hand, as the century wore on, the state accelerated – both intentionally and unwittingly at various times – the means by which some colonists hoped that te reo would eventually be extinguished. The threat to te reo had become so great that by the 1890s the consensus was that its fate, along with that of its speakers, was sealed. If this narrative of Māori as the classic example of a dying race was true[15] – and it appears most people by this time believed that was the case[16] – there was correspondingly no chance the language would outlive its speakers.

However, the relationship between tangata whenua and te reo worked differently from an indigenous perspective – as encapsulated in the whaka-tauki 'Ka ngaro te reo, ka ngaro taua, pera i te ngaro o te moa (If the language be lost, man will be lost, as dead as the moa)'.[17] The language and the people were indivisible so far as most Māori were concerned. This was no stubborn ideological position; on the contrary, the possibility of Māori without te reo was inconceivable.

There is a tendency to place too much store on the standard portrayal of yet another indigenous language being jostled and pushed to the point of extinction, as though it were some acquiescent cultural relic rendered suddenly helpless when confronted with the vigorous expansion of the language of the coloniser; or as though the arrival of English was the equivalent of some linguistic Big Bang that led to a cultural constellation emerging in the colony, and which cast te reo from the centre of the Māori universe into oblivion. Such depictions form part of the metanarrative of a 'fatal impact',[18] which not only overrides the nuanced history of te reo in the nineteenth century but positions Māori more generally in this period as passive indigenes, in contrast to the more assertive and implicitly culturally superior Europeans.[19] The fatal impact argument also risks overlooking the significance of Māori agency, which in this era manifested itself continually in encounters with the coloniser. The architecture of traditional Māori culture and society demonstrated its ability not only to withstand and sometimes even repel particular aspects of the British imperial onslaught,[20] but to adapt and modify itself to survive in the following century and beyond.

Three main themes are explored at various points in this book. The first is how the disruption inflicted on Māori society as a consequence of British colonisation both preceded and precipitated the breakdown in the use of te reo. The dogmatic pursuit by almost all branches of settler society throughout the century to 'civilise' Māori inevitably had an effect on te reo, frequently as a consequence of incursions taking place elsewhere in the culture. It becomes necessary at certain junctures to explore the overall apparatus of British colonisation during this era in order to develop a clearer understanding of how te reo's fate was enmeshed with it. The modernisation that accompanied British intervention in some cases had the effect of widening the rift between the Māori and settler societies throughout the century, with political, economic, cultural and linguistic power shifting steadily into the hands of the European core while Māori were being shunted further to the periphery. Te reo was unavoidably caught up in this process.

Secondly, there are numerous examples in this era of colonists learning te reo, translating English publications into the Māori language and taking steps to ensure te reo had, and then maintained, a presence in places such as the church, native schools and even branches of the government. However, while these might appear to be exceptions to the general grain of colonisation having an adverse effect on indigenous languages, the existence of such seemingly opposing trends ironically reinforced rather than undermined the coloniser's assault on te reo.[21] What look like individual fragments of support for te reo Māori take on an entirely different complexion when fitted into the overall colonial mosaic.

And finally, the effectiveness of successive nineteenth-century governments in eroding te reo's place in the country was achieved precisely because these administrations largely avoided formal efforts to ban the language outright. Instead, they put in place more subtle and definitely more effective measures to squeeze out the indigenous language and supplant it with that of the coloniser. Anyone searching for signs of outright prohibitions during this period will inevitably end up in a very short historical cul-de-sac; it is in the more circuitous routes of the policies of the state and other institutions to 'save and civilize the remnant of the Maori Race'[22] that the coloniser's stranglehold on te reo was progressively tightened. When Sir James Henare testified before the Waitangi Tribunal during the te reo Māori claim in 1985, he was asked about the fact that there was no official policy in the nineteenth century specifically outlawing te reo. He stated emphatically, 'The facts are incontrovertible. If there was no such policy there was an extremely effective gentlemen's agreement!'[23] An almost innate European aversion to te reo made it unnecessary to legislate prohibitions against the language: cultural and social pressures were a far more practical means of evisceration.

This book follows a mainly chronological sequence in addressing these themes and developments, with the occasional divergence. The opening chapter surveys the state of te reo Māori around 1800 and assembles some of the surviving fragments of information that suggest how Māori perceived the language at that time – perceptions that often differed in important ways from European notions of the nature of language. From this time, te reo had experienced intermittent encounters with outside languages, mainly English. Initially these were meetings on the margins, with occasional visits from whalers and sealers and slightly more frequent engagements with traders, almost exclusively in coastal parts of the country. In the hinterland the situation was very different: probably the majority of Māori had no contact at all with a language other than the one they were born to.

The nature of the world that te reo faced in the early colonial era has survived in its most immutable form in text; and it was the introduction of text to Māori society that was to lead to the biggest revolution in te reo. Writing was the medium of the coloniser, and it initially filtered and then reconfigured elements of Māori language and culture in ways that had momentous effects on the retention and transmission of te reo, especially once it started to appear widely in written form. This was also the commencement of the trend towards the greater standardisation of te reo in text, and although the process never reached the point of absolute uniformity, some of the more pronounced dialectical variations across the country were eventually narrowed down – in written form at least – in the process.

As the demographic balance of the colony shifted in favour of the settler population from the middle of the century, te reo Māori was portrayed more overtly by Europeans as a language that belonged to the country's less civilised past, and one that had little purpose in its increasingly anglicised future. When would-be anthropologists among the settlers considered te reo from this time, it was almost as if the language were some museum exhibit whose form could be studied and whose origins offered ample opportunities for imaginative speculation, but which had little purpose in the modern world of the Victorian era. Te reo was regarded as an anachronism, and the sooner Māori appreciated this fact and discarded it, the better.

The use of te reo could not just be switched off. From the inception of the colonial state in 1840, te reo and English were used by the government when communicating with Māori communities. By the second half of the nineteenth century, teams of translators from iwi across the country were trained and employed to handle the volumes of work arising from the requirement that the state be bilingual in certain areas of its activity. As the European population in New Zealand outgrew the Māori population, the proportionate role of te reo in the apparatus of the state diminished. And while the government employed translators to ensure that Māori understood its intent, it was also responsible for policies that effectively evicted the language from the education system and marginalised it in many other areas in society.

As te reo descended the path towards a likely terminal destination, there were diversions along the way, giving the occasional flicker of an impression that the language was still holding its own if not quite flourishing. Emerging Māori political and religious movements used te reo as the main medium of communicating their faiths and philosophies and, in more subtle ways, to signify the indigeneity of these movements. This affirmed and accentuated te reo's function as the language of religious rite and political ritual for Māori in the colonial era, just at the point where its role as the vernacular of Māori was becoming much more vulnerable to the forces of English.

This book concludes with an overview of the state of te reo as the century drew to a close – a time when all things Māori appeared to be going through their death throes. Given the dire condition of the Māori population by the 1890s, it is hardly surprising that this was when te reo reached its nadir. Yet a handful of people at the time refused to see the fate of the Māori language and population as being sealed: 'the case, though desperate, is not absolutely hopeless,' John Thornton, headmaster of Te Aute College, insisted in the winter of 1899. 'It is plainly our duty to do what in us lies to avert the threatened calamity.'[24] Just how forlorn things had become by the end of the 1800s can be seen in the fact that over a century later the threat of that calamity facing te reo has still not been expunged, and anything like a full recovery is still far from certain.

This work is less concerned with the minutiae of orthography, the quality of translations, grammatical evolution and related issues over the century. From time to time, such topics do arise – Henry Williams' translation of the Treaty of Waitangi is an obvious example – but in general, they are more incidental to some of the cultural, social, political, economic and other developments that altered the course of te reo's history and are the primary focus of this book.

A NOTE ON TRANSLATION

Translations for words in te reo that appear in this book are provided in the glossary. For longer extracts, or where there is a specific meaning attached to a segment, translations are included within the text.

ACKNOWLEDGEMENTS

There is a Ngāpuhi whakataukī that asserts that 'the whole of the body speaks through the mouth'.[25] This means that behind the voice is so much else that contributes to it. In a sense, the same principle applies to this book. Several people (some no longer with us) have contributed in numerous ways to the writing of this book – providing translations, discussing various ideas about language and offering invaluable cultural perspectives. They are listed here in alphabetical order.

Dr Richard Benton, Te Taurawhiri i te reo Māori Māori Language Commission; Dr Teena Brown Pulu, Auckland University of Technology; Professor Peter Cleave; Sir Toby Curtis; Erana Foster, Auckland University of Technology; Erima Henare, Chairman, Te Taurawhiri i te reo Māori; Maaki Howard, Auckland University of Technology; Matanuku Kaa; Professor Tania Ka`ai, Auckland University of Technology; Professor Pare Keiha, Auckland University of Technology; Dr Karena Kelly, Victoria University of Wellington; Hohepa Kereopa; Jason King, Auckland University of Technology; Te Haumihiata Mason, Te Taurawhiri i te reo Māori; Associate Professor Hinematau McNeill, Auckland University of Technology; Professor John Moorfield, Auckland University of Technology; Dr Dean Mahuta, Auckland University of Technology; Professor Margaret

Mutu, University of Auckland; Dr Wayne Ngata, Te Taurawhiri i te reo Māori; Dr Lachlan Paterson, University of Otago; Taina Pohatu, Te Whare Wānanga o Aotearoa; Robert Pouwhare, Auckland University of Technology; Ngamaru Raerino; David Rankin; Graham Rankin; Professor Michael P.J. Reilly, University of Otago; Professor Poia Rewi, University of Otago; Tom Roa, University of Waikato; Rachel Scott, Otago University Press; Mere-Hēni Simcock-Reweti, Te Taurawhiri i te reo Māori; Dr Valance Smith, Auckland University of Technology; Gillian Tewsley; Dr Ranginui Walker; Jack Wihongi.

CHAPTER 1

'He taonga tuku iho ngā tūpuna'

1800

A small group of manuhiri, all clad in heavy dark coats, bunch slightly closer together as a cold drizzle drifts in through the valley. Then the sharp sound of the karanga cuts through the gloom, calling these visitors towards the marae[1] where the tūpāpaku is lying in state. The manuhiri shuffle slowly and mournfully along the marae ātea – a prologue to the central part of this rite, the whaikōrero (a formal oration ritual), where speeches are exchanged, beginning with honouring the deceased and invoking the ancestors before unfurling in various directions. It is at solemn ceremonies such as this tangihanga where ritual and language coalesce into a single cultural experience and where the ties linking te reo to a much earlier period in the country's history appear to be at their strongest and most audible.

It is easy to be seduced by this sense of seamless continuity with the past, especially in the ambience of an old rural marae with its lichen-mottled wharenui, the worn and flaking exterior slowly being reclaimed by nature. The sombre sepia photographs of departed whanau in the dim interior tug at the deepest and most visceral sensations of history and tradition. Tangihanga have been played out across the country at places like this for centuries,[2] each one echoing the elements of those that have preceded it, like some apostolic succession. There is a specific topography of tradition evident here, in which te reo is one of the central organising features. However, its function also extends to providing a full-strength antidote to the culturally whitewashed modern world that exists just beyond the marae, where te reo is more likely to be constricted or made anomalous. At the marae, te reo maintains its elevated, even sanctified status.

In some ways the ritualised use of te reo Māori in practices such as tangihanga serves to consecrate the language by reprising centuries-old traditions and evoking the intimate cultural sentiments attached to those traditions. The language therefore becomes the main means by which the culture is made authoritative, partly through its ancient paternity, and partly through the links that it provides with the traditional era.[3]

Yet in certain fundamental respects the connection between the Māori language of 1800 and te reo of today is disjointed. Admittedly, the grammar has remained much as it was two centuries ago, and the lexicon has survived even though it has since been augmented enormously to accommodate the demands of a rapidly modernising society.[4] It is probable too that the principal pronunciation traits resemble those that were prevalent in the early nineteenth century.[5] What separates the language of 1800 from its modern incarnation, however, is the context in which it was nestled.

In 1800, te reo was not just the dominant language in New Zealand, it was the only language for Māori. With some very minor exceptions there was no conception of an alternative language, and so from the perspective of most Māori at that time it was the universal human language. Moreover, for Māori it was an entirely oral language, which had profound cultural and social implications for how knowledge was transmitted and stored, and who in communities took on these roles. And because Māori society was still overwhelmingly isolated from the rest of the world, te reo did not need to be held up by the sorts of political and social props that supported national languages in parts of Europe, for example, where the cultures connected to those languages had evolved mechanisms to preserve them in the face of linguistic competition from their neighbours.

What is noticeable is the extent to which te reo was entwined in the culture and society that it occupied: it could even be possible to argue that the language was the culture and the culture was the language. Te reo was the means of constructing meaning, and was part of the collective psyche.[6] When giving evidence before the Waitangi Tribunal for its 1986 report on the te reo Māori claim, Sir James Henare encapsulated the notion of te reo extending far beyond a means of communication and into the realm of identity and metaphysics: 'The language is the core of our Maori culture and mana. Ko te reo te mauri o te mana Maori (The language is the life force of the mana Maori). If the language dies, as some predict, what do we have left to us?' For Henare, te reo was 'the very soul of the Maori people'[7] – what John Rangihau described as 'a reo wairua, a spiritual language'.[8]

The conventional notion of 'language' as a functional means of communication[9] therefore has some limitations when it comes to describing te reo. Undoubtedly, in 1800, Māori did not see te reo as a language in the sense that the term is popularly understood today. First, it had historical resonance in that it connected the world of the present with those of the ancestors – it was 'he kōrero tuku iho', words handed down,[10] and 'he taonga tuku iho ngā tūpuna', a gift from the ancestors,[11] and served as a conduit linking the spiritual and physical worlds.[12]

To Māori at the beginning of the nineteenth century, te reo was also an entity that possessed a mauri – loosely translated as a life force – that vitalised the language and infused it with elements of a personality, which required it to be treated with respect. Individual words often had their own whakapapa and were a means of reaching into the past. The words spoken by Māori in 1800 were the same words their ancestors would have used generations earlier, and thus had acquired a certain amount of reverence. And because te reo had a mauri, individuals could connect to it with their own mauri, making a symbiotic link between language and its speaker in which each contributed to the mauri of the other.[13] Some words were not just revered but were regarded as sacred, particularly depending on who was using them and in what setting. Yate cited the example of a tohunga reciting a karakia, the words of which were 'held too sacred to be made known to any but the initiated'.[14] These included some of the language associated with rites and prohibitions, as well as kōrero tipuna – the act of talking about ancestors – which was regarded as sacred[15] to the extent that during kōrero tīpuna, eating and certain other activities were prohibited.[16]

Such facets of the perception of te reo may appear too esoteric for modern Western sensibilities, but there is some basis for te reo having emerged in this form and with these traits. Words can give the user a sense of power over their environment, even if solely because the act of naming something is to command some form of authority over it.[17] Words can evoke images and associations in the imagination, and for Māori society at the beginning of the nineteenth century the spoken word was still the only means of expressing ideas about not just the the physical world, but also the divine. It was no wonder, then, that the belief in words having potentially mystic or binding powers was accepted by Māori. The potency of the curse was a frequent testimony to this. Reverend Samuel Marsden, who is credited with introducing Christianity to New Zealand in 1814, observed the severity with which curses were regarded among Māori:

> The greatest insult that can be offered to a chief is to make use of bad language to him, and particularly to curse him, as when this is done they are always apprehensive the curse pronounced will come upon them. Hence it rarely happens that the New Zealanders who are men of

rank make use of bad language one to another as the Europeans do, but are cautious in what they say. When this is done it is not infrequently productive of serious consequences, as the friends of the person who has been abused will take up the quarrel and punish the offender.[18]

Curses were one of the more common causes of wars;[19] they gave rise to a volatile concoction of offence and fear in roughly equal measure. One nineteenth-century example is the case of a young man who, 'seeing the perspiration dropping from the cheek of a chief as he was running, in great haste, remarked that "the vapour rose from his head like the steam of an oven". This expression was regarded as a great curse, and caused a war which exterminated the tribe to which the young man belonged.'[20] The danger of the power of words being evoked through their inappropriate use gave rise to whakataukī such as 'He tau rākau e tae ate karo; he tao kī e kore e taea' (A wooden spear may be parried, but not the shaft of the tongue).[21]

Te reo could be flourished as well as feared. Experienced speakers, wielding it wisely, could deliver forceful oratorical blasts. The Wesleyan missionary James Buller witnessed such speeches up close and was impressed:

> Their memories are tenacious: every word, sentence, or image is skilfully
> chosen, from their copious language, to make impression upon the
> minds of their hearers. Their traditions and myths, their songs, proverbs,
> and fables, contained, for the Maori orator, a mine of wealth. Repetition
> never palls, provided it be pointed and pertinent … One after another,
> the speakers will spring to their feet, and, with spear or mere in hand,
> and the dog-skin mat, or the silken kaitaka, waving from the shoulder,
> they move up and down with a stately and firm step, which quickens
> into a run when passion is invoked. Hours pass in this way. Whether
> regard be had to their choice of natural images, their impassioned appeal,
> or their graceful action, no one can deny the oratorical power they put
> forth.[22]

In such settings, speaking was raised to an act of highly nuanced performance that adhered to an intricate set of conventions[23] and allowed each speaker to establish their intellectual and leadership credentials before the group and among the other speakers – in keeping with the notion of 'Ko te kai a te rangatira, he kōrero' (Oratory is the food of leaders).[24] What made the content of these orations so compelling was the way speaker drew on the metaphors, allusions and allegories to heighten their rhetoric and embellish the content. To this the speaker could add methods of controlling emphasis, pace and rhythm, such as the frequent use of repetition in storytelling, which enabled the speaker 'to slow down the speed, and to allow space for waiting, looking, experiencing the passage of time or of the gradual development of an action'.[25]

Oratory was very much a two-way process – the speaker had to be constantly aware of how the audience was reacting: 'From moment to moment, they see the effect of their words in their faces and postures … they would carefully avoid anything distasteful to their listeners and build up what they know their audience will enjoy, whether in sorrow or delight, to its highest pitch.'[26] 'Distasteful' in this context did not equate with despondent or forceful; it was more a case of veering away from topics that might cause offence or that might affect the mana (prestige or status) of the audience. At the same time, the speaker could not afford simply to please the audience if it resulted in him appearing in any way weak or ineffective. After all, there was his own mana and that of the group on whose behalf he was orating to be protected also. And it was not just what was said, but how it was said that mattered. Intonation and physical cues played a large part in how the message was communicated. As Leinani Melville explains about their oral culture:

> A listener knew what the speaker meant by perhaps the rise of an eyebrow, an expression of the face, a tilt of the head, or a description moulded with fingers. It has often been said, 'Tie a *kanaka's* hands and you will have him tongue-tied.' Many words had double, triple, and quadruple meanings, some not even remotely connected with each other. The same word pronounced one way meant one thing, yet pronounced differently it meant something else. The purport of a word depended not only upon inflection but also upon the words with which it was accompanied in a sentence.[27]

Apirana Ngata observed in 1940 that his people still liked committing spoken words to memory rather than reading them, because 'it was nearer to the old-time narrative of adept raconteurs or of poetical and priestly reciters. More than that, the genius of the race preferred education through the ear, conveyed by artists through intonation and gesticulation.'[28] The extent to which such non-verbal elements were a critical part of languages like te reo meant that any effort at transcription inevitably eviscerated much of the meaning. The bare bones of the text could never flesh out the tenor and substance brought to bear on the content by the manner of the oral delivery – especially as the non-verbal elements of te reo had become somewhat codified over time.[29] Subsequent efforts at 'preserving' Māori culture and language through transcribing spoken material invariably ended up diminishing its value and disfiguring its character. Te reo did not evolve over seven centuries as a static language, embalmed in text and shaped to fit the cultural expectations of the European world. It was a language that breathed – metaphysically as well as literally – in an exclusively Māori realm. Attempts to convert it to text could only have a suffocating effect on its cultural integrity.

Te reo Māori, while it is an oral language, nonetheless possessed its own literature (provided the term 'literature' is not applied too narrowly). In what was a remarkably modern view for the time, New Zealand typographer and historian of printing Coupland Harding told an audience at the Wellington Philosophical Society in 1892 that 'the song, the proverb, the fable, or the history inscribed in set form of words upon the tablet of the human memory is as truly literature as if with an iron pen and lead it were graven in the rock for ever'. He noted how oral cultures were popularly considered 'barbarous' and 'the productions of savages, untrustworthy historically, and scientifically worthless', yet, he argued, the Polynesian genealogies were 'paralleled by the classic traditions of civilised Greece and Rome' and therefore 'the offhand criticism which would reject Polynesian poetry as worthless must, to be consistent, pass a similar verdict on the "Iliad" and the "Odyssey"'.[30] Unlike most European literature, the authorship of Māori literature was usually anonymous.[31] The authority of what was contained in that literature, and the way in which it enforced Māori cultural and social mores, mattered overwhelmingly more in most instances than the authority of whoever brought that literature into being (if that individual was even remembered).

It was not that Europeans were entirely ignorant of these features of te reo; it was just that this was an age on the cusp of modern anthropology, where efforts to mimic the precision of science were spilling over into the study of cultures. When it came to the examination of languages, for example, the emphasis among European scholars was tilting to a more clinical form of analysis in which the elements of a language were increasingly dissected and scrutinised like sterile specimens. The more stylistic literary attributes, and especially any esoteric aspects, were often pushed aside in the process, as though they were extraneous debris.

So pervasive was the enthusiasm for this quasi-scientific method that some feared that even English was gradually moving to becoming 'a language which has no uncertainty, no whims of idiom, no cumbrous forms, no fitful shimmer of many hued significance, no hoary archaisms … a patent de-odorized and non-resonant language, which effects the purpose of communication as perfectly and rapidly as algebraic signs'.[32] (It was the same fear that Dickens channelled through the character of Gradgrind in *Hard Times*.) What chance was there of capturing te reo's vitality, subtlety, wit, character, metaphors, allusions, ethereal textures and its many other nuances in text by English anthropologists in this era when the 'academic' approach, particularly to indigenous languages, was potentially at risk of being reduced to barren inventories of cultural classifications? This is an important consideration when reviewing the contemporary accounts that survey te reo and its role in traditional Māori society. How New Zealand's indigenous language was filtered through the embryonic academic language of European observers, and the extent to which these writers stripped away those things – such as the umbilical connection between language and spirituality – that they regarded as superfluous (not to mention overlooking the many things they failed to identify about te reo in the first place) requires these sources to be tempered with a dose of discretion. They are useful but far from definitive.

CIVILISATIONS

In the Māori world the spiritual dimension of te reo was widely felt and never far from the surface. It was 'the skull beneath the skin of the culture'[33] and surfaced often – as in the case of rites such as whaikōrero where the language became the means, among much else, of articulating and achieving a communion with the dead.[34] The dead were revered[35] and considered tapu, and so summoning their names, their memory or their presence in some form turned te reo into a sacred entity in its own right. It was not just the fact of the names being evoked, but the manner of their evocation through the specific words or phrases used that transfigured the language into a sacred form. In practice, this meant that stretches of the boundary between the sacred and secular use of te reo were porous[36] and, as a result, strictures about the use of it emerged. Certain words and names were designated as tapu and only able to be given voice by, for example, a tohunga.[37] To the extent that te reo was used in sacred rites and traditions and that there were occasionally supernatural sanctions applied to certain words, the language was part of the moral and social order for Māori in the beginning of the nineteenth century. The speakers themselves became tapu through being involved in the whaikōrero process. For some iwi, when the speaker got up to do the tauparapara (the initial recitation at the commencement of whaikōrero)[38] they would remain tapu from that point until a waiata was performed (usually by the women), followed by a haka done by the men. Only then would the speaker be noa (free from tapu). If this process was not adhered to strictly, then 'all your kōrero [talk] means nothing', and the speaker was left open to challenge by others over their status and what they had said.[39] Far from whaikōrero being a convoluted ritual that had calcified into a tradition honoured for the sake of formality, it had serious diplomatic and political purposes for Māori society at the turn of the nineteenth century. The words spoken, the context in which they were framed and the manner of their delivery indicated the authority and influence of the community the speakers were representing. As the Tūhoe tohunga Hohepa Kereopa succinctly put it, 'The marae is as strong as the people who whaikōrero in it.'[40]

Such finely tuned linguistic gradients relating to the processes such as whaikōrero were generally beyond the awareness of most Europeans in the nineteenth century. Some found it easier to resort to pejorative designations such as 'primitive', 'savage' and 'barbarian'[41] to describe the indigenous people, culture and language of the country while, in contrast, proudly picturing themselves as the social and intellectual counterpoint, charged by Providence with bringing the blessings of European civilisation to Māori.[42] They believed that the indigenous savages embodied 'all the exotic, untutored qualities that the forces of civil society strove so hard to control',[43] and lacked the rule of law, a centralised system of government[44] and the other trappings of the civilised world. Had they ventured to look beyond the veil of their own presumptions they would have discovered that not only was Māori society a civilisation in its own right, it equalled and in some areas superseded European civilisation. The language that categorised aspects of the natural world is one area where te reo was at least a match for languages of the so-called civilised world. There were, for example, 14 words in te reo to distinguish various categories of pounamu (Europeans in the nineteenth century did not get beyond two or three), 47 words denoting as many species of kūmara (Europeans managed to identify just a few), and almost 60 terms for particular astronomical features.[45]

Early nineteenth-century Europeans were generally unaware of the detailed knowledge or specific vocabulary of Māori civilisation and assumed, out of some inherent cultural bias, that te reo was in most ways inferior to English. 'The language of a savage people,' Scottish writer and literary critic George Craik concluded imperiously, 'is necessarily in all cases a poor and imperfect instrument for the expression of thought.'[46] Te reo was 'a language of simple ideas'[47] in the view of one visitor to New Zealand in the 1830s, and was one of the obstacles thwarting the civilisation of Māori. The trader Joel Polack expressed this view of civilisation in forthright terms. 'The influence of a refined society,' he suggested, 'cannot, at present, be felt by the native surrounded by his own primitive habits in his country. The civilized man cannot urge the claims due to an enlightened taste and elegant education or manners; the native understands them not.'[48] Charles Terry, a settler who later became an Auckland newspaper editor and amateur antiquarian, lamented in 1842 that insufficient efforts had been made in the preceding decades to introduce the English language in New Zealand; had English supplanted te reo earlier on, that 'would have more certainly insured the early civilization of the natives'.[49]

In an attempt to give such views a more academic gloss, the doctor, interpreter and one-time government official Edward Shortland surveyed wider Polynesian history and society and drew various inferences from the scope of his material and the manner in which he conflated it. In the volume that emerged from this research, *Maori Religion and Mythology*, published towards the end of his career in 1882, he held fast to the sort of conjecture about te reo that had been popular among some Europeans since the 1830s. 'The Polynesian language appears to have retained a very primitive form, remaining fixed and stationary' was his estimation of it. In his mind, he linked the alleged primitiveness of the language to the limited intellectual development of its speakers. 'There is a notable mental condition of the Polynesian to which we desire to direct attention,' he advised his readers. 'The Maori has a very limited notion of the abstract. All his ideas take naturally a concrete form. This inaptitude to conceive any abstract notions was, it is believed, the early mental condition of man.'[50]

The shared blind spot in these various commentaries was filled in by the conviction that te reo was a vestige of a stone-age culture that had survived solely because of its isolation from the rest of the world. It was the means by which primitives uttered basic bursts of ideas to each other, and in some sense it was responsible for holding Māori captive to their barbaric, intellectually impoverished and uncultivated lives. Until European settlement commenced in New Zealand in the second decade of the nineteenth century, te reo was the single language of an entire civilisation. Every aspect of that civilisation – its politics, diplomacy, arts, history, science, religion and mythology – was wrapped up in that language, and no part of the civilisation existed outside of the language. This put te reo in a vulnerable position when the Māori civilisation came into contact with the civilisation of a recidivist coloniser. Moreover, in 1800 te reo was not one of two languages in the country, let alone the minority or endangered language that it would later be shunted into. Rather, at this point in its history it was as confident and muscular as any language that was so deeply ingrained in its culture and whose status seemed beyond any conceivable threat. Everything about Māori culture and society was preserved in its words and revived and animated when it was spoken. Te reo was at once the means by which knowledge was communicated and the repository of that knowledge.

LANGUAGE AND SOCIETY

Some sense of the proportion and structure of Māori society in 1800 is useful at this juncture to give a general impression of the environment te reo occupied on the verge of a century of tumultuous change. Estimates of the Māori population in this era vary considerably, and remain a point of contention. Johann Forster, who visited New Zealand on the *Resolution* in 1773, estimated the number of Māori to be around 100,000, although he conceded that 'we rather think our estimate to fall short of the true population'.[51] It was not until 1817 that the next informed approximation was calculated, this time by John Nicholas, who put the Māori population at 150,000 – a figure which, he implied, took into account the effects of recently arrived diseases.[52] By 1834, when the country's indigenous population had already begun to be depleted by wars and disease, Reverend William Williams suggested to Dandeson Coates, the Church Missionary Society (CMS) lay secretary in London, that based on his extensive tours through the country, the North Island Māori population was 105,400; and, extrapolating from this, the country's Māori population was 'small, not exceeding 200,000'.[53] This was an exaggeration: the more probable estimate was just over 100,000 in 1800. The population was formed, in the eyes of one Colonial Office official in 1839, of 'a people composed of numerous dispersed and petty tribes, who possess few political relations to each other, and are incompetent to act or even deliberate in concert'.[54] Although there is some truth to this, the perspective is that of someone whose sources of information were limited to other Britons who had been to New Zealand and who had written about the country's indigenous population during the 1820s and 1830s; it did not reflect the essence of how Māori society was organised or how it functioned, and it showed little advance on the knowledge of that society obtained at the beginning of the century, as represented in John Savage's précis published in 1807:

> As this country is divided into small principalities, whose chieftains are almost constantly at war with each other, the wandering of the natives is prevented by its being rendered unsafe; a bond of society is therefore formed for the safety and protection of the members of each principality. This society is divided into classes, each distinguished by devices variously tattooed on their faces and persons. These classes consist in those educated for the priesthood, or the performance of their religious ceremonies; others – to arms, by far the most numerous class; and the remainder may be considered the cannaille, or vulgar multitude.[55]

Although the constituent parts of Māori society are easily assembled and their roles can be roughly sketched out, as Savage attempted in cursory fashion, the nature of their mutual interaction is much more involved. Relations within and between whanau, hapū and iwi could be fluid and idiosyncratic, with any arbitrary rule likely to be marked by a slew of exceptions. In the standard rendition of Māori social structure, the hierarchy of entities stems from waka, which were a confederation of iwi based on descent from one of the legendary migratory vessels that brought the first Polynesians to New Zealand. The next level down is the iwi, which in turn consisted of hapū, and each hapū is made up of a collection of whānau, all bound by familial links in varying proximities to each other.[56] The constant evolution and growth of Māori communities meant that the overall social structure was not tightly fixed into these categories.[57] At the beginning of the nineteenth century, for example, some former hapū had grown into iwi, while others were in an indeterminate state of transition.[58] Moreover, while iwi were frequently represented as a single political body, they could be riven by internal conflict, sometimes erupting into war.[59] By 1800 there were around 50 politically autonomous iwi, each of which traced its descent from one of the migratory waka,[60] but it was the hapū that were the basic social and political entity in Māori society[61] and that Europeans frequently mislabelled.[62]

The identity of individuals, as well as of hapū and iwi, was tethered to the terrain and could be expressed through the formula of the pepeha, which was another of those linguistic devices where history, territory, tradition, identity, politics, place and a sense of sanctity converged. The precise conventions that were applied to pepeha varied among iwi – which in itself became a linguistic identifying factor – and their content, while it usually remained succinct, could still incorporate proverbs, witticisms, charms, boasts, metaphors, communication with ancestors, and figures of speech.[63] They were linguistic vignettes that were capable of encapsulating myriad shades of the identity and character of the speaker.

Leadership was another area where the definitions and rules put in print by colonists did not always capture the essence of how Māori society functioned. Chiefs, for example, assumed their role mainly through primogeniture, but the weaknesses of that system (which Gibbon suggested in Rome's case offered 'the fairest scope for ridicule')[64] were compensated for by the need for leaders to prove their worth.[65] In effect, the constitutional basis of Māori leadership had an inbuilt system of checks and balances. Again, rigid British categorisation[66] did not always fit the reality of Māori society as it functioned at the turn of the nineteenth century.

In most European societies, the workings of their political systems were circumscribed by the written word: constitutions, charters, declarations, regulations, statutes, histories detailing precedents and other such texts delineated the boundaries of power and the manner in which authority was devolved among the various strata of the system of rule. Māori society had to meet the same requirements relying solely on the spoken word. This placed an immense burden on certain individuals within hapū and iwi being able to recall precedent, argue about ancestry, evoke history, draw on myth and legend and articulate the political points that would ensure the constitutional apparatus of society continued to function. And frequently, these discussions were preceded by a separate series of debates over who would be sanctioned to speak on such weighty issues, and in what sequence. Such procedures were seldom routine or regarded as mere formalities. Each circumstance could require recollection of a specific corpus of whakapapa or precedent, and so the extent of the knowledge held by those making the decisions could be vast – and it had to be; choosing the wrong leader or making the wrong alliance could have lethal implications for the entire community. Te reo, exclusively in its spoken form, was the sole constitutional and legal instrument the community would depend on for the most prudent political decisions to be made, and for the systems of rule to continue to function as effectively as possible. It was as good an example as any of the maxim that 'the word *is* a deed'.[67] In such oral cultures, all deeds were necessarily preceded by the spoken word.

WHAKAPAPA AND HISTORY

The Polynesians who migrated to New Zealand and formed the society that was to become known as Māori arrived roughly around 1250 AD,[68] and by the mid-fourteenth century the migrations ceased. The language, history and culture of these migrants was the main cargo they brought with them, and evolved in complete isolation from the rest of the world until the first Europeans set foot in New Zealand in 1769; according to one visitor to New Zealand in 1793, most Māori still 'had no idea of any other Country'.[69] Within this society – spread relatively sparsely over some 268,000 square kilometres of territory[70] – it was inevitable that dialectical and pronunciation variations would emerge. Regional differences in vocabulary, pronunciation and (less often) grammar could indicate where a person was from and their tribal affiliation,[71] and it is likely that, over time, some of these differences were accentuated as a result of reduced contact between communities as they fanned out after the migratory phase concluded.

Physical distance and isolation can lead to political and social dissociation, but for centuries, Māori society maintained a degree of political unity that was fortified by the memorising and use of whakapapa. These served as 'a long chain of interlocking conversations between members of the group', resulting in 'all beliefs and values, all forms of knowledge, [being] communicated between individuals in face-to-face contact; and ... stored only in human memory'.[72] What people remembered became vital to defining and manoeuvring through social, political and generational relationships.

At a superficial level, whakapapa were family trees – a list of generations that stretched back sufficiently to dissolve into the realm of deities.[73] But they were at the core of Māori history and formed the linkages to otherwise disparate communities and events; indeed, apart from whakapapa, it could be argued that there was no such thing as 'Māori history' at all, only tribal history.[74] Whakapapa became possibly the sole source of a Māori metanarrative of history, in which discrete historical events, groups, trends and phenomena at hapū or iwi level were carefully assimilated into a single, overarching, trans-iwi master narrative – a version of history that aspired to universality[75] except that the wrinkled texture of regional differences were never quite flattened out completely. The migratory legends illustrate this point. Most hapū and iwi pinpointed their origins to a particular voyaging waka, and were aware of who were the descendants around the country of the other migratory vessels. The location where a community's particular ancestral waka landed was often memorialised thereafter as that community's geographical genesis. However, a few hapū and iwi had whakapapa that preceded the arrival of these waka. The Taranaki iwi of Ngā Rauru, for example, place emphasis on earlier narratives when assembling their tribal histories.[76] The iwi's migratory waka is the *Aotea*,[77] but when a transcription of Ngā Rauru's history was undertaken there were 200 lines of text detailing the iwi's history[78] before Toi Te Huatahi, who was said to have arrived on the *Aotea*.[79]

Whakapapa also had political implications, including determining rank and succession within a community,[80] and familial connections with other communities could have a bearing on whether they were regarded as friend or foe. Given such serious practical implications, the requirement to learn and remember whakapapa was widespread in Māori society, and not limited to a few experts.

Relationships and lines of descent were of course at the core of whakapapa, but other types of whakapapa applied to non-human areas, such as the pedigree of plants and animals (which in most cases, like their human counterparts, had divine origins). These whakapapa could also draw connections between species, resulting in the creation of a 'folk taxonomy' and 'ecosystem maps of culturally important resources'.[81] Te reo itself was seen as the creation of Tānenuiārangi, the deity who was the offspring of Ranginui and Papatūānuku – the sky father and earth mother – who were central to the Māori creation myths.[82] Therefore, to speak te reo was to use a gift given directly by a deity, and one that was part of creation. This connectedness broadened to encompass the natural world. Tohunga could transform their use of te reo to enable them to talk to other parts of creation – shellfish, trees, or just about anything else.[83] The parameters of the language were the parameters of the physical and spiritual world, and everything within those boundaries was interconnected through whakapapa.

All these forms of whakapapa – seemingly about to collapse under the sheer weight of their historical detail and a latticed network of relationships – were the framework on which Māori society was built. Without them, the society would not have existed or survived in the form that it did. With them, Māori culture was imbued with a sophisticated system of politics, history, diplomacy, religion, economics and ecology that was a stabilising influence on the society yet allowed social and cultural evolution and innovation to occur.[84] Whakapapa also fostered what became 'one of the two finest oral historical traditions in the world'.[85]

Such detailed systems of knowledge required many individuals in each community – especially tohunga, kaumātua and rangatira – to commit vast sequences of information to memory. In 1869 the Bishop of Wellington commented on the extent of such undertakings; he observed that Māori were '"born disciples of inductive science". Never did I meet with men more averse to hasty generalizations themselves, and more keen in showing up *our* tendency thereto,' and that:

> As specimens of their intellectual power, I would say that their cosmogony is only inferior to the Mosaic, deriving matter from mind, and creation from no material atoms. I would say that their mode of expressing 'Eternity' is in itself a clear and grand conception:– 'No tua iho whakarere a mua tonu atu' ('That which exists before the stream of Time infinitely onwards').[86]

According to the early twentieth-century ethnographer Elsdon Best, the acquisition and transmission of this knowledge took place in the whare wānanga. 'The term *wananga*,' he explained,

> is applied to teachings that are held to be *tapu* – occult lore, esoteric knowledge; and *whare wananga* means the *wananga* house, or house of knowledge. This world was originally barren of superior forms of knowledge, hence Tane ascended to the Toi o nga Rangi (the uppermost of the twelve heavens) in order to obtain from Io, the Supreme Being, the three famous *kete o te wananga*, or baskets of knowledge.[87]

Best cited two examples which, although taken from the 1890s, are indicative of the sort of discipline applied to memorising material that would have been typical for certain individuals within every Māori community for centuries. In the first example, he obtained from 'an old native' in Ruatahuna the lyrics of 406 songs 'together with much information of an explanatory nature pertaining to them', and all done by memory. In the second example, a Māori giving evidence before the Land Commission at Ruatoki in relation to a land claim provided a genealogy extending back 34 generations, with 'innumerable branch lines, of a multitude of affinitive ramifications'. So detailed was this presentation – again, done entirely from the man's memory – that it took three days to present to the commission, and contained specifics on the history, occupations and relationships of over 1400 individuals.[88]

Such testimony relating to whakapapa and iwi histories was not only overflowing with detail, it also proved reliable when tested.[89] In a letter to geologist Julius von Haast in 1885, James West Stack, a clergyman and interpreter, gave his assessment of the accuracy of Māori myths relating to the creation of the world, in which the transmission of centuries of oral history was able to be verified by cross-referencing it with published material dealing with legends on similar topics from other parts of Polynesia:

> I think the Maori traditions very reliable. It is a curious fact that the mythological legends related by Gill in his *Myths and Songs of the South Pacific* are identical with the Maori. They were preserved here by oral tradition, and with such exactness, that after the lapse of centuries the legends of the offshoot correspond with those of the original stock. This seems to me to afford satisfactory proof of the reliability of their traditions, for if they could preserve those relating to one subject, why not another? The historical traditions are consistent and hang together, and I see no reason to discredit them.[90]

These legends included those relating to 'land-raising'[91] – stories about islands being fished up or thrown down by ancestors, which were widespread in Polynesian mythology[92] and which arrived with the Polynesian migrants to New Zealand and were then passed down through Māori society for approximately the next seven centuries with no opportunity for cross-referencing or correction. The ability to maintain these accounts in identical form for such a long period, relying solely on oral transmission, was unequalled in most other cultures in the world.

Oral histories were summoned frequently for political purposes, too, giving purchase to arguments – as Polack noted on one occasion, when describing a chief from Tolaga Bay who was able to 'recite minutely in prose the feats of reckless valour that had conferred a lasting renown on his race and tribe' as part of an assertion of the political and military status of his community.[93] Without such histories to draw on, what else could gild an individual's or community's reputation in such a way? Some Europeans dismissed these types of pronouncements as a betrayal of the speaker's vanity, but they were more part of long-established political rituals, relying on a mix of performance and elaborate compositional capabilities to assert a political position.

Whakapapa memorised in such minute detail could act as cues to explain and reinforce specific social structures and relations: they were, in a way, the 'charters' of social organisation and institutions rather than just faithful historical accounts of genealogies.[94] They could also be called on whenever some precedent was needed to tackle a particular challenge in the social order. This was precisely why these vast repositories of knowledge passed down orally were so stringently maintained: they had direct repercussions, especially in the political and economic spheres. If the imperative to hold on to certain branches of knowledge weakened over time, it was only because its practical use had subsided. The most striking example of the loss of an entire body of knowledge in traditional Māori society was that relating to trans-ocean navigation: it may have been passed down for centuries after the first Polynesians migrated to New Zealand but, by the time of European arrival, it had long since ceased to be of any practical use at all in a country with a landmass that was so vast. At some period, this knowledge had been cut loose to drift away into that great expanse of historical amnesia, from where – existing only in oral form – it became irretrievable.[95]

In all this consideration of the byzantine nature and multitudinous purposes of Māori oral histories before the full onslaught of European colonisation, some account must be taken of the fact that history itself is a culturally determined notion. In the hands of subsequent European historians, much of this oral inheritance was either 'reduced to fantasy' or, when scrutinised more closely, 'regularly excluded as unreliable and fickle'.[96] This cultural gulf is evident in something as fundamental as the distinction between myth and 'proper' history. Myths, by definition in Western scholarship, are fictional, lack any basis for verification, and were often fabricated to fulfil the deep-rooted collective psychological needs of a community.[97] Sir Api Mahuika provided a vital corrective to such presumptions, noting that 'people who are not Māori have a propensity to interpret what for us is a fact by calling it a myth'. He used the example of Māui, who is typically described as a mythical character, and explained that:

> For us, as Ngāti Porou, Maui is an ancestor, to which we all have a
> whakapapa to Maui Tikitiki-a-Taranga. Some people would say, 'You

know, Māori are reifying this person.' But the reality for us is that such is the skill and ability of this person that it is almost impossible to say that Maui is just something else.[98]

This is not just a case of *Māori* culture having possessed different (and, from a European perspective, inferior) probative values. Instead, it reflects an entirely alternative system of knowledge. The epistemology of truth as an 'embodied knowledge' rooted in experience, received knowledge and individual perspective trumped any effort to verify history through assembling material evidence. This difference extended to how knowledge was constructed, transmitted and valued,[99] and in some ways made traditional *Māori* knowledge, including its expression through te reo, incompatible with the approach to knowledge that was about to be introduced by the coloniser.

THE SACRED WORD

Any Māori being raised in 1800 would have been taught that all knowledge was sacred to varying degrees.[100] It is probable that, in some cases, this sanctity diminished as European colonisation bit deeper into the country,[101] but even in the late nineteenth century the indefatigable Victorian compiler of Māori traditions, John White, recalled the reaction of a tohunga who realised he may have disclosed a bit too much information during their discussions. White recounted how his informant

> was so terrified at the idea of having divulged so much to me ... that he dreamt the spirits of his ancestors met him, each with an adze in his hand, and, passing him, each struck his adze into the ground; at each stroke, rats issued forth from the holes. This he interpreted, that for his divulging Maori secrets he was to be eaten alive by rats. After this dream, I could not get the old priest, for any consideration, to proceed with his teaching.[102]

Just two generations earlier, even the slight insights that White managed to secure from this tohunga would have been impossible to obtain – so revered and guarded was such knowledge. Even as European culture began to penetrate more of the country's hinterland in the latter decades of the century, some knowledge was still shielded from curious outsiders, as German naturalist Ernst Dieffenbach discovered in the early 1840s. '[C]ertain karakia, or invocations,' he observed, 'are less generally known, and a stranger obtains them with difficulty, as they are only handed down amongst the tohunga, or priests, from father to son.'[103]

Because this knowledge could only be communicated orally, the sense of the potency of words was correspondingly heightened. In addition, words in te reo were conduits to the essence of a person and so, when articulated, became 'symbols of thought',[104] potentially relaying simultaneously direct meaning, metaphorical meaning, the mana of the person speaking them and the mana of the person being spoken about.[105] Te reo was precisely the sort of language that Heidegger described as 'the house of Being. In its home man dwells. Those who think and those who create with words are the guardians of this home. Their guardianship accomplishes the manifestation of Being insofar as they bring the manifestation to language and maintain it in language through their speech.'[106]

This house was about to be entered by another culture, however – one that had accumulated centuries of experience at imprinting its dominance in almost every part of the world where it took root. And for its part, te reo's evolution in complete isolation from the rest of the world had left it ill equipped to handle the approaching encounter with the English language and its colonising protagonists. Although no one in Māori society had any way of knowing it, the period around 1800 was the highwater mark of te reo. Just a smattering of Europeans had prodded and probed the coast of parts of New Zealand in this period, and none had yet settled. Still, as Savage sailed from New Zealand after his brief visit in 1805, he assembled a list of the country's favourable attributes, which he covetously foresaw held out 'great inducements for colonization' at some future time.[107] As it turned out, the point when New Zealand would succumb to more invasive forms of involvement by colonisers was much closer at hand than Savage or anyone else had even an inkling of at the beginning of the century, and te reo's greatest source of security – its isolation – was about to come to an end. By 1800, when several Europeans had already briefly visited New Zealand's shores, there was no prospect of te reo remaining an island entire of itself. But in joining the continent of languages, it was involuntarily dragged into a sort of Darwinian struggle for survival that continues to the present day.

CHAPTER 2

'A strange medley'
End of eighteenth century to 1814

History does not fall conveniently into chronological compartments. A period such as 'the nineteenth century' cannot just be torn out from the entangled fabric of which it is a part and analysed in neatly clipped isolation. This applies to the history of te reo in this era: its earlier brushes with the outside world were the curtain-raiser for the language's turbulent experiences in the nineteenth century, and so deserve some consideration.

From the omniscience of the present, it is easy to see a sad inevitability in the fate of te reo Māori in the nineteenth century – from primacy to perishing in just 10 decades, with each act of diminution dovetailing into the next. And after all, doesn't colonisation always end in this, with the preordained triumph of the coloniser and the correspondingly doleful prognosis for the indigenous peoples and their cultures? Certainly, the story of te reo in this period is overall one of decline. However, fixating on the fact of this decline – the metanarrative of a 'Great Retreat' in the face of colonisers intent on the rampant Europeanisation of the country – risks masking the intricate crosscultural imbroglios of this era, and ascribing culpability where it may not lie. It also risks underplaying the role of Māori agency in the changes that occurred. The nature of how the literate world of Europe first engaged with Māori society is far more nuanced than the generalised accounts would suggest.

METAMORPHOSIS

The first fragments of text attached to New Zealand were written by the Dutch hydrographer Franz Jacobszoon Visscher,[1] who served as chief pilot for Abel Tasman during their 1642 expedition on behalf of the Dutch East India Company to locate the fabled Great Southern Continent.[2] The continent, as they found out, was not there to be discovered, but Visscher's nib did outline stretches of the coast of the North and South Islands.[3] The map was cartographically unremarkable[4] but symbolically momentous.[5] Visscher's penning and naming the curves of the coast represented the point when literacy reached New Zealand's shores – literally. It also signified that nascent European curiosity in so-called unclaimed territories that all too often slipped from the paper and into practice. In New Zealand's case, the social and cultural landscape of Māori would eventually convulse under the burden of British colonisation – but not just yet. The few hastily written names that Visscher attached to his map also constituted the first assault on te reo. The map made its way back to the archives of the Dutch East Indies Company[6] and within 30 years details of Tasman's 'discovery' of New Zealand had been published in England.[7] Cook was familiar with Tasman's journal and made specific reference to it during his first voyage to New Zealand.[8]

This journey of text from Tasman and Visscher to Cook was a prime example of how the written word, as opposed to its oral counterparts, was transportable, translatable, impersonal, immune to the fickleness of memory, and had a lifespan that exceeded that of any individual. No wonder Milton wrote (around the time of Tasman's Pacific voyage) that 'books are not absolutely dead things, but do contain a potency of life in them … they do preserve as in a vial the purest efficacy and extraction of that living intellect that bred them'.[9] Here was the depth of Europe's faith in the written word captured in a single sentence.

Of course, it did not occur to anyone in Europe that the indigenous occupants of the land Tasman and his crew sighted might have already named the geographical features of the land they inhabited. The act of assigning names to the geography, fauna, flora and even the peoples of the non-European world and then putting these names in print for dissemination was part of the Enlightenment's 'textualising of the world'.[10] The intention was 'to make the globe an object to be understood through the powerful gaze of Europeans'. Knowledge itself became a culturally privileged possession, and insights were the exclusive preserve of the 'discoverer'.[11] Those things being discovered, on the other hand, were regarded as static exhibits.

The Māori naming of the country was far more extensive than Tasman appears to have imagined. 'Every part of the country was owned and named. Not only were the large mountains, rivers, and plains named, but every hillock, streamlet and valley. These names frequently contained allusions to persons or events, and served to perpetuate the memory of them and to preserve the history of the past,' one missionary later noted.[12] The combination of geographical features and names served as the 'survey pegs of memory' by which a tribe's history was recorded and history was kept always in the present.[13] In the 1880s the Cornish missionary William Colenso, who had arrived in New Zealand in 1834, offered a surprisingly forthright explanation of the significance of Māori placenames in the face of the unrelenting English renaming of the country's terrain:

> That the Maori people had very many highly significant names for things
> in general, is pretty well known to those who are well acquainted with
> their language; although, on account of their plainness, some could only
> be translated into English by an euphemism. Just so it always was with
> their names for persons and for places. It is not, however, with reference
> to the meaning, the utility, or the beauty of such Maori names in their
> estimation, that I [...] write, – but of the errors of Europeans respecting
> them [...] The two languages differ so widely in their construction.
> Twenty, or more, orthographical errors may occur in the columns of
> an English Daily Newspaper, without any one becoming or causing a
> serious error, – that is, making an entire change in the meaning of the
> word, the sentence, or the subject; or, even causing the word or words so
> spelt erroneously to mean anything else, or to be wholly misunderstood;
> but such is not the case in Maori, – here every orthographical error is
> more or less of a serious one; and as it is in the writing, so it is in the
> pronunciation, and, consequently, in the meaning and etymology.[14]

The nuances of pronunciation in te reo and the various shadings of meaning that were dependent on their context in phrases often defied easy translation into English. This became another reason why colonists preferred renaming to translating.

It was more than a century after Tasman's cursory survey of a few small fragments of New Zealand's coast that one of the Enlightenment's greatest explorers, Captain James Cook, commenced a much more thorough exploration of the country in 1769 and on two return trips in the 1770s. The emphasis of the voyages was primarily scientific, which in addition to producing charts and maps required the systematic description of whatever was seen, the collection of samples where possible, the measurement of dimensions, and making comparisons and deductions.[15] Cook had also been secretly instructed that during the course of the first expedition, if the opportunity arose while in the South Pacific, he was 'to observe the Genius, Temper, Disposition and Number of the Natives, if there be any',[16] extending scientific observation and categorisation to other human beings. The botanist on board Cook's ship HMS *Endeavour*, Joseph Banks, obliged, producing descriptions of Māori[17] that were not dissimilar in essence to his descriptions of animals. This was entirely normal scientific practice in this era, and was in keeping with Banks' personal view that Māori were 'a race of beings placed so infinitely below us in the order of Nature'.[18] European intellectual ascendency demanded that there be such an order of beings, with Europeans naturally set on its pinnacle. Even before New Zealand had been sighted by the *Endeavour*'s crew, their relationship with Māori was preordained by these almost innate presumptions of cultural and intellectual superiority.[19] And among all the other compiling, codifying, scrutinising and interpreting that was going on, Cook's expeditions over that decade would result in the first effort at 'textualising' the Māori world, with the pivotal transposition of samples of te reo from the verbal to the written realm and, once committed to paper, its translation into English.

In March 1770, with the assistance of the *Endeavour*'s translator Tupaia[20] (who was from Ra`iatea in the Society Islands), Banks made a list of 43 words, comprising mainly terms for parts of the body, and numbers from one to 10.[21] The list was in four columns: the first containing the English words; the second and third the translations of these from te reo in the North and South islands respectively; and the final column listed the equivalent words in Tahitian, which Banks added for comparative purposes. By way of commentary, he noted that the dialectical differences between various parts of the country were slight but that, in certain locations, a particle was sometimes added before or after a noun. He recorded one such occasion that illustrates a method Europeans used to describe Māori linguistic knowledge:

The Genius of the Language especialy in the Southern parts is to add some particle before a noun as we do 'the' or 'a'; 'the' was generaly *He*, or *Ko*; they also often add to the end of any word, especialy if it is in answer to a question, the word *Oeia* which signifies yes, realy, or certainly. This sometimes led our gentlemen into most longwinded words, one only of which I shall mention as an example. In the Bay of Islands a very remarkable Island was calld by the natives *Motu Aro*: some of our gentlemen askd the name of this from one of the Natives, Who answerd I suppose as usual *Kemotu aro*; the Gentleman not hearing well the word repeated his question, on which the Indian again repeated his answer, adding *Oeia* to the end of the name which made it *Kemotuaroeiea*: this way at least and no other can I account for that Island being calld in the Log book &c *Cumattiwarroweia*.[22]

On the same expedition the *Endeavour*'s botanical illustrator, Sydney Parkinson, produced his own *Vocabulary of the New Zealand Tongue* which, although similar in content to Banks', was slightly more comprehensive (with 67 entries) and resembled lists he had compiled for the lexicons of other parts of the Pacific.[23]

The 26-year-old naturalist William Anderson, who was on Cook's last voyage to New Zealand in the *Resolution* in 1776, also wrote down a Māori vocabulary of 21 words that would meet only the most rudimentary communication requirements for any future visitor to New Zealand. Of more interest than his list of words, though, is Anderson's commentary on the language itself. He noted that 'their language is far from being harsh or disagreeable though the pronunciation is frequently guttural, and whatever qualitys in any other is requisite to make it musical certainly obtain a considerable degree here'. Anderson judged that the Māori language was, in general, inferior to European languages. He then recommended what he believed was necessary to redeem the culture – the sort of suggestion that would echo much more loudly into the following century in both the policy and practice of the coloniser. 'Nothing would be more humane,' he concluded, 'nor I think more worthy a great nation, than to endeavour to remove such a number of our fellow creatures from the situation they are now in and which is actually little superior to that of the Brute creation.'[24] Civilisation was the only antidote to Māori barbarism in Anderson's view, and no doubt the 'deficient' language of Māori, as he described it, was one of those aspects of the culture that he considered would have to be expunged in order to allow the country to advance. It was the sort of formula for progress that was habitually propagated by Europeans during this era.[25]

MAPPING TE REO

Seven years after Cook departed New Zealand for the final time, the English antiquary and palaeographer Thomas Astle published what would be the most important work of his career: *The Origin and Progress of Writing*. In its opening lines, Astle laid out the general position held by Europeans in this era on the status of writing, asserting: 'The noblest acquisition of mankind is

SPEECH, and the most useful art is WRITING. The first, eminently distinguishes MAN from the brute creation; the second, from uncivilized savages.' Astle equated the stages by which non-literate civilisations developed writing with their evolution into higher states of civilisation.[26]

The civilising power of literacy was undoubtedly one of the main weapons in the armoury of British imperial expansion. It enabled the definition, classification, quantification and regulation of indigenous peoples and their cultures while dismantling and reconstructing some of those cultures in a form that was more acceptable to the coloniser. But although history eventually bore out Astle's faith in the inevitable triumph of the written word (especially in its most advanced form, English),[27] the route to that end, especially in the most distant regions of Britain's colonial tinkering, was a circuitous one and far removed from the chest-thumping, flag-waving images of imperial dominance that Britain liked to project in later decades. In the early period of contact, cultural compromise was common, especially where indigenous groups in the vicinity enjoyed a demographic dominance. One such example was recorded on Norfolk Island by its British administrator, Lieutenant-Governor Philip King, in November 1793. Two Māori had been brought there to assist with the island's flax processing industry, but their expert advice would be of use only if they could be understood – and despite all the self-confident assurances about the superiority of the English language, when you needed commercial advice from experts in treating flax, such cultural conceit would not get you very far. King's journal entry on this issue is revelatory in two important ways. First, it showed that in those parts of the world where the British presence was stretched to its thinnest, a fleeting cultural equilibrium could, and indeed had to be reached with indigenous cultures. It also revealed that King was aware of the Māori vocabularies that had been produced during Cook's voyages and that he augmented these, based on the additional knowledge of te reo that he and others had accumulated since:

> It may be expected that after a six months acquaintance, that we should
> not be ignorant of each others Language. Myself and some of the
> Officers, (who were so kind as to communicate the information they
> obtained from our visitors) could make our ideas known, and tolerable
> well understood by them; They, by intermixing what English words
> they knew, with what we knew of their language could make themselves
> sufficiently understood by us; During the time they were here, I did not
> possess any of Captain Cooks Voyages; but since their departure, I find

from his Second Voyage, that it has a great similitude, to the general language spoken in those seas. The Vocabulary which I have added to this Journal, was collected by myself and the Surgeon, and is, I believe, very correct, particularly the Numerals. Much other information was given us by our two friends, but as it may be liable to great error I forbear repeating it.[28]

King's *Vocabulary*, which he completed with the help of his Māori informants and a colleague on Norfolk Island, was by far the most comprehensive that had been produced to that time, with the equivalent of 199 English words listed in te reo Māori.[29] At times, it was a clumsy and laborious process: King had to explain some terms at length, then ask for a translation, establish that it was a match for the word he was describing, and finally transcribe it in a phonetic manner, as was the precedent established on Cook's voyages; the orthography of te reo was still decades away from standardisation. King's method eventually resulted in a handwritten list of words and translations, accompanied by the occasional explanatory note, which took up several leaves of his journal.

And then, in the middle of this fairly pedestrian lexicographical inventory, the glint of a minor cultural epiphany flickers on the page. One of the groupings of words King had prepared pertained to various categories of family membership. All was going well as he wrote down their Māori equivalents – until he got to the word 'orphan'. There is no comment made by King in his journal about this but, pointedly, the space for the translation was left empty. The term 'orphan', in the common English sense of the term,[30] was a category that existed in Māori society only as a designation that a child's parents were dead.[31] In practice, the whāngai system ensured that all children who had lost their parents were brought up from that moment by others in the community.[32] Abandoned orphans of British parents, of the type that Māori may have seen on Norfolk Island, would have been unfamiliar and socially unacceptable to them, and so no word had ever emerged in te reo to describe an orphan in the English sense. That someone of King's political standing produced this *Vocabulary* testifies to the sense some Britons had that they were in the orbit of a language and culture that could not just be brushed aside to make way for the accession of English. For the short term at least, te reo was a language that they would have to come to terms with in one way or another.

There is an ironic coda to King's *Vocabulary* involving one of his main Māori sources, Tuki Tahua. In 1793 Tuki drew a map of New Zealand,[33] at first with chalk on the floor of the governor's house on Norfolk Island, and then on a piece of paper with pencil.[34] William Chapman, King's secretary, added the names to the map as Tuki dictated them.[35] In addition to incorporating boundaries, the coastline, placenames and the location of a few important sites, the map also showed a metaphysical path along which the souls of the dead[36] travelled to Hawaiki. One and a half centuries after Visscher had labelled parts of New Zealand, one of its indigenous occupants had done something similar. This was an ambiguous development. Tuki's map reclaimed the Māori names for parts of the country that in some cases had already been given English replacements, and was also symbolic of Māori entering the world of writing.

This was no straightforward transaction of knowledge. In map-making there was an intersection between drawing and words, but there was also a tinge of prophecy. The creators of maps read, saw, imagined and visualised territories as they were, but also in anticipation of how they might be.[37] The lines and labels that these cartographers traced eventually shifted from the page to the ground, becoming boundaries that defined the dominions of savage and civilised, chaos and order and, most significantly, past and future. Rather than being a culturally inert representation of the landscape, from the outset maps refracted images of the world as it was socially constructed by their makers.[38]

Maps of New Zealand in this period viewed the country as a 'new' land – at least culturally. Māori were already being seen as a relic of a primitive age[39] and so the placenames and their histories associated with those locations were easily written over by cartographers who preferred designations that would be familiar and reassuring to the new British presence in the region.[40] The act of naming was culturally highly invasive, and the colonists knew it. '*Names* of places, too, should be changed,' insisted Edward Gibbon Wakefield in 1849, on the basis that 'they make part of the moral atmosphere of the country'. With a bullish British preference for names like 'Nelson' and 'Wellington' that supposedly resonated with the greatness of the empire,[41] traditional Māori placenames stood little chance of surviving in print once the mapmakers set to work. Maps were where the forces of linguistic conquest mustered, and where literacy and the politics of domination first began to mix.

BREACHING THE LINES

It is a strange feature of both the first vocabularies of te reo and those maps of New Zealand that contained the original Māori placenames that they were created outside of the country. This might seem inconsequential, but it suggests the strong bond between language and power. The British presence in the region was numerically slight: the entire population of New South Wales – the nearest British colony – in 1800 was only around 5000.[42] These migrants to the South Pacific were not an isolated and segregated group but an outer branch of a global system of European and especially British economic and cultural imperialism – a system that was rapidly encroaching into the non-European areas of the world by the turn of the nineteenth century.[43] Even the emerging notion of English as an international language was a flexing of that imperialist attitude.[44] And because the earliest transfers of te reo into text often occurred outside New Zealand – either on ships or in neighbouring Australian colonies – it became easier for British power to take shape within the transcribed forms of the language.[45] It was as though English possessed a viral quality that allowed it to infect other languages, almost imperceptibly at first, as a precursor to inflicting much wider damage as time – and colonisation – progressed. Even slight incursions such as the various vocabularies that were produced had significance out of all proportion to their extent. There was a prevailing belief in Europe that a nation should be unified by a common language. Once a second language was added to the society its linguistic sovereignty could be disturbed, resulting in an imbalance in power relationships and disruptions to the established ways of projecting social and cultural identity.[46] For Britain, its empire accordingly needed a common language – even if only at an administrative level – to act as a unifying force in what was otherwise a diverse collection of culturally and linguistically dissimilar territories. Britain was projecting the cultural unity that the English language gave it onto those other parts of the world where it was asserting a commercial or terrestrial interest. The connection between an ethnic and cultural group and a specific territory also existed in traditional Māori society, embodied in the term 'tangata whenua'[47] (literally, people of the land) – a statement of political sovereignty, territorial dominion and cultural homogeneity – and reinforced through concepts such as mana whenua, tūrangawaewae and te ahikā.

Despite these shared notions of language being seen as a vital social unifier, there was a fundamental difference at play. Te reo was rooted exclusively in New Zealand and had no prospects of flourishing anywhere else in the world. By contrast, English, although anchored to its home country, had a remarkable capacity to clone itself in other territories, usually on the back of British imperial expansion.[48] The English essayist Thomas De Quincey in the early nineteenth century captured the vigorous optimism of this linguistic encroachment when he described the English language as 'travelling fast towards the fulfilment of its destiny … within the thirty last years [it] has run through all the stages of infancy into the first stage of maturity … [It] is running forward towards its ultimate mission of eating up, like Aaron's rod, all other languages. Even the German and the Spanish will inevitably sink before it.'[49] The metaphor of English as a spreading organism was an apt one, especially in light of Friedrich Nietzsche's later appraisal of the expansion of European culture into other parts of the world, in which he insisted that there was no alternative but for 'advanced' cultures to overrun 'savage regions'. 'Attempts to give an organism duration without the goal of reproduction destroy it,'[50] was his characteristically brutal conclusion on the matter.

As English – the most nomadic of the world's languages – migrated to New Zealand, it brought with it the means for the coloniser to encode and then reproduce the sorts of unequal relationships that were embedded in English and that it had previously used to coerce other populations.[51] But while these traits may have become part of the DNA of English, at the beginning of the nineteenth century you could be forgiven for thinking that the linguistic colonisation of te reo by English had anything of the certainty of this irrepressible organic expansionism. The stopover of the missionary vessel *Duff*[52] is a case in point. Its diversion to New Zealand to pick up some timber in 1800 led to one of those typically awkward linguistic encounters of the period, with Māori and European communicating clumsily using hand signals, facial gestures and, in the case of the visitors, the odd Tahitian word thrown in – anything to get the message across. This already faltering interaction between the two peoples was further prejudiced on the British side by their fear of the reputed cruelty of New Zealand's indigenous inhabitants. As the vessel approached the country's coast, for example, a violent storm caused great anxiety on board among the missionaries and crew as the *Duff* was tossed close to rocks. 'Our situation was reduced to a state of desperation!' Reverend William Smith later wrote. 'No probability of escaping the dreadful consequences of total wreck, and the more dreadful still of being torn to pieces by cannibals, if even we should arrive safe on shore.'[53] The following day the tempest was replaced by a gentle breeze, which enabled the ship to glide into the mouth of the Thames River that evening. At daybreak the next morning around five Māori reached the ship in a canoe, and as they drew near the ship's captain, William Wilson, called out to them in Tahitian, 'Harree Mai, Harre Mai te Pahhii' (Welcome to the canoe).[54] Wilson's intent was clear even if his language was not (pahhii – or pahī – was a less commonly used term for a large ocean-going canoe),[55] and the visitors climbed onto the deck. However, 'not being able to confer with them by language,' as Smith recorded, 'we had recourse to signs; by which we made them understand the object of our pursuit, who then directed us to sail south a considerable distance up the country, where we should find an abundance of trees of all descriptions, and also that a ship was there.' So fraught had the communication become between Māori and these visitors that Smith concluded, 'By their behaviour, I had reason to imagine that the great majority had never seen a European before.'[56] The brevity of such stopovers in New Zealand, coupled with the knowledge that there were no immediate plans to establish a mission, appears to have dissuaded visiting missionaries from learning even the rudiments of te reo. At the beginning of the nineteenth century, before large-scale whaling and sealing began, the very few Europeans who reached New Zealand tended to remain for only a few days and had no plans to return; there was almost no motive for them to learn the language spoken by Māori.

To cast these almost transient visitations as an indication of the slender and vulnerable nature of British involvement in New Zealand, nevertheless, would be to belie the distinction between the frailty that characterised the expeditions of these early emissaries of English and the intrusive strength of the language itself. The fact that English had reached New Zealand and was now lapping on its shores was already a harbinger of the erosion of te reo that would follow. It was a pattern with a well-established precedent. Even the rare instances of Europeans learning te reo at the start of the century were part of a shortlived anomaly. As much as they saw commercial benefit in speaking in the most rudimentary way the language of their trading partners in New Zealand, to many Māori it was that much more obvious that their commercial future depended on becoming familiar with English, even if there was no great urgency to do so right away.[57]

And no great powers of premonition would have been needed to see this. The expansion of English into other territories had started with similarly small steps. In India, British officials had made no attempt to eradicate local languages; the scale of the challenge alone might have been a deterrent there. Instead, English was introduced as the language of the colonial governing elite and of higher education (serving a similar function as Latin had in medieval Europe),[58] and spread among indigenous groups because of the perceived advantages it brought them.[59] Similar structures that emphasised English at the top of a linguistic hierarchy appeared in parts of the Caribbean, South Africa, West Africa, South Asia and in other parts of the Pacific.

What the imperial advocates of English could not have known was that once the language took root in some colonies, its dominance would outlast the empire that planted it. In Australia, New Zealand, Canada, the United States, South Africa and other former colonies the language transformed from a lingua franca to the new mother tongue for most of the populations.[60] And over time, English insinuated itself further, becoming a means of constructing identities, constituting knowledge systems, contextualising cultures and conferring civilisation on 'The Other'.[61] For some, it was a colonial scar that persisted well into the postcolonial era.

As for the status of te reo Māori as lodged in the minds of European visitors to New Zealand in the early nineteenth century, it tended to be lumped in with more general stereotypes about its speakers. How, after all, could te reo be perceived as anything other than the crude means of expression of a primitive people, when Māori themselves were painted as being culturally underdeveloped, socially barbarous and, in some cases, more animal than human? New South Wales Governor Lachlan Macquarie was in no doubt as to the qualities of Māori: he described them (and all the other Polynesians) in an 1810 despatch to London as 'in general a very treacherous race of people, and not to be trusted'.[62] Three years later, he issued a General Order that cautioned the masters and crews of ships visiting New Zealand about the risks of falling as 'a sacrifice to the indiscriminate revenge of the natives'.[63] This kind of attitude to Māori was more colourfully captured in the press; in 1811, for example, the *Sydney Gazette* warned extravagantly of the 'fury of the merciless hordes of savages that infest that barbarous coast' of New Zealand.[64] Māori cannibalism, above all else, accentuated for most Europeans this divide between savage and civilised. Depictions of the 'revolting barbarism' of Māori, and their 'degraded state',[65] rounded off the battery of condemnations. There could surely be nothing redeeming in the language spoken by such 'beasts'.[66]

It was not all acrimony and recriminations being hurled at Māori. Commerce, in particular, was a great leveller of the more hysterical charges that were being made. King pleaded the case for greater trade with Māori in 1805. In a letter to the Secretary of State for War and the Colonies he observed: 'The New Zealanders ... are found a very tractable people; hence there is every reason to expect that the assistance they may derive from them, if encouraged and liberally treated, will greatly facilitate their pursuits.' Already, the governor pointed out, several ships had berthed in the Bay of Islands, and had never, 'as far as I have learn'd, had any altercation with the natives, but have received every kind office and assistance in procuring their wood and water, &c., at a very cheap rate.'[67] And when John Savage sailed into the Bay of Islands in September of that year, his initial impressions were at once at odds with all those hoarsely recited rumours from British sailors about the ferocity of Māori: 'In a country that has been described as being peopled by a race of cannibals, you are agreeably surprised by the appearance of the natives, who betray no symptom of savage ferocity.' Such initial observations, he noted in his journal, 'tend forcibly to remove the prejudices you have imbibed from former accounts of this country and its inhabitants.'[68]

Neither of these stereotypes – Māori as barbarian or as compliant native – allowed for even the possibility of te reo being maintained as the means of communication in the longer term for visitors to New Zealand. Both considered te reo implicitly a language of the past. It went without question that English would eventually spread into New Zealand and displace the country's indigenous tongue, just as British arrivals would quash the 'deluded', 'barbarous superstition'[69] and 'the obscene customs and notions of the natives'[70] that tied Māori to a less enlightened past. Linguistic colonisation was every bit as important as its political and territorial relatives.

Six years after Marsden's first visit to New Zealand he was already able to look back with satisfaction at the advance of British values, which included the inroads English was making. 'Much has been done already towards the civilization of the natives in those parts of N. Zealand with which we have had any communication,' he informed CMS secretary Josiah Pratt in 1820, 'and nothing has tended more to this object than the chiefs and their sons visiting N.S. Wales ... I have some very fine youths with me now, who are acquiring the English language very fast.'[71] Two decades before the formal British assertion of sovereignty over New Zealand, the colonisation of the country was already well under way.

The belief that British imperial expansion in the nineteenth century was a blessing for those countries fortunate enough to come into its embrace has long since fallen from favour. More sober critiques now emphasise the rupturing effects on the colonised. Language was frequently on the frontline of this clash of cultures, as English – both spoken and written – served as the first instrument of colonial conquest. Among the opening shots were the documents that some Māori working on British ships were obliged to sign in the early nineteenth century as a condition of their employment.

The background to these early engagements by Māori with written text was the abusive treatment many were receiving on British vessels.[72] Cases of exploitation had become so frequent that in December 1813 Macquarie issued a proclamation that regulated the actions of any British ship operating in New Zealand waters and allowed for a fine to be imposed on vessels whose captain or crew breached the basic rights of any Māori serving on board.[73] This meant that working relationships became slightly more formalised, as Māori crew signed contracts with the captains of trading ships. Māori could end up serving on ships and being kept away from home for several months or even years at a time. The missionary Thomas Kendall, when lobbying for greater rights for Māori crew on trading vessels, pointed out to the authorities in Sydney that it was well known about Māori that 'after they have been some time from their home they are exceedingly desirous to return, and every unkind disappointment of their wishes tends greatly to excite their resentment'. Their returning home was at the discretion of the captain, who could always fall back on the employment contracts with their Māori crew (which the Māori usually signed with a cross) to enforce their will. Kendall drew attention to the crux of the problem with these crosscultural arrangements: 'It cannot be supposed that [Māori] are acquainted with the binding nature of an article at the time they sign it, and they must in certain cases on this very account deem the restraint a great hardship upon them.'[74] This was a harsh lesson in how text worked,[75] not only for the immediate consequences to those Māori who discovered that a mark on a piece of paper could constitute an enforceable obligation (a principle utterly alien to anything in their cultural experience), but also because it gave them a taste of the universalist attitude[76] of the British – the conviction that the British way applied everywhere, while other cultures were expected to yield because of their presumed inferiority.

ENGLISH GOING NATIVE

At the opposite end of the scale to these often unfortunate Māori encounters with the periphery of the European world were those few men who immersed themselves completely in Māori communities in New Zealand in the early nineteenth century and became fluent in te reo in the process. Thomas Taylor was one such man. An illiterate convict, he had absconded with three others while the ship – the *Hunter* – that was transporting them had stopped off at Waihou to pick up a supply of timber in 1799. Later known somewhat derogatorily as a Pākehā-Māori,[77] Taylor's name has survived in the historical records mainly through his encounters with subsequent European visitors to the Thames region, including those on the *El Plumier* in March 1801 and on the *Royal Admiral* the following month.[78] Taylor's conversations on board the *Royal Admiral*, summarised by the missionaries on the vessel, contained details about Māori customs, religion, agriculture, social structure, family relationships and other intelligence that gave them some insight into the nature of the country's indigenous people.[79]

It is nearly impossible to assess how proficient in te reo those few Europeans who spent time in Māori communities in this era were. But when sealer Robert Murray was picked up by the *Governor Bligh* and returned to Sydney in August 1810, after having spent several months marooned in a Māori settlement in the Foveaux Strait area, he claimed that he had become 'tolerably conversant in the native language', which he described as 'totally different from that of the Bay of Islands'. To be able to make such a distinction between dialects of the same language suggests that Murray had acquired at least enough vocabulary and grammar to be reasonably conversant with his Māori colleagues[80] (although equally, he may have made this statement as a boast or to conceal his own limited knowledge of the language spoken by Māori living in Sydney, who were almost exclusively from the Far North).

Murray probably spoke te reo in complete sentences rather than in stuttering utterances such as the captain of the *Duff* had relied on. He was a long-term visitor rather than a permanent resident of his host community[81] and so was on the periphery of the popular understanding of what a Pākehā-Māori was: he may have lived with the natives for some time, but he had not 'gone native'.[82] The contemporary European view of Pākehā-Māori was that they were in some sense betrayers of their race; they had consciously forgone civilisation for savagery, which went against the popular view that European civilisation was what all other people on Earth aspired to. White European supremacy was the moral and political consensus of the age.[83] The progress of civilisation depended on the axiomatic belief in the transition from savage to civilised society.[84] But Pākehā-Māori, rather than having any civilising effects on their new communities, were seen as having become 'more degraded than the natives'.[85] They were lost, apparently absorbed into an 'inferior' culture and, having 'gone native', had shown that European identity was anything but the watertight perimeter most people believed it to be; instead it was culturally porous and had allowed a few Europeans to leak through to join the ranks of the barbarians.[86] John Nicholas, who accompanied Samuel Marsden to New Zealand on the cleric's first visit to the country in 1814, offered as good a summation as any of the 'respectable' European opinion on the calibre of those of their countrymen who had abandoned civilisation in favour of life in Māori society:

> The persons who at distant intervals resorted … [to New Zealand], were men … of callous hearts, who were as little disposed to conciliate the friendship of the rude inhabitants, as they were to pay a due regard to their own character; and, in addition to this, the odium thrown on the natives themselves, by being viewed as ferocious cannibals, served, as it were, to interdict any cordial communication with them. Dreaded by the good, and assailed by the worthless, their real dispositions were not ascertained; the former dared not venture to civilize them, the latter only added to their ferocity. Too long had they continued in this state of obnoxious barbarism.[87]

Yet, as the example of Thomas Taylor shows, those Europeans who had chosen for whatever reason to live in Māori communities were not thereafter divorced from the rest of the world and abandoned to their sinful life. On the contrary, they sometimes acted as cultural and linguistic intermediaries,[88] marrying the commercial and communication needs of two peoples who otherwise struggled to comprehend the world of the other. Pākehā-Māori occupied a middle ground where the binary notion of civilised and primitive dissolved.[89] But the status of these Pākehā-Māori remained ambiguous. Yes, they lived in and by the rules of their adoptive community, yet they were also apart from it, not only ethnically but culturally and linguistically. They were exposed and weak in the community they lived in, often as a minority of one; but they could negotiate in the language of the trader, and this made them someone to be protected by their community as a commercial asset. They came to represent a type of cultural synthesis, embodying the traits and histories of their past and present environs, including the necessity of these immigrants learning to speak te reo.

This was no happy equilibrium, however. Men like Taylor may have appeared to be at the complete mercy of their volatile hosts[90] but – to paraphrase Louis Antoine de Bougainville – 'the English were at their strongest when they appeared, at least to themselves, the most weak'.[91] The outward signs of Pākehā-Māori being transformed were obvious, including their clothing, the acquisition by some of moko (tattoo) and, of course, their speaking te reo. But in less visible ways their presence also transformed the communities in which they lived. Taylor was a conduit to trade with the outside world, and his Māori hosts would have come to realise that they themselves would have to master the only language that British traders and migrants could understand[92] if they were to prosper through trade. In the longer term, leaving communication and growing commercial opportunities to just one or two individuals who arrived in the region by accident was just too precarious. If the traders were not going to learn te reo, then the only option was for Māori to earn English,[93] and it was Pākehā-Māori like Taylor who unwittingly forced this realisation on the Māori communities they lived in.

This phase of the expansion of English into New Zealand was so slight that it did not appear to be displacing te reo. This is an important point: there was no way chiefs could know how British colonisation and the English language worked together like the hook and jab of a boxer – unpredictable and random in appearance, but coordinated at a subconscious, almost instinctive level to deliver the knockout blow to the indigenous language. In the early nineteenth century, Māori would not have felt that their language could ever be threatened; after all, they had no experience or even conception of a language being endangered. There was no precedent for them to draw on.

For the few more upstanding Englishmen, the consequences – moral and cultural – of the engagements between Māori and the riff-raff of the European world were highly undesirable. When George Clarke jnr visited a Māori settlement in Otago he complained that its inhabitants 'appeared to be in a miserable condition', which he suspected was due to the fact that 'more than in any other part of the country they had suffered by their intercourse with the very roughest of whalers and sealers, and altogether they were in a more pitiable state than any of the tribes in the Northern Island'. Their population, physique and morals had deteriorated in his view and, as a corollary, linguistically, 'The very jargon they spoke in their common talk with Europeans was a strange medley of bad French, bad English and low Māori.'[94] The significance of this for the future of te reo in the nineteenth century lies in the uncompromising expectation by Clarke and some of his contemporaries that a more standardised form of English ought eventually to prevail in New Zealand – and the sooner the better, if the level of Clarke's frustration is any indicator. It was not enough that people from different cultures managed to communicate through a pidgin language. Such a spectrum of language contact that incorporated more than two languages (while missionaries were still struggling just to contend with English and Māori), and which carried with it the chance of the breakdown of existing social structures – ironically sometimes the very indigenous structures the missionaries themselves were attempting to modify – was something to be actively prevented. Pidgin languages (and their creole successors) potentially undermined the authority of 'standard' English by orienting their speakers to a different source of linguistic and social influence, and by destabilising the exclusivity of standard forms of English as the language of religion, of European moral authority[95] and, later, of political jurisdiction.[96]

'A WORK OF VAST MAGNITUDE'

Of the cast of individuals and groups that had some involvement in New Zealand in the beginning of the nineteenth century, the missionaries had more of an instrumental role than any other group in the remodelling of te reo Māori into a written language, and in the way Europeans engaged with the language. This transformation of te reo did not take place through a gradual accretion of events over several decades. Within five years of the first missionaries arriving in New Zealand, the groundwork was laid for the revolution of the language: they brought about a rapid, profound and irreversible change to te reo. And Samuel Marsden was central to the initial pace of this change.

Marsden's plans for establishing a mission in New Zealand were initially roused after meeting a delegation of Māori led by the Ngāpuhi chief Te Pahi in Port Jackson in 1805. Marsden considered Te Pahi 'a man of high rank and influence in his own country' and someone who 'possessed a clear, strong and comprehensive mind, and was anxious to gain what knowledge he could of our laws and customs'.[97] Marsden's gratification at this meeting was founded on the sense that he was introducing 'a noble and intelligent race' to the 'blessings of civilization and the knowledge of the Christian religion', through 'introducing the chiefs into civil society at Port Jackson'.[98] He pictured Te Pahi's curiosity about the wider world as the first step in a well-trodden path by which the savage would be subordinated to the dictates of civilised European society. At the same time, Christianity would further liberate Māori from the stultifying strictures of pagan tradition. The 'communion of the soul with God and its eternal salvation … [were] the only objects worth living for'[99] in the minds of all upright Christians, and would replace the worldly will of the chiefs and the superstitious grip of the tohunga.[100] For Marsden and his cohorts, the force of civilisation's gravitational pull on the barbarian was inevitable. There were no 'ifs' in his mind about this occurring – there was just the firm conviction of 'when'.

Māori were inclined to approach these encounters with a measure of shrewdness that does not always make it to the surface in contemporary European accounts. They were not blinded by any great moral light emanating from Marsden's pronouncements on civilisation. For Te Pahi, and almost all of those who followed him to Sydney, the civilising effects of the English language were not an end in themselves – or at least not a priority. English was a commodity and a means of accessing the world of the one European empire that had a global reach. Any chief worth his salt would have appreciated the opportunities that might come from closer diplomatic relations with the agents of this empire – even those like Marsden, who were on its outer extremities. Each of these views happily accommodated the other: Marsden cherished the thought of souls from New Zealand entering his civilisation–Christianity nexus, and Māori like Te Pahi saw it as an entrée into an immense commercial and technological emporium.[101]

The shortcomings of te reo would have been obvious to Marsden. It suffered from the twin impediments of being a 'primitive' language (at least on the basis of being a language spoken by a people perceived as primitives), and an oral language that was therefore unable to provide the architecture of civilisation that literacy offered. New South Wales became the satellite location from where Marsden made some of his early experimental attempts at modernising Māori society. He formed a 'Seminary' at his home in Parramatta 'for the instruction of New Zealanders'. Nothing would better 'enlarge the minds … of the natives', he believed, 'than to witness the advantages of civilized life'. The numbers of Māori at the seminary ranged from around six to 10 at any one time, and they were taught the basics of agriculture, together with 'moral and religious instruction'.[102] Here, knowledge and literacy coalesced, especially in the case of moral instruction. There was no alternative.

What has sometimes been overlooked in analyses of Christianity's entry into New Zealand is that the faith was one based entirely on the written word. Like Muslims and Jews, Christians are Ahl al-Kitāb, People of the Book – and a single volume at that. This presented a fundamental challenge to missionaries attempting to make converts: in what way should they communicate the message of the Bible to Māori? There was no single best answer as the first batch of missionaries departed for the Bay of Islands in 1814, but it was becoming clear that in order to convert Māori, their language would have to be converted into written form. With the meagre number of missionaries available to minister to potentially tens of thousands of Māori, Marsden had understandably given little if any thought to becoming an evangelist for English.[103]

Although many Māori were interested in the spiritual message of the missionaries, some of them, such as Ngāpuhi chief Ruatara, tended to keep one eye gazing heavenwards while the other was trained on the technology, assets and trade they knew would follow in the wake of a missionary arrival. For Ruatara, there was no ambiguity in this stance. He was initially the most zealous of the Northland chiefs to embrace the temporal gains that he saw on offer through Marsden, and he made a measured show of interest in the spiritual side of the European world as well, when necessary. While he was in New South Wales in August 1814, Ruatara requested that his half-brother, who had accompanied him on the trip, stay behind with Marsden so that the boy 'might be instructed in useful knowledge'. The reverend described Ruatara's relative as 'a very fine intelligent youth, exceedingly well disposed and industrious. This youth is next in authority, and will succeed Duaterra [Ruatara] in his estates,' and importantly, in the context of an emerging missionary 'policy' on te reo, Marsden added: 'I intend him to remain till he can speak the English language, and gain a knowledge of agriculture.'[104] Marsden saw some proficiency in English and a knowledge of British agricultural methods as a means to a civilised, Christian end (civilisation and Christianity were inseparable in his mind),[105] whereas Ruatara viewed literacy and agricultural knowledge as ends in themselves – they were the complementary 'commodities' that would bring him rapid economic growth and presumably the enhanced political power and mana he anticipated would come with it.

Marsden's plan was to direct the Anglican mission in New Zealand from Sydney; the missionaries on the ground would manage the mission's day-to-day affairs and would feed back to him their requirements, experiences and expectations. The triumvirate that made up this body of missionaries comprised William Hall, John King and their leader, Kendall. None was an ordained minister; Hall and King were tradespeople (a carpenter and a shoemaker respectively), and Kendall was a teacher. On 14 March 1814[106] the *Active* sailed from Sydney for New Zealand with Kendall and Hall on board.[107] A fortnight on, while the ship sought shelter in a bay on the Australian coast, Kendall wrote a letter that he would send to CMS secretary Josiah Pratt when he returned to Sydney around five months later. In it, he outlined his intentions for when he reached New Zealand, and he borrowed a line from Marsden about promoting good relations with Māori[108] as a prelude to his plans for the language:

> Our object at this time is 'to promote a friendly intercourse with the natives of New Zealand.' I also wish to procure a native of New Zealand who is acquainted with the English language as a kind of companion, that I may be enabled to proceed with the New Zealand vocabulary which I have now in hand. I am told some of the natives of New Zealand can speak the English language tolerably well; one of these would therefore be of great assistance to me. I have already collected several words, chiefly from a young chief whose name is To-i [Tuhi] and whom I have clothed and fed for several weeks past; but he knows so little of English that I have not been able to make much progress, although he does all in his power to assist me.[109]

Kendall kept a record of his earliest efforts at introducing English to Māori as a written as well as a spoken language. In July 1814, the first attempt at something resembling English school lessons in New Zealand was made – the embryo of literacy in the country:

> I had some cards of letters and monosyllables by me, such as are used by the lower classes in Doctor Bell's system of education, and I proposed to give each of the natives some fishhooks for every page they should learn correctly upon my arrival in New South Wales. At this they expressed the greatest satisfaction, and my little pupil Depero [Ripiro] seemed transported with the idea of possessing some riches which he should have to show his mother and his uncle Kangwha [Kangaroa] upon his return to his native land. The natives pronounce with difficulty the letters C, G, H, J, X, and Z. The remainder of the English alphabet they

can articulate very well. It is my intention in my little vocabulary of the language to substitute K for the C.[110]

Kendall was not just teaching, he was learning. He was developing his planned vocabulary, which was still a rough draft and incomplete. As he got 'better acquainted with the language', he suggested, 'I have no doubt but I shall find it necessary to make many corrections of my own words.' Initially his main source of vocabulary was a work that had been produced by the London Missionary Society missionary John Eyre,[111] 'containing several thousands of words in Manuscript from which I or any future servant of the Society may expect great assistance'. Eyre's work was a dictionary of Tahitian, but in Kendall's rather hasty assessment this was no great impediment. 'There can be no doubt,' he argued, 'but the Language of the New Zealanders and Otaheitians and indeed of most of the natives of the South Sea Islands is radically the same. I have observed that A New Zealander can understand a Native of Otaheite, Bolabola, or Owhyhee in the course of a very few days.'[112]

Kendall soon discovered that the dictionary was insufficient even for the most basic conversation with Māori. Faced with the pressing need to become more fluent in te reo, he quickly jotted down a few rudimentary phrases. Among the examples he gathered were 'Ire mi kiki [Haere mai ki te kai] Come & eat', and 'Emmera Ho my why [E mara homai (he) wai], Bring me some water'.[113] Yes, the spelling was inconsistent (for example, the 'ai' diphthong in te reo was spelt variously with an 'i' or 'y', as in English), and no attempt was made to deduce any grammatical rules from the phrases he recorded, but it was another early step at encasing te reo in text – an advance that was all the more important because of the number of translated words that he mustered: 322 in total, along with 17 short phrases designed to allow other Europeans (well, missionaries anyway) to begin communicating with Māori.[114]

This was always going to be a stop-gap measure. Acquiring full fluency in te reo was at the forefront of Kendall's thoughts, and he even committed his concerns to God in prayer. On 12 July, as a group of Māori on board the *Active* watched the missionaries undertaking their morning devotional exercises, Kendall prayed that

> the petitions which they heard but which they did not understand may be accepted by the most High God: And that he will bless our endeavours to acquire such a knowledge of their Language as will enable us in time to make known the glad tidings of the Gospel and direct the Attention of

these poor benighted heathens to that Saviour who alone can enlighten their darkness.[115]

Proselytising was utterly dependent on language, hence Kendall's earnest plea for divine assistance in learning te reo. To be able to speak to potential converts in their own tongue would be inestimably advantageous to the mission.

But then, so too would it be helpful if Māori learned to speak English – and on this side of the linguistic ledger, progress initially looked promising. Kendall reported in a satisfied manner that those Māori he had been instructing had 'learned the English alphabet in five or six days', and that one of them had 'also written several copies of letters'.[116] The system Kendall was using to teach English was based on the ideas of Andrew Bell (1753–1832), an Anglican minister and educationalist whose influential 1797 book *An Experiment in Education* contained novel suggestions about how to make boys into 'good scholars, good men, and good Christians'.[117] It was a system he had devised while running an institution in Madras for the illegitimate and orphaned sons of British officers, and it relied on people being taught to help each other to improve their skills. Uncommonly, for the period, Kendall's system eschewed corporal punishment and favoured a reward system instead (he offered fishhooks to his students when they successfully completed a task).

No mission is an island, and during his exploratory journey to the Bay of Islands, Kendall found that the little English that Māori had already acquired was coloured by the calibre of visiting Europeans they had met. The missionary found himself chastising Tuhi 'for making use of some bad language which he had learnt from the seamen'. Whetoi,[118] another chief accompanying them, commended Kendall's stance and then (possibly with some mischievous intent) 'repeated the blasphemous expressions of Englishmen, saying they were no good. "Yes" and "no" (he said) were good words to make use of'.[119]

When Kendall and Hall returned to New South Wales in August unharmed by New Zealand's feared indigenes, Marsden was more confident than ever in the success of his planned mission to the country. In November he sought from the colony's governor a four-month leave of absence from his duties in Parramatta in order to plant a CMS mission in the Bay of Islands. The leave was 'happily' granted,[120] and he prepared for his departure. Among the passengers on the voyage were Kendall, Hall and King and their respective families, along with the chiefs Hongi, Korokoro, Tuhi, Tuhi's brother and Ruatara.[121] It was a high-powered group of leaders, which reflected favourably on Marsden's status.[122] The editor of the *Sydney Gazette* was in no doubt as to the merits of Marsden's mission:

> The *Active* … is expected to sail on a return voyage to New Zealand, in three weeks or a month, for the excellent purpose, as we understand, of setting down several Gentlemen of the Church Missionary Society, to commence the benign labour of opening the minds of the natives to those benevolent and just conceptions which adorn the Christian Religion, and which in a region of cannibals, will, it is much to be hoped, soon display its benefits.[123]

But in all the enthusiastic anticipation about the mission, Marsden was nonetheless clear about the scale of the task ahead of him. In what was a prophetic comment, he said: 'The civilisation of the natives of New Zealand, and the introduction of the Gospel among them, is a work of vast magnitude.'[124] It was precisely because of the great sense of destiny he had for the New Zealand mission that he did not allow this commitment to get carried away with wispy idealism. He wrote that it was his 'full intention of accompanying the settlers to New Zealand, in order to aid them in their first establishment and to give them as much influence as possible amongst the natives'.[125] A practical start was all he hoped for.

The Māori accompanying the missionaries from New South Wales on this voyage occupied some of the many spare hours on the trip by singing. John Nicholas made notes of a few of these songs and, probably unknowingly, produced the first transcription of Māori lyrics, including one which he described as 'a low, soft, and plaintive air … not without harmony, and has that similarity to our chanting'. This particular song was about a man carving a canoe, who fled when a group of enemies approached him. He was pursued and eventually caught and put to death. 'Many of the expressions in this song,' Nicholas observed, 'possess a remarkable degree of natural tenderness, and a kind of piteous melancholy runs through the whole of it.' The parts were sung alternately by different Māori in the group, giving the song an effect that was 'not uninteresting to the sympathetic philanthropist'.[126] The orthography that Nicholas used was almost entirely his own – an inevitable characteristic of all early attempts at transcribing te reo, where there were few other available examples to base any standardised conventions on. Nicholas's effort was generally phonetic – which depended on how the transcriber heard the words – but also contained English idiosyncrasies such as the fricative 'th', which was highly unlikely to have been a feature of te reo's pronunciation. Nicholas eventually published the text of the song in the following form:

Nohohannah marharrar hannah hoko hetu
Tetarrah thumu thumu, hotha na whackah
Ho murthar tui; tupu farkar edo, teeah mi
Nah teyawhah carmuthu rah hecahhow
Taradee, artukee to parrah tar nepha
Whyesho attua no, wharho towriver tuwhy
Ta-isha mi hare, emow narwhackah; towhu.
Huah tari karhah tacotangheetanghee
Pheeu athu farkar wharhow; mo to
Iree farkar attah taparreeparree whackee
Why takee eree keeree; tarmarthui ruru po
Whatthu tackah rarunghah kecoranghee
Pukee uhahu reekee kecotanghah my
No rafarrafar taho yonghee tahonghahruru
Totarrah how mattah reekee phi yapoo ha.[127]

Entertaining as these songs may have been, they did not alleviate the underlying fear of Māori in the minds of the other passengers and crew on board. For most Europeans heading to New Zealand, engaging with Māori was still laden with risk, and Marsden was not exempt from such apprehensions. On 15 December, near North Cape, he gathered some of the Māori on board the *Active* in preparation for them going on shore, 'so that they might open an intercourse between us and the Natives'. The boat that was lowered was heavily armed so its occupants could defend themselves if attacked, but 'Before the boat had reached the land, a canoe appeared alongside the *Active*, with plenty of fish; and, shortly afterward, a Chief followed from the shore, who immediately came on board with his son.' Marsden entered in his journal: 'We were now quite free from all fear, as the Natives seemed desirous to show their attention to us by every possible means in their power. I then informed the Chief that we wanted some hogs and potatoes.'[128] The incongruity of the world's most malleable, persistent and invasive language gaining a foothold in New Zealand with the aid of individuals who would flinch at the slightest quiver of Māori militarism in a way encapsulates this phase of the advent of English to the country: it was able to squeeze out other languages in places where it got established in the first place, but that act of getting established could be a haphazard undertaking with no certitude as to when or how it would happen.

Ten days later Marsden was in his cabin in the Bay of Islands, preparing to deliver his sermon a few hundred metres away at Oihi. That morning when he stood on the deck of the *Active* looking towards the shore, he saw the British flag flying and took it as being 'the signal for the dawn of civilization, liberty, and religion in that dark and benighted land'. He added, 'I never viewed the British colours with more gratification, and flattered myself they would never be removed till the natives of that island enjoyed all the happiness of British subjects.'[129] The desire to save souls momentarily gave way to a more patriotic type of mission, replete with the trappings of civilisation, the rule of law – and the implicit requirement for literacy that these entailed.

On shore, Marsden and the other missionaries from the *Active* were led to a makeshift pulpit. His account of the scene gives a sense of how he saw his utterances in English being anticipated and received by the local community, and of the consequence with which he viewed his sermon:

> The inhabitants of the town with the women and children and a number of other chiefs formed a circle round the whole. A very solemn silence prevailed – the sight was truly impressive. I got up and began the service with singing the Old Hundred Psalm, and felt my very soul melt within me when I viewed my congregation and considered the state we were in.
>
> After reading the service, during which the natives stood up and sat down at the signal given by the motion of Korokoro's switch which was regulated by the movements of the Europeans, it being Christmas Day, I preached from the second chapter of St. Luke's Gospel, the tenth verse: 'Behold I bring you glad tidings of great joy.' The natives told Duaterra [Ruatara] they could not understand what I meant. He replied they were not to mind that now for they would understand by and by, and that he would explain my meaning as far as he could. When I had done preaching he informed them what I had been talking about. Duaterra was very much pleased that he had been able to make all the necessary preparations for the performance of Divine service in so short a time, and we felt much obliged to him for his attention. He was extremely anxious to convince us that he would do everything for us that lay in his power and that the good of his country was his principal consideration. In the above manner the Gospel has been introduced into New Zealand, and I fervently pray that the glory of it may never depart from its inhabitants till time shall be no more.[130]

The sermon was almost certainly the longest oration given in English in New Zealand to this time. The passage from Luke relayed the details of Christ's birth. Since it was written, it had been translated from Aramaic and Hebrew to Greek, then had ended up in Western Europe locked in Latin for centuries until the Reformation released it into the popular languages of the day, including English. Now, through Ruatara's interpretation of the essence of Marsden's sermon, something of this message had been translated into te reo, which thus became part of an ancient lineage.

An illustration published in the Auckland *Weekly News*[131] in 1964, of Marsden's Christmas Day service at Oihi in the Bay of Islands 150 years earlier, depicted an image of the fleshy-faced reverend, draped in his vestments, delivering a Christian service to a congregation of deferential if rather puzzled Māori. It quickly became part of New Zealand's historical iconography, a graphic representation of one of the longstanding legends of the country's evolution into a nation state. The symbolism of two peoples fusing into one hybridised and happy cultural entity was embellished by the consecration of *Metrosideros excelsa* – the pōhutukawa – as a de facto Christmas tree. 'For here in Aotearoa the Pohutukawa blooms whilst in the opposite part of the world the brilliant Star of Bethlehem ushers in the birthday of Jesus Christ. Thus the Pakeha gave the Pohutukawa a second name, The Christmas Tree, for it is at this time of Christmas that the Pohutukawa is seen blooming in all its beauty and glory' was the cloying explanation of this tree's status in the Department of Maori Affairs' quarterly magazine *Te Ao Hou: The New World* in 1973. The pōhutukawa was elevated in this belaboured version to being part of an arboreal apostolic succession: 'the Pohutukawa welcomed our ancestors to their new home. In 1814, Samuel Marsden preached the first sermon when our ancestors heard The Good News, on Christmas Day'; and for good measure the point was made that 'at the time when the Pohutukawa was again in bloom, in 1928, a Maori was consecrated the first Bishop of Aotearoa'.[132]

The historical events at the heart of this confection are well documented, but how they should be interpreted is another matter. Looked at from the position of the coloniser, this was a sermon delivered to Māori by Marsden, with Ruatara serving as organiser and cultural intermediary. However, this view ignores a vital point: that most of the Māori present at the sermon would not have understood a word of what Marsden was saying. The role of language transforms the interpretation of Marsden's message at Oihi: instead of being an improvised church service, this was, from a Māori perspective, 'a political meeting [hui] … again choreographed by the leading chiefs of the area, particularly Ruatara. At this hui, Ruatara, the most chiefly Maori who spoke English, got to speak to the people about the white strangers now coming to live – at his behest – in this place.' Suddenly the power of language shifts the balance, converting the event from a religious to a political one: 'By their actions, the crowd indicated that Māori on the day upheld Ruatara's words (rather than Marsden's which they did not understand). In other words, in helping to attract the curious crowds, Marsden unwittingly became Ruatara's helper as Ruatara persuaded the people to accept his – Ruatara's – futuristic plans.'[133] So significant was this language barrier that it is possible some of those in the 'congregation' did not even appreciate the religiosity of the event. It was only later that presumptions about the significance to Māori of this sermon were carved into the national memory. The exclusivity of te reo in New Zealand made the sense of this encounter entirely different: Ruatara, not the parson, was at the centre of Marsden's appearance before the multitudes at Oihi. As with so much of history, the reflection of events depends on the viewpoint.

The interim effect of Marsden and his fellow proselytisers founding the country's first mission was that te reo was temporarily cleft into two geographic zones as far as the colonisers were concerned: the Bay of Islands, and the rest of the country. Over the next few years, within the orbit of the fledgling mission at Rangihoua and then Paihia, te reo became a written language; and within the mission station itself, the first community of English speakers was established. In the rest of New Zealand it was te reo as usual, in its traditional form; most Māori had yet to see a European, let alone be exposed to the transfiguration of their language into a written form or translated into another language altogether. Te reo still had the weight of numbers over English – but not internationally; and as New Zealand was being drawn rapidly into the English-speaking international realm, that numerical superiority was more chimerical than most – Māori or European – would have realised.

CHAPTER 3

'E mate ana matou i te pukapuka kore'
1815 to mid-1830s

WHOSE KUKI?

Being important in traditional Māori society meant you got remembered, and, like some Newtonian principle, the more important a person was, the longer the blaze of their reputation trailed behind them, in some cases for generations after they had died. In the early nineteenth century there was one man whose status – uniquely – spanned both Māori and European history: James Cook. By the 1820s Cook was a lionised figure in Britain[1] – an explorer, empire-enlarger, hero and, ultimately, a martyr. His prominence is still being perpetuated in print and elsewhere. There was a minor industry in published accounts of Cook's expeditions which simultaneously cultivated and reinforced his eminence in the pantheon of great British explorers.[2] And although Cook's accomplishments were exceptional, the sustenance of his reputation through books was commonplace. In the European world, this was the chief means by which reputations were maintained.

At the same time, the mana of Cook and his feats permeated the oral histories in Māori communities that he visited. Augustus Earle, an artist who spent eight months in New Zealand from late October 1827, noted in his journal a series of convivial meetings he had with the Ngāti Manu chief Te Whareumu (whom Earle called 'George') in Kororareka in the Bay of Islands: 'Our friend George generally paid us a visit after the business of the day was over, and took a cup of tea … while he sipped his beverage, we lit our pipes, and managed, with our slight knowledge of his language, together with his imperfect English, to keep up a sort of conversation.' Earle could not have acquired more than a modicum of te reo in the short time he had been in the country, and so presumably it was Te Whareumu who was the more bilingual of the two. Still, they maintained a steady friendship for most of Earle's stay in New Zealand. As Earle later put it, 'Sometimes this was rather wearisome; but occasionally it became interesting in the extreme.'

One instance of this was when Te Whareumu told him that 'when Captain Cook touched here, he [Te Whareumu] was a little child; but … his mother (old Turero, who was then with him,) remembered his coming well.'[3] There was clearly a degree of esteem in being able to claim descent from someone who had seen the great explorer in the flesh.

When Joel Polack landed in Poverty Bay in October 1769, 66 years after Cook had been there, the trader met Manutai whom he described as the 'grandson of Te Ratu, a principal chief'.[4] Despite some ambiguity about Te Ratu's exact identity,[5] the description that had been passed on to Manutai was the hallmark of an indigenous group encountering The Other for the first time and trying to contextualise features of this foreign arrival in a language that did not yet stretch to encompass what they had witnessed:

> Cook's ship was at first taken for a bird by the natives; and many remarks passed among them as to the beauty and size of its wings, as the sails of this novel specimen in ornithology were supposed to be. But on seeing a smaller bird, unfledged (without sails), descending into the water, and a number of party-coloured beings, but apparently in the human shape, also descending, the bird was regarded as a houseful of divinities. Nothing could exceed the astonishment of the people.[6]

It is interesting to note that, while the terminology used to describe European ships was widespread in Māori society by the mid-1830s, especially in coastal settlements,[7] the account that Manutai relayed to Polack remained faithful to the type of language that had been used in the late 1760s – an indication of just how disciplined the transmission of oral histories was.

The bearing that whakapapa had on Māori oral histories was disclosed when Polack discussed the local reminiscences of Cook. One chief asked him 'if Cook was my father or uncle', to which he replied diplomatically that 'proud as I should be of the relationship, I could not boast of being so nearly connected, but that I belonged to the same tribe of Europeans, and was born under the same venerable chieftain'. The next question put to Polack was 'if Kuki [Cook] had been a great chief in his own country Ingerani. I answered that no name was held in greater estimation, and that the benefit he did his tribe in making known to them countries, the existence of which they were previously to his time ignorant of, would cause his services to be cherished by future tribes yet unborn.'[8]

What is most notable of all about these histories of Cook's visits to parts of New Zealand is that they were created, carried and communicated by Māori for Māori. The examples that Earle and Polack relayed show that this history had become indigenised: Māori had taken curatorial control of the material and structured it in accordance with the particular architecture of oral history that their culture utilised. And the term 'maori' is used advisedly here – yes, it refers to the ethnic group, but it also had application as an adjective, meaning ordinary, normal, or belonging to the community.[9] This definition extended to self-identification once Europeans began to arrive; the term was used to designate 'the ordinary people of the land'.[10] These accounts of meetings with Cook had been configured in a way that made them a normal part of the corpus of Māori oral history for those communities with some history of encounter with the captain. Even Cook's name had been appropriated as 'Kuki' and was now woven into the lexicon of New Zealand's indigenous culture. It would therefore be simplistic to presume that European ways of seeing the world (expressed in English) naturally dominated Māori ways of seeing the world (expressed in te reo) whenever the two met.

'BY UNIVERSAL CONFESSION'

By the beginning of the nineteenth century, officials and administrators in Britain's imperial jewel, India, were crystallising their views about indigenous knowledge and languages in a way that was to emerge as conventional wisdom wherever else British commercial or political interests were taking hold. It was the conviction of Charles Grant, chairman of the British East India Company, that 'the Hindoos would … be glad to possess the language of their masters, the language which always gives weight and consequence to the natives who have any acquaintance with it',[11] as he put it in 1813. James Mill,[12] a senior official in the company, argued 11 years later that the country's indigenous population should be taught 'useful knowledge' as opposed to 'Hindu knowledge' in schools[13] as one way of divesting them of a 'destructive' culture in which 'their minds were enchained more intolerably than their bodies'.[14] This in turn influenced Lord William Bentinck, governor-general of India, who proposed that 'the great object of the British government ought to be the promotion of European literature and science among the natives of India; and that all the funds appropriated for the purpose of education would be best employed on English education alone'.[15]

None of these men was a match, however, for the most vociferous crusader for the propagation of English in Britain's colonial possessions in this era. Thomas Babington Macaulay, who served assecretary to the Board of Control (which oversaw the British East India Company), wielded a kind of blunt cultural tyranny in India, premised on an unwavering belief in the inherent superiority of British civilisation and the English language. His famous minute on the issue encapsulated a generation of ideas that had been taking shape among British policymakers on how their language fitted in with those of indigenous cultures in territories where they had established an interest. The short answer was that it did not – at least judging by Macaulay's position:

> Whoever knows [English] has ready access to all the vast intellectual wealth, which all the wisest nations of the earth have created and hoarded in the course of ninety generations. It may be safely said, that the literature now extant in that language is of far greater value than all the literature which three hundred years ago was extant in all the languages of the world together. The question now before us is simply whether, when it is in our power to teach this language, we shall teach languages, by which, by universal confession, there are not books on any subject which deserve to be compared to our own; whether, when we can teach European science, we shall teach systems which, by universal confession, whenever they differ from those of Europe, differ for the worse … I have never found one among them who could deny that a single shelf of a good European library was worth the whole native literature of India and Arabia.[16]

Macaulay ruled out indigenous language, knowledge and traditions of learning altogether on the basis that they were demonstrably inferior in almost every aspect compared with the European (and specifically British) alternative.[17]

Such a general view about the inferiority of indigenous peoples and their cultures had been radiating throughout the British world for at least half a century. These peoples were the 'wild untutored cousin'[18] of Europe, intellectually and culturally static,[19] and encumbered by 'pre-Newtonian science and technology, and … pre-Newtonian attitudes towards the physical world'.[20] The philosophical footing for this perception of the non-European world had been set by Thomas Hobbes in 1651 in a statement that became a manifesto for all advocates of the superiority of European civilisation, the final line of which was recited ad nauseum as a rhetorical warning of what the civilised world was up against:

In such condition there is no place for industry, because the fruit thereof is uncertain, and consequently no culture of the earth, no navigation nor use of the commodities that may be imported by sea, no commodious building, no instruments of moving and removing such things as require much force, no knowledge of the face of the earth; no account of time, no arts, no letters, no society, and, which is worst of all, continual fear and danger of violent death, and the life of man solitary, poor, nasty, brutish, and short.[21]

Ironically, intellectual ideas in Europe about the uncivilised essence of indigenous peoples in other parts of the world were central to Europe's sense of its own superior civilisation.[22] Places where people still lived in a so-called savage state were a reminder of how far Europe had progressed.[23] It was as though, if primitivism did not exist, Europe would have had to create it as something to define itself against.

As Europe began to encroach into New Zealand in a more concerted way after Marsden's initial visit in 1814, it was inevitable that this embedded mentality of cultural superiority would have some bearing on how the coloniser would regard a language such as te reo. Whatever short-term concessions to te reo were held up as examples of European charity or altruism, the objective of the British in New Zealand – even if they themselves did not always realise it – was to 'depose "primitive" cultures and install variants of their own religious, social, political and economic regimes. This was the standard price levied for entering the world known by Europe.'[24]

Signs of this European superiority complex – some obvious and some less so – are sprinkled throughout most accounts written by visitors to New Zealand in the first half of the nineteenth century. On the evening of 19 March 1814, Marsden looked at a group of Māori he was encamped with and described them 'lying in all directions like a flock of sheep upon the grass'. Unable to sleep, at three o'clock the next morning he got up and wandered around the camp. 'Never did I behold the blessed advantages of civilization in a more grateful light than now' was the thought that came to him as he contemplated those Māori sleeping on the ground 'like the beasts of the field'.[25] This sort of crude (although not ill-spirited in Marsden's case) characterisation of Māori as somehow closer to the animal kingdom than the human one was not exclusive to the visiting cleric. Māori were described variously as being wild animals,[26] beastly[27] and inhuman,[28] and with a language that was grunted,[29] growled,[30] roared,[31] howled[32] and screeched[33] rather than spoken.

This is what te reo increasingly had to contend with as small streams of Europeans meandered into the country in the following decades: the near-universal brutalisation and primitivisation of all things Māori, and the establishment of the English language and British culture as prerequisites for the propagation of European civilisation in New Zealand. The fact that these attitudes towards te reo and its native speakers are not more prominent and explicit in the written historical records of the era is not because they were a minority view (they were not); rather, it is because such pejorative attitudes towards indigenous cultures – and the corresponding elitism among those lucky enough to have been born a Briton – were widespread in the settler psyche. The obligation to convert the savage to the civilised was self-evident. Towards the end of the century, British prime minister William Gladstone ebulliently summarised this pervasive spirit of the age: 'The sentiment of empire may be called innate in every Briton,' he proclaimed. 'If there are exceptions, they are like those of men born blind or lame among us. It is part of our patrimony: born with our birth, dying only with our death; incorporating itself in the first elements of our knowledge, and interwoven with all our habits of mental action upon public affairs.'[34] This was the type of pugnacious rhetoric that wallowed in the grandeur of the British Empire, revealing in the process the extremities to which British imperial thinking had reached – from being a conscious political programme to a compulsive instinct. What had started out as a mixture commercial opportunism, religious ambition and administrative expansion had mutated into something of a national genetic trait in which the supplanting of inferior cultures – if not the societies they belonged to – was just part of the natural order of things.

COLLABORATION

The whole process was going to be very slow, though. Evolution trumped revolution in the contest of cultures, and besides, if you had the sort of ingrained confidence that Gladstone possessed, the triumph of English and of the civilisation to which it was implicitly wedded was inevitable anyway. The initial steps that missionaries took from 1814 to control the country's language (both Māori and English) might appear small in scale and stumbling in execution, but they were vital to the larger strides that came later. And they were to become one of the important turning points in the history of te reo.

For almost half a century, te reo's relationship with English had been neither deep nor lasting. Short episodes of communication, driven mainly by impromptu trading opportunities, were all that drove Europeans visiting New Zealand to acquire a few phrases of te reo, and a handful of Māori to reciprocate with some essential utterances in English. But around 1815, these very casual linguistic liaisons started to change. A hint of this came as Marsden was readying himself to depart from the Bay of Islands in February of that year. He had resolved to purchase land for the mission that had just been established. The purchase was, he conceded, 'as far as possible a legal settlement'. He had to make this concession because there was no precise survey,[35] no titles, and no system of land registration, so such arrangements were unavoidably ad hoc in nature and uncertain in tenure. Despite this, a document was drawn up and signed 'in the presence of a number of chiefs from different districts'[36] who had assembled at Rangihoua. Kendall and Nicholas signed on behalf of the Church Missionary Society, and then, as Nicholas noted, it remained only for the chiefs who had dominion over the land (Te Uriokanae and Wharemokaikai) to add their names to the document. They could have drawn an 'X' but this would not have distinguished their signatures from anyone else's.[37] The way around this – devised by Hongi, who was present at the negotiations – was an ingenious and 'perfectly original'[38] fusion of European literacy and traditional Māori culture, as Nicholas described:

> For this purpose, the ingenuity of Shunghi [Hongi] furnished a ready contrivance; and that chief drawing upon the deeds a complete representation of the *Amoco* [tā moko], or tattooing of Gunnah's [Te Uriokanae] countenance, to which the latter set his mark, it served as the ratifying symbol of the agreement. These deeds Mr. Kendall and myself witnessed on the part of the settlers; and a native, whom they called a carpenter, drew the *amoco* of one of his cheeks, as a corresponding testimony for the New Zealanders.[39]

Marsden saw this as a form of guarantee. Through this procedure, Te Uriokanae and Wharemokaikai 'publicly declared that the land was no longer theirs, but the sole property of the white people and was tabooed for their use'. Addressing the 'signature', Marsden described it as containing 'all the curves and lines which are tatooed on the chief's face and their singular and curious drawings or figures'.[40]

Hongi's elegant solution to the need for an individualised signature on what he realised was a politically and historically important document was an approach to literacy using a forerunner of writing. There was no phonetic element in the symbol; instead, the pictogram encapsulated a particular idea[41] – in this case, the mana of the person it represented, and his agreement to what was written on the paper. This revealed something of the urge some Māori had to use literacy as a means of asserting their authority in the culture of Europeans. At the same time, that authority was indigenous. Tā moko were a sign of status and identity to Māori[42] and, as such, Hongi's suggestion was about reaching a cultural accommodation with both the language and the system of writing of the British arrivals, rather than allowing Māori culture to be completely subverted by this new form of language confronting them.

The missionaries' approach to te reo in this period showed signs of their adapting to the language rather than just trampling over it, and in this they had the backing of their organisation's policy on the issue. Until now, the missionaries had had only limited engagement with te reo – a few had made an effort to produce brief lists of Māori words and their English equivalents, and a very small number of chiefs had learned to speak English while in New South Wales, but that was it. From 1815, CMS headquarters in London began instructing its men in foreign fields to get to work translating religious material in indigenous languages. 'As soon as possible, devote yourself to the proclamation of the Gospel in the Susoo tongue' was Pratt's clarion call to missionaries in West Africa; and to another working in Nepal he wrote, 'We should think … you well employed if you could translate the Scriptures into the Thibet tongue.'[43] In August 1815 Pratt penned a similar request to Kendall: 'We shall hope to hear that you have made proficiency in the New Zealand tongue; and that the way will be thus prepared by you for the Translation of the Scriptures.' And in a tone that betrays the most overbearing kind of colonial condescension, he added that he hoped 'the little New Zealanders will, under your kind and paternal care, first learn the rudiments of their own tongue out of the Book of God'.[44] This was the first sign of something resembling a policy on te reo devised by the coloniser – even if it came from a branch of the imperial apparatus that was chronically underfunded[45] and staffed by lay missionaries, many of whom had only a modest education.

The main impediment to this policy was that Pratt's ambition had temporarily overtaken the means of the CMS to enact it. Kendall at times felt out of his depth: 'I can speak to them in their own tongue, as yet, but very imperfectly,' he admitted to Marsden in May. He suggested that trained ministers be despatched to New Zealand to assist with the Great Commission in this corner of the world, and also that the mission be supplied with a few 'Persons of Talent to assist in fixing the Language. I and my colleagues sensible of our weakness call for help.'[46] But with funds scarce back in London[47] and the turn-around time for correspondence between New Zealand and England being upwards of eight months, Kendall opted to tackle the language issue on his own. Stretching his abilities to their limits and beyond, he composed *A Korao [kōrero] no New Zealand, or, The New Zealander's first book: being an attempt to compose some lessons for the instruction of the natives*[48] – a small work, measuring 145mm by 105mm and extending to just 54 pages, consisting of an alphabet, numbers, a basic vocabulary, some suggestions for pronunciation, and a few essential sentences.

As the first concerted effort to produce a work of this type, and by someone with no training in this field, the representation of te reo in *A Korao no New Zealand* was inevitably erratic. Kendall's idiosyncratic transcriptions of the Māori words he heard can be ascribed to a broad range of factors: he was working in a small dialectical pocket of te reo as spoken in the Bay of Islands,[49] so some of the words betray a parochial terminology or accent; it is possible that those Māori he approached to assist him modified their pronunciation and simplified their phrases to help the missionary;[50] he relied on a limited number of informants, and so any peculiar individual pronunciation traits they may have possessed may have coloured his transcriptions; his spelling was swayed by the Tahitian orthography that he had access to,[51] coupled with his own English-influenced improvisations, and was far from standardised; and how he heard te reo would undoubtedly have affected his choice of spellings. The way the sounds of the language came across to the ears of European transcribers was a central issue. In 1946 Patrick Smyth, the Ngāpuhi headmaster of St Stephen's Native Boys' School, attributed the difficulties of these early attempts at transcribing te reo to its elevated aesthetic qualities – as he described it in a passage of somewhat overwrought literary filigree:

> The Maori language of the present day is recognized as a most euphonious one, representing the sound of a quietly running stream heard from a distance. Its music is continually commented upon. We can but dream of what its beauty must have been before its contact with the European language, and the entry of inevitable harshness consequent upon the effort to transfer its oral beauty to print in an alphabet

supplied from a foreign tongue. A complete representation was of course impossible, but with the experience of years the harshness softened, as much of the liquid and soothing tone was gained in utterance by the scholars who learnt the Maori tongue.[52]

Some of Kendall's orthographical choices (subsequently adopted by others) came in for some spurious criticism for their alleged effects on Māori speech. William Brown, settler and later politician, argued in 1845 that the 'apparently natural defect in their [Māori] organs of speech has been consolidated and rendered permanent from the missionaries having discarded the letters b, c, d, f, g, j, l q, s, v, x, y, z, from the alphabet.'[53] This notion is of course preposterous; but the fact that the suggestion was even made, let alone appeared in print, points to how little was understood about te reo even decades after Kendall's book was released.

At the time of its publication, though, Kendall was hardly preoccupied with the effects of *A Korao no New Zealand* on Māori speech. He had struggled to assemble the work, which was written after he had spent less than a year in New Zealand – and he knew it. He wrote to Pratt to suggest, with a hint of frustration, that 'if a Clergyman of my own country could be prevailed on to come he could better cooperate in fixing the Native language, as we should better agree in method and arrangement of letters than two persons who had been accustomed to speak different Languages'.[54] Kendall's understandable lack of expertise in this field – which he openly acknowledged was the crux of the problem with his book – was soon identified by others. His missionary colleague William Hall confirmed to Pratt in a rather uncollegial letter in August 1816 that Kendall's work was of very limited value. 'There has been a small book printed at Port Jackson for the use of the school, composed of words and sentences out of our vocabulary, which Mr. Kendall has put together,' he advised the CMS secretary, 'and although very defective yet it will be of some use, if it were but to teach them the alphabet and a beginning for further improvement.'[55]

If the CMS could not afford to send a qualified linguist to New Zealand, the only option Kendall could see was to work with one in England. The man who took on the task to produce a more reliable book on te reo Māori was Samuel Lee, who in 1819 became professor of Arabic (and later Hebrew) at Cambridge University, and who had achieved recognition for authoring a Hebrew grammar and lexicon and for translating the Book of Job.[56] Lee was also a devout Christian and, according to his daughter, 'omitted no opportunity of inculcating spiritual truth, or ever failed to respond to the motives which carry a missionary into a far country'.[57] The challenge to produce a book on the Māori language that was properly chiselled into shape by someone with his particular academic skills surely must have appealed to him.

Pratt and fellow CMS secretary Edward Bickersteth appear to have been the conduit between Kendall and Lee. In March 1818 they wrote to Kendall, letting him know that 'Our Orientalist, Mr Lee, is making use of Tooi [Tuai] & Teeterree [Tītere] (who have recently arrived) to form a complete Grammar & Vocabulary of the New Zealand Language', and that his *A Korao no New Zealand* 'furnishes him with important assistance'. As with some earlier (and much more modest) efforts at building a basic working knowledge of te reo, Māori were called on for help. But in this case, although the assistance of Tuai and Tītere was no doubt invaluable, their limited knowledge of English[58] and the fact that they soon fell ill and had to return to New Zealand[59] left Lee feeling that more progress needed to be made before his work was publishable.

The missionary administrators appear, at this stage, to have been concerned only with translating the Bible and catechisms[60] into te reo. No mention was made of teaching Māori to read these works in English – this presumably would happen at some later date. As they told Kendall, 'We much approve of your plan of beginning to instruct the children *first* [emphasis added] in their own language, as being the most likely way to interest them.'[61]

There was much more happening here – probably more than the missionary officials realised – than merely the conversion of a traditional spoken language into a written form. Transcribing aspects of an oral culture tended to cause reverberations back in the oral realm itself. This was the start of a 'metropolitan te reo' – a language that would eventually be pantribal in its standardised use of vocabulary and that would also signify a shift in power[62] from the traditional setting, where memorised material was master, to this emerging environment where authority was connected much more closely with the ability to read and write. At the same time, this augmented form of te reo melded traditional knowledge with 'international' knowledge in ways that were sometimes almost seamless. European ideas could now merge with Māori knowledge in text,[63] internationalising the culture in the process. The printed page, as was being discovered, was never a culturally neutral place. In addition, the written word carried with it a level of authority that seemed hard to replicate in oral culture[64] – the information embodied in text was fixed, and was not subject to change through arguments or pleas. Māori oral culture depended heavily on the mana of the person speaking as well as the circumstance in which something was being said, and to whom. In contrast, the written word, particularly in its printed and published version, was silent yet authoritative. Indeed, the fact of something being printed was, in itself, its own attestation of status and authority. And even if you had cause to doubt the content of a text, whom did you address? At whom did you aim your rhetoric? The answer was at an inanimate object that could not talk back but was capable of 'speaking'. Text may have been silent, but it was also utterly immune to the most powerful oratory. Such was the paradoxical and confounding nature of the written word that confronted oral cultures.

At first glance, printed materials were the slowest form of communication – slower than handwritten text, and with nowhere near the instantaneity of the spoken word. Printed texts – even those as seemingly innocuous as the type of dictionary and grammar that Lee and Kendall were working on – held one advantage that greatly augmented the speed and scope of their impact: they could mass-produce information without changing the form of that information in the slightest.[65] This was also the commencement of a new notion about the vocabulary, idiom, pronunciation and grammar of te reo: that all the shades of variety in these areas of the language could be boiled down into a single, standardised and supposedly 'correct' version. It was an approach to te reo that was fortified by the fact that representatives of the colonising power, with all its implicit authority, were behind this drive to uniformity. The notion of correctness with respect to pronunciation, vocabulary and so forth was an external incursion that, once applied, would continue to have a bearing on how te reo appeared in text thereafter. There is practically no evidence of pre-European Māori having a sense of the 'correct' version of te reo, or of one version having status over another, in the manner that had bedevilled English for centuries.

The gradual emergence and acceptance of the idea of a 'correct' te reo Māori – buttressed by the efforts missionaries were making to standardise the printed form of the language – could well have been a factor in the eventual reduction of some of the more extreme dialectical differences in the language up until this time. The uniformity that came with printing probably also contributed to a narrowing in the range of pronunciation. And although this standardisation diminished te reo's dialectical richness, Colenso – who was observing this change taking place – detected some longer-term benefits for the language in the process:

I regret to say, that this pure and ingenious Maori nomenclature did not last very long, it gradually died away, partly through the carelessness and the ignorance of the foreign settlers, and partly through the clear capacious memory of the Maori by which they were enabled to remember the *patois* names of common things, &c., as used by the early settlers and visitors, and in doing so not un-frequently escaped more or less of ill-words. Moreover the Maoris in the earliest days of the Colony, and for some time previous, were very prone to abandon pure Maori among themselves for the incorrect broken Maori of the settlers; for as the Maoris had considered them, *at first*, as being a superior race, they largely took up their errors in common talk and pronunciation as well as in other matters; and had it not been for their obtaining a written language through the Church-of-England Missionaries, and also had books printed in correct Maori by them, the Maori language would have soon become irretrievably lost; – even as it is at present the loss is very great among themselves, more than most Maori scholars are aware, and it is daily becoming more contracted and corrupt.[66]

This assessment highlights just how invasive the early European colonisation of New Zealand was on te reo – even if Colenso was inclined to overstate the case. Purists might have lamented the adulteration of the country's indigenous language, but the fact of colonisation made these initial attempts at 'fixing' the written vocabulary and orthography of te reo an inevitable result of European tampering with an oral language.

Dialectical variations were apparent in the early nineteenth century even to those Europeans who were far from proficient in the indigenous language. Robert Maunsell, the missionary who went on to produce a Māori grammar, detected differences in dialect even in a geographical area as compact as the eastern and western banks of Lake Taupo;[67] and as he travelled elsewhere around the country, the variety in te reo that he heard was so great that he believed the country must have been settled in distinct migratory waves.[68] Maunsell was most familiar with the Waikato dialect: this was the region he was most closely associated with and that he was therefore able to research to a greater depth[69] – in the same way as Kendall's work was inflected by the Ngāpuhi dialect.[70]

Perhaps the most evident contrast between dialects was captured by the Wesleyan missionary James Watkin, who established the first mission station in the South Island, in Waikouaiti (near present-day Dunedin). While he was in Sydney, Watkin had been invited to the region in 1839 by two Otakou chiefs, Karetai and Taiaroa, who 'desired schools for their children in order that they might read and write like the Maori children of the North Island'.[71] Watkin had supplies of the books printed by the missionaries in the Bay of Islands, but he discovered that they were of little use to him because the dialect spoken in this part of the South Island differed so greatly from that of Northland.[72] His planned school was thus without books – so Watkin was forced to prepare his own. This was a project he was enthusiastic about. He wrote, 'I have printed several books with the pen, and they are much prized. I think many of the people here will soon learn to read. I intend to teach them the writing of the printed characters at the same time.'[73] The first work he published was *He Puka Ako i te Korero Maori* – a 19-page work containing prayers and hymns, printed at the Wesleyan Mission at Mangungu in 1841.[74]

Although the geographical location of a European transcribing or translating English works into te reo would have betrayed local dialectical predilections, their act of putting the language on paper – especially using the increasingly standardised missionary orthography – would have started the process of whittling away some of the more extreme dialectical differences in parts of the country.[75] And as the century progressed, 'corrected' copies of works translated into te reo led to even greater uniformity in published versions of the language, and a consequent reduction in dialectical variety in print. It is impossible to know the exact degree to which such developments either caused or correlated with a narrowing of the dialectical range in spoken te reo, but it is certain that this trend in print would not have aided the maintenance of these variations in the spoken language.

The arrival of the printed book in te reo introduced a symbiotic relationship between Māori society and text. The more literate that Māori readers became, the more they could use printed material to expand their perceptions and knowledge; and as these mental horizons broadened, the demand for texts increased.[76] In the process of this cycle of growing reading and increasing demand for printed works, the expression of mainly European cultural and ideological values that all books brought with them[77] continued surreptitiously to colonise the minds of indigenous readers. In Europe, where the Reformation coincided with and co-opted the new technology of printing, the political, religious, economic, cultural and philosophical changes that came about with the advent of Protestantism have tended to overwhelm the contribution that printing made to these changes – as though books and tracts were little more than a means of communicating disruptive intellectual changes.[78] In New Zealand, the impact of the introduction of printing was more pronounced and more directly traceable as the *source* of changes to the country's culture and society, rather than merely as the vehicle of communication. This was primarily because the topics of the early texts in te reo were almost exclusively biblical: ideology, spirituality and theology were both the means and the ends of the first printed works in the language.

Lee must have had more than an inkling of the effect that his translation work would have in this regard, given his stated intent that his 'sole motive' in his translation work in general was 'the advancement of Divine truth, and of the honour of Him to whom we owe it'.[79] But as Lee was no longer so closely associated with the CMS because of his new university appointment, the society decided to develop a clearer plan when drawing on his expertise, to make the best use of his time. While Kendall continued to revise existing works and create new ones in te reo – such as a catechism which he sent to London in December 1818 – his superiors appear not to have passed on his work to Lee to revise, thus sparing the professor for what were regarded as more urgent translation tasks. Kendall's frustration with this apparent logjam may have been one of the factors influencing his decision to go to England in 1820 with two chiefs – Hongi and Waikato – to meet Lee and finalise his *Grammar and Vocabulary of the Language of New Zealand*.[80] Of the two chiefs, Hongi, it was said, 'understands somewhat of English, but does not speak it, as he has lived very much with his own people, and his intercourse with the Settlers has been chiefly in his native tongue', while Waikato 'understands English tolerably well, and can make himself understood therein, having had more intercourse with our countrymen than Shunghee [Hongi]'.[81]

Lee had made plain his purpose for getting involved in the project: 'The furtherance of the Mission, sent out to New Zealand, for the double purpose of civilizing and evangelizing the Natives of that country' and, specifically, 'the instruction of the European Missionary in the Language of New Zealand; whereby he may be enabled to communicate the blessings of Christian Instruction and Civil Improvement.'[82] Lee laid out clearly the linguistic approaches he had in mind for tackling the systematic conversion of te reo into a written form, in a way that Māori would understand:

> With respect to the New Zealanders, care has been taken to represent their language in a manner as simple and unembarrassed as the nature of the subject and materials would admit. In doing this, the first point aimed at, was, to make the Alphabet as simple and comprehensive as possible, by giving the vowels and consonants such names and powers as were not likely to be burthensome to the memory or perplexing to the

understanding: and for this end, the division into vowels, diphthongs, and consonants, as well as the names of each, as laid down in the Sanscrit Grammars, has been preferred; though the scantiness of the New-Zealand sounds has made it impracticable to follow their arrangement in every particular: it was not possible to illustrate every sound by English examples: some are therefore left to be learnt from the mouths of Natives.[83]

The result of Lee's endeavour was a 230-page book, starting with an alphabet and progressing through elements of grammar, a 45-page section on sample phrases for conversation and six pages of prayers and creeds, before reaching the vocabulary, which occupied the final roughly 100 pages of the book.

The 1820 edition of *The Missionary Register* praised the work of Lee and Kendall as representing another momentous stride in the advancing march of Christianity into the heathen corners of the world. It described *A Grammar and Vocabulary of the Language of New Zealand* as the first such undertaking for that country that was 'fixed on scientific principles',[84] with the hope that this standardisation of te reo in written form would assist in opening up Māori society to the message of the Gospel in the near future.[85]

Lee may have been an expert in grammar and linguistics generally, but he was not a speaker of te reo, and this – together with possibly too little time available to work on *A Grammar and Vocabulary of the New Zealand Language*, and Kendall's still limited knowledge of te reo – meant that the resulting book was not quite the ideal encapsulation of the basics of the Māori language and grammar that its supporters had claimed. Neither was Lee's abiding hope – that the work would standardise the orthography of te reo – to be realised in this publication.[86] There were shortcomings, for example, in the attempts made to standardise the use of certain consonants in te reo, where subtle differences in pronunciation were missed by those transcribing them.[87]

The deficiencies of the book soon became apparent. In 1823, while Marsden was on a visit to New Zealand, he had cause to refer to *A Grammar and Vocabulary of the New Zealand Language* and made an uncharacteristically caustic assessment of its value. After spending the best part of a day in a house in Paihia reading through the work, he declared it to be 'very imperfect', before setting forth what he felt were its main shortcomings:

The rules laid down in the Grammar for the orthography and pronunciation of the language are not simple enough for the missionaries to comprehend. They cannot retain in their memories the sound of the vowels as laid down in the rules of the Grammar, and consequently the pronunciation, so as the natives can understand them. The changing [of] the English pronunciation of the vowels has created very great confusion amongst the whole.

This was no nuanced appraisal punctuated with cautiously qualified doubts, but a denouncement plain and simple. In its present state, Marsden saw the book as nearly useless. His remedy was to raise his concerns with Kendall directly, with a view to wholesale changes being made to it. 'I am sure I should despair,' he suggested, 'of ever being able either to write or speak the New Zealand language according to the rules in the Grammar.'[88] The following year the missionary Henry Williams, who had recently arrived in New Zealand and was having to depend on *A Grammar and Vocabulary of the New Zealand Language* to learn te reo, felt compelled to mention in a letter to his brother-in-law how he and his fellow missionaries had found the work: '[We] have condemned the book called "The Grammar." I cannot tell what share Professor Lee may have had in the composition thereof, but it certainly appears far from simplicity.'[89]

No doubt stung by the criticism of the book that he had poured so much effort into producing – criticism that must have felt amplified in the claustrophobic confines of the missionary community in the Bay of Islands – Kendall wrote to Lee in 1825, highlighting another side to the work:

It has been doubted by some whether the plan you adopted in the *New Zealand Grammar* is a proper one or not, but I am glad to inform you that the Church and Wesleyan missionaries after trying other methods now generally agree that yours best suits the idiom of the New Zealand language. The fact is that the *New Zealand Grammar and Vocabulary* which was compiled under your inspection may be considerably improved, but neither the sounds of the vowels, nor the orthography, can be changed for the better.

There was a concession of sorts here about the limitations of the book, but Kendall was aware – perhaps more so than any of his colleagues in New Zealand – that it would take years before any one of them had sufficient fluency to be able to attempt a translation of the Bible. 'The New Zealand language is very imperfectly understood,' he continued.

A man may be tempted to make the language to correspond with his own ideas of it, but time will convince him, in such a case, of his error. It will be found that the sounds of the vowels not only express the names of them, but each sound has a particular meaning which is applied to all the purposes of language, and therefore each sound must be carefully preserved throughout and each letter must keep its place in writing or print, or else the language will never be understood, nor can it be taught.[90]

Within 15 years the history of this episode was being revised: the responsibility for the shortcomings of these works was now placed, perversely, at the feet of Māori. Charles Terry, for example, framed the development of te reo in written form in an especially slanted way in an attempt to exculpate the missionaries from any charge of incompetence:

The Missionaries, on their first arrival in the islands, were obliged to learn the Native language, and that by rote, from an ignorant, untutored savage, whose knowledge of his own language was confined to speech; for the New Zealanders had, then, no characters … by which they had been accustomed to convey their ideas, or to record their history and traditions. The sound, alone, was the guide to the Missionary, for the orthography of words, without any knowledge of the etymology of the language; and hence, the present written language of New Zealand, has, for its sole origin and authors, the Missionaries.[91]

All the bumpy twists and turns that had gone into the creation of the *New Zealand Grammar and Vocabulary* were ironed out in this reconstructed interpretation. Readers of Terry's works[92] were reminded of the dividing line that separated savage from civilised, and of how missionary altruism had triumphed over Māori atavism – in part through the introduction of literacy to Māori society.

WHITHER TE REO?

The irony of all this furrowed-brow academic activity invested in reconstructing te reo Māori in a written form was that once *A Grammar and Vocabulary of the New Zealand Language* was completed, typeset, and copies printed for use in New Zealand,[93] there was no other published material in te reo for the newly literate Māori of the Bay of Islands to read. It was as though an instruction manual had been created for a product that was yet to arrive. For the missionaries, who were maintaining their monopoly on written te reo for the time being, the next step was glaringly obvious: print religious material in te reo as the major plank of their plans to advance the mission.

The great Bible translator and leading Reformation figure William Tyndale had emphasised in the early sixteenth century the importance of producing religious literature in the vernacular of the local population, and it was a message that still resonated in the nineteenth century. 'I perceived how that [sic] it is impossible to establish the lay people in any truth except the Scripture were plainly laid before their eyes in their mother tongue.'[94] But just when the impetus seemed to be building to churn out the standard corpus of missionary tracts and biblical extracts in the country's indigenous language – the type of programme that had been implemented in several other mission fields – the prospects for the full gamut of publications in te reo were abruptly reined in. The edict came from Marsden for a compromise approach in which some books in te reo would be prepared but there would be an expectation that Māori students attending the mission schools would acquire at least some familiarity with English. This swing in policy away from having reading materials and instruction exclusively in te reo stemmed partly from the frustrations that had accompanied the production of *A Grammar and Vocabulary of the New Zealand Language*. The ongoing debate over how to spell words in te reo, together with mounting dissatisfaction with the book that Kendall and Lee had written, had pushed Marsden to reconsider the best linguistic approach to evangelising Māori. In the spring of 1823, during another of his visits to the mission in New Zealand, he consolidated his thinking on the best way to spread the Word – by words – among Māori.

First he tackled the contentious issue of the inconsistency of the current orthography of te reo. Because Māori were 'so quick in learning our language and could pronounce the vowels so well according to our custom', Marsden concluded it would be best to retain the English pronunciation of the vowels used in transcribing te reo, rather than to shift to an alternative option that Kendall had been toying with. And then came the decision that, through a convoluted chain of events, would end up drastically destabilising te reo whenever it came into contact with missionary teachers: Marsden recommended that 'all the English terms for such things as the natives had never seen should be introduced into the New Zealand language – that a sheep should be called a sheep, a cow a cow, etc. If we did not do this the New Zealanders would give their names by comparison, and probably it would require three or more words in some things to express what we do in one.'[95] Marsden saw this as the most pragmatic option, and preferable to relying on missionaries to create a phonetically similar neologisms for use by Māori.

In this way, thin slivers of linguistic hybridity were now piercing te reo's lexicon, and not just as part of the natural process that occurs when two languages collide in one geographical space, but also because it was specifically willed by the group that monopolised literacy. This was an early reminder that in the contest of English and te reo (which was already well under way by the 1820s), the language that was politically and culturally more authoritative[96] was the one that did not have to rely on adopting words from the other. Such hybridity was therefore hardly a linguistically, culturally or politically neutral development.[97] The idea that this type of augmentation of a language through borrowing foreign words occurs simply to resolve a deficit in terminology is not borne out by history. Instead, for the language being colonised, it was a strategy – and possibly the only strategy – for survival,[98] while confirming the dominance of the language of the coloniser.

This conviction of the superiority of English in New Zealand was emphasised by Marsden. Underlying his various recommendations for the orthography and vocabulary of te reo was his attitude towards what he believed was its underlying inadequacy: 'The New Zealand language is … very impure, and that impurity would increase by allowing them to give names to animals, etc., but if we retained our own terms and interwove our language with theirs, this would tend to make their language more chaste. At present it is very unchaste and offensive.'[99] The paradox of enhancing a language's 'chastity', or purity, by impregnating it with foreign words was apparently lost on the parson.

The immediate result of Marsden's meddling in the written form of te reo was the decision to publish a new vocabulary – one that would retain the English pronunciation of the vowels and would be augmented with English words for anything that did not already have an exact equivalent in te reo. Kendall was asked to carry out this task, and appeared eager to accept the challenge,[100] despite the fact that his personal relationships with most other New Zealand missionaries were all but severed by this time as he had, in his own words, 'almost completely turned from a Christian to a Heathen.'[101]

Even after he parted ways permanently with the mission in New Zealand, Kendall still clung stubbornly to his zeal for improving his text on te reo. In 1827, while living in Sydney, he made contact with Marsden and showed him the manuscript he had prepared for the second edition of *A Grammar and Vocabulary of the New Zealand Language*. Marsden, though, seems to have had a change of heart about Kendall's involvement in this undertaking. Kendall reported to his former superiors in London that Marsden 'appears to be afraid of committing it or any of my labours to the press lest by so doing the missionaries who are now at New Zealand should be discouraged'. Kendall's ruined reputation in the eyes of the missionaries was the one obstacle that prevented the possibility of his ongoing refinement of te reo from gaining wider circulation. 'I have made the New Zealand language my delightful study during the whole of the past fourteen years, and cannot give it up' was his pathetic admission to the CMS secretary in October of 1827,[102] and he endeavoured to verify this claim by offering a commentary on how te reo had been evolving as a written language since his departure from New Zealand:

> I perceive the missionaries in their late publication have discarded the consonants b, d, f, j, l, s, v, y, and z. I could wish to be favoured with Professor Lee's candid opinion as to the propriety of discarding these consonants which would be so useful in transcribing all foreign names, especially Scripture names. If Professor Lee should coincide with the missionaries I will discard them also, but I cannot consent to do it until I hear from him. It has been acknowledged by all that the Grammar which was published seven years ago has been very useful. I should hope that the present one, which has been improved and corrected throughout, will also be useful, having seven years' experience in addition to the seven preceding ones.[103]

Kendall's solicitations were met with a stony silence. Lee had long since shifted the focus of his work to his Hebrew Grammar,[104] and the New Zealand mission had grown in the intervening years and had been supplemented with a group of Wesleyan missionaries who were making their own efforts to tackle te reo. Kendall, meanwhile, barely managed to scrape together enough funds to print privately just a few pages of his revised grammar towards the end of 1827,[105] and it made no material difference to the work on te reo that had been gathering pace over the previous five years.

WHOSE LANGUAGE WAS IT NOW?

Later Jesus appeared to the Eleven as they were eating; he rebuked them for their lack of faith and their stubborn refusal to believe those who had seen him after he had risen. He said to them, 'Go into all the world and preach the gospel to all creation. Whoever believes and is baptized will be saved, but whoever does not believe will be condemned.'
— MARK 16: 14–16.[106]

No people were ever converted but by preaching to them in their own tongue. — A.S. THOMSON[107]

Christ's exhortation to His followers to spread the message of salvation throughout the world made Christianity one of the great proselytising religions. The effort to secure converts among Māori had practically stalled in New Zealand after Marsden's Christmas sermon at Te Oihi ('for fifteen years the missionaries were like men crying in the wilderness' is how one writer in the 1850s described the dismal situation during this time).[108] For the missionaries, the absence of their book in te reo was a critical drawback. The obvious next step, then, was to produce a translation of at least part of the Bible (translating the more than 788,000 words of the entire work was well beyond the capacity of a handful of missionaries who were at best just partially fluent in te reo).

Rendering the Scriptures in te reo was an act of cultural miscegenation: the words and grammar of one culture were being inculcated – in printed form – with the lore and spirituality of another, and then fed back to the former as the single, non-negotiable truth of the coloniser's culture. Whose language was it now? The words and grammar belonged to Māori, but the concepts they conveyed did not. The answer can be looked at from two angles: either te reo was being used by the missionaries to dismantle some of the traditional beliefs of its Māori speakers; or the language was expanding to draw new ideas from the outside world into its culture. Bits of both of these perspectives were at play during this stage of te reo's evolution.

The representation of the introduction of 'Western' religious texts to a non-literate society is generally couched in terms of a process whereby those who produce the texts control the process; and that the content of those texts is thereafter the intellectual and cultural property of the coloniser. In such a scheme, the indigenous population merely 'benefits' or 'improves' from having access to the text; beyond that, they have no proprietary claim to the content of the text.

Look at this from the indigenous perspective and a different picture emerges. Various Māori communities, for example, took the religious literature that the missionaries were disseminating among them and made it part of their own traditions, rather than exclusively that of the coloniser. When an improved translation of the Bible in te reo was published in 1887 – with many of the previous awkward attempts at translation supposedly resolved – the response was 'disastrous'; stock of the new Scriptures proved 'virtually unsaleable'.[109] For all their faults, the earlier editions had become part of Māori text culture and, consequently, some people felt the revised edition was an aberration. Colenso was alert to this approach by some Māori to written texts dealing with sacred topics: he pointed out that there could be difficulties with 'unnecessary alterations of texts … [to] a people sensitive to ancient songs, or recitals of histories'.[110] This at the very least suggests how Māori society was able not only to assimilate new ideas and technologies, but to allow these to become part of its own evolving culture – instead of these new elements remaining as a foreign appendage. Alterations to the grammar and vocabulary of the Bible in te reo later in the century were seen as almost a violation of 'traditional' Māori culture, so far as many Māori were concerned. Therefore, determining what constitutes traditional is not always a case of drawing an unwavering line of demarcation between European and Māori.

As if the waters were not already muddied enough by the cross-currents of language and culture, there was the issue of the Anglican Church being both a denomination and the state church of Britain (and its empire) – a union that in some ways gave a political taint to the work of the CMS missionaries in New Zealand.[111] Whose master were they serving? (It was a valid question, especially considering Christ's injunction about serving two masters.) Some caution needs to be exercised when evaluating whether the translation of parts of the Bible constituted an act of cultural or even political imperialism.[112] These notions have become so broad in their application that they now tend to be used to describe 'any instance where awareness of the wider world represented by the West has influenced indigenous cultural change', with the implication that such change has worked against the interests of the peoples being colonised.[113] The situation on the ground in New Zealand was far more nuanced than this. Māori and missionaries occupied the same colonial space, and the cultural influence, as in other parts of the world, could go both ways.[114]

Nothing in this area was clear-cut. The desire to save souls extended into the urge to civilise Māori and, in particular, to offer them a specifically British form of civilisation.[115] The leaders of the CMS had been aware from the organisation's inception of the risks of arbitrarily imposing a British cultural regime on indigenous peoples. It had always been in favour of preaching the Gospel 'in a manner to be understood by the natives'.[116] One of its founders, Reverend Henry Venn, had long been an advocate of indigenous churches.[117] He described 'the European element in a native church' as a 'great snare and hindrance to its growth', and in order to avoid a 'collision of the races' in the mission field, he advocated for largely independent and self-governing indigenous church administrations.[118] When it came to colonising enterprises, this was about as far away as possible from the image of missionaries obsessed with eliminating all vestiges of the indigenous cultures that they encountered to further the cause of British commercial and imperial strategies. Yes, there were the usual set of 'abominations'[119] to which the missionaries were implacably opposed – cannibalism, infanticide, warfare, general promiscuity and, especially, idolatry – but there were also limits to what these missionaries wished to alter about Māori society. Even because of the sheer weight of numbers, te reo was one of those facets of the culture that could be tackled only gradually. Marsden had instructed that English words be introduced for anything that was new to Māori society – but this was likely to happen eventually anyway, without the need for a directive on the matter (as had been happening to English for centuries).[120] Otherwise, the onus would be on the missionaries to adjust to te reo; any expectations of Māori embracing English en masse lay far in the future.

Unexpectedly, the task of translating portions of the Bible into te reo fell to one of the least educated of the missionaries in New Zealand. James Shepherd (whom Marsden considered 'truly pious and his heart engaged in the work')[121] had a natural gift for languages,[122] and combined this with a firm conviction on the still contentious issue of whether conversion ought to be preceded by civilisation – one of the most hotly debated issues among missionaries in the South Pacific. 'I think,' he informed Marsden, 'the Gospel will prove the only means of civilizing the heathen … I say Evangelization precedes Civilization.'[123] The problem with this aim, as the 1824 *Missionary Register* pointed out, was that while missionaries were regularly visiting Māori settlements to provide schooling and religious instruction, there was not yet any Christian text that could be left with these communities to reinforce the lessons. 'With this view,' the author of the *Missionary Register* reported,

Mr. Shepherd is paying particular regard to the preparation, in the New-Zealand Tongue, of portions of Scripture, for the use of the children and adults who may learn to read; and the conviction is gathering strength among the Labourers, that a direct and unwearied communication of the Gospel to the Natives must henceforth, more than it has yet done, accompany and promote the efforts for their civilization.[124]

So, although he was a successful horticulturalist in the mission station, Shepherd turned to translation in order to assist in the harvest of souls. He produced an account of the 'Creation, Fall and Recovery of man' and immediately followed this with a translation of the Gospel of St John,[125] filling a need that had become obvious to all involved in the New Zealand mission. Until this time, Māori children in the mission schools were in the anomalous position of acquiring their literacy through Kendall's *Grammar and Vocabulary*, after which, one missionary regretted, these students were left stranded and had nothing further to read.[126] Shepherd's rough translations were the first important step in addressing this deficit in reading material for Māori.

The mission schools were at the core of the efforts to transmit written te reo among Māori communities, and they proved especially effective at it. In the same year as Marsden had preached his first sermon in New Zealand, his parent organisation, the Church Missionary Society, established a fund to set up schools 'among the heathen'. The thinking behind the initiative was laid bare in its January 1814 report in the *Missionary Register*: 'The instruction of children facilitates access to their parents, secures their friendship and conveys information to them through unsuspected channels. The minds of children are more susceptible and less under the influence of habit and prejudice than those of their parents.'[127] This principle of working through students to effect change in their parents was made explicit by John Philip, the superintendent of missions of the London Missionary Society (LMS) in South Africa, who wrote that 'the children of barbarous tribes ... [might] raise up [sic] to cultivate and humanise their parents, and become the elements of a society that will soon be able to supply its own wants, advocate their own rights, and diffuse the blessings of civilisation among the tribes ...'[128]

This dissemination of literacy – which in the early stages of the European presence in New Zealand was almost synonymous with the spread of Christianity – proved so effective that written te reo acquired a life of its own in a number of Māori communities. William Brown, an early settler and later a member of New Zealand's Legislative Council, attributed this era of the rapid spread of literacy predominantly to Māori being easily taught and 'most eager to obtain information'. Some missionary teachers claimed that their Māori students were learning the basics of reading and writing in a fortnight, and that the expansion of literacy into areas where no missionaries had been was almost as swift as in places where missionary instruction was provided. Brown noted that, 'If one native in a tribe can read and write, he will not be long in teaching the others. The desire to obtain this information engrosses their whole thoughts, and they will continue for days with their slates in their hands, and soon make satisfactory progress.'[129]

Initially the missionaries taught only a small number of people of various ages, but by the late 1820s they were establishing a more formal style of schooling – one that would have been familiar to the English.[130] The rationale for Māori parents encouraging their children to attend these mission schools was plain to Kendall: '[T]hey believe that education is valuable as it bears upon the temporal interests of mankind. Their commercial disposition induces them to believe this.'[131] Regardless of the initial motive, once students saw te reo in a written form, the burgeoning possibilities of language in text became their own incentive.

For the Word to be spread in the schools and beyond, however, its translators would need better knowledge of te reo. Shepherd was suitably modest when he informed Marsden in 1822 about his preparation of segments of the Bible in te reo: 'I some times do a little Gardening &c, Converse with the Natives, learn the Language, and translate part of the Scriptures. I have thought, that to make preparations for the Scriptures to be read and conversed upon, is the only means to do good to the New Zealanders.'[132] With the damage Kendall had inflicted on the New Zealand mission still a long way from being repaired, and Kendall's own increasingly obsessive devotion to his flawed book on te reo, Shepherd's offer to produce a reasonably reliable version of segments from the Bible must have looked to missionary officials like a move in the direction of resuscitating the evangelisation of New Zealand.

PERPETUAL MOTION

There was a fresh mood of optimism among missionaries involved in translating and printing religious material in te reo in the 1820s. The mission overall was still 'in an infant state, and hitherto has effected little,' as Reverend Richard Davis conceded, but 'Now we have a brighter prospect. There is scarcely one individual who cannot proclaim to the natives in their own tongue the Lamb of God that taketh away the sin of the world.'[133]

By 1827, 13 long years after the establishment of the first mission in New Zealand, portions of the Bible in te reo were finally being prepared for publication, and the printing presses were about to produce Christian literature for Māori in their own language. In August, Davis joyfully reported that 400 copies of a small volume (31 pages) had been printed in Sydney. This work contained the first three chapters of Genesis, the first chapter of St John's Gospel, 17 verses of the twentieth chapter of Exodus, 30 verses of the fifth chapter of St Matthew's Gospel, the Lord's Prayer and seven hymns. The cost of this exercise was a hefty £41, which Davis thought could be reduced substantially if a printing press were sent to New Zealand.[134]

In the meantime, more texts from the Bible were being translated into te reo and despatched to Sydney for publication. Reverend William Yate oversaw the publication of a 117-page volume of selected books from the Bible, which included 19 hymns, and parts of the Anglican liturgy and catechism.[135] One of the results of this burst of translation was that orthographically, by the early 1830s, written te reo had moved away from some of the clumsier and more inconsistent traits that had marred Kendall's early work on the language, towards a form that has roughly remained in place since.[136] In the religious and cultural spheres, the significance to Māori of the mounting quantity of translated material was considerable. As Yate described it, 'Nothing could exceed the gratification with which these books were received on my return, by those who could read them. They were willing to receive them as wages, or to purchase them with any thing they possessed of a saleable nature.'[137] The missionaries' long-held faith in te reo as the most appropriate language to disseminate the message of Christianity was finally being validated. 'The Liturgy of the Church of England, as translated into the language of New Zealand, has been, next to the preaching of the Gospel and the use of the Holy Scriptures, one of the most efficacious means of Christian instruction,' Yate observed with confidence.

> It is so simple, expresses so well the wants, both temporal and spiritual, of the people and, like the Bible, from whence a large part of it is derived, it so exactly meets every case that it comes home to the experience, the heart, and the conscience; tends to awaken the unconverted; and is a source of comfort and consolation to the distressed sinner under his convictions, while the more advanced are edified by the spirituality of its petitions.[138]

It was impossible for the other missionaries not to notice, as well, what Yate called 'the thirst for knowledge, which has been excited among the New Zealanders'. Māori communities were so enthusiastic about acquiring literacy (still exclusively in te reo) by the early 1830s that the missionaries no longer needed to promote it – as Yate proudly recorded:

> Every [Māori] … now wishes to learn to read and write … [is] willing
> to pay for the requisite materials; that is, to purchase books and slates,
> for the purpose of instruction. Many native villages have two schools
> established, under the direction of a lad who has previously received
> his instruction from the Missionaries themselves. It is scarcely to be
> expected that there should be much order or classification in a school
> commenced and conducted by an untutored man, whose whole previous
> life has been disorder and irregularity … But let the plan upon which
> they have conducted their schools be what it may, very many, some
> hundreds, have learned to read and write in them; to read so as to
> understand and to be understood; and to write a good bold hand upon a
> slate.[139]

This was one of the crucial developments in the spread of te reo in printed form. Since they had arrived in the Bay of Islands, the reach of the missionaries had seldom stretched far from their sleeves. Their small, vulnerable settlements depended largely on the patronage of local chiefs, some of whom were intermittently locked in hostilities with neighbouring communities. This meant that opportunities to reach further afield were often curtailed. The tyranny of being at the mercy of a fickle benefactor had the effect of confining the spread of literacy to very localised areas (in addition to making the mission stations themselves linguistic ghettos – the only places where English was spoken conversationally).

Then, as if through some act of divine intervention, written te reo found a way of spreading of its own volition. Some of the Māori who had been taught by the missionaries belonged to distant tribes but had been taken captive in wars and made slaves[140] of communities in the Bay of Islands. Yate noted that these 'slaves', when they were 'liberated', would take their newfound faith back to their home communities. Hence, he wrote, 'in some of our distant journeys, we have met with the most agreeable surprises. When we have been telling them of some of the first principles or truths of our holy religion, what has been our astonishment, to hear them say, "We know all that!" and, upon examination, to find that they really had obtained no contemptible degree of knowledge.'[141]

What the missionaries did not quite appreciate at first about this phenomenon was that the spread of Christianity to Māori by Māori was rapidly making the faith a pantribal movement, especially from the early 1830s onwards as the pace of conversions picked up. This inevitably had political as well as religious implications for Māori society. Having a new, shared set of codified moral and, to a lesser extent, social beliefs in some ways offered the potential to transcend existing intertribal animosities, and loosened the political and social structures that bound individuals to tribal lore. And the fact that these new teachings were articulated and practised in te reo grafted elements of Christianity directly onto the language that was once the exclusive stock of traditional Māori beliefs.

In the course of such changes, the authority held by those who offered instruction in traditional beliefs in each hapū and iwi – the tohunga, kaumātua, kuia and rangatira – was slowly being altered. The elements of this tradition were not disposed of straight away, and most elements of orality retained their privileged status, but some perceptions were being modified by the introduced faith – as Edward Shortland, a doctor, administrator and amateur linguist, discovered while travelling through the country in the early 1840s. 'When the New Zealander becomes a professing Christian,' he remarked, 'it is not a consequence that he at once abandons his former belief. He continues, at least in a great majority of cases, to believe in the reality of the *Atua* of his fathers. But he believes the Christ to be a more powerful *Atua,* and of a better nature; and therefore he no longer dreads the *Atua Maori*.'[142] Polack similarly witnessed that Māori 'admit that the Atua no Europi, or God of the Europeans, has power over them'.[143]

It was now becoming apparent that not having the traditional Māori religious beliefs set down in text was a disadvantage for the country's indigenous culture. The attributes of various divinities had begun to diverge among the tribes, and details of the mythologies were becoming confused or fragmented as a result. Portions of stories could be enhanced or played down, depending on the person relaying them and the circumstances that they were being used to address. This malleability seems to have been a permitted part of traditional Māori religion, and it migrated on occasion to the new converts to Christianity. Polack provided an example of how the religion of the Book could be transplanted to the Māori religion of memory and speech: 'One venerable sage assured me, that he had beheld the God of the *white man*, and described the several comets he had seen, within his own memory, and that of his parent.'[144] The fact that Christianity was a religion in te reo, so far as most Māori who came into contact with it were concerned, made it that much easier for such amalgams to occur.

Siding with te reo Māori as the language of choice to convert Māori had yielded dividends for the missionaries (notwithstanding the heresies that incidentally got included among some converts' beliefs), but this success turned out to be the source of many unexpected consequences. One of these emerged around the late 1820s, when the missionaries effectively tried to place a cordon around New Zealand's indigenous language. Rather than attempting a mass linguistic conversion to English – which a few of them had toyed with in the late 1810s and early 1820s – the country's missionaries were now increasingly attributing the inroads they were making into Māori society to their own growing familiarity with the language of their converts. The consequent irony was that the missionaries – later typically depicted somewhat arbitrarily as an invasive colonising force[145] – were applying the brakes on the introduction of English. It was an approach that worked hand in hand with the CMS's policy in New Zealand during this era of having te reo as the sole language of instruction in its schools.[146]

'E MATE ANA MATOU I TE PUKAPUKA KORE'

As the missionaries became increasingly fluent in te reo, their translations of the religious works and basic teaching materials necessary to advance their cause both improved in accuracy and grew in volume. By 1830 the Anglican printing presses in Sydney were producing hundreds of copies of texts from the liturgy, as well as catechisms, biblical extracts and spelling books to be shipped to New Zealand. Then, in 1837, the real triumph for the missionaries came when an entire translated New Testament – mainly the work of Yate, Colenso, Shepherd and William Williams – was published (it was not until 1858 that the whole Bible appeared in te reo). It seemed as though, wherever missionaries travelled through the country, the fervour for books in Māori communities was unquenchable. William Wade, an Anglican missionary who was also a printer, recalled visiting remote (to Europeans) Māori settlements and regretting that while the inhabitants were 'destitute' of books, he had none to supply. 'Their cry was the same as in almost every place we staid at, – Books, books, "E mate ana matou i te pukapuka kore," We are ill (or dead) for want of books. The thing wanted was not food for the body, but a book.'[147] When Yate reported back to his superiors in London, he informed them that such was the demand for religious texts among Māori that: 'One earnestly requested a copy of the Gospels, offering a large pig as payment; another proposed to save his wages to purchase it, &c. Another said that his heart was sick for the Word of God, and that he desired it more than axes and blankets.' He cited these types of example to strengthen his case for more support from 'the Christians of England' to get printed religious matter to Māori as speedily as possible.[148]

It is possible to get carried away with a generalised impression of Māori as 'stone-age native[s] … naïve, grateful, enthusiastic, or oppressed', and appearing as 'hapless recipients, while the colonizer is the active decision-maker'.[149] Such narratives were widespread in the British Empire in the nineteenth century,[150] and something of the residue of this sentiment has survived in more recent portrayals of this era. To a degree this is unavoidable, especially as there is a dearth of written Māori records from this period[151] to counterbalance the numerous European accounts that have survived. With such lopsidedness in source material, establishing Māori motives can be challenging, but is not impossible. Vestiges of indigenous agency remain, even if it takes some adjustment of perspective to bring them into focus. For example, the notion that Māori rushed to lap up the literacy being served by the missionaries ignores the fact that the missionary presence until at least the 1840s was often contingent on the assent of local chiefs. If a chief decided he did not want a missionary presence in his area,[152] the mission could be expelled in an instant – as happened to the Wesleyan mission at Whangaroa in 1827. The patronage of chiefs, as Marsden knew all too well with Ruatara, was vital to the survival of missions. It was therefore the chiefs who initially sanctioned the introduction and dissemination of te reo in text form, rather than missionaries having a free hand among the haplessly appreciative natives.

The notion that Europeans possessed superior knowledge and wisdom that they graciously consented to share with indigenous peoples was another popular misconception among settlers.[153] The spread of literacy among Māori would have served as a form of moral reassurance to armchair colonists back in Britain: it was the spectre of indomitable Western superiority matched with native passivity[154] once again materialising. From the coloniser's perspective, indigenous peoples appeared to abandon their self-determination when they leapt to embrace the superior knowledge of the coloniser. This thinking reflected the latent desire for a sort of intellectual feudalism, with the natives bonded to the colonial educator and simultaneously acquiring European skills and knowledge, yet denied the possibility of asserting greater self-determination based on what they had gleaned from the colonists.

A clear sign that Māori would not fall into the stereotype of acquiescent natives fawning over the great white missionaries, teachers and, later, other categories of coloniser, however, was that some Māori employed their newly acquired literacy and related knowledge to establish and expand their own commercial enterprises, noticeably in the areas of agriculture and trade.[155] Māori were using literacy to control their economic destiny, rather than allowing others to use literacy to control them.[156]

In the bustle of the 1820s and early 1830s, when missionary attention was concentrated on rendering as much of the Bible as possible in te reo, it is easy to lose sight of the fact that all this activity was confined to a narrow and very direct area of translation: converting existing written words and phrases from one language into another. In a sense, this was the most straightforward and 'mechanical' type of translation that could be undertaken. There was no requirement to capture the specific mannerisms, intonation or any of the range of non-textual cues that accompany spoken language; instead, what the missionaries had been doing since arriving was translating text into text.[157] So while the religious ideas contained in these texts were new to most Māori – in many instances even revolutionary, and to some extent culturally subversive – they were also at times regarded with scepticism,[158] even among those Māori who actively supported a missionary presence in their area.[159] Again, the relationship between coloniser and colonised was not a straightforward one of European dominance and Māori submission.

In any case, it was not as though the early missionaries to New Zealand were the fount of great academic knowledge; some, like Shepherd, even struggled to write in English, and most were not ordained ministers but tradespeople, typically with few specialised skills.[160] Indeed, missionaries frequently were dependent on the hospitality of their host communities for their very survival.[161] It is hard to imagine Māori, in such circumstances, gazing on their foodless, shelterless, sometimes culturally disoriented and occasionally frightened European guests and expecting much in the way of wisdom from them.

Given these considerations, the pendulum now appears to swing towards the proposition that Māori were extracting whatever benefits they could derive from having their language converted into text, while enduring as few as possible of the cultural incursions that typically accompanied the introduction of the language of a coloniser. Eventually, though, pendulums come to a standstill in the centre, representing a sometimes shortlived equilibrium. In this case, independence from European intellectual hegemony was counterbalanced by enthusiasm for the religious ideas contained in printed texts and for the revolutionary possibilities that writing held more generally. The intricacies of these cross-currents defy any single overarching characterisation of the way te reo was evolving through contact mainly with missionaries. And although the consequences of the Māori encounter with English were to be sweeping, they were neither initially swift nor dominated solely by European proselytisers.

'SH'

The botched efforts of Europeans in their first attempts to convert sounds in te reo into text were to be expected – after all, the ones who were doing the transcribing had no training or experience in this area,[162] and the circumstances they were working in were seldom conducive to producing a careful and systematic orthography. John Nicholas's 1817 account of his visit to New Zealand made the point that 'the Missionaries would not only differ from each other in the spelling of the same words, but likewise in the pronunciation of them; a circumstance which must always happen when a new language is to be learned with no other standard of instruction than the ear.'[163]

In the span of roughly a decade, the range of spellings inevitably narrowed in published te reo as the importance of uniformity became more apparent,[164] and as the opinions of a greater number of European 'hearers' of te reo converged on the issue of how they would transcribe what they were hearing. But for some arrivals to the country the missionary efforts at spelling Māori words were still unsatisfactory – as an 1834 entry in the journal of the English visitor Edward Markham reveals: 'I trotted on Thirty Miles to the Mission Station of Kiddy Kiddy, but the Missionaries in their writings exclude the "D" from their Language because the Letter 'R' will answer as well in some Districts as Kirri Kirri, and Wirri Nacky [Whirinaki] instead of Widdy Nacky thus making the Language poorer instead of enriching it.'[165] The possibility that Markham was the one mishearing some words seems not to have entered his consideration, and this was precisely the point – there was still no consensus among Europeans about the exact pronunciation of the words they were hearing spoken by Māori, let alone how they were to be represented in text.

Print is permanent, however, and by the early 1830s the gulf between the more uniform version of written te reo being produced at that time and the previous variants that had been published in Britain and New South Wales was widening, to the point where the editors of the Church Missionary Society's annual proceedings felt it necessary to provide an explanation of the way words in te reo were now appearing – often in a substantially modified form – in their reports.

> a very material change has been made in the Spelling [of te reo]. The old Orthography has hitherto been followed in the Publications of the Society, while the new one is employed by the Missionaries. As that used by them appears to be now, in a considerable degree, settled, it has been judged advisable to introduce it into print. The difference, however, between the two forms of Spelling is so great, that it has been found requisite to insert the following Vocabulary of the terms most frequently occurring in the communications of the Missionaries, to enable our Readers to recognise those heretofore employed under the form in which they now appear.[166]

To illustrate the point, and to assist those pedants who may have been following changes in the orthography of te reo that had occurred over successive issues of the CMS publications, the editors of the 1831 *Church Missionary Record* provided a revised vocabulary. This offers a useful indication of the nature and extent of changes that had been occurring in written te reo since the mid-1810s, as the following sample shows.

Old Spelling	*New Spelling*
Ahoodoo-Pa (sepulchre)	U'dupa
Amoko (the tattooing)	Moko
Areekee (Priest)	Ariki
Hippah (Fortification)	E Pa
Koko (a tool)	Koko
Koomeras (sweet potatoes)	Kumara
Taboo (to make sacred)	Tapu
Whydua (Spirit)	Waidua[167]

It was not yet a finalised version of the spelling – that was still more than a century away – but it represented an extraordinary consolidation of orthography over a fairly condensed period of time, especially considering the lack of training by those involved in first transcribing te reo to text.

It would be easy to see, in the period from 1815 to 1830, that there was a natural sifting and sorting process whereby the missionaries' self-doubting but determined efforts to produce a written version of an indigenous language resulted in the emergence of a fairly uniform spelling. In general this is what happened, but in the process at least one localised pronunciation trait was lost. This was the sibilant 'sh',[168] which appeared commonly in the published works of Europeans who had visited the Bay of Islands in the 1810s and 1820s. It has been suggested recently that 'Ngāpuhi simply did not differentiate between SH and H … But H and SH sounds did sound different to Kendall, so he wrote them down as he heard them.'[169] A similar point on the prevalence of 'sh' in some words in te reo was made as early 1838, when Polack feigned a scientific air as he concluded that 'the auricular organs of the English visitors, generally speaking, appears to have been rather obtuse', whereas the French apparently had no such difficulties.[170]

The preponderance of 'sh' in various European attempts at transcribing certain words from the Ngāpuhi dialect suggests that the alleged inability by so many of these writers to distinguish sounds is unlikely, by itself, to account for the frequency with which this specific orthographical feature appeared in so many books, journals, and correspondence from this period. Moreover, if Kendall was the principal source of this uniform error, then presumably, those who followed it faithfully would have made similar efforts to copy the other examples of the distinct spelling of te reo that Kendall devised. And, although the 'sh' sound appears fairly consistently in their works, there is considerable variation of spelling among those writers who attempted to transcribe certain words that they heard in te reo. Earle, for example, titled a watercolour he painted in Northland, 'The residence of Shulitea chief of Kororadika, Bay of Islands, New Zealand'.[171] Shulitea was Te Whareumu, who sometimes styled himself as 'King George'.[172] Not only was this spelling not used by Kendall for Te Whareumu, but there is no evidence that Earle was familiar with Kendall's works in te reo, so it is not as though the artist was conforming to some sort of convention laid down by the missionary translators. Earle also used the 'sh' sibilant for Hongi (Shunghie),[173] which was similar sounding (although, importantly, differently spelt) to Shunghee, as written by Marsden[174] and Kendall;[175] while Butler[176] and Craik[177] both spelt Hongi the same way as Earle (Shunghie), although Butler also spelt it Shungee on occasion.[178] Shepherd wrote the great chief's name as 'Shone'.[179] Other variants included Shunghee,[180] Shungi[181] and Shongi. This last example is slightly more significant in that it was the spelling used by Eruera

Pare Hongi, who was a nephew of Hongi Hika,[182] and one of the first Māori known to have written a letter in te reo[183] – though, of course, this spelling was just as likely to have been the consequence of missionary instruction.

There were other words that were written as 'sh', such as Shukianga for Hokianga (both Butler[184] and Alexander McCrae[185] used this form) and the variant Shukeangha (which was used by Marsden),[186] both of which give some indication of the geographical spread of 'sh'. Hoshee was used for Oihi (by Marsden),[187] and Shoroe for Horoia (by Kendall).[188] Lee, in the preface to the 1820 *Grammar and Vocabulary*, offered this explanation for the appearance of 'sh':

> There is one peculiarity in the pronunciation of the New-Zealand
> Language, which should here be noticed, and which could not be marked
> in the Alphabet. When two vowels concur, the combined sound becomes
> that of the English *sh*; ex. gr. *E ongi, A salute*, is pronounced *Shongi*; and
> so of every combination, in which the indefinite article *e* precedes a
> vowel.[189]

As a variant of this, Maunsell, in his 1842 *Grammar of the New Zealand Language*, explained that the letter 'h' in te reo was pronounced the same as in English, but added: 'A gentle sibilancy accompanies its pronunciation amongst Ngapuhi, which some speakers erroneously confound with *sh*.'[190] A more obvious explanation for the frequent occurrence of the 'sh' sound in text in this period is that this affricated sound was definitely pronounced by Māori in parts of Northland.[191] Even in the early twentieth century, the 's' sound persisted in some dialects, albeit on loan words.[192] It is also evident, if the orthography of printed te reo is anything to go by, that by the mid-nineteenth century the 'sh' ceased to be used widely.

What cannot be known with any certainty about the fading of the 'sh' sound during the nineteenth century[193] is the extent to which the standardisation of te reo, imposed by its appearance in print, contributed to its decline – especially from the 1820s.[194] The editor of Henry Williams' early journals concluded: 'The C.M.S. missionaries soon discovered that the ['sh'] sound was not a sibilant, and made various attempts to capture it in an adequate symbol. Hence it appears, first as, e. g., *E'Okianga*, later as *'Hokianga*, and finally as *Hokianga*.' This process bears the hallmarks of linguistic standardisation occurring in parts of Northland. The dialectical variation of te reo was clearly being curtailed in print, but it is also possible that this insistence on uniformity had its effect on various Māori communities, resulting in a similar reduction of dialectical variation in spoken te reo.[195]

There were bound to be transitory stages in the process of bringing greater orthographic consistency to written te reo, and the use of an apostrophe before an initial 'h' (as in 'Hongi, and 'Hokianga)[196] and, less often, before a medial 'h' (as in ha'hunga)[197] was a case of this. One explanation for the appearance of apostrophes in these words was that they were 'a symbol of a variant of the Ngapuhi dialect', and that they represented 'a very similar sound to the *shewa* in the Hebrew language, which in English transliteration can be seen in the word *qetal*, where the vowel *e* is very, very short and the accent is on the last syllable. So the Maori sound can be represented by *Whongi* for the normal *Hongi*.'[198] By the close of the century, 'sh' had slipped from almost all printed Māori texts, and from spoken te reo as well. Whether the former development led to the latter is difficult to determine; nonetheless, it cannot be discounted as a possible influence in the language's evolution.

TE REO ELSEWHERE

If there is a sizeable amount of detail about te reo in Northland during the 1820s and into the 1830s, it is because that is where the frontline of the encounter with English was at its most conspicuous, and where the incursions of English and of literacy were at their deepest. But how was te reo faring in the rest of New Zealand? In the early 1830s, roughly three quarters of Māori had never even seen a missionary (at least not a European one), although word of their presence had spread throughout almost the whole country.[199] 'Natives living around the base of Tongariro, at Poverty Bay, and on the banks of the Mokau, and Wanganui rivers, all knew that a small body of unarmed men had taken up their abode in Hongi's territory [Northland]' is how one mid-nineteenth-century writer described it.

> New Zealanders [Māori], who went to and from the north, brought
> with them occasionally religious books, and always news of the sayings
> and doings of the missionaries. Masters of whalers reported that the
> aborigines far away from the mission stations prayed night and morning
> in nasal psalmody, and chanted Christian psalms to heathen tunes.

The reputation of missionaries among Māori communities – that preceded their arrival in some instances by hundreds of kilometres and several years – was that they were a different class from sailors and Pākehā-Māori. According to the rumours that circulated through many hapū, missionaries 'kept schools, and instructed persons to write on paper words which others seeing comprehended, gave books for nothing, performed a ceremony called baptism, opposed war, promoted peace, cultivated new sorts of food, preached against cannibalism, and of a God who did good and not evil'.[200]

Absent from this inventory of what the new culture had to offer was its language. Perhaps this is what made the ways of the coloniser more beguiling than disagreeable to so many Māori: that these new types of thinking and doing were permeating New Zealand almost exclusively in the language of its indigenous occupants. It is as though there was an unspoken presumption among Māori that foreign arrivals would have to learn te reo if they wished to function. Even as the 1830s progressed, it must have looked inconceivable to Māori – given the numerical proportions of the two peoples – that they would ever have to become fluent speakers of English. If anything, te reo appeared more secure exactly because it had not fallen at the first sign of English; on the contrary, it was the native speakers of English who looked to be doing most of the linguistic compromise.

Measuring the spread of written Māori into other parts of the country by the early 1830s with any sort of accuracy is impossible; zealous estimations are generally all that survive. During a visit to Rotorua in 1831 – a distance of about 450 kilometres from the Bay of Islands – Henry Williams described in his journal how a group of Māori gathered around him, one of whom asked him what was the meaning of the letters that he had been writing. 'I wrote them down for him,' Williams noted, 'and in half an hour he knew them all, and was teaching several outside. Numbers of others came, until I had no paper left of any description on which to write a copy. At length they brought small pieces, to have the letters written for them, and about two hundred, old and young, were soon employed teaching and learning the letters with the greatest possible interest.'[201] Reverend Joseph Orton assessed in 1833 that there were people in almost every village in Northland who could read and write.[202] The same year, the *Missionary Register* likewise reported that every village in the region contained literate Māori, and that schools were being established by Māori without any missionary prompting.[203] And on the East Coast, there was a 'literacy fever', with demand for teachers and books easily exceeding supply.[204]

If you relied on the breathless enthusiasm of such accounts, as most settlers did, you could be forgiven for imagining that te reo was being revolutionised as a text-based language. The diffusion of te reo in written form needs some context, at least to prevent seeing the phenomenon as the death sentence of Māori oral culture. First, a comfortable majority of Māori still did not read, and so the effects of literacy were not as comprehensive as some of the published reports of the period implied.[205] Second, te reo was the exclusive language of communication within Māori communities, and it was also the sole language used in cultural practices and rites. The appearance of te reo in print did nothing to undermine this, and even by the mid-1840s the vast majority of Māori still could not speak or read English.[206] And third, the works that appeared in printed form in te reo were limited in range in this era, and were almost exclusively religious: their application to the day-to-day life of Māori communities was confined to consideration of sacred matters.

Then there is the perception that some Māori had of books during this period. The missionaries promoted the printed Scriptures for the value of their content, but for some of the recipients of these texts, the books themselves were venerated as sacred artefacts. They had value among Māori communities as quasi-magical talismans, aids to supernatural practices, and even as signs of social status – and various other non-literary purposes.[207] In 1832 Richard Davis expressed his exasperation that, just at the point where indigenous superstition looked to be losing ground, those Māori 'who know not a letter wish to possess themselves of a copy of the translated Scriptures, because they consider it possesses a peculiar virtue of protecting them from the power of evil Spirits'.[208] The power of the book as physical object – as opposed to its content – indicates how the dissemination of books cannot be used as a reliable measure of the spread of literacy.

The year after Davis wrote of his anxiety about the possession of books becoming a form of idolatry, Henry Williams recorded in his journal an occasion when he received a bundle of letters from a ship. Those Māori who were present were impressed that others who were travelling with Williams were able to read the letters. The onlookers were 'struck with wonder at hearing as they described it a book speak; for though they expect that a European can perform any extraordinary thing, yet they cannot understand how that a New Zealand youth can possess the same power'.[209] Language that could be 'carried' on paper (when previously it had only ever been spoken) was mildly miraculous to those Māori who were encountering literacy for the first time, and the notion of printed texts possessing supernatural powers was therefore readily formed. Perhaps the most telling example of the power of books as physical objects comes from an episode captured by George Clarke jnr. He recalled how many of the Māori he came across

> thought it highly proper that they should be armed with books. It might be an old ship's almanac, or a cast-away novel, or even a few stitched leaves of old newspapers. What did it matter? A book was a book, and every one knew that to hold a book was part of the ceremony in the new Karakia. Still there were a score or two who could read, and one of the most touching things was to see their books. Leaves of cartridge paper folded and stitched like a pamphlet, but written all through with the prayers of the Liturgy, or a chapter or two from the New Testament.[210]

These accounts of the spread of literacy among Māori reveal a particular dimension of the social history of te reo's earliest period in print. Religious texts were used – as they had been in other cultures at various times – as a means of confronting the uncertainties of colonialism, both through the content of their text and in more token ways through their mere physical presence. And because it was still only religious material that was appearing in books in te reo, the distinction was blurred between the sacred ideas held within a book and the sanctity of the book as an object in its own right.

The challenges that books threw up to the traditional basis of Māori society – questioning and even overturning long-accepted truths, proposing new ways of living and believing, and sometimes undermining existing power structures and political allegiances – inevitably resulted in more volatile social and cultural conditions prevailing in some communities.[211] Meanwhile, the mounting signs of European commercial, religious, social and religious influence, especially in parts of Northland, removed any sense of the certainty of Māori political authority born of demographic dominance alone.

There were early signs that the country's indigenous language and culture were succumbing to those of the settler. As an example, the status of tohunga – those men (and occasionally women) who held so much specialist and sacred knowledge – was being undermined by the new forms of knowledge introduced by settlers; by the texts circulating in te reo in an increasing number of Māori communities, which were offering an alternative belief system; and by the powerlessness of most tohunga to combat new diseases, which brought to the fore their apparent spiritual impotence. From the

British perspective these were all changes for the better, arousing centuries-old hopes about colonies transforming into utopias.[212] The displacement of elements of traditional indigenous culture with recently introduced European ways pointed at the very least to a better, more civilised future.[213] An English captain visiting Paihia early in 1833 found that even the work of the local mission school in educating approximately 70 Māori from the area was contributing to the utopian tint of the country, led by the dual prongs of Christianity and literacy. He described how he was

> much gratified to observe … all ranks and ages, Chiefs and subjects, old and young, bond and free, receiving and communicating instruction, with a degree of decorum and regularity which would have reflected credit on a school of the same kind even in England. Catechisms, reading, spelling, writing on slates from dictation, and ciphering, formed the employment of the upper classes, while the lowest were engaged in learning the alphabet and forming letters. The former disinclination of the Natives to attend School has now happily entirely subsided, and given place to an anxiety for instruction, which appears to be rapidly extending.[214]

These changes may have appeared to the colonists unambiguously as improvements, but they were also subversive: the Māori cultural confidence that had been so obvious in the 1820s was receding, albeit so gradually that it would have been barely perceptible to most people.

One symptom of this change was that the relative values of te reo and English was undergoing a process of re-evaluation. Te reo was still the preferred language of instruction for missionaries in their schools and was not openly disparaged, but the forces of modernisation[215] were effectively driving a wedge into the Māori world whereby various elements of the culture were judged to be either 'acceptable' or 'unacceptable' in the view of the coloniser. Some aspects of the traditional Māori world, such as rāranga or weaving, were considered nothing more than a harmless craft[216] and so were permitted to continue, while at the other end of the scale Europeans were unanimous in their opinion that traditional practices such as cannibalism were irreducibly primitive[217] and must be purged from the culture. But where did te reo fit in this spectrum of European approval?

Part of the answer to this lies in the general sense of superiority that many settlers had when they looked on their Māori compatriots. Te reo was easily lumped in with all the other 'primitive' aspects of the culture[218] that some Europeans were openly hostile to. The Catholic Bishop Jean Baptiste Pompallier illustrated how contemptuous these attitudes could be in an account that was ostensibly about an attempt at converting Māori, but which has undertones of the prevailing notions of European cultural ascendency:

> In the familiar conversations I held with these people [a group of Māori], when visiting them, it was easy for me to point out their ignorance to them. Not unfrequently they saw it in an instant by the questions I asked them, which forced them to look for a first principle. If I asked them to give me the genealogy of their god, they became lost in their ideas and their answers. As they quoted in succession the names of these ancestors, I wrote them down before their eyes with a pencil on a bit of paper, and sometimes they would repeat names which were already written down, assigning as a father to an ancient god someone whom they had already classed as being one of his offspring and divine posterity. When I pointed out to them the incoherence, the contradictions and the viciousness of their religious theories, the people who were listening began to laugh at their wise men and priests, who were arguing with me in public. Then, quite humiliated, each one confessed his ignorance.[219]

On the edges of the Māori world, it is easy to see how doubt and disorder were beginning to displace dominance, and how a vague sense of uneasiness was gnawing away at many of the old certainties.[220] As a result, te reo, and the culture it gave voice to, were in a much more precarious position by the mid-1830s than the proportion of the language's speakers would suggest. The preconditioning phase[221] of te reo's subsequent decline was under way.

CHAPTER 4

'A mere language of tradition'
Mid-1830s to c. 1850

'THE CIRCLE WIDENS YEARLY'

In the 1830s New Zealand was in the early phase of becoming what was regarded as a 'white colony'.[1] But ironically, as the flow of immigrants from Britain gathered pace during the decade, so too did the impression among Europeans that the country was darkening. In the 1810s and 1820s, most things Māori were at least tolerated, if not fully accepted, by the few missionaries, traders and settlers living in New Zealand. This forbearance extended to te reo, which at the opening of the 1830s was still not only the dominant language numerically, but the language that those who intended to engage with Māori had to acquire.

This period could be seen as a Golden Age for te reo – evidence, if any was needed, that the language could hold its own with any newcomers and that, given the right circumstances, Europeans would be prepared to learn to speak te reo to a reasonably high standard of fluency without Māori necessarily having to reciprocate with English to the same extent. In this era, there was a particular attitude towards indigenous peoples – a sense of 'psychological superiority'[2] – that was burrowing away in the minds of many settlers in the territories where British imperial activity was unfurling, and that would eventually have an effect on how Europeans saw te reo (among much else) in New Zealand.

As the experience of other parts of the burgeoning British Empire had revealed, it would be only a matter of time before this tolerance of things Māori started to wane and the European superiority complex manifested itself. In other parts of the world, overt antipathy towards indigenous groups was already in evidence. In 1821 Sir Stamford Raffles, who had founded the city of Singapore two years earlier, detected such a shift in the way Britons regarded non-European peoples. 'It is very certain,' he wrote, 'that on the first discovery of what we term savage nations, philosophers went beyond all reason and truth in favour of *uncivilized* happiness; but it is no less certain, that of late years, the tide of prejudice has run equally strong in the opposite direction.'[3]

In New Zealand, the concerted case for the British government to take serious measures to protect Māori from the ravages of colonisation would be argued for the final time in the 1830s, primarily by missionary groups concerned that the burgeoning presence of other Europeans in the country was undoing some of their accomplishments. Otherwise, a new and more domineering mood was appearing in New Zealand. British imperialism was seen by its agents as the light that would shine into the 'dark' places of the world. Instead of affording some semblance of protection to indigenous cultures (and their languages), colonialists were increasingly driven by an ideology that espoused the abolition of 'savage customs'[4] and the promulgation in these societies of their own moral, cultural and scientific values.[5]

In areas of British intervention around the world, this newly invigorated commitment to civilising was having an impact on indigenous languages, especially as teaching in English was coming to be regarded as a moral as much as a practical imperative. The consequence of this change in attitude was not always a sudden rush to instruction in English, however. If nothing else, in New Zealand's case at least, the sheer logistical obstacles to achieving such a transition to a new language made any immediate change impossible; so in the interim te reo and English looked in general to be cohabiting the same geographical space.[6] The appearance of a harmonious partnership, though, existed only on the surface.[7] The ascendency of English, at least in the countries where British imperial interests had established a foothold, was becoming ever more certain during this time. In 1838 the English antiquarian Edwin Guest drew on this spirit of the age to make a sanguine prediction about the global future of the language:

> Before another century has gone by it [English] will, at the present rate of increase, be spoken by hundreds of millions! Of the five great temperate regions, *three* – North America, South Africa, and Australia – are fast peopling with our race, and some, now living, will see them overspread with a population claiming in our language the same interest as ourselves. That language, too, is rapidly becoming the great medium of civilisation, the language of law and literature to the Hindoo, of commerce to the African, of religion to the scattered islanders of the Pacific. The range of its influence, even at the present day, is greater than ever was that of the Greek, the Latin, or the Arabic; and the circle widens yearly. Though it

were not our mother tongue, it would still, of all living languages, be
the one most worthy of our study and our cultivation, as bearing most
directly on the happiness of mankind.[8]

Guest's conclusion contains a noticeable strain of Benthamite utilitarianism,
as though the confident expansion of English around the world was some
fixed universal social principle that would lead to the betterment of all
peoples.[9] Its spread was not always going to be easy, but both the inevitability
and the benefits of its impending universality were unquestioned.

Polack echoed Guest's forecast that same year in New Zealand when
he wrote about the rate at which Māori were acquiring English, which had
recently surged: 'Many natives speak our language pretty well, from the
intercourse derived from serving as seamen and servants to the Europeans.
Doubtless in the course of two or three generations, the native language will
become obsolete, in favour of the English.'[10] In the eyes of these colonists,
English was shifting from being a complementary skill possessed by an
expanding number of Māori to a language that was supplanting te reo. And
if the pattern of acquisition of English among other indigenous groups
was anything to go by, it was a shift that would most likely occur in two
important phases. The first was increased use of English when Māori and
settlers were communicating: this was an inevitable development as tens
of thousands of British migrants poured into the country in the 1840s and
1850s, almost all of whom could not speak te reo and, unlike the previous
generation of settlers, saw little reason to do so. The second phase was more
invasive, as English progressively became the language of communication
within Māori communities. This was a far slower and more uneven process,
and the indigenous language never succumbed completely to the foreign
usurper in New Zealand in the nineteenth century.

The commencement of formal British rule in 1840 was an important
catalyst for both these changes. When Charles Terry assessed the future of
the new colony, one of his suggestions was that 'the Government … should
enforce education of the native children, in English, as well as in their
vernacular language. It will be the most certain means of rendering them
useful and valuable auxiliaries to the Europeans in every capacity.'[11] English,
in this context, was implicitly the language not only of progress but of Māori
servitude.

In the years leading up to 1840 te reo was still the principal language of the
country – if published works are anything to go by. By the late 1830s, there

were two printing presses operating in New Zealand – used by the Anglicans and, from 1836, their Wesleyan counterparts – producing religious texts in te reo in unprecedented quantities, and with reduced production costs and faster dissemination than the previous arrangement in which almost all the texts for Māori were printed in Sydney. Colenso, in particular, was publishing volumes of mainly religious works on an industrial scale from the late 1830s – a feat made all the more amazing considering he relied on a rundown Stanhope hand press[12] that he pushed to its limits to meet the voracious demand among Māori for printed material. The first major work to emerge from his printery in Paihia was the New Testament in te reo – 'an event that caused a great sensation at the time, both in New Zealand and at Home',[13] as Colenso proudly recollected. Wesleyan missionary Nathaniel Turner saw the publication of this important work as forestalling the spread of Catholicism among Māori. He wrote in his journal: 'No book will counteract the errors of Popery like the New Testament of the Lord Jesus.'[14] And as interdenominational chauvinism extended into Māori communities, printed works in te reo were used by the different factions as authorities to back up their various stances.

Between March 1836 and December 1837, 5000 copies of the New Testament came off Colenso's press, and over the next five years this output was augmented with other publications. As some indication of the fervid pace at which Colenso and a few assistants worked, in 1835 they printed 2000 copies of the Epistles to the Ephesians and the Philippians and 1000 copies of St Luke's Gospel. Four years later, a batch of 10,000 primers on how to read te reo were distributed and, in 1840, 20,000 copies of a prayer and hymn book, 11,000 copies of the Psalms, 10,000 copies of a catechism, 6000 prayerbooks and 10,000 portions of Daniel and Jonah from the Old Testament.[15] From frustrating beginnings in 1835, dealing with faulty parts and lacking essential supplies, by the end of 1840 the Paihia press had produced an astonishing 5.5 million pages of text in te reo.[16] Colenso was deluging the market with books in Māori but the demand was nowhere near satiated.

This mass production of texts in te reo occasionally drew criticism from outside observers such as the journalist Samuel Martin, who – probably like other settlers – was puzzled and angered that almost all the written material Māori were reading was in te reo. His caustic response made his feelings on the matter clear: 'The missionaries have hitherto, with a most extraordinary and ignorant pertinacity, set their face against every attempt at teaching

English to the natives, vainly endeavouring, by lame translations of garbled extracts from the Scriptures, to convey to them a knowledge of religion.'[17]

There were a few exceptions to the all-te reo publishing programme. In May 1836 the first work in English was printed by the missionary press in Paihia. *Report of the Formation and Establishment of the New Zealand Temperance Society*[18] – 'a small unpretentious book of eight pages', as Colenso described it[19] – was the first bilingual publication in New Zealand; and it was another canary-in-the-coalmine development nudging English closer to being a substitute for te reo, even though an insignificant number of copies were produced, and it was not intended for a Māori readership.

'CONSTANTLY SENDING LETTERS'

The Māori demand for religious works in te reo went hand in hand with a fairly sudden acceleration in the number of Māori converts to Christianity. After years of the Anglicans and Wesleyans struggling to secure even one or two converts, by 1842 the Anglicans alone could claim a staggering 35,000 Māori adherents.[20] Among other factors, the power of the printed word in te reo was fundamental in this great cultural shift. And while it is notoriously difficult to assess the authenticity of a person's faith, Māori enthusiasm for Christianity was frequently more than skin deep, judging by their often rapturous expressions of interest in these books, and because many of the religious books they acquired were so well read that they wore out.[21]

The fact of all these religious publications appearing only in te reo for more than a quarter of a century and being consumed eagerly by thousands, even tens of thousands of Māori, was bound to leave its mark on the country's indigenous culture and language. Christianity acted as a cultural implant that became part of the body politic of several Māori communities, to an extent that would not have been anywhere near the case if the missionaries had gone down the path of teaching Māori to speak and read English from the outset. In 1800 Christianity was indisputably not a part of Māori culture, but could the same claim be made in the 1840s? By that time it was still an 'imported' religion (as opposed to the traditional alternative), but such a binary delineation of 'indigenous' and 'European' ignores the degree to which the message of the Gospels had taken hold and was en route to becoming a spiritual and cultural element that was fused to Māori society, instead of remaining an ill-fitting colonial accessory. It was a development that had been effected partly through te reo serving as the medium of cultural change, rather than a language resisting outside influences. This indication of te reo's cultural adaptability was to be a key element in its survival through the remainder of the century.

And the changes did not stop there. The confluence of indigenous language and colonising culture was altering te reo itself – first through the increasing standardisation of the language (at least in printed form), but then more noticeably in the expansion of its vocabulary through the addition of neologisms. Supplementing a language with new words occurs for a variety of reasons,[22] but usually the increments are slight and slow to occur. The first Polynesian arrivals in New Zealand, for example, would have had to create words for the new fauna, flora and other unfamiliar aspects of the natural world that they encountered. With the arrival of a new and intricate culture in New Zealand from the early nineteenth century, the process of word creation mushroomed at an unprecedented rate.

This was not a neutral process – because of its effects, and because of those in control of it. It was initially the missionaries who conjured up the words necessary to translate the copious names and concepts in the Bible into te reo. This resulted in the at times ironic situation of a neologised form of te reo being thrust on Māori by the coloniser instead of being produced by the native speakers themselves.[23] At the same time, it would have been noticeable to those Māori who were acquiring some fluency in English that this was a one-way process: while te reo's vocabulary was proliferating with new words converted from English, English had little need to borrow from te reo.[24] This was a potentially destabilising factor for the country's indigenous language,[25] in that there is a power that is exerted and maintained by those who create any sort of knowledge and, to the same extent, there is a powerlessness in those languages that are not in full control of their own lexicon.[26] In his 1949 dystopian novel *1984*, George Orwell addressed the cultural and intellectual power of word creation. The Ministry of Truth's lexicographer Symes, when discussing 'Newspeak', explained how his department was 'getting the language into its final shape'.

> When we've finished with it, people like you will have to learn it all over again. You think, I dare say, that our chief job is inventing new words. But not a bit of it! We're destroying words … In your heart you'd prefer to stick to Oldspeak, with all its vagueness and its useless shades of meaning. You don't grasp the beauty of the destruction of words … Don't you see that the whole aim of Newspeak is to narrow the range of thought?[27]

This sort of displacement was starting to happen in te reo around this time. Old words were not necessarily 'destroyed' in the Orwellian sense, but their application could be modified or limited while new, settler-created words in te reo proliferated.

Eventually, many of the neologisms introduced into New Zealand's indigenous language, mainly by the missionaries in the 1820s and 1830s, were assimilated into te reo and became regarded by Māori as 'ordinary'. For that period of time when an avalanche of new words descended on the language, the disruption – not only to te reo itself but to Māori knowledge, perceptions and beliefs – was considerable. There was no clenched-fisted coercion in this process; on the contrary, it was more a form of intellectual colonisation by tacit consent, in so far as it addressed for Māori readers a shortfall in the existing vocabulary of te reo.

To some settlers, this missionary-led enhancement of the vocabulary of te reo was deserving of ridicule. One example of this view appeared in a letter to the editor of an Auckland newspaper in 1843, which mocked efforts to accommodate new terms in te reo:

> In fact, a student shall take up a copy of the New Testament in what is
> called a translation into Maori, and after he has got sufficient insight into
> the trick, he will find somewhere about a quarter of the words, divested
> of their false orthography, are English words borrowed, but, like a stolen
> horse, so cropped and doctored, concealed in a disguise so grotesque and
> startling, that their most familiar friends cannot recognise them.[28]

While one correspondent to the paper described this assessment as 'nonsense' and 'a palpable display of ignorance',[29] it nevertheless revealed that there was open hostility among some sectors of settler society towards the modernisation of the nation's indigenous language. The consensus among this group was that te reo was best left to die out altogether.

The shift from te reo being read to also being written was another important stage in the evolution of the language. Scottish lawyer-cum-merchant William Brown was mildly astonished at how quickly Māori were learning to read and write. In the early 1840s he recalled a visit he had made to Thames, where he came across a group of around 20 Māori catching and curing eels. 'On looking into their huts,' he wrote,

> I observed some of them were busy with their slates, and found that they
> were learning to read and write. They are constantly sending letters to
> each other, and some idea of the extent of their correspondence may be

gathered from the fact that the postmaster at the Bay of Islands informed me that he had seen a bundle of native letters a foot square, in his office, at one time. Some of these letters do the writers great credit, exhibiting much good feeling as well as mental ability.[30]

R.G. Jameson, an Australian official who visited New Zealand in 1840, was impressed at how swiftly and proficiently young Māori in particular were acquiring literacy:

> Their favourite amusement is writing upon a slate, or sending letters on puka pukas to their friends. The style of their epistles is quaint, igurative [sic], and full of repetitions and expressions of courtesy; but I have seen one addressed by a female catechist to the daughter of a missionary, which, in the correctness of its style and the propriety of its sentiments, would bear a comparison with any European letter.

For the younger generation of Māori in many communities, to be without these skills was considered to be 'a mark of inferiority, against which their pride revolts'.[31]

Two things stand out from Jameson's observation. The first is that the spread of literacy in te reo was beyond the control of anyone – either those who wished to advance it or those who might have favoured its curtailing. The second point is that this was a generational development: Jameson could not help but notice: 'The old chiefs, whose minds have been moulded by the savage customs of their youth, are for the most part passive spectators of the changes that are daily going on.'[32] Māori youth, on the other hand, were rapidly embracing literacy at a rate which, in a decade or two, would overrun the perception of te reo as exclusively a spoken language in most Māori communities. It was now on the cusp of becoming accepted among Māori as a written language as well. This meant that knowledge could be stored, transmitted, built on and deployed in ways that undermined or, at the very least, redefined many of the traditional ways of storing and using knowledge.

An example of this hybridity between the Māori and European worlds was the practice some Māori employed of personifying the letters they wrote to other Māori, imbuing them with aspects of a living entity with its own personality, as though the letters possessed some of the traits that tohunga held. This manifested itself in phrases such as 'Nau mai, haere atu e taku reta ki te kawa kōrero', which translates as 'Welcome and farewell, my letter, on your way to convey greetings and news.'[33] When Māori wrote in te reo to Europeans, however – notably to those in a position of authority or who were able to wield some influence – they would adapt their style to suit the expectations of their addressees.[34] This ability to modify styles of prose, content and thematic material showed a sophistication in letter writing that surpassed that of most Europeans at the time.

To those Māori who may have been concerned about literacy arriving in their communities, this form of colonisation was proceeding at a relentless pace. As early as 1842, the rate at which various Māori communities were acquiring literacy exceeded that of settlers in their vicinity. At times this produced unexpected dynamics – as an incident that Jameson recorded in 1840 reveals:

> It was related to me by an individual who had passed some time in
> Mercury Bay, that some English sawyers had requested their employer
> to teach them reading and writing, being ashamed of their inferiority in
> these respects to the young New Zealanders, who were taunting them
> all day long with defects which they deemed wholly unpardonable in a
> white man.[35]

From the point of view of the missionaries who had toiled for decades to transform te reo into a written language, this period of mass adoption of literacy by Māori must have felt like a vindication of their efforts. But self-congratulatory thoughts of this nature would have missed the point. Literacy in te reo was now emerging as a fixture of Māori society rather than a skill loaned from another culture. This possession and control of literacy by Māori made it a de facto part of New Zealand's indigenous culture, and to that extent it lessened the coloniser's control of that culture.

TE REO OFFICIALLY

It was not until 1987 that parliament passed an Act that belatedly made te reo an official language of New Zealand.[36] By that time te reo had all but been expunged from state communication, and even when occasionally some token deference was required to be paid to the country's indigenous language, it was a concession sometimes honoured more in the breach than the observance. The previous year the Waitangi Tribunal had warned that 'urgent action' was needed if te reo was to survive[37] and, as if by instinct, officials and politicians leapt to legislation as the panacea.

A very different situation prevailed a century and a half earlier. The strictures of statutes were not needed to ensure that te reo was a language used by the organs of empire operating in New Zealand. Practicality dictated that any message from British officials to Māori needed to be conveyed in te reo as well as English – and this practice continued in diminishing degrees for the rest of the nineteenth century.

The first major example of this was the 1835 Declaration of Independence,[38] contrived by the generally ineffectual[39] first (and only) British Resident to New Zealand, James Busby. The declaration was an assertion on paper of the sovereignty of those chiefs who signed the agreement, and it aimed to create a confederation of tribes that would govern the country and pass laws. Although it was dismissed by the governor of New South Wales, Sir George Gipps,[40] and was given the faintest acknowledgment but no endorsement by Lord Glenelg, the Secretary of State for War and the Colonies,[41] Busby and the chiefs who gave their consent to the declaration saw it as possessing some constitutional gravitas. This belief would have been fortified by the fact that Busby was a representative of the Crown – even if his declaration was an initiative of his own creation and done without the instruction or authorisation, let alone the approval, of his superiors.

There was no doubt in Busby's mind that this declaration had to be translated into te reo, and that the translated version would hold the same weight as the English version. There has been some debate regarding the quality of the translation,[42] the extent to which Māori were involved in augmenting rather than merely copying the text of the declaration in te reo and, specifically, the degree to which Henry Williams' translation of its English text into te reo was aided by Māori.[43] Support for the suggestion that there was some Māori input into the translation rides on 'the quality of its language and expression', which were in 'formal Ngapuhi idiolect'.[44] But what is important is that the precedent had now been established for bilingual versions of official documents to be produced in New Zealand – a requirement based on pragmatism rather than any sentimental affection for te reo among Crown representatives.

That was in New Zealand. In London, the centre of the British imperial web, the version of the Declaration of Independence in te reo that arrived in the Colonial Office in early 1836 would have been incomprehensible and therefore inconsequential to officials. Te reo was just another of those 'native' languages on the periphery of the empire[45] – at worst an obstacle to civilisation, and at best an anthropological novelty. If a document was of any importance it would have to be in English.

One of the consequences of the de facto policy in the emerging nation state of New Zealand of using te reo in constitutional documentation was that the language remained a focus of the mobilisation of Māori political identity to a greater extent than if English had been the sole language employed. Thus, while the linguistic core–periphery dynamic corresponded with imperial English and colonised te reo respectively,[46] in New Zealand the distinction was more clouded, particularly in the first half of the nineteenth century when Māori were still the majority population.[47] Ironically, as the machine of empire accelerated its activities in New Zealand from 1833, its local policy of communicating with Māori in te reo – at least in text – arrested the decline of the language, mitigating many of its other actions that were to prove so debilitating to te reo.

Outside of New Zealand, the British response to indigenous cultures more generally from the late 1830s and into the 1840s[48] was a muddle of humanitarianism, commercial imperatives that were seen by some as grubby but unavoidable, colonial paternalism, the desire to secure converts to Christianity, the wish to civilise, and the political requirement to protect British interests overseas. The form and extent of official British intervention in New Zealand in the foreseeable future – with all the anticipated implications it would have for the country's indigenous culture and language – would to an extent be determined by the recommendations in the House of Commons Select Committee on Aboriginal Tribes in British Settlements, which reported on its hearings in 1837.[49]

The general tone of the committee's findings started out as one of caution. The British public, its members suggested, were indifferent to the sufferings endured by indigenous peoples as a result of British imperial expansion. The committee alleged that

> no effort … has yet been made to check the progress of oppression in our colonies. In an age distinguished for its liberality, its enlightened sentiment, and its Christian zeal, atrocities, the most daring and dreadful in their character, which, even in a darker era of the world's history, would have excited universal horror, have passed unnoticed and unreproved.[50]

Soon the language became more forthright. The committee acknow-ledged, in terms as forceful as any that had previously been used in a government publication dealing with this topic, that:

The injuries we have inflicted, the oppression we have exercised, the cruelties we have committed, the vices we have fostered, the desolation and utter ruin we have caused, stand in strange and melancholy contrast with the enlarged and generous exertions we have made for the advancement of civil freedom, for the moral and intellectual improvement of mankind, and for the furtherance of that sacred truth, which alone can permanently elevate and civilize mankind.[51]

Finding an equilibrium between the presumed benefits and injuries resulting from colonial intervention was no easy task, and the select committee, understandably, was unable to provide a formula that would satisfy the apprehensions and ambitions of those on either side of the debate. It did, however, touch on issues of indigenous languages in a way that acknowledged rudimentarily the threats posed by the advance of English into British areas of colonial interest. Among the committee's general suggestions, for example, was that written state or constitutional documents – such as treaties – with indigenous peoples be approached with the utmost caution. 'A ready pretext for complaint will be found in the ambiguity of the language in which their agreements must be drawn up, and in the superior sagacity which the European will exercise in framing, in interpreting, and in evading them,' the committee warned, before adding that 'the safety and welfare of an uncivilized race require that their relations with their more cultivated neighbours should be diminished rather than multiplied'.[52] Try telling that to the land-trading organisations, merchants and settlers who were already directing their covetous gaze in New Zealand's direction. In their minds, the suggestion of less rather than more commercial intervention was anathema. And it must have been equally galling to some officials who were to be appointed to colonies with a sizeable indigenous population to be told that their duties 'should consist, first, in cultivating a personal knowledge of the natives, and a personal intercourse with them; and with that view these officers should be expected to acquire an adequate familiarity with the native language'.[53] At this time, only Busby was employed by the British government in New Zealand,[54] and his knowledge of te reo was limited; he depended on missionaries to translate for him. Marrying London's official intent with actions on the ground in remote areas of interest was neither easy to achieve nor to enforce[55] – illustrating the gulf between policy and practice in these areas. Similarly, the committee's other recommendations – on restricting emigration to New Zealand – held little sway among potential settlers, many of whom were being drawn to live in the country by the New

Zealand Association, formed the same year as the committee reported its findings, and which aimed to systematically settle vast tracts of territory it would purchase from Māori.[56]

In the New Zealand Association (which became the New Zealand Company in May 1839), some of the worst fears of the 1837 House of Commons select committee came to fruition. From the outset, the organisation had shown little regard for the culture or interests of Māori. Its founder, Edward Gibbon Wakefield, saw indigenous peoples generally as having their 'natural inclinations' unrestrained by law or honour – something that separated them from the civilised peoples of the world,[57] while his son Edward Jerningham Wakefield snidely cast Māori as savages whose only chance for redemption would be if their territories were settled by colonists so that, over time, they would acquire 'the knowledge, habits, desires, and comforts, of their civilized neighbours'; otherwise, they would remain barbarians.[58] Such sentiments were more than just the venting of personal prejudices: they shaped, to some extent, the approach to Māori taken by the company when it came to purchasing land in the southern and western areas of the North Island in 1839. To start off with, Māori society had no concept of the permanent alienation of land.[59] Yes, there had been several transactions between Māori and European before this time, mainly of small parcels of territory, but the idea that one person could own a section of land in perpetuity, and to the exclusion of all others with some ancestral or cultural claim to the site, was still a foreign notion to them. This difference in perspective would eventually put these Māori vendors on a collision course with company agents.

In order to communicate its intentions to Māori, in 1839 the company drew on the services of Richard 'Dicky' Barrett – a former sailor and whaler who possessed a low level of literacy in English but was reasonably fluent in te reo (in addition to being familiar with many of the Māori leaders in areas where the company had an eye on land it wished to acquire).[60] Barrett was devoted to the company's plans, partly because of the prospects he saw for his own business ventures in Wellington once company settlers started arriving there in large numbers, and partly because of the generous fee of £400 that the agents promised him for translating and negotiating a particular purchase with Māori vendors in Wellington and Taranaki.[61] Te reo would have a central role in these transactions, especially as the vast majority of Māori in this region spoke very little or no English. The deed of sale was drawn up in English and was unnecessarily verbose,[62] possibly because its authors were attempting to mimic legal prose.[63] The placenames in the deed, provided by Māori, were dictated by Barrett to Edward Jerningham, who transcribed them. Many names were misspelt; an iwi, Ngāti Ruanui, was described as a geographical feature; and boundaries were only vaguely delineated.[64] There was plainly no commitment to accuracy in translation. George Clarke jnr, in his review of Barrett's efforts, wrote how it 'soon became clear that Barrett's qualification to interpret, was that he spoke whaler Maori, a jargon that bears much the same relation to the real language of the Maoris as the pigeon English of the Chinese does to our mother tongue', and that his translations 'had been of a very hasty and hugger-mugger character'.[65] Fifteen years later, the Crown's land purchase officer, Donald McLean, testified before a parliamentary select committee that Barrett was 'not competent to translate the deeds'.[66] But as land sharks circled the country from the late 1830s, good translations were hardly a priority. To their mind English was the only language that counted, and translation of land deeds into te reo was a cynical formality aimed at assuring British officials back in London that no native rights were being harmed in these deals.

As the virtues of New Zealand's systematic colonisation were being extolled by Wakefield's propagandists in England, and as his agents plotted their purchases of Māori land (or 'waste land' as the New Zealand Company dismissively referred to most of its acquisitions),[67] the House of Lords set up a select committee to deal exclusively with New Zealand. The committee issued its report in April 1838.[68] The testimony before this committee predictably reflected the respective areas of interest of those who appeared before it, but in the midst of their usually pedestrian responses to the questions put to them, at odd moments small revelations about the status of te reo in New Zealand would leap out. In the vexatious area of land purchases, for example, John Watkins – an Australian surgeon who visited New Zealand between 1833 and 1834 – testified how the oral aspect of Māori society still dominated in transactions over territory. The deeds for these deals were often written exclusively in English, and chiefs would go to their local missionary, whom they usually trusted, for advice on these sales and for translations of the accompanying documentation. Next, a chief would consult with all his relatives to gain their collective consent to the offer. This would be followed by a meeting between the buyer and vendors, at which the latter would all give their assent verbally, in te reo. According to Watkins, the Māori he saw engaged in such exchanges were 'as competent to deal with an European as another European would be', and every detail of the transaction would be examined 'very minutely'.[69] It seems that text and talk combined effectively in such cases, with neither party coming out the worse for it in terms of the agreements made – provided the parties adhered to them. And with the strict disciplines of Māori oral culture still functioning, the land deals that chiefs entered into were understood by their communities and were enforced in every detail[70] (even if the same standards were not always upheld by some European buyers).[71] It should be noted, however, that these predominantly oral transactions that Watkins observed took place between chiefs and individual Europeans rather than commercial land-trading enterprises or British officials.

In some cases before the late 1830s, sale and purchase agreements were translated into te reo, but it seems that the Māori preference for the authority of oral agreements prevailed and they paid little attention to storing the written and signed copies.[72] This raises an interesting distinction because many Māori were coming to regard the text of the Bible as extremely important and something to be treasured – materially as well as for its content. So why the discrepancy – why cherish religious texts yet neglect commercial ones? Part of the answer may be historical. There was a well-established precedent in Māori society for oral agreements about land occupation, and perhaps they saw the deals with European purchasers as an extension of these. Moreover, there was an implicit sanctity in the physicality of religious texts[73] that was absent in the more temporal realm of land trading.

So Māori were making use of literacy when they felt it was needed, rather than employing it in every facet of life solely because it was deemed obligatory. As the number of settlers increased and the interactions between Māori and European become more frequent and at times more entangled, the reach of literacy extended further into Māori society, and it played a greater role in delineating aspects of the commercial and social relationships between Māori and settlers. A letter in te reo that was sent to Marsden by a chief in 1837 (and that was presented in evidence before the 1838 select committee by Dandeson Coates, lay secretary of the CMS) illustrates the sort of transactions where literacy and society overlapped in New Zealand during this period. The contemporary English translation[74] reads, in part:

Sir,
Will you give us a law? This is the purport of my address to you.

1. If we say, let the cultivations be fenced, and a man, through laziness, does not fence, should pigs get into his plantations, is it right for him to kill them? Do you give us a law in this matter?

2. Again; should pigs get into fenced land, is it right to kill, or rather to tie them till the damage they have done is paid for? Will you give us a law in this?

3. Again; should the husband of a woman die, and she afterward wishes to be married to another, should the natives of unchanged heart bring a fight against us, would it be right for us to stand up to resist them on account of their wrongful interference? Will you give us a law in this also?

4. Again, in our wickedness, one man has two wives; but after he has listened to Christ, he puts away one of them, and gives her to another man to wife. Now, should a fight be brought against us, are we in this case to stand up to fight? Give us a law in this.

5. Again, should two men strive one with the other? Give us a law in this. My (*ritenga*) law is, to collect all the people together, and judge them for their unlawful fighting, and also for wrongfully killing pigs. Therefore I say, that the man who kills pigs for trespassing on his plantation, having neglected to fence, had better pay for the pigs so killed. Will you give us a law in this? Fenced cultivations, when trespassed on, should be paid for. These only are the things which cause us to err – women, pigs, and fighting one with another.[75]

Here was a sample of the type of political thought, expressed in te reo, that was probably prevalent among Māori. It provides a snapshot of the aspirations and frustrations that some Māori were experiencing during this period, and shows an orientation towards the sort of order that they imagined British rule might bring, while revealing some of the challenges they were confronting. And it shows how in areas that even a decade earlier would have been addressed orally by Māori, producing arguments in text was becoming imperative. This letter, and the fact that it found its way into a submission to a House of Lords select committee, also shows how Māori were being drawn, through literacy, into the workings of the administrative and governmental apparatus of the British Empire, with consequences that would be far-reaching for te reo and Māori culture and society more generally.

THE PEOPLE ARE THE LANGUAGE

It is at about this time that the weight of population shifts in New Zealand began to affect the country's linguistic terrain much more noticeably. With the sharp rise in influx of Britons from the end of the 1830s,[76] English was elbowing its way more boisterously into parts of New Zealand society where once te reo Māori had been predominant.[77] And if the adage is true that the strength of a language is the strength of its speakers, then there was the scent of another serious problem for te reo in the wind at this same time: depopulation.

What the Musket Wars had started in the first decade of the nineteenth century, bequeathing a death toll of upwards of 20,000 Māori,[78] epidemics such as measles and influenza had continued in the 1830s: up to 50 per cent of the population of 1800 Ngāi Tahu, for example, were wiped out.[79] Indigenous populations and cultures wilting in the course of colonisation was nothing new for Europe's imperial nations,[80] of course, but in New Zealand as early as 1837, the decline in the number of Māori – and therefore of native speakers of te reo – was so pronounced that Busby asked his superiors in June 'how far this depopulation of the country, which has at least been rapid in proportion to the increase of its intercourse with the whites, was originated by the latter, and may be justly chargeable to them?' To the puzzled British Resident there was no obvious explanation for what was happening: 'all the apparent causes which are in operation, are quite inadequate to account for the rapid disappearance of the people' was his summary of the crisis.[81] Maybe the declining Māori population was a mystery to Busby, but this extract aroused consternation among others – including the Wesleyan minister Reverend John Beecham[82] who, in his response a few months later, argued that Māori could be saved from impending termination by a more tangible, albeit radical measure:

> If it be true, that 'all the *apparent* causes which are in operation, *are quite inadequate* to account for the rapid disappearance of the people;' and that the natives are doomed, by some mysterious decree of Heaven, rapidly to waste away without any *visible* cause, in the presence of white men, who have gone among them with no other view than to do them good; the only course by which our Government or Parliament could hope to meet the case would be, not to found a Colony, but to banish henceforth every white man, good as well as bad, from the shores of New-Zealand.[83]

This was a King Canute-type response: Beecham was convinced of his own rectitude but was trying to hold back a tide that had swamped just about every other territory where Britons were establishing settlements. If Beecham had taken a step back from the waterline he would have seen the improbability of his position. An alternative solution was needed to halt and then reverse the decline in the Māori population.[84]

Beecham was right in that the attitudes of some colonists towards Māori would do nothing to arrest New Zealand's plummeting native population.[85] While he and a few of his fellow missionaries were advocating restricting British immigration, and although the House of Commons select committee had suggested in 1837 that the odd official should learn the indigenous language of the country, others, including advocates of the New Zealand Association, were nothing short of vulgar in their assessment of Māori. One of these disparaging voices was that of Montague Hawtrey, an Anglican minister and one-time neighbour of Wakefield,[86] who advised 'Englishmen' about to embark for New Zealand that they 'should be prepared' and needed to steady themselves for their initial encounters with Māori:

> you will probably find them dirty, intrusive, violent, thievish, restless, already perhaps affected by the low habits of the most degraded of your countrymen, having manners and customs of their own utterly at variance with all your ideas of right and wrong, and displaying the most extraordinary ignorance about things which to you are perfectly familiar.[87]

It is hard to imagine anyone who held such attitudes toward Māori having even the slightest desire to protect te reo; on the contrary, they were likely to see the language as being just as degraded as its speakers.

Beecham's fear was Hawtrey's desire. The latter saw the triumphant British colonisation of New Zealand as ordained by providence; he believed that 'no power on earth can prevent Europeans from being the agents by which it is to attain this position, or from sharing largely in the benefits to be derived from it'.[88] Māori culture would be swept aside for their own best interests, and where the culture was expunged, so too would the language be. Beecham hoped, vainly as it turned out, that the Hawtreys of this world would be excluded from New Zealand before further damage was inflicted on Māori as a result of their presence.

Sir James Stephen, who became permanent head of the Colonial Office in 1836, was reponsible for navigating the British government's position on

Māori. Stephen, who had been heavily involved in the abolitionist movement (he had drafted the legislation that abolished slavery in Britain), was far more concerned about the fate of indigenous peoples across the empire than any of his predecessors had been. So when the British government finally and reluctantly yielded to the inevitability of drawing up a treaty to establish a British administration in New Zealand,[89] Stephen was at pains in the instructions he drafted for this treaty[90] to have Māori interests protected as much as possible.[91] This included the requirement that Māori give 'free and intelligent consent' to the treaty's provisions – which at the very least would require a version of the agreement to be produced in their language.[92] But beyond just requiring a translation of the treaty's text, the British government wanted to ensure its terms were comprehended by the Māori signatories, as the instructions make plain:

> The natives may, probably, regard with distrust a proposal which may carry on the face of it the appearance of humiliation on their side, and of a formidable encroachment on ours; and their ignorance even of the technical terms in which that proposal must be conveyed, may enhance their aversion to an arrangement of which they may be unable to comprehend the exact meaning, or the probable results. These, however, are impediments to be gradually overcome by the exercise, on your part, of mildness, justice, and perfect sincerity in your intercourse with them. You will, I trust, find powerful auxiliaries amongst the missionaries, who have won and deserved their confidence, and amongst the older British residents who have studied their character, and acquired their language.[93]

And as it turned out, most chiefs who signed the Treaty of Waitangi (as it was known, from the location of its inaugural signing) nominated to put their mark or sign their name on the version in te reo,[94] which had been translated mainly by Henry Williams.[95] As interest in the treaty was resuscitated in the late twentieth century, a plethora of books, journal articles and theses examined the translation, often in excruciating detail. However, when the treaty was considered from another perspective – that of the chiefs who signed it – it was not a written document produced exclusively by British officials but an oral agreement produced in te reo by representatives of the Crown, and so was in some ways an extension of traditional Māori oral culture. In most cases the treaty was heard (rather than read) in te reo by its signatories and those of their hapū who were present when copies of the agreement were brought to them for their assent, so assessments about what the chiefs understood they were agreeing to would have to include not only what the text of the treaty said in te reo but also whatever was discussed between the chiefs and those conveying the agreement to them. The entirety of the discussions would have constituted the agreement – meaning that each group of signatories would have had their own individual understanding of its terms.

It is also important to avoid interpreting the presence of signatures, moko or other marks written by those chiefs who gave their assent to the treaty as evidence or even indicators of literacy among these 'signatories'. Although this has been a standard, if crude measurement applied in other societies,[96] its application to Māori is unreliable because some communities learned to read well before they learned to write. And of those chiefs who signed their name as opposed to making some other mark, the degree of fluency in their handwriting might show that they could write only their names – and possibly nothing else;[97] or that after years of reading they had only just begun to learn to write.

So while the debate about the treaty's intended meaning has been overwhelmingly text-focused, with constitutional specialists combing through the phrases and words looking for some new speck of meaning or interpretation, this is very much the sort of analysis that is carried out in the culture of the coloniser. Those chiefs who consented to the treaty were much more likely to have interpreted it as an oral agreement.[98] In addition, for some, if not most Māori signatories, the treaty was likely to have had a tenor of sanctity, partly because so much written text in te reo was of a religious nature, and partly because, in most instances, copies of the treaty were presented to chiefs and explained to them by missionaries. Again, this is an aspect of te reo woven into the Māori view of the treaty that was informed by a combination of an oral approach to agreements, especially if made in te reo, with the recent introduction of te reo in written form. It also serves as a repudiation to the assumptions that the binding power of the written statements stood in contrast to the weaker 'flexibility of oral accommodations'.[99] If anything, the oral version was more robust in that it belonged to a culture that preserved information in the memory.[100] In more recent assessments of the treaty's meaning, the Crown's recollection of what was discussed and agreed on in 1840 has relied on documentary evidence, whereas numerous Māori communities have been able to call on the oral histories of the negotiations and signings, recounted over generations, which have enhanced enormously the understanding of what the agreement meant (and means) to the parties to it.[101]

THE STATE TAKES ON TE REO

Golden ages tend to glisten more brightly from the distance of hindsight, but the main missionary movements operating in New Zealand in the first half of the 1840s[102] were in the rare position of being able to bask in their own success as it happened.[103] After nearly three decdes of sowing the seed of the Gospels on what must at times have felt like exceedingly barren ground, suddenly Māori Christian communities were sprouting up everywhere, nourished by the tens of thousands of biblical texts that were in circulation by then. And to gild things even further, the missionaries were operating in a newly forged nation state, which for the Anglicans meant they were once again the state church, with all the informal as well as formal benefits that came with that status.[104] The enormous investment in translating and printing works in te reo that had been building since the mid-1810s was finally paying dividends. And in the absence of any government-run education regime, the missionary schools had become the state school system by default – and one in which Māori students easily outnumbered Europeans. The Anglican Church, which ran the vast majority of native schools, had already taken steps to centralise their organisation[105] and to fund it, despite the considerable financial burden this was placing on the church's already stretched resources.[106] By the mid-1840s the state deemed it the right time to take over some of the responsibilities for the colony's schooling that the churches had been shouldering. It employed its superior administrative and financial resources to manage the nation's education.

The first direct attack on te reo by an act of state intervention in education was in 1847 when Governor George Grey introduced the Education Ordinance. On the surface, the wording of the ordinance appeared innocuous enough, and its initial impact was slight. In addition to its commitment to fund and monitor a new state school system, the government reassured colonists that 'instruction in the English language shall form a necessary part of the system'.[107] This commitment to English as the sole medium of instruction ran deep – so deep that students could opt out of religious instruction (which was a provision in the ordinance) but had no such choice when it came to the language they were taught in. This was presented as a measure to promote Māori welfare[108] rather than anything more pernicious, although it was later seen as one of the first formal state moves towards English-language domination in New Zealand.[109]

The context for the 1847 Education Ordinance had been laid three years earlier by Governor Robert FitzRoy who, with strong devotion to the prevailing ideas in this period about Māori improvement, stressed – through another ordinance – the need for Māori to be 'instructed in the English language and in English arts and usages' as a remedy to the 'great disasters that have fallen upon uncivilized nations on being brought into contact with Colonists from the nations of Europe'.[110]

During the mid-1840s, St John's Native Teachers' School[111] in Auckland had been exemplifying this shift to English as the language of instruction for Māori. Founded by the Anglican Bishop George Selwyn, the school set clear guidelines for Māori who were to be trained as teachers and, in keeping with the thinking of the era, linked the ability to speak English with greater civilisation:

1. No teacher is admissible into the First Class, who does not pledge himself to adopt English habits, to divide his house into rooms, to abstain from smoking, to take care of his wife and children, and attend to their improvement, – to wear English clothes constantly, and, above all, to be regular in his attendance at Church and School.

2. The Second Class is composed of those who are candidates for admission into the first.

3. The Third Class consists of those who wish to learn English but have not yet made up their minds to give up native habits.[112]

The Wesleyans, never far behind, chose to follow a similar course in training Māori teachers. A meeting held in Auckland in 1844, chaired by the superintendent for the Wesleyan schools in the region, unanimously passed a resolution declaring it 'very desirable to instruct a selected number of the natives of New Zealand in our language, with a view to having access to the stores of the English literature, and also to their becoming more efficient teachers of their countrymen in matters of … civilization'.[113] The alternative was for the country's indigenous youth to suffer 'the degradation of being brought up as Maoris'.[114]

Children who were the offspring of Māori and European parents were also brought into this civilising mission. One report stressed the importance of schools that accommodated such children: 'How many half-castes, for want of such institutions, have been brought up in the barbarous habits of the dark race from which they derive half-kindred, presenting too often the painful picture of an Anglo-Maori with all the tastes, habits, and feelings of the savage.'[115]

FitzRoy's 1844 ordinance was intended to assist with this civilising/ anglicising process, and to avert those 'great disasters' that had been inflicted on other indigenous peoples faced with British colonisation; he would achieve both 'by assimilating as speedily as possible the habits and usages of the Native to those of the European population'.[116] To this end, the trustees of Māori land were directed to use the proceeds from the lease of their land to establish schools 'for the instruction of the Native people in the English language, and for a systematic course of industrial and moral training in English usages and English arts'.[117] What started as this small-scale effort to set up a handful of English-medium schools reached its logical conclusion with Grey's state-directed policy for English to be the language of education throughout the colony.

Grey's move was all the more injurious to Māori because language is not just a means of communication: it is a culture-shaper that is socially and politically constructed. In addition, educating one culture entirely in the language of another has the potential to sever the continuity of history of the former culture. The introduced language of instruction has the potential to inject new ways of thinking that, deliberately or otherwise, override older ways.[118] In New Zealand, this shift tied Māori politically much more directly in to the language of the empire, drawing them into a regime in which ethnicity was subsumed by an emerging sense of imperial nationalism that was pantribal, monolingual and – increasingly in the twentieth century – non-tribal.[119]

Grey had been mulling over his assimilationist programme even before he arrived in New Zealand. While he was still in Australia, he argued that the prospects of that country's indigenous population would be improved if they were brought into the field of British rule and colonial schooling rather than maintaining their traditional systems: 'for many races who were at one period subject to the most barbarous laws, have, since new institutions have been introduced amongst them, taken their rank among the civilized nations of the earth' was how he justified his stance.[120] And as governor of New Zealand, Grey had greater authority to implement his plans for assimilating indigenous peoples. As an example, when a parcel of land was granted for a government school run by the Wesleyans in the Auckland suburb of Three Kings in 1850, the grant deed specified that the school would operate 'for the education of children of our subjects of both races and of children of our poor and destitute persons being inhabitants of the Islands in the Pacific Ocean', and that the government would continue to support the school 'so long as religious education, industrial training and instruction in the English language shall be given to youths educated therein'.[121] Te reo was nowhere to be seen on this deed.

Te reo itself was undergoing changes, not only through the substantial extension of its vocabulary with the addition of neologisms but also through small alterations in its role in what was a rapidly modernising society. In the 1840s it was still the principal language of spoken communication in Māori society, as it always had been, but the loud signal sent to Māori by the Education Ordinance and subsequent government policy was that English, the language of the empire, was becoming the state-sanctioned language of New Zealand. This, coupled with the explosive rise in British immigrants (from 2000 at the beginning of the 1840s to around 20,000 by the end of the decade),[122] altered te reo's ancient and seemingly immutable equilibrium. Now, more than at any previous time, te reo was a language whose position was being determined by another culture, and whose appearance in certain spheres was a negotiated one, with most of the negotiations in mid-century going against Māori. In such ways did the language slip in small increments from dominance in the country. In the realms of government, the military, church and commerce, English made its exclusivity felt. Te reo speakers would have to adapt to this fact or be excluded from involvement in those areas: the choice was often that stark.

Yet this assimilation did not follow a straightforward trajectory of Māori simply moving closer to the world of the settlers. In contrast to the increasing cultural contact between Māori and European in the early 1800s, by the 1840s the two groups were showing an inclination to retreat more to their own communities. William Swainson, the colony's sagacious attorney-general, was a witness to this process of separation:

Of their [the Māori] language … the colonists themselves are, for the most part, as ignorant as the people of England. For the purposes of trade, the natives constantly, and in large numbers, frequent our English settlements: but the two races really live apart; and, with the exception of the missionaries and a few isolated settlers, few have sufficient knowledge of the language, superstitions, and social life of the native race.[123]

This increasing isolation became another source of pressure on te reo. For Māori to enter the fold of the fast-expanding settler world from the end of the 1840s, speaking English was a vital skill. Apart from a smattering of missionaries still searching the hinterland for souls to save, the days were gone when British arrivals struggled to acquire some fluency in te reo as quickly as possible. The fragile English-speaking ghettos in the Bay of Islands and Whangaroa in the 1820s had long since burst their seams, and across the country, colonies of settler communities – where English was the dominant language – were spreading and becoming both more populous and more culturally assertive.

This, then, was one of several routes by which te reo started on its journey to decline over the remainder of the century. There is a risk in seeing such developments in too formulaic a way, as though the correct quantities of circumstance, political will and cultural assertion – all lined up in their predetermined sequence – might produce the inevitable linguistic demise, with all the certainty of a scientific experiment that has been verified through frequent repetition. This is how some structuralists tend to view this type of situation anyway: with the complex web of interrelations between all the elements involved – in this case in the fate of an indigenous language – forming part of a large, overarching system, with any variations in the process that might appear on the surface belying those constant, 'natural' laws of cultural domination that operate underneath.[124]

This was how the situation was often perceived in the country during this period. One mid-nineteenth-century writer portrayed the spread of European civilisation in New Zealand as being 'like geological changes on the earth's surface ... noiseless, and unheeded by men busied with their daily cares', and added, '[only] by extending our researches over several years [can] we distinctly detect what escaped our narrower investigation'.[125] There is some merit in this way of looking at the history of te reo over the course of the nineteenth century – particularly as the general patterns of its retreat are not dissimilar to those that other indigenous languages faced with the intrusion of English during the colonial period.[126] However, structuralists wrongly assume that language is a discrete entity that can be examined in relative isolation, like some specimen in a test-tube, and that its responses to certain stimuli are predictable precisely because they conform to previous patterns evident elsewhere.[127] The fallacy of language as a self-contained cultural unit is apparent when two languages and their attendant cultures come into contact with each other and intermingle, as happened in New Zealand with te reo and English.[128] From the earliest period of British intervention, te reo's vocabulary, the ways in which the language was used, the places where it was employed ceremonially or formally and the knowledge it carried were slowly being inculcated with the words, the ways of thinking, the 'technology' of literacy, and some of the cultural protocols of the coloniser.[129] Māori language absorbed and became the sum of everything that was known to it and that it was drawing in from English speakers;[130] and so it was a party to certain stages in its own modernisation, constantly adapting to ensure it remained relevant to the period. This evolutionary process for te reo accelerated during phases when it was incorporating large numbers of concepts and vocabulary from the settler culture. It was a development in the language that to an equal extent reflected and modified changing Māori perceptions of the world.[131] Just over a decade later, the colony's chief justice, William Martin, observed this cultural transition; he depicted it as though it were complete. 'The Natives,' he pronounced,

> have gradually abandoned old usages, adopted our dress and our modes of cultivating the ground ... Nor has the moral growth of the race been less apparent. They have readily given land for schools ... In every part of the country, efforts have been made by them to establish some mode of settling their disputes by law, and to frame and enforce regulations for repressing drunkenness and immorality, and for securing good order amongst themselves.

The swiftness of this apparent metamorphosis was just as telling: 'The success of this great undertaking,' Martin concluded, 'has been such as no man in the Colony anticipated twenty years back.'[132]

In the end there was no grand plan by which it was ordained that te reo would experience the changes that it did when New Zealand became a Crown colony. Neither the 1847 Education Ordinance nor earlier government policies had brought about alterations to te reo on their own, just as the influx of settlers did not, in itself, lead to the asphyxiation of the language. Neither was there an uninterrupted linear progression in these developments. Instead, te reo's evolution, and its retreat in parts of the country, were the result of the chaos of history, with its inadvertent diversions, its chance events and its unexpected cultural collisions shaping the language's fortunes throughout the century. Statutory punctuation points such as the Education Ordinance, while they were undoubtedly important in the history of te reo, were as much markers that reflected existing cultural trends as they were efforts at altering the status quo. Moreover, they were a response to what was believed to be the entropic state of traditional Māori society, rather than conscious acts of suppression or subversion.

An incident in 1844 involving Selwyn showed that colonisation does not always follow a predictable course. As he toured the country, he discovered that in several districts 'there was a growing indifference to religion [among Māori], and a neglect of the opportunities of instruction, which the natives had formerly prized so highly'.[133] Had the attraction of elements of the European world begun to wane for Māori? Maunsell (who incidentally had once been taught by Samuel Lee at the CMS Training College at Islington in London) could also not help but notice a change in attitude in certain Māori communities towards the religion and the school instruction that the missionaries were providing. He lamented that it was 'impossible to conceal from oneself that our progress is not so strong or lively as it was formerly', and that some Māori were now less willing to travel long distances to attend schools – which was cause for 'anxiety'.[134] Maunsell's fellow cleric Octavius Hadfield attributed this mounting indifference at least partly to the system of education that the missionaries were providing (which he described as 'wholly inadequate'), and conceded that when it came to ideas for a remedy among his colleagues, the cupboard was bare.[135] The 'problem' (if it can be defined as such) was much broader, though. The general presumption by settlers that Māori would succumb unquestioningly to the influence of Europeans ignored the resilience of Māori culture and language.

GOING TO PRESS

The colonial government in New Zealand strived to engage with the country's large, diverse and in many ways disconnected indigenous population. While disseminating basic government policy and agricultural information with Māori was the ostensible purpose of the various newspapers – some bilingual, some exclusively in te reo – there were a number of cultural and linguistic side-effects of the state's foray into the newspaper business. First, the government made itself the principal source of national information for Māori communities, thus often creating a shared sense of selected national issues in a way that transcended iwi boundaries and was generally free of parochial slants on some subjects. Moreover, these newspapers presented a particular view of the settler world and the country as a whole for their Māori readers.[136] And inevitably they were also propaganda devices.[137] The ideology of the colonial state achieved another advance through these papers: the information they propagated was centralised, vetted by officials where necessary and, through the advice they offered, presented a vision of the future of the country that was carefully prescribed by the state.[138] Moreover, the newspapers were in part responsible for popularising the use of the name 'Maori'; previously, Europeans had used the term 'native', and the indigenous population had tended to identify themselves according to their hapū or iwi affiliation.[139]

The civilising mission was, of course, seldom far from the surface whenever the state engaged with Māori. As an example, when visiting British soldier Tyrone Power[140] wrote about the formation of a newspaper for Māori in the second half of the 1840s, he expressed a hope that there would be:

A column ... devoted to the fashions, and to music and the fine arts, for the purpose of getting rid, as soon as possible, of the shark oil and kokowai, or red ochre, as well as to substitute other songs and dances for the discordant and barbarous 'hakas' and 'waiatas' at present in vogue. The Maories can nearly all read, and are inordinately fond of news and gossip; so that a well-conducted periodical would have much success among them, and would tend greatly to their improvement.[141]

The first regular edition of a Māori newspaper was published by the government on 1 January 1842, and another 48 editions followed over the next four years. *Te Karere o Niu Tireni* (the New Zealand Messenger) focused on government announcements and news about the colony's laws, and it also included advertisements. In keeping with the state's desire to assimilate Māori, the stated purpose of the newspaper was 'that the Maori people would come to know the ways and customs of the Pakeha and the Pakeha would also come to know the customs of the Maori people'.[142]

The New Zealand Company's main settlement in Wellington – which was always eager to argue the case for its superiority over the colonial government in the capital, Auckland – produced its own Māori newspaper and made a point of stating that it was no official initiative. A Māori working in the office of the *New Zealand Gazette and Wellington Spectator* had taught himself typesetting and printing. Then, the editor recalled, one day he 'presented us with a most creditable production, entitled the *New Zealand Messenger*, and composed and printed entirely by himself, and without suggestion from any one that we are aware of'. The standard of te reo in the publication was said to be good, and it was promoted as 'the first attempt yet made in these islands by a native to communicate through the press, in his own language, with his fellow countrymen'. The company hoped that, within a few years, the newspaper would lead to better relations between Māori and settlers, and that it would encourage further Māori involvement in trade in the region.[143] This was the same modernising programme that the company's adversaries in Auckland were promulgating.

The Anglo-Maori Warder, published privately in Auckland, appeared only during 1848 and, true to its title, was a bilingual newspaper: the majority of its content was in English, with the final page in te reo. What makes this newspaper such an important development is that it was among the very first works in te reo (albeit only partially) to be published as a commercial venture. It is therefore something of a linguistic weathervane, pointing in a very general way to the extent of Māori literacy in te reo in the late 1840s.

Having tackled a rebellion in Northland by 1846, the government re-entered the Māori newspaper business in 1849 with the publication of *The Maori Messenger – Ko te Karere Maori*. It was most likely edited and translated by George Clarke, who had been Protector of Aborigines until the office was disbanded by Grey in 1846.[144] The pages in this newspaper each had four columns, in English and te reo alternately – a feature that 'helped not only to spread a knowledge of the English tongue, but induced many of the colonists to subscribe and take an interest in whatever might benefit the aborigines'. There were restrictions on content that was overtly political; the focus was instead on issues such as 'the cultivation of land and flax and the management of sheep and cattle'.[145] As well, there were articles on travels through parts of New Zealand, offering the sort of detail that some Māori communities would have had little familiarity with. In small ways Māori were acquiring knowledge through this newspaper about the history and culture of other hapū and iwi. At the same time, for settler readers, it added weight to the impression that a hybridised Māori culture existed.

Some settlers were frustrated with the very idea of newspapers in te reo – especially in the New Zealand Company settlement of Wellington. The *New Zealand Gazette and Wellington Spectator*, which served as the company's mouthpiece, was firmly in the camp of those opposed to te reo being supported in any way by the state (even though the government had backed its own shortlived attempt at a newspaper in te reo). In 1843 the editor of the *New Zealand Gazette and Wellington Spectator* quoted the New South Wales governor George Grey, who argued that the experiences of other colonies all showed that 'the existence of two different races in a country, one of which, from any local circumstances, is considered inferior to the other, is one of the greatest evils under which a nation can labour'. The *Gazette* extrapolated this theme so it applied to two languages in one country; and it criticised the missionaries not only for teaching in te reo, but for adding new words to its vocabulary. The problem was plainly expressed: 'For animals, objects, substances, &c. utterly unknown to the Aborigines, before their intercourse with Europeans, they had, of course, no corresponding words in their language; therefore, the missionaries have added greatly to the vocabulary, by *creating Maori words* ... [which are] unintelligible to the natives.' The proposed remedy was for Māori and European children to be schooled together so that the indigenous pupils would not only learn English but would 'be taught to learn our habits and our wants, and thus amalgamate with the emigrants'.[146] If the government continued to publish newspapers in te reo, this would hold back the process of assimilation.

Eventually Grey, during his first term as New Zealand governor, lived up to his word as an ardent assimilationist by terminating publication of the government's recently founded the *Native Gazette*, which had been the main conduit of official information to Māori in te reo. There were only small expressions of concern at this act – the main one from the Committee of the New Zealand Aborigines Protection Society, which expressed its 'deep regret' that this route of communication with Māori had been shut off. The society also favoured assimilation, but it proposed a different means to that end. According to the committee, the *Native Gazette* had afforded 'the finest opportunity of civilizing a semi-barbarous race ever possessed in any country', and had now been 'abandoned and destroyed by Governor Grey, in his hasty zeal to overturn all the Native measures of his philanthropic predecessor, without having substituted any other publication tending to improve the native mind'.[147] Despite such protestations, the course was set for reduced government commitment to publishing newspapers in te reo – although for the remainder of the century new state-funded titles continued to appear intermittently.

THE NOMADIC ORIGINS OF TE REO

The first Polynesians arrived in New Zealand around the late thirteenth century,[148] bringing with them a Polynesian language that eventually evolved into te reo.[149] Modern scholarship has reached a consensus on this, but in the nineteenth century te reo's pedigree – along with that of its native speakers – was much more wildly speculated on and hotly contested. At one level such exercises – which resulted in a flurry of published papers and public lectures – were something of a hobby for many of those involved. They provided an opportunity for amateurs to feign having conceived a theory of some academic consequence and to be part of the pursuit to track down the mysterious source of the language; and in the absence of modern analytical techniques, all sorts of conjectural conclusions were arrived at. Most of these undertakings now seem quaint and even slightly amusing – a form of armchair anthropological exploration, like the safari-suited, pith-helmeted adventurer hacking his way through a forbidding jungle in a quest for discovery, but without the associated physical deprivations.

At another, more serious level, this was an area of activity where the control of te reo was being wrested away from Māori. Europeans were not just adding words to the language (although that process was still relentless) but were now tracing te reo's origins, its route to New Zealand, its relationships with other language families, and contextualising it in linguistic schemes[150] about which most Māori had not even the faintest idea. This was part of a much more far-reaching reconstruction of te reo by the coloniser. This transformation, which already encompassed the conversion of te reo into a written language, the increased standardisation of its spelling and uniformity of its pronunciation and grammar, now included the classification of te reo as part of a romanticised construction of New Zealand's traditional Māori past.

All this tampering with te reo – including the speculation on its origins – was part of the process of making 'the unknown and strange knowable' to the coloniser. This had been the case in colonial India, where 'The knowledge of languages [by the British] was necessary to … create other forms of knowledge about the people they were ruling. This knowledge was to enable the British to classify, categorize, and bound the vast social world that was India so that it could be controlled.' This control of the way language was used, understood and classified thus served the 'larger colonial project'.[151] And there is no reason to believe that this imperialist approach to indigenous knowledge was any different to that applied in other British colonies, such as New Zealand.

Most analyses of the origins of te reo were based on a specific perception of the basic ethnic composition of the world. James Crawford, a farmer-turned-politician who exemplified the Victorian gentleman scholar, began his study of the language of Māori in this way. Crawford had been president of the Wellington Philosophical Society and a governor of the New Zealand

Institute, and had published papers on topics ranging from botany, geology, engineering and language, to agriculture, history, economics and railways.[152] Unimpeded by detailed research, he observed that: 'The inhabitants of the globe appear to be divided into races of three colours, viz., the white, the black, and the brown. The latter includes the vast population of the Chinese Empire, the Malays, the aboriginal inhabitants of Madagascar, the red men of North America, the Maoris.' Shifting then to Polynesia, he noted: 'Throughout the vast range of the Pacific Ocean, from the Sandwich Islands to New Zealand, we find a brown race, speaking a language which is substantially the same, and holding similar views as to religion.'[153]

The first theory Crawford examined in his quest to determine the origin of Māori and their language was that 'Malay or Japanese vessels had been driven eastward, and had gradually peopled the islands of Oceania,' as he summed it up. It was an idea that he dismissed on the basis that 'if this were the true theory, we should find the people and the language to be Malay or Japanese, which they are not'. It was all common sense, really. Crawford conceded that there was some connection between the languages of the Malay and the Māori, 'but that it is so slight that, supposing the Maoris to have been originally Malays, a vast term of years must have passed away to admit of the great divergence that now exists between the two languages'.[154] Part of the basis for this linguistic link – and here is where the theory slipped into the dubious realm of anthopologic typology – was Crawford's dependence on matching physical characteristics of ethnic groups to support his theory. He detected 'a resemblance in figure and in colour, and the gravity and politeness which are said to be characteristics of the Malay may be distinctly traced in the Maori'.[155]

Samuel Marsden, in a moment of idle speculation, had also written about the origin of Māori; he was inclined to think that they 'have sprung from some dispersed Jews, at some period or other, from their religious superstitions and customs, and have by some means got into the island from Asia'. His rationale for this was that Māori, 'like the Jews … will buy and sell anything they have got'; and in addition to this appalling stereotype, he saw traits of Māori culture resembling Old Testament Judaism.[156] As a side note to this theory, in the preface to his *Grammar of the New Zealand Language*, first published in 1842,[157] missionary Robert Maunsell noted that there were a few similarities between 'the fundamental principles of the Hebrew language and those of Maori'.[158] Although this was written in the wake of the views of Marsden and others regarding the possible Jewish genesis of Māori,

Maunsell's references in his work to Hebrew was primarily methodological – a response to having to devise a grammar for a language which, like Hebrew, was sometimes an ill fit with the conventional European grammars that he had some familiarity with.[159]

Another would-be scholar, John Turnbull Thomson, proposed that Māori could be traced to the Dravidian races of southern India, and from there they had migrated to Madagascar, and then to the Pacific (to which Crawford responded with uncharacteristic modesty that he was 'not competent to give an opinion on this theory, as I know nothing of the Dravidians').[160] The Dravidian connection was assessed by William Vaux, an antiquarian who worked for the British Museum, who pointed out that this view was, 'obviously, at variance with the Negro theory – for the Dravidians are certainly descendants of a Yellow race, who… drove the Negro people out of the country; and have, except accidentally, nothing in common with the Negroes'. Vaux thought it far more probable that Māori were

> in part, offsprings of the Tibetan and Ultra-Kīngitanga races … perhaps, now represented by the Bajow or *Oranglaut*; – ('Men of the Sea') the more so, that these tribes are, in an especial manner, 'Sea-nomads' … In this way, no doubt, it will be quite possible for New Zealand to have been peopled – only, that unless this took place, at a very remote period we should unquestionably find much more modern Malay in the Maori language.[161]

For good measure, Crawford offered up his own variant on the Malay hypothesis. 'A friend of mine in New Zealand,' he wrote, 'who is an expert in the Maori language, suggests that the race came from Java. In all the islands the tradition is, that the people came from Hawaiki. My friend suggests that this means little Java – "Java-iti," "Hawa-iti." This is another form of the Malay theory.'[162]

German geologist Ferdinand von Hochstetter was less convinced by the proposed Malay connection with Māori. He drew on a general impression of both peoples as the basis for his deduction: 'It is worthy of remark that neither in the social habits of the Polynesians, nor in the original mode of their government, is the slightest trace of influence from abroad, or of an intermixture with other nations to be observed. In vain we search for foreign elements in their language, for a connection of the Māori tongue with the Malay language.'[163]

Ideas about the origins of te reo – and its speakers – continued to be tossed around throughout the century, becoming ever more 'confusing, contradictory, and in some cases absurd'.[164] The missionary William Ellis, in his three-volume work *Polynesian Researches*, argued that 'A tabular view of a number of words in the Malayan, Asiatic, or the Madagasse, the American, and the Polynesian languages, would probably show, that at some remote period ... colonies from some of them, originally peopled, in part or altogether, the others.' From the 'striking analogy' between the languages of these dispersed peoples, Ellis concluded that 'they were originally one people, or that they had emigrated from the same source'.[165] Auckland entrepreneur and former soldier-sailor Coleman Phillips contributed to this theory; he claimed that 'Indian writers, also, have often been struck with the resemblance of many Polynesian habits and customs to those of the Hindoos. It will thus be seen that, when fairly investigated, the origin of the Polynesian islanders will not be a very difficult problem to solve.'[166] The problem was proving anything but easy to solve, as the hypotheses and speculation continued to pile up.

Word similarities appeared to offer the best clue as to where te reo originated. As long as a word from one exotic culture appeared to resemble that of another, maybe there was the germ of a connection to be uncovered. A typical paper, published in 1897, reveals how these linguistic dots were being joined:

> The Yap people [from the Caroline Islands] have a plentiful stock of folk-lore, and a very elaborate astronomical system. In old days they seem to have been great conquerors and navigators, sending trading and fighting expeditions up to Pulawat or Enderby Island, and as far even as Ruk and the East Mortlocks, in search of the *taik*, a noted cosmetic in Micronesia, made up of finely-scraped and powdered turmeric root done up in neat little cones. This word is found in Māori *takou* (red ochre), in the Peruvian *takeu* (red clay), and in the North Marquesan *taiki*, and in New Hebrides *tei*, *teik*, id. (a red, vermilion, or crimson colour).[167]

Some considered this approach to tracing the lineage of a language so important because it was the sort of anthropological record 'which cannot be falsified' – as historian Richard Taylor erroneously argued in 1855. Taylor considered Africa a candidate for the ultimate source of te reo, although, paradoxically, he qualified his examples by stating that he was not intending to draw any inference from them.[168] One of the examples Taylor located to support his African thesis was the Moroccan word 'door', which he explained 'is a cave made in the earth to keep wheat in, and is entered by a small door or opening on the top, which is closed by a large stone or block of wood. This is precisely the description of the New Zealand *dua* or *rua,* which is made to hold the kumara.'[169] The same approach was used for the word 'sun', which in te reo is 'ra'. Taylor now moved from the Moroccans to elsewhere in Africa and then Asia, as he located similar-sounding terms:

> The Coptic one is the same; the Egyptian *rah*; and hence, perhaps, the origin of the East Indian word Rajah Maha. The great rajah or prince, *Maha*, is a New Zealand word for a multitude; the sun being the light of heaven, the prince that of the multitude. So the New Zealand word *rangatira*, or chief, when dissected, is *ra-nga-tira*, which simply means the light of companies, or assemblies of men.[170]

These were convoluted lines of pursuit, but they were difficult to disprove and seemed, at some rudimentary level, at least, to be plausible.

When the linguistic similarities dried up, Taylor went one step further: he conflated artistic designs among otherwise disparate cultures to make linguistic connections. He dismissed the link between Malay and te reo on the basis that there were no grounds to trace te reo's origins in this direction 'beyond the resemblance of a very few words' (an irony that obviously escaped him, given that such tenuous resemblances were the partial basis of his own theories). The affinity between the Māori and Sanskrit, he felt, was considerably closer, 'as well as their customs; the widow sacrificing her life at the husband's death is a remarkable agreement. The figures sculptured on the caves of Elora and Salsette bear a singular resemblance to the Maori hei tiki in their form.'[171] This appears, from the modern standpoint, to be clutching at academic straws, but in the absence of more developed anthropological and linguistic techniques of analysis, and without the benefit of more than a century of intervening scholarship, such conclusions were perhaps the best that could be hoped for.

One of the more extravagant theories on the origin of the Māori language and culture was that they essentially had no origin beyond their immediate Polynesian precursors. Von Hochstetter, who concocted this theory, dismissed broader geographical or cultural influences as being found 'wanting', and contended that 'neither in the social habits of the Polynesians, nor in the original mode of their government, is the slightest trace of influence from abroad, or of an intermixture with other nations to be observed. In vain we search for foreign elements in their language, for a connection of the Maori tongue with the Malay language.' All that was left was the possibility that the Polynesian culture and language somehow spontaneously appeared – a notion that von Hochstetter did not shy away from:

> the mythology of the Polynesian tribes … cannot be interpreted as the issue of a remoter and older system, but must be considered as original to them. The Polynesians, we must conclude, had their own sphere of creation, and science has at yet not been able to reduce the different spheres of creation to one common centre.[172]

A specific offshoot of this conjectural branch of research was the notion of the Aryan origin of the Māori.[173] The chief advocate of this theory was former soldier, official, and enthusiastic (if fanciful) anthropologist Edward Tregear.[174] Although his main thesis now reads like a Victorian curio from a mind in which imaginative excess compensated for academic deficiency, it does reveal the lengths to which te reo could become distanced from its historical settings and mythologised by Europeans. Picking up a few shreds of argument from German philologist Max Müller's 1860 work, *A History of Ancient Sanskrit Literature*,[175] Tregear constructed an entire history of Māori that, at least to some readers, looked plausible.[176] Early on in his 107-page testament to this theory, *The Aryan Maori*,[177] Tregear's absolute faith in his position was made plain:

I now proceed to assert –

Positively,

1. That the Maori is an Aryan.

2. That his language and traditions prove him to be the descendant of a pastoral people, afterwards warlike and migratory.

3. That his language has preserved, in an almost inconceivable purity, the speech of his Aryan forefathers, and compared with which the Greek and Latin tongues are mere corruptions.

4   That this language has embalmed the memory of animals, implements &c., the actual sight of which has been lost to the Maori to centuries.[178]

Although the notion of Māori being the descendants of a supposed Aryan race was met with near incredulity by specialists in philology – as much for its audaciousness as its ineptitude[179] – the interest it generated and the opinions it influenced[180] show how far te reo as a field of enquiry had become the intellectual commodity of the colonists. Tregear's thesis also served as a basis for a developing national identity, and what could be better for the cause of a homogeneous New Zealandness than the suggestion that the country's indigenous population – as one newspaper editor put it – 'belong to the same race as ourselves'.[181]

Most of these Victorian scholars appear to have had an aversion – intentional or otherwise – to fieldwork, and an almost total absence of Māori informants. This demonstrates how little value was placed on Māori knowledge by European researchers. Instead, the language of the country's indigenous inhabitants was the subject of imperial gaze from afar, in the same way as any other antiquity might be: it was in the dim, book-lined private studies and in the country's libraries that te reo was objectified in the image crafted by the coloniser.

All this research and conjecture about te reo's origins contributed to an emerging hierarchy in the status of language and knowledge in the colony.[182] Frequently, in the various assessments made of te reo, values were applied to it that confirmed its inferiority to English in the opinion of the colonists. They judged it as being unable to make any useful contribution to the country's future. And as the settler population increased, the perception of te reo's worth to the newly minted nation diminished in proportion – to the point where some immigrants regarded te reo as a barrier to national progress: as Selwyn noted, as early as 1844, 'Some of our settlers are in a great hurry to abolish the native language and substitute English.'[183] As the century progressed, this antipathy not only persisted but hardened in certain instances.

Ernst Dieffenbach, the German geologist who was brought to the colony by the New Zealand Company in 1841, captured some of this mounting settler hostility to Māori culture, and what it was like for Māori on the receiving end of it – including the pressures it exerted on te reo:

> Placed amongst a European colonial community, a native, when he ceases to be an object of curiosity to us, is little regarded, unless he gives us his aid as our servant; and even as such he often finds himself curtailed in the recompense of his labour. He is soon made sensible of the differences of rank, and perceives that he is not treated as one who is made of the same flesh and blood as his master. Of all the better enjoyments of civilized life he is deprived, as in colonial society every one gives up his mind solely to the acquisition of money ... *he is expected to*

forget his language; in fact, all the sacrifices are on his side … he will by degrees be taught the value of civilization, and be able to appreciate its manifold advantages, without entailing on himself its miseries only.[184]

The strong settler expectation, from roughly the point when New Zealand became a British colony, that Māori shift to become English speakers was audacious, and for two main reasons: Māori still outnumbered non-Māori in the colony at the beginning of the 1840s by a ratio of almost 50 to one;[185] and only two decades earlier, Europeans who decided to live in New Zealand took it almost for granted that they would need to become reasonably fluent in te reo.

What had changed since the 1820s was that settler society was fast finding its feet. The Europeans no longer depended on Māori patronage for their survival, and as their population grew, so did their cultural confidence. In the 1820s the number of native English speakers in New Zealand might have been around 100 to 200: by the end of the 1840s the figure was approaching 20,000. This population surge showed no signs of abating, and it led to a perception that the future belonged to the settlers: Māori were now cast as a remnant of an earlier, 'primitive' and waning culture. The prescription for the country's progress seemed obvious to many Europeans, as one newspaper argued in 1843 in an article that also stressed the necessary fate of te reo in this development:

It is an immense object for the future as well as the present, to amalgamate the native with the emigrant … [by] teaching the English language, and accustoming the native New Zealander to the habits and wants of our social relations … Amalgamation, by one language, must be their pole-star; and civilization by the early impressions of schooling and training, and not encouraging the habit or separation of tribes, will be the sure forerunners of real and not nominal Christianity.[186]

The press in Wellington were making this supposed association between language and European civilisation more explicit by the 1840s; views about the indigenous population tended to be expressed in a more forthright manner there than in Auckland-based newspapers. An 1845 opinion piece in the *New Zealand Spectator and Cook's Strait Guardian* insisted that 'One of the first measures indispensable to any successful attempt to bring the natives within the pale of civilization, is to teach them our language, and so far as we can, to cause them to forget their own … It is nothing less, in short, than to change the nature of the savage, and to raise him to the level and standard of civilization.' It was not just the civilising of Māori that was at stake by allowing te reo to persist unchecked: even the country's race relations were supposedly being jeopardised by the unfettered use of te reo among Māori. 'As long as the native language is maintained,' this journalist argued, 'so long a most effectual impediment is placed between the two races.'[187] Te reo was 'a mere language of tradition'[188] that was too 'vague and indefinite'[189] to be of use in the nation's future. After all, it had 'sufficed for the requirements of a barbarous race, but it can never be made an instrument of refined spiritual thought, or become adapted to the higher purposes of life … There does not seem sufficient compass in the language to give impressive conceptions of the great work of human redemption.'[190] Such attitudes are just a small sample of the invective that was heaped on te reo by some – though certainly not all – of those Europeans who had made New Zealand their home. It was ironic, therefore, that one of the main defences against the popular assaults on te reo was a European institution, and a government department at that: the Protectorate of Aborigines.

Formed by Lieutenant-Governor Hobson in 1840 on the instruction of the Colonial Office,[191] the Protectorate of Aborigines was charged with carefully defending Māori 'in the observance of their own customs' until they reached the stage where 'they can be brought within the pale of civilized life, and trained to the adoption of its habits'.[192] It was a broad and culturally ambiguous mandate, and the protectorate attracted the criticism of a large portion of the settler community because its staff were seen as being too pro-Māori. An observer writing in 1846 noted that this alleged leaning towards Māori interests was inevitable: 'it is quite natural to suppose, that their feelings would soon come to be identified with those of their *proteges,* and that they would look upon them as a lawyer looks upon his client, namely, as one whom he was bound to protect whether right or wrong, and at all hazards. Were they to act otherwise, it would be considered a dereliction of duty on their part.'[193] For his part the Protector, George Clarke, ensured that, among much else, he guarded te reo against being displaced too suddenly by English. Clarke was, after all, also a missionary, and he was very well aware that practically all the religious material that Māori were reading, and that was still having such a profound effect on Māori society through the spread of Christianity, was in te reo. The language could not, therefore, simply be abandoned in favour of one that few Māori spoke, let alone read.

To this end, the missionaries and others made every effort to promote te reo Māori as one of the two shared languages of the colony, rather than just the language of the colonised indigenous population. There was a small but symbolic example of this ambition at the ceremony to lay the foundation stone for St Paul's Church in Auckland on 28 July 1841. For the benefit of Māori attending the event, Clarke translated and read out Hobson's speech in te reo. The colonial administration thus gave equal recognition to both languages. Predictably, the reponse of some Europeans to this bilingualism was less than charitable. Charles Terry wrote that it was 'very much to be regretted that during the many years since the establishment of the Missionaries, on the North Island, their attention and efforts have not been directed, to teach, generally, the Native youths the English language'.[194]

As the uncompromising culture of the colonists (the Protectorate of Aborigines notwithstanding) was looking to remove te reo not only as the dominant language of the country but as a spoken and so-called 'living' language[195] within Māori society, te reo was being romanticised by some of the colony's more imaginative writers. This was one of those telltale signs that the language was already well on its way to being seen as a dusty artefact of a primeval and fading culture. The Druids in England had undergone a similar sort of treatment,[196] and now it was the turn of Māori to have their culture rendered archaic and nostalgic in a picturesque and poetic sense. (That some colonists likened Māori to Druids[197] only goes to show how far this artificial and formulaic depiction of the Other could be taken.[198]) The portrayal of te reo was shifting from being the language of savages and barbarians to something exotic, antique, Arcadian – and tamed. It was the return of the Noble Savage, only with slightly less savage in some people's estimation. This gave rise to remarks such as that from a visitor to a Māori community who initially found te reo 'sounding strongly guttural from some of the speakers in the vehemence of debate', but was later drawn by how it was also 'musical and agreeable to the ear', and 'in the mouth of a young and pretty woman I dare say it may be soft and persuasive'.[199] The entire language was being reduced to an aural trinket. The artist George French Angas, when he attended evening prayers, jotted down in his journal how he took pleasure in listening to Māori partake in their supplications 'in their soft and simple language'. The effect was 'pleasing, as their voices, chanting the evening hymn, sounded at a distance, through the dull and dewy night'.[200] Here the sublime landscape of a Caspar David Friedrich painting blended with the placated but still exotic natives and their language.

William Marshall, a sailor and impassioned missionary supporter who visited the country in 1834, attended a Māori church service and was 'struck with amazement, and very very deeply affected, at the eloquent pathos of their voices'. He did not understand te reo, but this was no obstacle as 'the difference of language was lost [in the] sound of … the unity of the sentiment expressed by the Church, and the tone in which that sentence was uttered, [which] seem to me the very echo of my own heart's lamentation'.[201] Māori culture and language were sentimentalised in this way – but the process of the colonial colouring of the language did not end there. Some writers went further, comparing te reo to the language of other mythologised cultures such as the Scottish Highlanders. When Governor Bowen visited the East Coast, for example, he was met with a fervent welcome by local Māori, which he described as being 'couched in language that might have been spoken by the Highland chieftains, Children of the Mist, when the clans were gathered together to declare for the unseen, unknown object of their imaginative romantic loyalty, full of the poetic fervour of one feeling common to all, yet strangely distinct, and true to the spirit of clanship'.[202] Writer and linguist John White compared Māori song poetry to the poems of the third-century Scottish King Ossian (transcribed in the mid-nineteenth century by James Macpherson, allegedly from an unbroken line of oral culture).[203]

Such accounts represented te reo not as one of the languages of a modernising New Zealand but as almost a linguistic confection from the primitive past. With the cultural importance largely stripped from some of the more saccharine depictions of te reo, it was left as little more than an affectation that added a touch of harmless exoticism to the nation's increasingly British cultural character. And because most Europeans did not understand te reo, it was that much easier for them to project onto it all the romanticised notions about Māori that were becoming voguish, especially towards the end of the century. Māori culture and language, as they were being constructed by the coloniser, could now serve yet another purpose: to accommodate the quixotic literary and aesthetic expectations of settler society.

Te reo was hardly remaining static in this period, though. The 'scriptural literacy' that was ushered in to Māori society from when the first missionaries had begun their translation work no longer held a monopoly on written forms of the language. As well as newspapers appearing in te reo from the 1840s, individuals such as White (who eventually published the multi-volume *Ancient History of the Maori: His mythology and traditions*)[204] started exploring the language and writing about it. White began composing a dictionary of te reo (although he ceased work on it in May 1847, having reached the letter 'k'),[205] and he was among the first of a small group of settlers involved in te reo translation who were outside the circle of missionaries. As a consequence, the character of the language in print underwent a small revolution: for the first time it was being used on a mass scale for secular purposes. This represented yet another stage in te reo's evolving response to some of the cultural and linguistic changes occurring.

Meanwhile, letter writing by Māori was emerging as another area of language adaptation especially among the younger members of Māori communities, who tended to be more literate than the preceding generation. This, coupled with journals that several Māori kept to record contemporary events and fragments of oral histories (a sort of contraction of conventional oral histories into written form), the proliferation of newspapers in te reo, and even the recording of commercial transactions[206] all broadened the application of the country's indigenous language in text. The fact that these developments were taking place almost exclusively in te reo must have confounded those fervent settler–civilisers[207] who saw Māori as having a future only in an English-speaking country. Other settlers, though, regarded the high rates of Māori literacy favourably. When, for example, a plan was announced in 1848 to publish a new newspaper in te reo, its European editors were 'glad to find that the Maories, with scarcely an exception, can read and write their own language, thereby making this publication available to every family and member of their respective tribes'.[208] There was an unspoken acceptance that, for the time being at least, New Zealand was a bilingual country, not by design but by virtue of the particular ways that Māori society had accommodated and responded to European settlement, and the extent to which they had adopted literacy in te reo.

However, the great demographic shift in the following decade, when Māori became a minority in New Zealand, would upset and then dismantle this equilibrium. Te reo could not be parted from the culture, history, ethnicity and identity of its speakers, and so when those speakers were no longer the prevalent population, the pressures on them to use the language of the new majority could only intensify.[209] Other changes were also taking place around this time that heightened these pressures, including the consolidation and extension of the powers of the colonial state, which conducted its public and official functions almost exclusively in English; the extension of English as the language of the national education system; and clear signs of the further social, political and economic marginalisation of Māori.[210]

The rise in Māori literacy had been swift and relatively steady since the 1820s, but any assumptions that this trend would continue unabated were unexpectedly dashed during the second half of the 1840s. This was sometimes opaquely hinted at,[211] such as in one missionary's report in 1844 that the 'state of things [is] more natural than it is flattering to the high expectations which we are apt to form.'[212] Māori literacy in te reo was still growing, only apparently at a slightly slower rate. But then came a much more candid and striking concession: 'Much effort has been used to keep up the Day Schools; but the complaint of the Native Teachers, that they cannot persuade the people to attend, is universal.'[213] Clearly a corner had been turned in the area of Māori education. But why?

For missionaries of any denominational persuasion, literacy had always been a means to an end – that end being conversion. It is likely that even by the early 1840s, some Māori were feeling that they had exhausted any educational benefits to be derived from the mission schools. Indeed, as they looked around at the British settlers flooding into the country, it would have become increasingly evident to Māori that they could not hope to prosper in this new world by relying on religious texts alone. However, the financially squeezed missions initially had neither the means nor, admittedly, the inclination to translate and publish secular works in te reo.[214]

This situation left Māori with only two alternatives: either retreat into their communities and somehow avert their gaze from the material and social changes taking place in New Zealand, or – and this was one of those shifts that would lead to a substantial change in the course of te reo's history – begin learning English. William Brown was adamant that if the missionaries had focused their attentions from the outset on instruction in English, Māori would have 'advanced' a lot further by the mid-1840s. Success in teaching in English, he argued, 'even in a few instances, would have done more for [Māori] civilization than teaching a hundred merely in their own language … before they can ever be expected to make any progress in knowledge, they must yet be taught English, or some other European language.'[215] And according to Samuel Martin, the missionaries were to blame for their illogical insistence on teaching literacy only in te reo. 'When I came first to this country,' he complained, 'several of us made an attempt to establish an English school. We spoke to the nearest Church missionary on the subject; but finding him inveterately opposed to it, we were obliged to abandon the idea.' Like Brown, Martin was convinced that until Māori were able to speak and read in English, 'they will make no further progress.'[216]

Eventually even the different denominations came around to a similar view. At the close of the nineteenth century, as Reverend William Morley was finishing his research on the history of Methodism in New Zealand, he conceded that it was 'a matter of regret that advantage had not been taken of the curiosity of the Maoris to give them ideas of other lands, and of industries, by the printed page'. With the benefit of hindsight that was not available to those missionaries working in New Zealand in the 1820s and 1830s, Morley concluded that 'instruction in English would have occupied [Māori] minds, extended their intellectual limits, and even made their religious faith more robust and enlightened'.[217]

The missionaries were not completely blind to this situation. They had made small efforts in some parts of the North Island in the 1840s to offer Māori students instruction in English, roughly in measure with the extent of European settlement in an area. In the Waikato region, where the settler presence was still relatively thin on the ground, the impetus to teach English was less pronounced than in other places[218] where Māori were in daily contact with sizeable numbers of Europeans and needed to acquire some knowledge of this introduced language. But at the back of their minds, the missionaries knew that if Māori learned to read and write in English, their assimilation into the European realm would accelerate and, consequently, the missionaries would be less able to keep Māori from the worldliness of settler society.

Overarching all these developments throughout the first decade of Britain's colonial rule was New Zealand's evolution as a nation state. The process was formally begun in 1840, but was given greater effect through constitutional and demographic developments in the 1850s. All the expected ingredients of a modern nation – a unitary political and legal system that was constitutionally prescribed, nominal equality among citizens, a collective sense of national identity and broadly universally shared values – militated against the two-language state that had persisted to the end of the decade.[219] The imperial ideology of the nineteenth-century British colony increasingly had little room for cultural or linguistic differentiation,[220] and so what in practice had been a bilingual country in the decade of the signing of the treaty was soon to be English-only at its core, with te reo (and its speakers) consigned progressively to the periphery.

CHAPTER 5

'Forge a way forward'

1850s to 1860s

'HAUNTED'

A large audience filed into the Council Chamber in Wellington on 26 September 1851 to hear an address by Governor George Grey, speaking in his capacity as president of the New Zealand Society. Formed just two months earlier, the society included among its stated aims: 'The collection and preservation of materials illustrative of the history of the native inhabitants, their language, customs, poetry and traditions.'[1] Already Māori culture was being regarded as something belonging to the past – an object to be scrutinised and picked over like any other archaeological artefact. Grey himself was a great collector, particularly of books, and acquired them in large quantities, albeit at times apparently indiscriminately.[2] His interest in New Zealand's indigenous culture and people was in some way an extension of his passion for collecting things that, like his books, were uncommon, exotic, and had a sense of antiquity about them.

Grey's lecture climaxed with a piece of highly embellished rhetoric that made clear the contrast between the country's Māori past and European future:

> We who stand in this country occupy an historical position of
> extraordinary interest: before us lies a future already brilliant with the
> light of a glorious morn, which we are to usher in to gladden unborn
> generations. Behind us lies a night of fearful gloom, unillumined by
> the light of written records, of picture memorials, of aught which can
> give a certain idea of the past, a few stray streaks of light in the form of
> tradition, of oral poetry, of carved records, are the only guides we have,
> and in the gloom of that night are fast fading out of view, although dim
> outlines of them are still visible, some of the most fearful spectres which
> bare ever stalked amongst mankind, in the hideous forms of idolatry,

human sacrifices, and cannibalism. The future will almost doubt that such gloomy forms of thought have haunted their then highly cultivated and civilized homes.[3]

And so it went on, with references to all the traits of traditional Māori society that Grey knew the audience would find distasteful, yet titillating. The purpose of the society, he reminded those present, was to preserve a record of this 'fast fading' culture so that future generations would have a notion of how a 'race ... could fall so low'.[4] The Māori world was being held up as an example of the dangers of veering away from civilisation; judging by the favourable reception he received, there were many others in the colony who shared the governor's views.

Such heavily paternalistic language was partly a reflection of Grey's personality, but it was also indicative of the overall thinking of a good portion of settler society – much of it fortified by dramatic demographic changes that were occurring. Just seven years after this speech was delivered, the census (the first to include Māori)[5] revealed that the number of Europeans living in New Zealand had soared to 59,328 while the Māori population continued to plummet, to just 55,336.[6] Settlers would have sensed well before the end of the decade that New Zealand was rapidly becoming a European nation; and this would have been accentuated by the fact that the Māori population included those living in the many communities located in remote rural areas, out of the sight of the main centres. It was at this time, for example, that publications promoting New Zealand as the 'Britain of the South'[7] started to emerge, contributing to the repositioning of New Zealand as an essentially European colony even while it was still (only just) a majority Māori country.

The demographic shift that was taking place from the 1850s further widened a divide that had already been apparent in New Zealand between its core and periphery. Political, economic, cultural and linguistic power was becoming ever more concentrated in the settler population, while Māori were being relegated increasingly to the outskirts in these areas.[8] This widening gap was as much a structural feature of the evolving state[9] as a series of ad hoc developments. Over the second half of the century, the legislature, judiciary, officials, religious bodies, the press and other groups that constituted the country's European 'core' developed positions, articulated opinions, formulated policies and made decisions that not only expressed a progressively hostile view towards te reo, but ingrained this view as a defining attribute of the state. And the fact that this disparaging attitude towards Māori culture, language and society in general was so deep-seated meant the state was seldom required to explicitly prohibit the use of te reo. The inherently dominating nature of the colonist core hastened the marginalisation of te reo: the attrition caused by the antipathy of various branches of the state towards the language would lead to its contraction far more effectively and smoothly than any attempt at direct prohibition would have achieved.

As the tectonic plates of state policy and practice continued to grind away at te reo, at an individual level the state's representatives sometimes came across as being well disposed towards the language. Grey himself embodied this apparent paradox: at the beginning of the 1850s, at the same time as he was playing a leading role in guiding the organs of government to an effectively English-only policy, he toured part of New Zealand, not only learning as much as he could about Māori culture and history but learning to speak te reo.

In the summer of 1849–50 the governor and a small entourage travelled from Auckland to Taranaki via Rotorua and Taupo. The group included two officials, an artist and two Māori – Pirikawau, a clerk in the Native Secretary's Office, who would serve as interpreter; and Ngāti Tūwharetoa chief Te Heuheu, who had travelled to Auckland for the express purpose of escorting the Europeans on the planned journey. George Cooper, Grey's assistant private secretary, kept a record of the expedition and published it in 1851 – appropriately, for the character of the expedition, in bilingual format, with English on the left-hand page and te reo on the right.[10] The translator is not identified in the book but it could have been Cooper working in conjunction with Pirikawau, whom he identified as 'a clerk in the Native Secretary's Office [and an] Interpreter'.[11]

This journey may well have confirmed Grey's existing prejudices about the value of te reo and its future role in the country. Throughout the trip they encountered numerous Māori settlements where the occupants, almost without exception, spoke only te reo – hence the need for the accompanying interpreters. Grey's entrenched views about te reo being a language of little utility, on the basis of its supposed limited capacity and primitive past,[12] were validated in his mind by what he saw on this expedition. He was struck by the squalor and material privations of the communities they visited. Opita, a settlement at the junction of the Ohinemuri and Waihou rivers, near Paeroa,[13] was depicted by Cooper as 'a wretched place, containing about a dozen miserable raupo houses all tumbling to pieces', where they 'found the natives in a very poor condition, not a living animal had they, save four geese, a hen with a brood of young chickens, and a few skeleton-looking dogs; they had neither potatoes nor kumeras but were living on fern root and a few eels which they catch now and then.' In similar vein Patetere, near present-day Putaruru, was 'a miserable place, containing about half a dozen small huts, inhabited by twenty or thirty of the most squalid-looking creatures I ever remember to have seen, nearly every one of whom is afflicted with the horrible cutaneous disease so common amongst the natives, to a disgusting extent'; and Te Puia, which was a few kilometres east of Lake Rotoiti, consisted of 'a few wretched little huts, and scarcely any cultivation … a more squalid, ill-conditioned place, I have rarely seen'.[14] Grey, who already equated te reo with barbarism and moral and cultural stagnation, could now add the dirt and destitution of Māori communities to the traits he associated with it. He did not claim that te reo was causative, but it was clearly correlative, and that was enough to firm up his conviction that the country's indigenous language and its culture should be superseded as soon as possible by English.

As Grey's expedition wound its way through the hinterland of the North Island, its members saw how te reo was adjusting to the culture of the settlers. In most places, European contact with Māori was limited to a missionary presence, either in a Māori settlement or somewhere in the vicinity. Unlike at some of the more established missions to the north, they sang hymns in te reo and the melodies were usually based on a traditional waiata. Cooper considered these 'rather unmusical to European ears' and 'a somewhat heathenish sound', but he noted that the missionaries had discovered by experience that relying on traditional Māori melodies was an easier way to introduce hymns than having to teach European music as well. This compromise was a temporary fix; even a passing visit through several settlements was enough for him to see that European tunes were gradually replacing traditional melodies.[15]

Such cross-cultural arrangements demonstrate that even when the language and melodies of a song were indigenous, the content and concepts of the language being used and the tendency away from traditional tunes were producing a cultural hybridity that made te reo's position precarious. After all, if the ideas and melodies of a song – in this case, hymns – oriented themselves to a general European archetype, the pressure on the language used to conform in a similar way would inevitably make itself felt. And because there was no counterbalancing force to this influence (apart from the relative isolation of most Māori communities) this apparent show of an indigenous adaptation of an English church service could more accurately be cast as the first stage in a transition *away* from indigenous Māori culture and language, rather than its outward appearance of new ideas being accommodated in te reo.

Far from being passive bystanders in this process, in many instances Māori were actively involved in directing it. Because of a chronic shortage in the 1850s of European missionaries who were fluent in te reo, Māori were being co-opted to assist in evangelising within their communities. In some parts of the country a Māori intermediary was appointed to every settlement in the circuit of the district's appointed missionary. Their duties, in the absence of regular missionary visitations, were to conduct two services a day (and three on Sundays), teach reading and writing in te reo, and carry out the general activities expected of missionaries.

What was most striking about this relationship was that the vestiges of European missionary power somehow filtered down to these Māori agents. These proxy missionaries, in conjunction with kaumātua in their communities, had the authority to impose church rules and to censure those who broke those rules – even to the extent of banishing them temporarily from the community. Cooper cited the example of a young man who violated some sanction and 'was not only prevented for a season from attending church service, &c, but was also temporarily expelled from the settlement altogether, being obliged to remain outside the fence day and night, with no house, nor indeed any covering save his blanket, and subsisting on such food as the others chose to give him, which he cooked for himself'. 'The poor fellow,' Cooper added, 'looked so lonely and miserable sitting by his fire, and almost cut off from all communication with his fellow creatures.'[16] This considerable power extended to instruction in the mission school, and while it was obviously approved of by the communities themselves, it derived in part from the perception that such rules had the blessing of the European missionaries. The role of te reo in this settler-dominated, Māori-co-opted missionary activity was ambiguous.

Presumably, as long as te reo was the sole language of teaching and religious services in these communities, its status as the main – or only – language spoken was likely to remain unaffected. However, the very structure that was assisting with te reo continuing as the language of European education and religious discourse was run by English-speakers. At a moment's notice, they could insist on switching to English as the main or even the only language used in schools. Moreover, as this informal power structure – with Europeans at its head – had quickly accrued authority and consolidated its position within various Māori communities, their chances of successfully defying it were becoming that much more difficult. This made the role of te reo, in missionary schools more than elsewhere, exceptionally vulnerable to policy changes – especially when such changes had the authority of the government to enforce them. This was a prime case of the cultural penetration by settler society of Māori communities laying the groundwork for English to subsume te reo. That this possibility was neither intentional nor premeditated to begin with does not detract from the potential threat it posed to te reo.

THE GOVERNOR LEARNS TE REO

Although the government increasingly regarded te reo as a handicap to Māori assimilation into settler society, Grey's intellectual curiosity was quickened by Māori culture and language. And to this private curiosity was added a public motive.[17] In his 1855 book *Polynesian Mythology*[18] he explained how, when he became the country's governor, he could 'neither successfully govern, nor hope to conciliate, a numerous and turbulent people, with whose language, manners, customs, religion, and modes of thought I was quite unacquainted'. Even with the assistance of a pool of highly skilled interpreters, Grey felt he was unable to communicate effectively with Māori, which was disappointing for him and disillusioning, he believed, for those Māori who met him. He therefore saw it as his 'duty' to learn to speak te reo 'with the least possible delay'.[19] His account of this undertaking was detailed and candid:

> But I soon found that this was a far more difficult matter than I had at first supposed. The language of the New Zealanders is a very difficult one to understand thoroughly: there was then no dictionary of it published (unless a vocabulary can be so called); there were no books published in the language which would enable me to study its construction; it varied altogether in form from any of the ancient or modern languages which I knew; and my thoughts and time were so occupied with the cares of the government ... that I could find but very few hours to devote to the acquisition of an unwritten and difficult language. I, however, did my best, and cheerfully devoted all my spare moments to a task, the accomplishment of which was necessary to enable me to perform properly every duty to my country and to the people I was appointed to govern.[20]

There had been several dictionaries and grammars produced by this time and it is inconceivable that Grey was unaware of them, so his claim that there was no material to help him learn the language was disingenuous. Nevertheless, the fact stands that no previous (or later) governor devoted so much effort to familiarising himself with te reo – although, as Grey conceded, his purpose in acquiring the language was at least in part driven by his desire to strengthen and broaden colonial rule.

One of the unintended consequences for Grey of learning to speak te reo was his discovery that Māori orators habitually relied on metaphors, allusions and figurative language when fashioning the content of their rhetoric, including in the addresses and appeals they made to him.[21] As governor, Grey felt that he could not allow 'so close a veil to remain drawn between myself and the aged and influential chiefs ... with whom it was necessary that I should hold the most unrestricted intercourse'.[22] He therefore set himself an additional task: to acquire some understanding of the traditions, legends, histories and mythologies of Māori, so that at least some of the metaphorical content he heard in speeches would resonate with him. In order to accomplish this, he drew on contacts he had made in various Māori communities, and he eventually produced an unprecedented volume of published material on pre-European Māori culture.

The body of knowledge that Grey produced was (and remains) invaluable. But it was amassed at a time when it was widely believed that Māori were disappearing – not just their culture and language, but the race itself. Grey's studies were as much an effort to embalm a disappearing culture as to create a resource that would help sustain its members during a period of vigorous colonisation. How he felt about the value of the culture that he was translating and transcribing was stated in his introduction to *Polynesian Mythology*. 'That their traditions are puerile, is true,' he informed his readers; 'that the religious faith of the races who trust in them is absurd, is a melancholy fact.' He believed nevertheless that there was some use in having an acquaintance with 'the mythological systems of barbarous or semi-barbarous races', even if it was for something as inconsequential as a perfunctory comparison with the mythologies of other cultures.[23]

One of the governor's main sources for his publications on Māori language, culture, history and mythology was Wiremu Maihi Te Rangikaheke;[24] and although Grey did not condescend to acknowledge him by name in his works, it was Te Rangikaheke who was principally responsible both for supplying content for the book and for tutoring the governor in te reo.[25]

Other sources Grey depended on were far less reliable. Parts of *Polynesian Mythology* were based on the stories that were being collected by John White, who sourced his material from around 300 Māori informants.[26] Occasionally White's imagination overtook his discipline. In one instance he produced a fictional composition that had the appearance of an authentic Māori oral tradition, which Grey subsequently incorporated into his own book.[27] Grey also wilfully altered names, places and the sequence of events, and he sometimes suppressed material that he regarded as too sexually explicit.[28]

The authority of Grey's *Polynesian Mythology* was thus fundamentally compromised, but for most readers, including later some Māori, it was a reliable source of material on their culture and history. Only someone with specific knowledge of the particular history concerned could detect the sections that were fabricated. Consequently, the translation of oral histories in te reo into printed English in this important case contributed to a body of knowledge emerging with the semblance of detail and accuracy, but that in many ways was a distortion of the culture from which it was ostensibly drawn.

Grey's role as a cultural mediator in this venture therefore cannot be underestimated. He exercised discretion over what material was included in his volumes, and was flexible about the standards he applied for the accuracy of his source material. Overall, he utilised a European measure (and an amateur one at that) of what was of value or importance when assessing aspects of Māori culture and history for inclusion in his publications, and inevitably, the resulting selectivity was bound to betray traces of cultural bias. Whether this was deliberate or unintentional in the numerous instances where it occurred is less important than the fact of this selectivity existing in these published works in the first place. The cultural mediation in such undertakings can be enormous, and extends even to areas as seemingly innocuous as the layout of the material on the pages of a book, which has the potential to distort the ways in which its content is interpreted by readers, and how knowledge is perceived to be prioritised.[29]

Overall, Grey's efforts at translating Māori culture, beliefs, histories, and even imagined thought processes into English served primarily to strengthen the position of English[30] by privileging it as an elite culture of text that could not only collate but format and structure the culture of the indigenous spoken word.[31] Like the efforts at producing portions of the Bible in te reo, acts of translation in colonial New Zealand were always culturally partisan, and Grey's anthropological pillaging was yet another step in the coloniser extending its cultural dominion over Māori.

WHOSE WHAREKURA?

Schooling was one of the primary means by which Grey hoped to modernise Māori society.[32] The failure of mission schools to move away quickly enough from teaching in te reo and the general lack of English in use in Māori communities certainly provided the governor with the impetus to develop his native schools policy. That English had not yet radiated out much from the main population centres of the colonists by the 1850s might appear surprising, considering that the country had now been settled by English speakers for almost four decades; it had been a British colony for more than 12 years; and, especially, the European population was on the verge of outnumbering Māori. Yet, as a report submitted to Grey about the Otawhao School in Te Awamutu in 1854 reveals, in much of rural New Zealand, Māori typically had only a minimal acquaintance with English, and te reo remained firmly ensconced as the mother tongue:

> Care appears to have been taken to ground the children in religious knowledge; but the answers given by the greater number were very imperfect, owing, apparently, in some degree, to the want of a ready command of the English language. The elder children can read the Scriptures in English remarkably well, and with correct pronunciation. The younger ones are making good progress. As to the meaning of what was read, the answers were less satisfactory. It appeared that many of the children either did not fully apprehend the meaning of the questions, (which were put in English) or that they had not a sufficient command of the language to answer readily. Very little systematic or efficient instruction in the English language appeared to have been given; although, in regard to the majority of these half-caste children, it is as necessary as for natives.[33]

At Maraetai, te reo's hold looked to be even stronger: Maunsell noted that 'The English language has not yet formed part of the general course of instruction.'[34] And at St Stephen's, a Māori girls' school, the students 'generally read and pronounce English well, considering the difficulty the natives have in acquiring this knowledge; but few of them are quick in turning sentences from their own language into English, or the contrary'.[35]

Te reo was obviously still the dominant language for Māori (including for the category of 'half-castes', which was mentioned much more frequently in official reports from the 1850s). However, the fact that there appears not to have been a deeper generational divide, which might have been expected given that so many Māori youth were learning English in schools, raises an important distinction between the respective roles and functions of language and literacy. When it came to literacy in te reo, the gulf between younger and older Māori in the 1840s had been noticeable. There was no apparent corresponding age difference, though, when it came to Māori knowledge of English. What this very generalised view suggests is that Māori were prepared to accommodate different ways of communicating and storing te reo, even if that included using the technology of the coloniser – and that, for a few decades, it was the younger generations to whom printed text appealed the most – but were far less inclined to relinquish their spoken language in favour of English, even when the state was pressing for precisely such a transition to occur.

It was not as though some areas of the country lagged behind others. Hadfield's 1855 report on a school for Māori in Otaki contained a glimpse of a trend in which – surprisingly to settlers – English-based education was beginning to be actively repudiated. This particular school was one of those that had been funded by the government on the basis that its students 'be taught the English language … receive religious instruction, and … be brought up in habits of industry'. At the beginning of 1854 there were 55 boys and 10 girls attending the school, and their progress was described as 'considerable', but by the following year there had been a conspicuous reversal and the numbers of children attending had started to decline. Hadfield attributed this to a series of causes. It is worth quoting his assessment in some detail as it provides an insight into the sort of developments that were occurring generally in those Māori communities that sent their children to the school – changes that were hardly restricted just to this region. Among other things, Hadfield determined that the reducing roll was due to:

1. The difficulty of obtaining schoolmasters who are both competent to teach Maori children and ready to exercise the patience necessary to success is a serious impediment to progress …

2. Sickness has impeded the progress of the school. In June, 1854, the measles visited it, and continued its violence during two months, till every one connected with the school had been attacked. This caused

the death of two boys; and occasioned much disorganisation in the establishment; several boys left when discipline was again enforced. The prevalence of this disease also induced many of the parents and relations of the boys to send for them; some of them did not return.

3. … parents desire to retain their children at home to assist them in work, especially in reference to their newly acquired property, such as horses and cattle, about which boys are found very useful …

…

7. The greatest obstacle now in the way of the success of schools is the apathy and indifference of parents. Boys are willing enough to come to school, but their parents like to have them near themselves. After much consideration I cannot but think that prejudices having their foundation in ignorance must eventually disappear; and that it is highly important to persevere in the only possible way of educating and civilising the Maori population.[36]

A lack of skilled teachers, health problems, economic changes and parents failing to see any immediate benefits for their children from attending school were all reasons contributing to declining school rolls in several Māori communities.

Māori boarding schools enabled students to be separated from their whānau to a much greater extent, and by 1858 there were around 800 Māori attending such institutions around the country.[37] Reports submitted to the government by these various schools indicated that these students were generally reaping the benefits of encounters with civilisation. Māori boarding schools were explicitly intended to act as 'so many centres from which education and a civilising influence should be imparted to the Native population generally' – a task that was becoming 'daily more important from the rapid increase of the English population among whom they live'.[38] And what is apparent from the schools themselves is that the intention to 'civilise' – of which instruction in English was at the core – was becoming the rule rather than the exception that it had been a decade or so earlier. Approving comments from officials – such as 'the usual routine of an elementary education has been pursued, and no means calculated to advance their civilization … has been neglected', and 'Native Schools [are a] powerful and indispensable means for the true civilisation and advancement of the Maori population'[39] – were common, and give some indication of how deep-set the role of the civilising mission was in the state education system. One report on the CMS boarding schools in Waikato, submitted to the governor in 1858, confidently asserted: 'These schools may therefore truly be considered centres of civilization, the influence of which is felt in every part of the District.'[40] In the longer term, te reo could not sit comfortably in a school system when the emphasis on modernising all facets of Māori life was so far at the forefront of education policies.

By the latter half of the 1850s, te reo was not just a minority language as a consequence of population shifts; it was also a language that was actively being marginalised by the country's state-funded schools, even if a few of the schools persisted in having classes in te reo as well. As an example, the chairman of the commissioners inspecting the schools during 1858 concluded his annual report to the ministry with a series of suggestions that had a bearing on the ascendency of English in schools. They included:

1. That a great duty rests with the General Government to promote the education of Native and Half-caste children, and that a considerable proportion of such funds as may be at the disposal of the Government for Native purposes should be dedicated to the object of Native education.

2. That Government ought not to be discouraged by past failures, insomuch as the very nature of the object to be accomplished obviously implies difficulties.

3. That English Masters and Mistresses should be invariably employed, and the teaching of the English language made the prominent feature of instruction.

   …

6. That upon these views being carried out in a sustained manner and enlightened spirit, the longevity and peaceableness of the Native race greatly depends.[41]

Hugh Carleton, a Member of the House of Representatives (and son-in-law of Henry Williams) went further in 1858. A report he wrote for Grey contained a more explicit assertion of how te reo ought to have little or no place in the future of the country's education system:

I consider that too much stress cannot be laid upon the acquirement of the English language. I believe that civilization cannot be advanced,

beyond a very short stage, through means of the aboriginal tongue …
There can be no doubt that words are suggestive of ideas, as well as ideas
of words. The Maori tongue sufficed for the requirements of a barbarous
race, but apparently would serve for little more.[42]

This was, of course, the long-held view of some Europeans of the value
of te reo in New Zealand and so was neither novel nor startling; but to
have it put so bluntly, and in a document that Grey saw fit to include as an
enclosure in a report he despatched to the British government, hints at the
governor's own sympathy with this sentiment. By itself, Carleton's statement
was merely the view of one politician – and not a very consequential
politician at that. But when considered in conjunction with all the other
assessments, recommendations and other similar opinions that denigrated
the worth of te reo, a trend emerges: a picture of te reo was being assembled
that portrayed the language as antiquated and inadequate for the needs of
modern Victorian New Zealand. There was nothing as brash as a ban on
te reo being proposed, but this was not because the level of official disdain
for the language was insufficiently high; rather, it was because the repeated
emphasis by politicians and officials of te reo's redundancy to the colony's
youth was gradually filtering through to school policy and was a far more
effective means of squeezing the language from the education system than
any state dictate. There was also less chance of an adverse reaction from the
targeted group than if some formal injunction were issued.

This incremental approach to eradicating te reo is evident in the Native
Schools Act 1858, which was a further effort by the government to direct the
way in which Māori were to be educated.[43] As with previous measures, there
was no specific exclusion of te reo in the legislation; but, pointedly, there was
a requirement that 'instruction in the English language and in the ordinary
subjects of primary English education, and Industrial training, shall form a
necessary part of the system to be pursued in every school to be aided under
this Act'.[44] Te reo may not have been prohibited but the message was clear:
English was the language in which subjects were to be taught in schools and,
by extension, it was signalled as the language of learning and progress in the
colony.

The policy of furthering the spread of English in Māori society was taken
up with even more conviction by Grey's successor, Governor Thomas Gore
Browne. Browne first made his views on te reo clear when addressing an
assembly of chiefs in Auckland in July 1860. War had broken out in Taranaki
four months earlier, and this had brought into sharper focus the fears of

an ethnic divide opening up and potentially splitting the country apart. Browne's speech was an open plea for national unity, but equally, it was a reassertion of the strong preference for linguistic assimilation, which for more than a decade had been embedding itself in most areas of government policy:

> I feel that the difference of language forms a great barrier between the Europeans and the Maories. Through not understanding each other there are frequent misapprehensions of what is said or intended: this is also one of the chief obstacles in the way of your participating in our English Councils, and in the consideration of laws for your guidance. To remedy this the various Missionary Bodies, assisted by the Government, have used every exertion to teach your children English, in order that they may speak the same language as the European inhabitants of the Colony.[45]

The impression given of Europeans and Māori in this period separated by a linguistic barrier was a misleading generalisation. In many cases the interests of the two races were interwoven, and linguistically, Browne's stark bichromatic divide was much more richly shaded. What he also either was unaware of or diminished in some of his statements was the extent to which, in some regions, te reo still dominated communication both within Māori communities and, crucially, between them and those Europeans on their periphery.

As tensions in Taranaki escalated during the 1860s, a small linguistic encounter took place that illustrates the fluidity of the boundaries between English and te reo. When the government called up local settlers to contribute to a militia force being established to fight those hapū in the area who had been identified as hostile, a few of the more informed Europeans in the region decided to make their views on the conflict known. One of these settlers, a Baptist minister, pointedly refused to serve in the militia, to which Māori in the vicinity responded by instructing him and his fellow opponents of the war to wear white scarfs to indicate to Māori troops that they should not be attacked. 'Thus distinguished,' as one historian described it two decades later, 'they were shaken hands with by each Maori, and a notice, signed by Te Rangitake and other chiefs, was posted up, declaring that the Baptist minister, Mr. Brown, and other enumerated persons, were to be respected, and that their property was to be strictly preserved.' And true to the word of the local Māori leaders, 'They and their children were safe while the fighting raged around them.'[46] This apparently inconsequential episode discloses something of how the use of te reo was evolving. First, Māori were now communicating with other Māori from the same iwi and hapū in te reo in its *written* form. This suggests either that the traditional ways of communicating were no longer being depended on in cases of urgency, or that where the matter was seen as sufficiently important, the dependability of a written message overrode that of a spoken one (or possibly elements of both applied). Regardless, the undermining of the oral routes of communication within Māori society in favour of written ones – which had been occurring with greater frequency as literacy continued its relentless advance – represented a shift in traditional linguistic practices. To a degree, this both preceded and precipitated further breakdowns in the traditional use of te reo among Māori. What also stands out from this example is that some Europeans on the fringes of Māori communities continued to communicate with their indigenous neighbours in te reo. The supposed great language barrier between Māori and Europeans, which occupied Browne's thoughts, was therefore overstated.

PAPER WARS

The fact that the mission schools were increasingly inclined to comply with the government's wishes by either primarily or exclusively teaching in English was indicative of the social developments of the time, in which English was emerging as the ascendant language in the colony. However, the ongoing emphasis on excluding te reo from schools was not universally accepted by Māori, and, given the government's increasingly didactic insistence on English-only instruction, together with the rise of Māori political groups based on fending off the intrusions of the coloniser, some sort of reaction to this policy was inevitable. One of the manifestations of this Māori resistance to the introduction or increase in English instruction was Māori parents withdrawing their children from schools altogether. In the 1860s there was a noticeable drop in the number of Māori attending local schools. Sometimes, the decline in an area appeared to be the result of other circumstances. In 1860 school inspector John Gorst reported that at Whatawhata, the entire student population left to attend a hui in the region and 'never returned'; while in Tapahina, two schools – one for boys and the other for girls – 'have recently been given up', as Gorst put it. Entire schools were closing – again, superficially on other pretexts. At Arowhenua a native school of 25 students shut its doors when the parents removed their children because the teacher got married; at Maungatautari, war forced the local school for Māori to close; and at Rangiaowhia, a school with 30 pupils closed down when its matron died and there was no one immediately available to replace her.[47]

This large-scale Māori withdrawal from the education regime of the coloniser was part of much broader developments taking place around this time, especially in the Waikato. Political changes in the areas that were under the jurisdiction of Kīngitanga (the King Movement) consolidated some of the resistance to English-based education from the start of the 1860s. The position that many Kīngitanga took was a direct response to a sense that the Māori world was under serious threat from the settler world burgeoning in its midst. It was the more avaricious land acquisition policies of the Crown, commencing in the second half of the 1800s, that alerted these communities to the danger they faced by accepting without question the path of cultural assimilation that had been laid out for them by the colonial state.

The Kīngitanga had a clear manifesto that it promulgated from its inception, and that found support across old tribal divisions. It was 'a land league to prevent the sale of land by aboriginal owners to the government, or the private sale of such land to individuals of the European or Pakeha race', and it expressed 'a desire to stop the rapid advance of European colonisation … a desire to introduce a code of laws suited to their own requirements … and chiefly, a desire to establish first in the Waikato, and afterwards gradually in all Maori districts, an independent sovereignty over all Maori and European residents in such districts' – as the Anglican missionary Reverend John Morgan succinctly explained it before a select committee of the House of Representatives. He was explicit about how Māori 'saw with fear the rapid advance of European colonisation and the earnest desire of the Pakeha to obtain possession of their lands'.[48] To expect those Māori to resist European political and territorial incursions while at the same time welcoming the education system run by the same coloniser, and delivered in the coloniser's language, was a step too far for those Māori whose land had been appropriated against their will.

The Kīngitanga drew in various iwi under broadly defined ambitions, and consolidated its status through several hui held in certain parts of the North Island. Francis Fenton, a former solicitor, had been appointed by the government as a magistrate charged with introducing British institutions in the Waikato region,[49] and observed at first hand in the late 1850s the arguments expressed by Māori leaders attending these hui both for and against this proposed pantribal movement.[50] Te reo was the language of this political discourse, and was also a great unifying force: it was an element of commonality between hapū and iwi in the face of serious and mounting threats appearing from outside their culture. Although tribal animosities continued to be a constant hindrance to Kīngitanga's expansion, the rituals associated with hui, and the strength of the debate about Kīngitanga, still all hinged on the use of te reo not just as a language of communication but, more noticeably now, as a distinctly Māori instrument of political expression.

Monumental diplomacy was often required by Kīngitanga advocates in their attempts to overcome situations where previously only discord existed between iwi. Its proponents – and those they were appealing to – had to resort to the most forceful, compelling and convincing rhetoric they were capable of flourishing in order to advance their respective views, and only in te reo could these requisite feats of oratory be accomplished. So among so much else, Kīngitanga provided further evidence to Māori (not that they necessarily needed much convincing) that te reo was the language of their political future, and was perfectly equipped to deal with the most pressing issues of the present. It was seen as not just equal to English but, in the moments of impassioned diplomacy and advocacy, plainly superior. So while settler society was happy to consign te reo to an unenlightened past and to regard its value as waning, those Māori involved in hui over the formation of Kīngitanga employed te reo very much as the language of their future. With such a sense of cultural reassertion it was little surprise that the schools that taught in English or, in some cases, were run by Europeans, were now being seen by many Māori in the Waikato region (and further afield in a few instances) as obstacles to Māori self-determination, rather than an entrée into the world of the settler. That settler world was, after all, the one responsible for tearing down traditional Māori political structures and enacting avaricious policies towards Māori land.[51]

Fenton, however, missed the point of the differences between English and te reo. Instead of seeing them as articulating vastly different ways of looking at the world, he regarded te reo simplistically as an inferior language. In 1861 he described how there was

> considerable difficulty … in the attempt to present in an intelligible
> manner the precise definitions, nice distinctions, and technicalities of
> the Law, through the medium of a rude language, which, though far
> from poor in expression or defective in structure, is better adapted for

narration or description of natural objects, than for dealing with abstract judgment of those who are skilled in the Maori tongue must determine.[52]

Overall, the government's response to Kīngitanga was not to compromise, let alone to contemplate the possibility of Māori political autonomy. As Fenton articulated it, the reason for Kīngitanga's emergence lay with its members' incomprehension of aspects of the inherently superior regime of the colonists. He recommended a myopic solution that set out how the government regarded English as the benchmark language of the state, against which te reo Māori had to measure up. 'The plan of placing the Maori and English in opposite pages,' he said, 'making the paragraphs correspond with each other, has been adopted for this reason ... that in case of obscurity in the Maori a reference to the English, on the opposite page, may at once afford the means of correcting misapprehension, by shewing what was intended to be conveyed.'[53]

All this was occurring against the backdrop of the formative stages of Kīngitanga, which Fenton accounted for – partially correctly – as the result of 'a growing perception in the Maori Race of their social wants'. His recommendation was that the government should 'with as little delay as possible, place within their [Māori] reach such information respecting our Laws and Institutions as may, with the Divine blessing, prove the means of directing their efforts to legitimate objects inducing results beneficial alike to both races'.[54] It could not have been made clearer that an alternative to the British system of rule was not even a matter for consideration.

No similar bar was put in place by the government, for example, on te reo, which was effectively a separate language, still spoken by around half the population. The country had demonstrated that it could function relatively effectively with two languages being spoken by its populace, but the possibility of two legal systems operating alongside each other in the state was nowhere near as tolerable to politicians or officials. Of course, tolerance towards te reo hinged on the belief that it, like Māori culture, was on a terminal trajectory, and so its existence could be countenanced in the meantime. Political autonomy, on the other hand, was considered counter to the interests of Māori and threatening to the sovereignty of the Crown, which made it a far more dangerous proposition. The distinction between the state's tacit acceptance of a two-language nation (in the interim) and its outright rejection of a two-sovereign nation reveals that political expediency and the commitment to the assimilation and civilisation of Māori were behind the state's tolerance of te reo.

But officials and politicians were not so naïve as to think that te reo was a politically neutral facet of Māori society. As the patina of presumed political and ethnic unity in New Zealand in the 1850s started to wear off in the 1860s, printed te reo became a tool that the state used to assist in promoting its causes among Māori – particularly those who were questioning where their political loyalties lay but had yet to make a firm commitment to Kīngitanga. As skirmishing spread through parts of Taranaki in the early 1860s, and as Kīngitanga simultaneously unfurled its political influence with mounting confidence among Māori communities in various parts of the North Island (but most strongly in Waikato), the government responded by deploying words as well as weapons. Through *The Maori Messenger – Ko te Karere Maori*, its main means of mass communication with Māori,[55] the government urged the country's indigenous population to resist the temptation to take up arms against the Crown. For a device of propaganda, the language was well chosen: it appealed to readers' logic and sense of fairness, and warned of the threat to civilisation and to Christian principles (playing on the missionaries' earlier success in converting Māori to the religion) that war would inevitably entail. The tenor of the writing was to plead rather than preach. A typical example (with its translation), incorporating all these traits, shows how printed te reo became part of the political frontline in the wars of the period:

The fullest information with respect to the disturbed state of Taranaki has been published in the 'Messenger' for the special perusal of our native readers. If those publications which contained an exact and true narrative of the origin of the present question between the Government and W. Kingi te Rangitake, have been carefully read by right thinking natives, the recent hostile demonstrations on the part of some of the Rangiaohia and Kawhia natives may well occasion them feelings of uneasiness. Calm and deliberate consideration must, however, make it apparent to all that there can be little to gain but much to lose by countenancing W. King's folly, or endorsing the murders recently committed by Ngatiruanui and Taranaki natives. What harm had the pakehas done to those tribes? The answer is, not any. We repeat it – not any, and challenge contradiction. Without the slightest provocation those mean people invaded the pakeha territory, plundered and burnt their houses, stole their cattle, devastated their farms, and cruelly murdered three unarmed settlers and two little boys! The latter were literally hacked to pieces. By whom were the little boys hacked to pieces? By men? Yes, by men, nearly all of whom have hitherto regularly assembled for Christian worship on the Sabbath day.

Ko nga korero mo nga mahi whakaoho-oho e mahia nei ki Taranaki, kua
oti te korero ki te *Karere Maori* hei tirohanga ma o matou hoa Maori. Kei
ena nupepa e mau ana te korero pono me nga tikanga o tera whawhai, o te
Kawanatanga o Wiremu Kingi Te Rangitake, me tona putake i tupu ake ai.
Na, me he mea kua ata korerotia marrietia aua korero e nga tangata Maori
whakaaro tika, tena e awangawanga te ngakau ki te mahi whakatupu
whawhai o etahi o nga tangata Maori o Rangiawhia o Kawhia, kua rangona
nei i roto i enei ra. Ki te ata huri huri marire, ka marama tenei whakaaro i
nga tangata katoa, ara, kahore he pai e hua mai i runga i te whakauru, ki te
mahi kuare a Wiremu Kingi i runga ranei i te whakatika ki te mahi kohuru
a Ngatiruanui a Taranaki, engari he kino anake ona hua, He aha koia te
hara o te Pakeha ki era iwi? Kahore kau, a ka tuaruatia ano e matou tenei
kupu, kahore kau ra he hara o te Pakeha. Kahore he take kahore he aha, i
whakatika pokanoa ai era iwi tutua. Heoi, whakatika noa ake, haere mai
aha ki runga ki to te Pakeha whenua, ko nga whare o nga Pakeha tahuna
ana e ratou ki te ahi, ko nga kau, riro atu te tango, whakamarakeraketia
ana nga paamu. Te kaati hoki i enei, na, tokotoru nga Pakeha Maori
kohurutia iho, tokorua hoki nga tamariki Pakeha, i kohurutia kinotia e
ratou; kahore kau he patu i te ringa o enei hunga, ko aua tamariki ra, he
mea tapahi kino ki te patiti a ngakongako noa. Na wai koia enei tamariki
i tapatapahi ki te patiti? Na te tangata ranei? Ae ra, na te tangata, na etahi
tangata ano e huihui ana ki te karakia i nga Ratapu katoa ka pahemo nei![56]

The necessity to publish in te reo was a reminder of still how little
English was permeating Māori society and, consequently, how the nation's
indigenous language was still the most tenacious obstacle to the government's
great civilising project. This boded ill for any hopes that future governments
might look more sympathetically on the language.

The government's attempts to smear Kīngitanga (in te reo) and dis-
courage more Māori from joining the movement only hardened Kīngitanga's
attitude towards the colonial state and any sign of its presence in Kīngitanga's territories – and this extended to an aversion to European-based
education. The consequences were swift. A report written in 1862 on schools
in the upper Waikato region, for example, noted that the education of Māori
children in that area was 'now totally neglected', leaving these pupils 'to run
about the villages with the dogs and pigs, wild, naked, and dirty'. Mission-
school attendance had dropped by half, and almost all the village schools
that once seemed so promising to European onlookers had closed, with 'no
effort and no desire to see them revived'. The young generation of Māori in
the area was doomed, in the opinion of officials, to 'growing up in ignorance
and barbarism'.[57]

It was not that Kīngitanga was opposed to education per se, but there was strong resistance among its leadership to government assistance of any sort in the areas over which it claimed jurisdiction. The popularity of this stance and its consequences on schooling among affected Māori is hard to measure. John Gorst's report on the situation indicates some ambivalence among Māori about these school closures; he predicted that the effects would be severe:

> A law has been passed and agreed to by them all, that no fresh European schools or schoolmasters shall be allowed within the King's dominions; to this law even William Thompson [Wiremu Tamihana, one of the founders of Kīngitanga] himself confesses that he has agreed. His own school at Matamata has dwindled down from sixty children to less than a dozen and though he regrets its downfall and would himself do anything to restore it, he positively refuses any assistance from the Government. Unless this state of things is very speedily changed, the next generation of Natives will be even worse educated than the present, and as ignorance increases the anarchy of the land will become still more difficult to cure.[58]

With the government and Kīngitanga both vying for the loyalty of such large numbers of Māori, printing presses were hauled out by both sides as part of an escalating propaganda war. For a Māori resistance movement, this was a new development. Kīngitanga's publication of its own newspaper from late 1861 represented a revolutionary (in several senses) deployment of te reo in printed form. Until now, te reo in publications had been used mainly to advance the interest of various groups of colonisers – first the missionaries, and later the state. Now, that same technology was being turned against the coloniser by a group of Māori who were challenging the Crown's absolute assertion of sovereignty over them.

The origin of using printed te reo explicitly for indigenous purposes can be traced back to a voyage to Austria made by two Māori – Wiremu Toetoe Tumohe and Te Hemara Rerehau Paraone – on the Austrian frigate *Novara* in January 1859.[59] They arrived in Vienna in October that year and began work at the State Printing House, where they soon became familiar with the various branches of printing as well as some aspects of illustration. The two focused on acquiring skills in printing for the next nine months.[60] When they left, they were given a printing press[61] which they brought back with them to Ngaruawahia after it had been assembled in Auckland. The press was used to print copies of *Te Hokioi*,[62] which became an early propaganda organ for Kīngitanga. One of its editors was Patara Te Tuhi, a cousin of

King Potatau – the first leader of Kīngitanga, who had died in June 1860. Te Tuhi, who was considered a moderate, argued in the paper for a limited and geographically restricted sovereignty for Kīngitanga[63] – a position that put him offside with other, more hard-line leaders in the movement.

Te Hokioi's output was erratic, as was its format, size and layout,[64] and in most cases its content did little more than reaffirm the partisan views of its readers. It was an important turning point in the control of te reo in its printed incarnation. Grey was initially inclined to dismiss Te Hokioi, in the hope that it would not gain extra notoriety through being the object of overt government opposition[65] (and possibly because the views expressed in the paper were not as provocative as those being aired by some other branches of Kīngitanga), but by late 1862 the government altered its position and despatched a printing press to Te Awamutu, where Gorst published a new newspaper in te reo, Te Pihoihoi Mokemoke i Runga i te Tuanui, expounding the government's position on a number of issues, as a counter-strike. Probably the best indication of how Kīngitanga regarded the potency of this official response is the fact that a Kīngitanga war party attacked the press in March 1863. By the end of the year, though, possibly because both paper and ink were in short supply, Te Hokioi also ceased production.[66] That particular battle ended in a draw.

The mounting adversity between Kīngitanga and the government over issues of land, sovereignty and culture is an obvious reason for Kīngitanga's rejection of the state school system. In Kīngitanga territories, state education and, to a much lesser extent, missionary-based education were seen as an arm of a regime that was trying to subjugate Māori and, consequently, whose presence was difficult to justify in regions where anti-Crown rhetoric and sentiment were becoming more boisterous. But this only partly explains why so many schools were closed in Māori communities, and it does not account for the decline in schools outside the areas where Kīngitanga held dominion. Māori were turning their back on schools in places that were not directly affected by this political crisis. George Cooper, the resident magistrate in Napier, portrayed Māori in that region as slipping away from the sort of settler-defined civilisation they had until only recently aspired to. Sexual morality was 'almost gone from among them', drunkenness was widespread, their religious convictions had almost disappeared, and when it came to education, it was 'hardly thought of, and, with rare exceptions, the children are growing up unable to read and write, presenting in this respect a marked contrast to their parents, who almost without exception can read, write, and cypher with fluency'.[67] The resistance to English-speaking schools in particular had spread to other regions in the late 1860s, inflamed to some extent by the wars that had flared across parts of the North Island and that were the result of the irruptive nature of Britain's colonisation of the country.

Whatever the reasons, European education was one of the early casualties. William White, a judge of the Native Land Court,[68] despaired at the reversal in attitudes towards schooling that had occurred since the 1830s and 1840s. By 1868, enthusiasm had been replaced by aversion. 'Education in this district is a dead letter,' he wrote despondently.

> I have done all in my power to impress upon the Natives the importance to them and their children that the education of the rising generation should be attended to, but, though assenting to my remarks, they will do nothing towards this object. During the last few months of last year, Mr. Matthews (the schoolmaster paid by Government) could seldom get the children to attend, though to meet their convenience several schools were established in the larger villages; no interest whatever was shown by either parents or children, until Mr. Matthews' services had to be dispensed with. Since that time, I cannot even get the Natives to converse attentively on the subject.[69]

The wars during this decade killed off most of the mission schools in Māori communities in the North Island, the majority of which were never revived afterwards – thus effectively ending the phase of missionary-dominated education.[70]

The government's will to consolidate English as the nation's main language was undiminished by the conflicts of the 1860s, however. If anything, the fighting strengthened the conviction of some legislators that their civilising programme had not gone far enough, and that their efforts to acculturate Māori into settler society needed to be stepped up.[71]

A SECULAR SOLUTION

To some of the more cynical politicians of the day, the missionaries had a poor track record when it came to teaching in English – especially after having spent more than two decades endeavouring to run schools completely in te reo. As some of the worst of the fighting in the New Zealand Wars abated, parliament again took aim at the issue of how Māori ought to be educated. This time, the state's assault on te reo in schools – and, by implication, on

Māori society more generally – would be launched without any missionary agency.[72] The first fruit of this renewed attempt to banish te reo from Māori education was the 1867 Native Schools Act, which superseded the outmoded prewar 1858 Native Schools Act. The importance of language in the proposed 1867 legislation was made clear when it was being debated in the House. The minister of native affairs, James Richmond, explained that, 'For a people in the position of the Maori race it was a first condition of their progress to put them in the way of learning the language of the inhabitants and Government of the Colony.'[73]

The statute provided for the establishment and funding of schools for 'children of the aboriginal native race and of half-castes being orphans or being the children of indigent persons', and for committees of local Māori in each education district to play a part in managing these schools in their area – although their powers were limited and their decisions could be vetoed by officials whenever it was felt necessary.[74] Part of the rationale for getting Māori involved in the revised native school system was financial: the government expected Māori communities in some instances to provide the land on which the schools would be built, and to contribute towards the teachers' salaries.[75] In addition, the government hoped that if Māori were making a clear commitment to the costs of schools in their area, they would better appreciate the value of the coloniser's education system.

The legislation also provided for special grants to be given to schools whose students demonstrated proficiency in English.[76] The central import-ance of using English in native schools was spelt out in the Act's final section: 'No school shall receive any grant unless it is shown … that the English language and the ordinary subjects of primary English education are taught by a competent teacher and that the instruction is carried on in the English language as far as practicable.' Exceptions to this would apply only in those 'remote districts' where it was 'found impossible to provide English teachers'.[77] This did not amount to a ban on te reo in schools (there was no injunction as to what language students should speak outside class times), but the effect was the same. Moreover, the fact that Māori parents would serve on the management committees required a high degree of complicity with the Act's anti-te reo (or pro-English, depending on which way you looked at it) stipulations.

One school inspector suggested a step-by-step approach to implementing the funding allocation for proficiency in English, as the best way of introducing English into schools where te reo was still the students' first

– and often only – language. He proposed that before any funding was withdrawn, some consideration should be given to the fact that English was 'one of the most difficult of languages' to learn, that it involved acquiring 'a habit of abstract thought and expression', and that it was necessary for these students to overcome 'the many prejudices such as that against industrial pursuits and habits ingrained from babyhood, which have to be overcome before a [Māori] pupil can in any way realise our European notions of a civilised being'.[78] Eradicating te reo (from schools in the first instance) was directly associated with civilising Māori. The government believed this was such a vital task for the colony to accomplish that it was preferable to exercise some flexibility in the system of funding Māori schools rather than terminating financial support as a punitive response to an insufficient presence of English in the schools. As the Kīngitanga response had shown, the state had to tread carefully when entering the world of its indigenous citizens: executing its will, but not in a manner that was unduly provocative.

Although its supporters felt that there was some altruism behind the 1867 Act,[79] there can be no doubt that it was based on calcifying settler opposition to Māori generally, and to their language and culture specifically. A typical example of this opposition was in a newspaper report on a hui in Wairoa in April 1867. The reporter, commenting on a haka performed by Māori at the hui, noted: 'Forty years of civilization ought to have taught these people the value of, at any rate, an appearance of decency but scrape a Maori, the most civilized, and the savage shows distinctly underneath.' The haka itself was described as 'an exhibition of the substratum of utter immorality, depravity, and obscenity, which forms the groundwork of the character of their race'. The answer to this 'savagery' was to change this degraded culture, and this would be achieved by 'taking in hand the education, *per force*, of the young growing saplings ... if the children be well trained the race will recover'.[80] Any mention of measures to protect the country's indigenous language or culture was met with a swift and shrill denouncement.

Such condemnation appeared, for example, in response to concerns raised by the London-based Aborigines Protection Society (not to be confused with the colony's by now defunct Office of the Protector of Aborigines) about policies that were detrimental towards native languages in British colonies[81] (of the sort exemplified in the 1867 Native Schools Act). One New Zealand newspaper editor wrote that the society's anxieties were the 'ill-considered' responses of 'well-meaning fanatics' who had made it their mission to protect 'barbarous or semi-barbarous races' against the interests of those civilising forces at work in the colonies.[82] There was no room for such misguided idealism in New Zealand, so far as this editor was concerned. The severity of the language he used indicated his depth of feeling on the matter. So-called Māori primitivism extended to the language they spoke, making its maintenance something that would counteract the colony's progress and improvement.

The series of reports on the nation's schools that preceded the passage of the legislation offer an insight into how the organs of state viewed te reo, not only in the school setting but in the wider community. One inspector wrote: 'from all that I can learn, there is at the present time a growing desire among the Maori to have their children instructed in the English language'. This desire, he deduced, had been brought about by increased interaction between Māori and Europeans in the preceding two years, which was 'daily convincing the Māoris of the disadvantage at which they are placed in respect of Europeans by their ignorance of the English language'.[83] According to this report it was Māori who were turning their backs on their own language. Officials were therefore not eviscerating te reo against the will of the indigenous population; on the contrary, it seemed to be the wish of Māori parents that schools teach only in English – something that happily coincided with the state's position on the matter.

According to some politicians, where previous governments had gone wrong in this area was by persisting in subsidising the native schools run by missionaries. Education in te reo had 'failed in [its] object', partly because of the missionaries' stubborn insistence in the 1820s and 1830s that English be excluded from the schools for Māori, and partly because officials believed that the missionaries had attempted to install a system of higher education for which 'the Natives were not sufficiently advanced, and which the religious bodies to whom the carrying it out was entrusted were unable to work out in its integrity'. And on top of everything else, there had been 'too much of the Bible taught, and too little of other subjects. They were taught moreover in their own language, whereas what they wished to learn was English,' according to William Rolleston, the under-secretary of native affairs. Henceforth, government assistance to mission-run schools for Māori should be based on the condition that the standard of English among Māori students was sufficiently high. This carrot came with a stick: one official recommending that 'no allowance should be made for any pupil who, after a certain stay [in a boarding school] did not at the periodical inspection exhibit a corresponding proficiency in the English language'.[84]

Within a year of the passage of the 1867 Act there were 17 schools around the country operating under its terms,[85] but still the rate of assimilation was not fast enough for some. One school inspector reporting on Māori education in Raglan felt that it was not entirely the fault of the 'simple Natives' that they did not appreciate the benefits of an English language-based education. He thought the problem ran deeper, to the very existence of racially separated schools. 'I believe it would be better, and far more efficient as well as economical,' he proposed, 'were one scheme provided for the education of the children of both races. I do not think that any Government scheme should pander to the pride of race assumed by some ignorant colonists who are not equal, in manners, birth, wealth, intelligence, or gentlemanly feeling, to the majority of the Maori race.' Such a system was unlikely to commence voluntarily; he suggested that 'compulsion or some other method must be had recourse to, to get both European and Maori children into school, for if they are allowed to grow up as at present and hitherto, no good to the State can come of them.'[86] The links between education in English, speaking English, and belonging to a single nation state were explicit in this report, and the drive to turn Māori into model subjects in the colony hinged on their first acquiring a fluent level of English. To use a phrase from the next century that was even more ironic in the 1860s, it was part of the Māori 'price of citizenship'.[87]

TE REO IN POWER

At this juncture, te reo's slide towards the status of an endangered language looked more certain than at any previous time. The cumulative effects of declining missionary involvement in offering schooling to Māori in te reo; legislation that discriminated heavily in favour of English in most areas of the government's operation; and a steadily congealing attitude towards te reo among settlers all connived to expel the language from the country's social landscape. And if te reo held on in some remote rural outposts then, like its ageing and declining number of speakers, it would remain as little more than a cultural relic – a slightly romantic or even quaint reminder of New Zealand's barbarous past that was also now doomed. The only 'decent' thing for the settler population to do now was to let Māori pass away into memory. In the unconscionable words of politician Isaac Featherston in 1856, when he proffered his assessment on the future of the country's indigenous inhabitants, 'The Maoris are dying out ... Our plain duty, as good, compassionate colonists, is to smooth down their dying pillow. Then history will have nothing to reproach us with.'[88] In addition to grossly underestimating history's power of reproach, Featherston, like many of his contemporaries, assumed that the decline of the culture would be like a receding tide – eventually emptying out of every crevice and exposing a very English-looking and English-sounding New Zealand. There were small eddies of te reo that remained, though – and not all the actions of the state in the 1850s and 1860s were consciously directed at their dispersal. Most notably, te reo had an ongoing, albeit ambiguous presence in the various (admittedly small) circles of the colony's government in this period.

The reasons for te reo's retention in some of the central organs of the colonising state appear at first opaque, especially as the trend to dislodge the language from the education system was gaining momentum and success during this time. The persistence of the language in the country's government was all the more surprising because the state had an overt ideological commitment to civilise Māori and exorcise them of the culture of their savage past. The two main underlying considerations to be kept in mind when assessing the nature of te reo's occasional role as a language of state authority are that its use was dictated by practicality rather than sentiment or a desire to preserve the language, and that the presence of te reo in parliament and in official documents was entirely at the discretion of the government. Te reo was thus held captive by the very people and institutions that were working towards its demise as a spoken language in the colony. Its outings were closely supervised and, predictably, the parameters of its use were heavily circumscribed. Besides, the settler administration, confident that English would soon be the country's sole language, was happy to make minor concessions to the language of the 'dying race'. In neither case, in the minds of politicians and officials, did the use of te reo in official documents run the remotest risk of a return to barbarism. It could be argued that the point at which the state was willing to employ te reo indicated that the state felt safe that the language was in no danger of reversing the inroads English was now making.

Perhaps there was also a more sinister side to the use of te reo in some of the nation's branches of government: being thrust into the centre of the apparatus of the state, its impotence would be exposed, and Māori themselves would come to realise that their language was ill suited to the modern world.[89] This might be a case of identifying a conspiracy where none exists, but it cannot be ruled out as a contributory motive – especially given the comments by the earliest Māori parliamentarians about the frustrations they felt at not being able to speak English in the House – that might help explain why the state extended what looked like a helping hand to te reo, instead of a clenched fist.

The government did not make frequent or consistent use of te reo in its printed form.[90] One of the first pieces of legislation published bilingually related to the regulation of native districts, and appeared in 1859 – after the New Zealand House of Representatives had already been churning out legislation for five years,[91] and had already passed important statutes that affected Māori.[92] This shows the low priority the government gave to te reo – and that not too much can be read into the state's apparent commitment to bilingualism.

The first Acts to be officially translated into te reo were pointedly preceded by an idealistic and paternalistic polemic on the benefits to Māori in assimilating into the ways of the colonists:

The Maori people have frequently been told that it is the earnest wish of the Governor, as the Queen's Representative, to encourage and assist to the utmost of his power those who are really desirous of elevating themselves and their people by the adoption of the civilised institutions of the Pakeha. A summary of the English Laws has been translated and placed in their hands for the purpose of enlightening them on these subjects, and they now possess the means of acquainting themselves with the principles of those just and wise laws which for so many generations have been the protection of the Pakeha and the glory of the English nation, and which every true Englishman obeys and loves, and is at all times ready to support and defend. The Acts referred to have been passed for the purpose of aiding the efforts of those Native tribes living apart from Europeans who wish to be governed and protected by the same laws as their Pakeha neighbours, and are prepared heartily to co-operate in carrying those laws into effect among themselves.

Kua tini nga meatanga atu ki nga tangata Maori, ko ta Te Kawana i tino whai ai ko te whakauru ko te whakakaha i te hunga e hiahia pono ana kia maranga ake i roto i te kuwaretanga kia hapainga hoki te iwi kia tangohia hei ritenga mana ko nga ritenga marama o te Pakeha. Te Kawana i pera ai, ko ia hoki to Te Kuini Ahua ki tenei whenua. Na, whakamaoritia ana tetahi Pukapuka whakarapopoto i nga Ture o Ingarani, tukua ana ki nga tangata Maori hei whakamarama ki era nga ritenga; takoto ana tenei kei tona aroaro nga korero whakaatuatu i nga putake o aua Ture tika, Ture

marama, i noho tika ai te Pakeha ka tini nei nga whakatupuranga tangata.
Koia hoki ko aua Ture ta to Ingarani Iwi i whakakororia ai. Koia hoki
ko taua Ture ta to Ingarani tangata pono i rongo tonu ai i matapopore
nui ai. Koia hoki ko taua Ture tana mea nui i waiho hei tiaki mona hei
hapai hoki mana. Waihoki ko enei nga Ture e rua ka korerotia nei, kua
whakatakotoria hei whakauru i era nga Iwi Maori e noho motuhake nei
i te Pakeha, a, hiahia ana kia waiho ko aua Ture tahi ano, e arahina nei e
tiakina nei o ratou hoa Pakeha, hei arahi hoki hei tiaki i a ratou, ara, i nga
Iwi ia e mea pono ana kia mahi tahi ki te hapai ki te whakamana i aua
Ture ki o ratou wahi.[93]

IN THE HOUSE

In the winter of 1860, shortly after tensions between the Crown and Māori
had spilt over into open conflict,[94] Governor Browne convened a meeting in
Auckland of 112 chiefs from around the country (about the same number
had declined the invitation) in what proved to be a futile attempt to bring
the fighting to an end or, failing that, to prevent it from spreading.[95] Browne
euphemistically described the event as 'an opportunity of discussing various
matters connected with the welfare and advancement of the two races
dwelling in New Zealand',[96] but despite affirmations of loyalty and solidarity
from many of the chiefs present, little of lasting effect was achieved by
the meeting. That is, except linguistically. This government-sponsored
conference was reported extensively in *The Maori Messenger* in both English
and te reo[97] – making it one of the most substantial translation efforts of a
government initiative published in this era.

The Maori Messenger reached as broad an audience as any other
publication in te reo (apart from the Bible) in the early 1860s, and because
it was disseminated so widely, politicians paid close attention to its
content. How influential it had become could be gauged by the bitterness
in the exchange of views in 1862 between some members of the House
of Representatives and the editors of the paper. *The Maori Messenger*
was accused of 'stereotyping and scattering through the whole country
misconceptions of a most dangerous kind',[98] and publishing statements that
were 'foolish', 'improper', 'untruthful' and 'disgraceful'. And in a reference to
the war that had recently broken out, Colenso, who was now a politician,
awkwardly suggested that 'to exclude powder and arms from the natives how
much more needful was it to exclude that much more powerful weapon –

the ill-directed pen.[99] It was not the fact that *The Maori Messenger* appeared bilingually that some found objectionable, but that some of the material it contained could be perceived as being unfavourable to government interests. And because te reo was the primary language for almost all Māori in this period, any controversy surrounding its content was likely to tilt opinions, even if only slightly, against the use of the language itself. What most likely prevented the state's translation of portions of its business into te reo from ceasing altogether was the acceptance – however grudging – among some politicians that translating some state documents into te reo was the most effective way of communicating to Māori communities and, in its absence, that important contribution to the assimilation of Māori would be lost.[100] The tacit trade-off seems to have been that this publication would continue to be issued in both English and te reo, but that the concession for having content in te reo was that it would serve the state's broadly assimilationist agenda – an arrangement that appeared to satisfy most politicians.

In 1865 parliament attempted to make its policies on translating legislation into te reo more consistent, after years of an ad hoc approach with little consideration of the relative importance of the documents selected for translation. In September a standing order was adopted that required that 'Speeches addressed to the House by His Excellency the Governor, and Bills introduced into the House specially affecting the Maoris, are translated into and printed in the Maori tongue for the information of Her Majesty's subjects of that race', and that 'All other papers are translated into and printed in Maori only by the order of the House upon motion'.[101]

Although at least a handful of Acts being printed in te reo might be interpreted as a small victory for the language, this decision must have made it quite clear to those Māori with an interest in the legislative process that this was still a system where only English mattered: if a person wanted to even be aware of the workings of the state, let alone be involved in its processes, they would need to be fluent in the language of the coloniser. This encounter between te reo and the state became more tangible when the Māori Representation Act was passed in 1867, opening up the possibility of Māori having a nominal role in parliament. Before that, Māori were positioned on the periphery in terms of not just their culture and language but their involvement in politics.

Until Māori representation was secured, parliament was even more disconnected from the country's indigenous people. Twelve years earlier, the Ngāti Rangiwewehi chief Te Rangikaheke doubted the legislative process of the coloniser could ever meet the needs of Māori. 'There is no recognition of the authority of the native people,' he wrote, 'no meeting of the two authorities … Suggestions have been made (with a view to giving natives a share in the administration of affairs), but to what purpose? The reply is, this island has lost its independence, it is enslaved, and the chiefs with it.'[102] So grim was this view of the nation's political structure from the point of view of Māori that Te Rangikaheke suggested local tribal leaders search for an alternative that would uphold 'the separate dignity and independence' of individual tribes.[103] Kīngitanga emerged as the most obvious response to this feeling of political disempowerment. John Morgan, who had closely followed the rise of the movement, later reported on the reasons for its formation; he noted that there was 'a desire to introduce a code of laws suited to their own requirements' and, above all, 'a desire to establish first in the Waikato, and afterwards gradually in all Maori districts, an independent sovereignty over all Maori and European residents in such districts.'[104]

The possibility of Māori representation in parliament was a solution to at least some of the concerns that were leading to separatist Māori bodies emerging, but as long as so few Māori met the threshold of property-owning entitlement to vote under existing legislation,[105] Māori representation looked unachievable in the foreseeable future. Still, some politicians continued to tap a seam of altruism and were keen that Māori not be shunted completely into the colony's political wilderness;[106] while others saw any move to power-sharing more cynically – as a means 'to pacify Māori'.[107]

The native minister, James FitzGerald, sought the opinion of half a dozen chiefs on the issue of fixed Māori representation in parliament in 1864, and received general endorsement for the proposal. The reply of one of those chiefs – Pohipi Tukairangi – was typical of most of the others:

> Friend Mr. Fitzgerald, this is our word to you and your companions, that you may open the doors of the Parliament to us, the great discussion house of New Zealand, for we are members of some of the tribes of this island. Let us be ushered in, so that you may hear some of the growling of the native dogs without mouths (i.e.) not allowed to have a voice in public affairs, so that eye may come in contact with eye and tooth with tooth of both Maori and European.[108]

The orality at the core of Māori culture is captured here with Tukairangi's emphasis on speaking rather than writing, and the striking metaphors he packed into his response to the minister.

After a tortuous route, the legislation to enfranchise some Māori was passed in 1867. The Maori Representation Act allowed for Māori males aged 21 and over (including 'half-castes') to vote for a Māori member of the House of Representatives. What constituted 'Māori', though, was jumbled in the legislation: only full-blooded Māori could stand for election, whereas both full-blooded Māori and half-castes were eligible to vote; the tendency by some officials to assign those with less Māori blood than half-castes to the general roll added further confusion.[109]

That most of the early crop of Māori members did not speak English fluently was a concern raised in relation to the efficacy of the seats overall, but this was overridden by the more pressing need to have that representation in the first place.[110] The language issue would presumably sort itself out over time (and no doubt, in the view of the existing members of the House, English would prevail), but until then, Māori members would continue to deliver their speeches before their fellow politicians 'in much the same way as traditional whaikōrero, calling on old alliances and past promises to deal with the problems of the present day and forge a way forward'. The result was speeches by Māori politicians that were 'noble, but they were repetitive, long-winded, and were at times misunderstood or ignored by Pākehā parliamentarians'.[111] A small gain in the form of guaranteed representation in parliament was more than offset by such a demonstrable marginalisation of te reo. The message that got through to aspiring Māori members of the House of Representatives in the remaining three decades of the nineteenth century was clear: if they wanted to make themselves heard in the House, they needed to be heard in English.

It was a clash of culture as well as language,[112] and some of the European members made sure they voiced their irritation about it. The difficulty that European politicians and officials experienced listening to speeches in te reo may have been a case of the boot being momentarily on the other foot, but that hardly deterred some of the more impatient MPs from grumbling about this supposed incursion.[113] One of the first elected Māori members in the House of Representatives, Mete Kingi, saw his role as a politician in a traditional sense and paid little deference to the arcane practices of the House. 'I have not been able to understand what has taken place in this House since I took my seat in it,' he said (in te reo), 'however I will speak my thoughts to you, and the thoughts of the Maori people, for I am an old man as far as conducting matters with my own people.'[114]

The language gulf was a source of frustration for some of the Māori members, too: one informed his European colleagues that 'the appearance of us who are called Maoris sitting here is this, we hear merely the words that are spoken, but we don't know the meaning; we are like a post standing, having neither voice nor ears.'[115] With sad predictability, the reaction of a few Europeans to the presence of Māori politicians in the House quickly descended into derision. In an account that was typical of contemporary commentaries on this issue, one journalist described

> the bewilderment of one of our Maori legislators when called upon
> to give his vote in the House of Representatives. The question was
> a proposed reduction of the honorarium paid to the members, and
> although the Maori M.H.R. had no doubt a tolerably clear insight into
> the merit of it, his anxiety perhaps arose from a fear of giving his vote
> against his intention … Just as the division took place, one of the Maori
> members (who appeared to be in blissful ignorance of the whole affair)
> seemed to hesitate as to which side he should follow as the members
> were filing past. Whips for each party got at him, and in broken Maori
> and equally broken English (why will Englishmen fancy a foreigner
> understands English better when it is mutilated?) were endeavouring to
> explain the merits of the question. The words 'Kaipai [sic] the utu,' 'They
> want to take away the utu,' 'Utu no good,' &c, served only to confound
> the sable legislator, who however at last, true to his native instincts,
> voted against the discontinuance of the payment.[116]

When Frederick Russell, member for the Northern Māori electorate (who had a European father and Māori mother) made his inaugural speech before the House, he claimed that some of the Māori members 'knew not what was said or done, not even in matters relating to Maori affairs'. The response by the member for Southern Māori illustrated the point: a journalist from the press gallery described how he 'made an attempt, in broken English, to say something, but the often repeated words "honourable members" was all that could be understood'.[117]

It was not long before some members began levelling criticism at the whole concept of specific Māori representation, holding up te reo in particular as some sort of insurmountable impediment. The accusations included that Māori members allegedly confused bills with Acts; some statutes were almost impossible to translate into te reo; Maori representation was, in general, a failure; Maori did not understand the legislative process; and many Māori found the very notion of special representation 'an insult'.[118] What politicians and officials – even those with some sympathy to the concept of Māori representation – resisted the most was the written material of parliament being translated into te reo – the very thing that Māori members themselves had sought.[119] The responses to their pleas for translation were a mixture of evasions and compromises: possibly bills directly affecting Māori might be translated; there was too little time and too few resources; summaries of legislation could be prepared;[120] and implicitly, that the onus fell on Māori to learn the language of government, rather than the government expend money and time on the language of just four members.

The trickle of te reo never dried up completely, though. Correspondence (with full translations) relating to the Crown's dealings with Māori were published in the *Appendices to the Journals of the House of Representatives*.[121] In 1868 for example, as part of the process of collecting and recording details of claims by Māori over confiscated lands, a printed form for the claimants was produced: *He Pukapuka tono ki Te Kooti Whakawa Whenua Maori, kia Whakawakia etahi Take Whenua*. But although written submissions were accepted, oral submissions were not. This reinforced the authority of the written word over the spoken alternative,[122] and excluded the oral political world of Māori from the colonial administration – in another example of te reo surviving but on the coloniser's terms.

Even the way the government translated documents into te reo was a matter of concern to more informed European observers – and, no doubt, to certain Māori readers. Colenso reminded an audience he was addressing in Hawke's Bay that Māori were 'great talkers among themselves' and 'would often spend their nights (and days too, in wet or cold weather, or on the arrival of visitors), talking and debating. They also excelled in minute description of every thing new they had seen.' The result, he said, was a language that was highly expressive and that was capable of accommodating new names and concepts, and deploying imagery and metaphor to enhance messages. Colenso recalled the letters of a Ngāti Porou chief that were 'copious, fluent, flexible, and euphonious' and that made every kind of description in te reo 'very easy' for other Māori to understand. The government's translations, on the other hand, were not of sufficient quality to make them intelligible and accessible to their intended readers. 'Why is it,' Colenso asked,

> that so many new words and phrases in broken-English are constantly being thrust forward in official Maori documents and papers as if they

were proper Maori words? Very sure I am of three things respecting such words and phrases: – 1. they are not understood by the bulk of the Maori people, if clearly by any among them: – 2. they are not required: – and – 3. the use of them is causing the sad deterioration of the noble Maori language. When a Gazette or a Proclamation, a new Act or an Advertisement, or perhaps a long Official letter, printed or written in 'Official' Maori, reaches a chief, or a Maori Village, the same is read over and over by the Maoris; and, at last, some one among them explains as well as he can each of those barbarous *patois* words and phrases to the people,—and, of course, with many ekings out of his own! But why not have printed or written the same in simple and plain Maori?[123]

Colenso identified a lack of skilled translators working for the government as the key problem, resulting in grammatical constructs in te reo that would never have been used in spoken language; unfamiliar loan words or compounds of existing words; technical and convoluted legal phrases in English translated more or less literally with no attention to their meaning in te reo; and even the use of Roman numerals such as C, D, L, V and X being used despite the fact that they were not part of the Māori alphabet.[124]

These uncoordinated and sometimes substandard efforts by the government to translate a tiny fraction of its publications into te reo in no way amounted to state support of the language. And as the Māori population continued to decline – from 55,336 in 1858 to around 47,000 by 1867[125] – there was even less political incentive to invest more time and funds in translation. It was only te reo's intractability in Māori communities that continued to force the government's hand and ensure that at least the most important government notices and legislation that directly affected Māori were translated. Otherwise, the government's commitment to civilising Māori, which was seen as even more urgent after nearly a decade of war with Māori, along with the surge in settlers who spoke only English, meant that te reo was barely noticed in the bulk of parliamentary publications, and hardly audible amid the din of spoken English in the various branches of the state. Hugh Carleton, a former inspector of native schools and, in 1867, a member of the House of Representatives, summed up the antipathy towards te reo that underlay so much of the government's approach to the 'Maori problem' – as it was seen by certain legislators – in 1867, when he addressed the ongoing war the state was waging against some Māori. He suggested that New Zealand would go bankrupt if the fighting continued for much longer, and so an alternative was urgently needed. Civilising Māori was Carleton's final solution, although, disturbingly, he aired the alternative of 'exterminating the natives' before admitting that such an idea 'could not for a moment be dreamed of' (even though he had just given voice to it in the House). Carleton argued that civilising Māori would be impossible if it was done through te reo, which he considered to be 'imperfect as a medium of thought'. The change he insisted was necessary, therefore, 'could only be eventually carried out by means of a perfect language'[126] – and of course that language was English.

WHAKAPAPA BOOKS

Te reo Māori continued to be uprooted in the European strongholds of the country and derided by some politicians. In addition, eager colonisers hoped that, on the Māori peripheries, the language would slowly wither as interaction with settler society progressively convinced Māori that their language was redundant.[127] For numerous Māori communities in the 1860s, this hope was turned on its head. Their core identity was located unambiguously in the Māori world;[128] the language and culture of the settlers was often remote and seldom seen or heard.

And what a difference this change of perspective makes. Instead of the nationwide prognosis of te reo's unrelenting decline, there were numerous sites of linguistic self-assurance dotted around the country. They may have generally been beyond the analytical stare of New Zealand's European population, but records of how, for example, Māori used text in te reo as a means of cultural expression give an impression of the indigenous culture still defining its own patterns of adjustment to literacy, and still wedded to te reo as the 'normal' language of its members.[129]

Since the late nineteenth century, the whakapapa books of some whānau have been among their most tapu possessions. These works, which combined genealogy, history, mythology, political statements, territorial information, cosmology and a range of other material,[130] began to emerge – in small numbers at first – in the 1850s and 1860s, and they are still produced today.[131] The sense of permanency that written text offered would have been more keenly appreciated as the Māori population continued to fall, and as evidence of the culture succumbing to the forces of colonisation was everywhere becoming increasingly apparent as the second half of the nineteenth century progressed.[132] For some, the whakapapa book must have looked like an uncomfortable act – at odds with centuries of oral traditions, and undermining the role of tohunga and others – but a necessary initiative nevertheless, if some of the most treasured information of hapū and iwi was to survive the advanced stages of colonisation.

One of the earliest surviving accounts of the creation of a whakapapa book offers a small insight into how Māori saw the state of their culture in this period. At a hui in the Wairarapa region in the late 1850s to discuss political and land issues, it was agreed that the three tohunga present would talk about the traditions of the area and its people. This was hardly unusual. What was unprecedented for this community, however (and probably most other Māori communities), was the suggestion that this valuable kōrero be transcribed and preserved in text. The task was taken up by Hoani Te Whatahoro, and the hui took place in January 1865 at Papawai (midway between Masterton and Martinborough).[133] The words of a tohunga were often regarded as sacred, and at times there were even strictures on who could approach a tohunga, let alone listen to what he had to say on something as important as the history and mythology of the community.[134] So where did the transcriber and, more importantly, the volume he was producing fit into this circle of sanctity? The answer represented a revolution in the tapu of the words of tohunga becoming noa (free from tapu). The permanence of text changed the dynamics of te reo's sacredness under certain circumstances, and the tohunga were the first to appreciate this: 'in olden times the house was closed by *karakia* to men outside and to those who would desecrate the house; now, because the talks were to be written, the house was open forever'[135] was the revolutionary admission of one of these tohunga in response to this development.

Because these whakapapa books, and most of those that followed, were written in te reo, it is easy to assume that they are the upholders of a branch of traditional Māori oral culture, albeit in a transcribed form. As these books were copied by others, though, the material was often edited, embellished and expanded with each copy that was made. In one case (and there is no reason to think it is unique) the notes were amplified to the point where they eventually contained four times as much text as the original.[136] That scale of enlargement, particularly occurring in a period of just a few decades, had no known precedent in the traditional, non-literate phase of Māori oral culture. Whakapapa books emerged as hybridised artefacts: part oral culture, part literate culture. And in that hybridised space, substantial changes to the type, amount, organisation and emphases of traditional Māori knowledge took place. Even the specific 'authorship' of oral histories and whakapapa was established often for the first time.[137] Ironically, the potential to store so much more material in text form, and to add to it comparatively effortlessly, increased the quantity and detail of that traditional knowledge, but at the expense of its orality. Over time, whakapapa books evolved from being transcriptions of an oral culture to substitutes for it, simultaneously diminishing the earlier discipline of committing to memory the details that were now deposited in text. The other irony about the emergence of whakapapa books is that these volumes ostensibly stored the details of oral history in a more lasting form[138] where they would be preserved from the fickleness or forgetfulness of human memory, and yet instead of faithfully reproducing oral recollections in text, they inflated their dimensions and altered their architecture. Like many disruptions to the normal transmission patterns of languages,[139] the consequences would take at least a generation to be noticed. So what looked at first to be a simple undertaking of cultural preservation in te reo through the creation of these volumes, turned out to be a more culturally and linguistically complex act, with implications that were unknown and indeed unknowable.

The emergence of whakapapa books, as with newspapers produced by Māori communities in te reo, was a case of Māori society adapting to the effects of colonisation in ways that modified their traditional culture yet firmly maintained the paramount position of their language. This was in spite of almost three decades of state policies aimed at trying to drive te reo towards the brink of extinction, and of unrelenting depopulation, rampant land loss, war, and spreading impoverishment. The language was emerging as one of the mainstays of Māori society – the single cultural trait that seemed almost immune to any assaults the coloniser might mount on it. But it was in the adjustments to new technologies and systems of communication that threats to te reo's apparent invulnerability lay.

The processes of rapid modernisation that the country was undergoing in this period – including the transition from a barter economy to a monied one; new production functions and technologies; changes in social dynamics, structures and values; the emergence of new political movements; shifts in educational requirements; and the greater concentration and centralisation of political power in the nation state – collectively contributed to te reo's persistence in the 1850s and 1860s being less a conscious act of resistance to European colonisation, and more just a matter of timing. Te reo would have to give way almost completely to English at the point where the forces of modernisation finally made this necessary,[140] and in the following century this is precisely what happened.

CHAPTER 6

Ngā Ātete

1870s to 1890s

DYING RACE, DYING LANGUAGE

The melancholy atmospherics for which the artist Charles Frederick Goldie received popular acclaim were seldom as thickly applied as in his 1913 portrait of Ngāti Awa kuia Pani. Her head is propped up by scrawny, heavily wrinkled hands as she stares disconsolately at the ground, her eyes glazed over with a mix of dread and despair. The reason for this extremely disconcerting apparition is hinted at in the portrait's title: *Memories: The Last of her Tribe*.[1] Goldie was indulging in one of his favourite themes: the imminent disappearance of Māori.[2] Far from this idea being some personal deduction, though, it was part of the received wisdom of the period.

From the 1870s onwards it was increasingly evident to nearly everyone in the country that Māori as an ethnic group were on the verge of annihilation. The causes of this were debated, as was the timing of its eventual occurrence, but the fact of impending obliteration was almost universally accepted. In January 1882 the doctor and Wellington city councillor Alfred Newman delivered a lecture in which he spoke authoritatively of the disturbing prognosis facing Māori. 'The increases or decrease of a race living in our midst must necessarily be a subject of vital interest to each of us,' he told his audience.

> That the Maoris as a whole are very rapidly decreasing, needs but little proof. Everyone who has lived long in the colony must admit the fact. The early statistics are of course very loose; but the number of the observers and their general unanimity of statement, forms a mass of evidence which there is no denying.[3]

Newman exposed the attitude of at least some Europeans towards this impending catastrophe when he calmly concluded: 'Taking all things into consideration, the disappearance of the race is scarcely subject for much regret. They are dying out in a quick, easy way, and are being supplanted by a superior race.'[4] Such a view, apparently devoid of any empathy, is indicative of how little Newman valued Māori as a people; and how highly he regarded his own culture. Māori were perceived as a barrier to the colony's progress – especially because of their annoying insistence on retaining ownership of what lands they had remaining in their possession – and so their demise would be of overall benefit to the country.[5] In the analysis of this situation offered by Newman and others there was conveniently no European culpability in this imminent 'extinction' – the rapid demise of Māori was attributable to a number of tenuous and dubious scientific causes rather than any purposeful act of destruction carried out by the state or anyone in it.[6] Two years later, the historian and lawyer Sir Walter Buller similarly claimed that 'the Maori race was dying out very rapidly', and estimated that within a generation 'there would only be a remnant left'.[7] This was, he believed, merely a case of nature demonstrating another of its cruel but unstoppable evolutionary twists.

Hovering over all of these crude and contemptuous attitudes about Māori was the spectre of social Darwinism – a relatively unrefined ideology which pitched ethnic groups against each other in a competitive fight for existence.[8] In the final three decades of the nineteenth century, advocates of imperialism, racism, Aryan supremacy,[9] anti-Semitism and eugenics had all begun employing social Darwinism in support of their respective causes;[10] its notions of the 'struggle for existence' and 'natural selection' earned it easy appeal among most categories of imperialists.[11]

One branch of the ideology flourished in the mind of Nietzsche, who in 1881 applied it to the European colonisation of the non-European world. '[E]veryone ought to say for himself: "better to go abroad, to seek to become master in new and savage regions"'[12] was how he saw social Darwinism operating in practice. At its heart, for Nietzsche and other advocates, the ideology had global implications. It tied all areas of the world in a single imperial project based on a specifically racial dimension:

> Whether we call it 'civilization,' or 'humanising,' or 'progress,'
> which now distinguishes the European ... behind all the moral and
> political foregrounds pointed to by such formulas, an immense
> PHYSIOLOGICAL PROCESS goes on, which is ever extending the
> process of the assimilation of Europeans, their increasing detachment
> from the conditions under which, climatically and hereditarily, united
> races originate, their increasing independence of every definite milieu ...
> that is to say, the slow emergence of an essentially SUPER-NATIONAL

and nomadic species of man, who possesses, physiologically speaking, a maximum of the art and power of adaptation as his typical distinction.[13]

Nietzsche's wording suggests that European colonisers were culturally predestined to dominate the peoples of the non-European world: there was little room for accommodation or compromise with colonised societies. British territorial encroachment may have been close to completion in New Zealand by the end of the nineteenth century, but the language of British cultural imperialism was as strident as ever. The empire's physical realm and commercial interests – unrivalled as they were – were the (profitable) symptoms of an underlying disposition to dominate. British politician William Gladstone had earlier summarised Britain's colonial expansion in quasi-biological terms in his 1878 essay 'England's mission', in which he suggested:

> The sentiment of empire may be called innate in every Briton. If there are exceptions, they are like those of men born blind or lame among us. It is part of our patrimony: born with our birth, dying only with our death; incorporating itself in the first elements of our knowledge, and interwoven with all our habits of mental action upon public affairs.[14]

The contemporary attitudes of settlers and the state towards te reo in New Zealand become clear when they are viewed in this context. All the callous deliberation by self-anointed experts about the Māori race dying out was in some respects a projection of their desire to utterly dominate the indigenous population: annihilation was domination in its most definite and irreversible form.

The sense by the early 1880s that this complete domination was imminent led to a shift in approach to Māori on the part of the politicians and officials, and made public opinion in some quarters even less sympathetic to Māori. Officials and ministers continued to work on land issues and other matters affecting Māori that fell under the heading of 'the native difficulty', but it was all to no purpose according to some settlers. As one newspaper editor put it in 1882:

> All the proudest tribes are humbled in the dust … The Maoris know as well as we do the rate at which they are approaching extinction. Anything like an organised opposition on their part is out of the question. A little talk, a little negotiation, and every native difficulty will disappear like the morning mist. This dying race should be tenderly treated. We, the strong, able to crush, should be kind to our brave but vanquished race.[15]

Ironically, it is possible that the very certainty of this demise blunted the civilising thrust of government policies on Māori for the previous four decades. Why expend funds and effort trying to modify a culture whose remaining time on earth was shortlived? Certainly the way the state grappled with te reo from the 1870s suggests that as the expectation spread that the Māori would soon disappear altogether, the earlier enthusiasm for expunging the language as part of the great civilising mission dwindled. Opportunities to stamp out te reo Māori in schools and other areas where the state exercised authority were less vigorously pursued, or were bypassed altogether. The European population were more inclined to treat te reo with pity instead of contempt. It was as though the culture of the coloniser was making peace with its dying adversary.

HINEMOA

Apart from its interest to a handful of people as a linguistic curio stored in the pages of dictionaries, grammars, histories and other texts that had been produced in te reo for more than half a century and were now archived in libraries and museums, the language of Māori belonged to another age in the minds of most of the population. The earlier deprecatory depictions of te reo had largely disappeared by the end of the nineteenth century. Now, as the sun set on the Māori race, there was a golden glow of romanticism and nostalgia cast over some depictions of te reo. A journalist attending a tangi in 1889 wrote, for example, of the 'beautiful poems full of noble thoughts, and dressed in the most expressive language' that were recited in te reo by the mourners. After decades of denigration and dismissal, some Europeans were belatedly discovering that there was so much more to the country's indigenous culture and language than they had appreciated. 'In the heroic work of colonisation – in the building up of a great nation – in our snow-clad peaks and noble valleys – in our burning lakes and burning mountains, and in the romantic legends of a dying race may be found inspiration enough for a hundred Illiads [sic]'[16] was how the *Auckland Star* theatrically put it.

James Cowan, historian, ethnologist and journalist, described the way traditional Maori 'poems' were 'couched in the most beautiful language and expressive imagery', containing 'the noble thoughts of a vanishing race'. Cowan believed that the reason why most of his fellow colonists had failed to appreciate te reo Māori and its oral literature was that they were familiar only with 'the Maori race from the few unpicturesque and often slovenly specimens whom they occasionally see in the city streets'. Had the majority of European New Zealanders attended a tangi or some other great gathering, he suggested, they would have been amazed at 'how poems of such delicate feeling and wealth of imagery should be found in the native language'.[17]

Perhaps the apogee of this recently acquired cloying affection for Māori culture and language was composer Alfred Hill's 1896 cantata *Hinemoa* (with libretto by Arthur Adams).[18] A review of one of its early performances by the Dunedin Choral Society suggested that the work would appeal to 'those who have not even superficially probed the mass of poetical phantasies and mystical lore with which Maori mythology and traditions are so richly invested'.[19] According to Cowan, this toe-dipping in Māori culture was part of an emerging 'craving'[20] for things Māori by a colonist population that was becoming more nationally aware. It was a form of indigeneity by proxy for New Zealand's European residents, and it came at the moment when the country's indigenous culture and language looked like disappearing. And this was the point. This sort of superficial affection for things Māori, along with the fashion for novelty borrowings (Hill even named his daughter Elsa Hinemoa) could occur because of the looming prospect that Māori would no longer be around to (re)claim cultural ownership of their language, mythology and history. These borrowings and appropriations were exercises in metaphorical tomb-raiding – only the doomed culture was taking a long time to expire.

Another European who approached te reo as little more than a moribund vocabulary to be picked over for useful linguistic trinkets was Native Land Court judge Thomas Smith, who had some knowledge of the language: the governor had asked him to translate Thomas Bracken's poem 'God Defend New Zealand' into te reo. Smith gave a lecture on 'Maori nomenclature' in Auckland in September 1892, in which he urged that the colonists, 'having adopted Maoriland as their home, and having expressed their wish to occupy it, upon equal terms with the original owners, ought not to allow the native names of places to fall into disuse, and finally be lost and forgotten' – especially the names for natural features; however, 'the Europeans,' he suggested, 'had a right to give their own names to the cities, roads, etc., which they had brought into existence.'[21]

This was a small part of the jostling for the possible roles te reo might play in the impending post-Māori New Zealand. European engagement with the Māori world had progressed in three general stages: from cultural exchange in the early decades to European cultural dominance over Māori from the 1850s and then, near the end of the century, a phase of cultural exploitation.[22] In this final stage, elements from Māori culture, including te reo, were subject to a process of identity stripping. Erroneous depictions[23] of Māori culture were becoming more common, including practices such as giving Māori names to houses in urban areas, with little awareness of their meaning. Europeans were appropriating te reo for superficial purposes, as a piece of cultural bric-a-brac to be discarded when it was no longer wanted.[24]

Of course it would be unrealistic to attempt to erect boundaries around te reo and presume that it could maintain its wholeness and continuity uninterrupted by the rampant colonisation surging around it: such expectations of linguistic purity tend to go hand-in-hand with the erosion of the language. However, what was occurring in the New Zealand as the end of the century neared was the clear degradation and marginalisation of te reo by the dominant culture; and these effects were compounded by the absence of any corrective influence, as the indigenous population seemed to be crumbling away to nothing. With the number of Māori falling from around 49,800 in 1874, to 42,650 just two decades later[25] – a decline of almost 15 per cent – their culture and language must have appeared near obsolete.[26]

A dying population was not the only threat. The marginalisation of Māori culture and language was accelerated with the onslaught of a second generation of settlers, who were more likely to be urban and therefore in even less contact with the Māori population, which was still overwhelmingly rural.[27] These new settlers were part of a more 'self-inventing' New Zealand society[28] in which there was no room for anything Māori except perhaps a few decorations, some postcards depicting sensuous Māori maidens and stern tattooed warrior chiefs,[29] and a handful of popular fiction and poetry[30] that either eulogised the passing of New Zealand's indigenous inhabitants or depicted the picturesque landscapes of 'Maoriland'[31] and its former occupants (whether noble savage or just plain savage) as the antithesis of modernity.[32] 'We stand in the parting of the ways. The young scion of New Zealand national life has begun to awake to a knowledge of itself,' wrote Henry Talbot-Tubbs, a classics professor at Auckland University College, in 1899; and, picking up the biological metaphor variously employed by Darwin and Nietzsche, the professor expounded on this point:

> There comes a time in the history of every colony – at least every colony of British origin – when the new country ceases to be a mere appanage of the old. The offshoot sends down roots of its own into a soil of its own,

and, finding there sufficiency of nourishment, no longer draws the sap from the parent stock. The connecting limb, atrophied, decays; the new life 'finds itself'.[33]

It was a cause of regret to Talbot-Tubbs that Māori still blighted the country. New Zealand had been throughout its colonial period, and still was, 'in close contact with a remote stage of human development, receiving … the stimulus of repulsion by what in it is savage'. The only concession, of sorts, was the patronisingly saccharine depiction of Māori as sometimes 'romantic, noble, uncontaminated'.[34] Either way, the impression of Talbot-Tubbs and many other writers at the turn of the century was that the country had outgrown its Māori past: there was no room left for the people and their culture, except in some limited ornamental capacity.

'ABSOLUTELY ASTONISHING'

The consequences of the indiscriminate Crown conquest and confiscation of Māori land, which had accelerated since the 1860s, was now yielding foreseeable results, including widespread impoverishment in Māori communities. This left them unable to continue partially funding native schools in their districts, so the government would have to bear the financial burden. To compensate for this, the Native Schools Amendment Act (1871) provided for Māori land on which schools were built to be vested in trusts, with some of the trustees being appointed by government.[35] Regardless of the motive, the effect of the amendment was that the government's grip on native schools tightened, and if some of the intelligence that was reaching officials was correct, greater control of Māori education – of which the 1871 Amendment Act was the latest step – was gradually advancing the anglicising cause.

In 1873 Native Land Court judge Frederick Maning wrote to his friend, native minister Donald McLean, offering his impression of at least one native school that demonstrated just how effective government policy had been in furthering English as the everyday spoken language of Māori:

> I have nothing to report except that if all your schools are going on
> as well as that at Wirinake there will soon be no Maories in New
> Zealand the small thieves are running about chattering English in a way
> absolutely unnatural to my eye and all have slates slung to their wrists

exactly in the way their great grandfathers used to sling the mere I can scarcely realise the whole business for the progress the desperate young villains is absolutely astonishing …[36]

Just how momentous this transformation was is suggested by the surprise Maning experienced at seeing young Māori speaking English: clearly, until then this had been a relatively rare occurrence. This supports the notion that, towards the end of the century, schools were once again at the frontline of linguistic change. It also bears out the theory that a group in a country that enjoys economic and political dominance – as Europeans in New Zealand did in this era – will be able to ensure their linguistic pre-eminence.[37] This is an important stage in introducing the language of the dominant culture as the mother tongue of the subordinate people.[38] In addition to the geographical advances that English was securing in New Zealand, it was making its presence felt among some younger Māori communities. It was still impossible to say at what point te reo would cease to be the first language spoken by Māori, but the probability of that happening was looking ever more certain.

The state imposition of English in schools was only part of the equation; there was evidently a growing enthusiasm among Māori in some regions for English to be taught in native schools. Spencer von Sturmer, Resident Magistrate in Hokianga, reported in 1872: 'There is a rapidly increasing desire amongst the people for the establishment of schools in their midst, for the education of their young men and children in the English language, as they begin to see that without such knowledge they will hold but a poor position in the future of the Colony.'[39] In some cases, entire Māori communities backed proposals for English to be the sole language of instruction in their schools. In June 1876 a petition presented to the House of Representatives by 'Wi Te Hakiro and 336 others' sought the creation of schools where Māori children from the age of two, just as they were beginning to speak, 'should be taught the English language, and all the knowledge which you the Europeans possess', with the hope that eventually 'our children will soon attain to the acquirements of the Europeans'. This petition was prompted partly by some of the attempts at education that had been implemented in Māori districts, which were seen by the local people as less than effective. 'Had our children received a good sound education,' the petitioners argued, 'it would have been for the benefit of both races and there would have been a return for the public moneys spent, and also for the lands of the Maoris given and the time spent, in the education of the children.'[40] The suggestions continued to flow, revealing how much consideration this community had put into the issues of language and education. Other recommendations included a shared playground for Māori and European children; a prohibition against te reo Māori being spoken at schools; and employing only teachers who only spoke English. Depending on the course the government decided to follow, the consequences were stark:

> it would be certain that in twenty-one years' time the Maori children would be on an equal footing as regards their education with the Europeans; but if the present system is to be continued, if our children were to be taught under it for a thousand years, they would [not] attain to what is called knowledge.[41]

At the other end of the spectrum of Māori opinion was the position of Kīngitanga. Its quest for political autonomy had leached into other areas, including education, where it had opposed the state's native schools altogether. This was a defiant position, but very quickly its members realised that it could be a case of cutting off their noses to spite their faces. Kīngitanga was consequently forced to run its own schools, which were conducted entirely in te reo, and endeavoured to protect them from outside interference by insisting that the government 'cease surveying, cease selling, cease erecting schools' in the territories over which it claimed to exercise its rule.[42] The government, for its part, did not force the issue, because it did not need to. By the mid-1880s, Kīngitanga's political potency had long since drained. This was manifested by a fall in membership; the authority of the king being increasingly ignored; and its former objections to the world of the coloniser dissolving. Kīngitanga's repudiation of native schools was no exception. An 1886 government report noted triumphantly that in the next six months, three more schools would be built in areas that were once under Kīngitanga's jurisdiction.[43] 'It is a matter for congratulation,' the official recorded, 'that the Natives have at last seen and acknowledged the importance of education for their children; and I hope that the example set by the Natives of the three settlements above mentioned will speedily be followed by those in other parts of my district where the juvenile Native population is numerous enough to warrant the establishment of schools.'[44] However, often it was not government policies but pressure from the local Māori community that brought about this reversal in attitude towards state schooling carried out in English. In these Māori communities, it was local kaumātua and rangatira who effectively were responsible for bringing schools back to their regions.[45]

As Māori enthusiasm for schools seemed to be on the ascent in the 1870s and 1880s, the government was consolidating its organisation of the schooling system in general. This was advanced considerably with the passage of the Education Act in 1877, which established the Education Department (it came into being two years later). Although it did not focus on Māori, the Act stated that 'any Maori shall be at liberty to send his children to a public school under this Act, subject to the regulations for the time being in force in such school'.[46] In practice, because the legislation made school attendance compulsory,[47] most Māori children would be brought into this regime at some point. Native schools were henceforth regarded as transitional institutions that would cease to serve their purpose once the assimilation process was complete. This was meant to bring about equality among the citizenry, but it was in fact a form of benign subjugation.[48] State schools would be 'entirely of a secular character', and would teach 'Reading, Writing, Arithmetic, English grammar and composition, Geography, History, Elementary science and drawing, Object lessons, Vocal music, and (in the case of girls) sewing and needlework, and the principles of domestic economy.'[49] Te reo would be nowhere in earshot.

'A CASE OF NOW OR NEVER'

The dichotomy between the state's commitment to Māori receiving as good an education as possible and its matching desire to expel te reo from schools had hardened from informal predilection into firm policy by the 1880s. In 1879, administration of the native schools had been transferred from the Native Department to the Department of Education, giving education officials much greater control over the syllabus and the language of instruction in native schools. And the following year, in what would turn out to be a fateful appointment, James Pope was made Inspector of Māori Schools.[50] Pope's long tenure in this role (23 years) and the policies he introduced and oversaw epitomised the state's sometime equivocal approach to te reo Māori in native schools – an approach that was built on the acknowledgement that te reo was still the mother tongue of practically all Māori children, but that it was also a perceived hindrance to their progress in what was now overwhelmingly and irrevocably an English-speaking colony. Pope's role in the introduction of English to the youngest generation of Māori is crucial in understanding how the transition to English becoming the mother tongue of at least some Māori got under way in the early twentieth century.

Native schools had become the Education Department's renewed focus for introducing civilisation and English into Māori communities after it concluded that the 'experiment' of Māori boarding schools, which it was hoped would inculcate students into European ways of life that they would then 'carry back … into the pā', had failed overall.[51] Pope, who was fluent in te reo, devoted himself to this revived mission with zeal. His civilising sentiment was further reinforced by his belief that the alternative for Māori was stark: to face extermination.

Pope's first major initiative on becoming inspector was to issue the Native Schools Code (1880),[52] which prescribed the sort of standardised curriculum that European schools already had in place.[53] The code also recommended that, where possible, married couples be appointed to teach at native schools; that the school buildings be of a standard equal to that of European schools; and that they promote the practice whereby some of the reading materials in English that were provided to Māori students (mainly English periodicals) were passed on to their parents. Some te reo would be permitted in classes, especially among the younger students for whom English was still a 'foreign' language. Te reo was depicted as a drawback that had to be tolerated in the interim where absolutely necessary, but with the clear understanding that the goal was its removal.

> It is not necessary that teachers should, at the time of their appointment, be acquainted with the Maori tongue. In all cases English is to be used by the teacher when he is instructing the senior classes. In the junior classes the Maori language maybe used for the purpose of making the children acquainted with the meanings of English words and sentences. The aim of the teacher, however, should be to dispense with the use of Maori as soon as possible.[54]

Pope's expressed ambition in eliminating te reo from the native schools was 'to bring an untutored but intelligent and high-spirited people into line with our civilisation'.[55]

Such was his enthusiasm for Māori education to be conducted in English that Pope wrote four textbooks for Māori students. There were other such publications that had preceded these,[56] but Pope's were the most widely used by the end of the century.[57] The link between the need to adopt European ways and subsequent health, happiness and prosperity (and even the survival) of Māori was unequivocal in Pope's publications.[58] Moreover, unlike some of their predecessors, these textbooks were exclusively in English, with only the odd word (such as 'tui' or 'pa') thrown in to provide some points of familiarity for its Māori readers.[59]

So while the number of native schools continued to increase in the 1880s (eight new ones were opened in 1888 alone),[60] they were increasingly 'native' by virtue of ethnicity only, rather than in language or curriculum.

> The work of teaching the Maoris to speak, write and understand English is in importance second only to that of making them acquainted with European customs and ways of thinking, and so fitting them for becoming orderly and law-abiding citizens. Indeed, it might be maintained that the first-named of these operations is the more important seeing that the knowledge of English ways can hardly be obtained by Natives unacquainted with the language. To teach the Natives English is therefore the raison d'etre of Native schools. If they do this work well their existence is justified; if not, there can be little advantage in maintaining a separate order of schools for this purpose.[61]

Pope was experienced enough to realise that changes currently being implemented in schools were unlikely to be as effective or as lasting if they were compromised; in this context, the main source of a compromised education was the ongoing presence of te reo in schools. He explained to the government how use of the indigenous language in schools was detrimental to Māori pupils, and he used the argument to justify the tough standards in English that he had begun to apply to native schools:

> Masters of Native schools are constantly hampered by the difficulty caused by their pupils' training in the use of Maori being continued along with the training in English that they are receiving from their teachers. It is hardly to be wondered at, then, if a Maori boy of fifteen, who has been six or seven years at school, is only tolerably successful in speaking and writing English. It seems to me, indeed, that the success achieved by our best schools is very remarkable, and that it speaks well for the intelligence and energy of the teachers. Nevertheless, no effort should be spared to secure improvement in this direction. With this end in view it has been decided to insist on a very stringent reading of the standards as far as English is concerned, and to allow no pupil to pass a standard who does not do well in that subject.[62]

In his reports to the government throughout the 1880s, Pope repeatedly stressed English as the cornerstone of his approach to improving the standards of native schools, and of enabling them to produce students who were better suited to life in the colony. 'English is the most important ... subject that the Native school teacher has to deal with,' he advised the minister in 1881. He prescribed a firm regime of introducing English to pupils at the youngest age, rather than gradually (if at all) as had frequently been the practice. 'It should always be remembered that the younger Maori children are, the more flexible are their organs of speech. A child of six or seven years of age may easily be taught to pronounce English almost faultlessly. A lad beginning to learn the tongue at the age of fourteen will always pronounce it with a strong Maori accent,' he wrote, as though even the 'Maori accent' was stigmatic and thus to be avoided. 'Hence,' he continued,

> a teacher can hardly bestow too much pains on his youngest class. He should never allow himself to think that a fairish pronunciation of words will do for the First Standard, and that, by-and-by, when the little ones get into a higher class, he will be able to make them pronounce English really well. It is indeed a case of now or never.[63]

His prescribed regime delivered the remedy Pope sought. By the late 1880s and early 1890s, the spread of English in native schools – at the expense of te reo – was noticeable in just about all regions of the country where these schools existed. In 1885 in Mangamuka, '[the] progressive improvement in the behaviour, dress, and English-speaking power of the children ... [was] very noticeable', and at Otago Heads, 'nearly all the Native children in attendance can speak English quite well, so that they might advantageously work for the public-school standards'.[64] Seven years later, inspectors reported that in Matata, 'Great strength was shown in some of the English work, the reading, and part of the writing'; in Rapaki, 'a persistent effort having evidently been made to induce a habit of answering every question by means of a complete English sentence'; in Waikouaiti, officials reported that the 'writing and the English deserve notice as being generally very good'.[65] English was making conspicuous advances among Māori youth throughout New Zealand, and te reo's greatest retreats among young native speakers were taking place in those districts that were closest to concentrations of Europeans. 'There,' Pope noted,

> the Maoris learn English in much the same way as they learn Maori; they 'pick it up.' And, no doubt, the public-school teachers of such Maori children would wonder what all the pother [sic] is about. 'Difficulty in teaching Maori children,' they would say; 'surely there is none! Maoris

learn just as readily as English children.' And this is quite true. Yet if these teachers had to deal with children that never, or hardly ever, heard a word of English out of school, they would then feel the difficulty in full force.[66]

By the end of the century, support among Māori parents for the native schools was growing in tandem with the renewed emphasis the schools were placing on English.[67] Far from engendering resistance, the marginalisation of te reo in the state's education system was seen by some Māori as an opportunity for them to improve their prospects of entering the economy and society of the coloniser, which now dominated the country.

Pope's ambition for what an ideal form of education for Māori might look like was fully manifested in the form of a boarding school in Pukehau in the Hawke's Bay region: Te Aute. The school's history in the final decades of the nineteenth century offers a case study in how the pursuit of 'improved' education for Māori left very little space for te reo. Founded in 1854 by Samuel Williams with the backing of Sir George Grey,[68] in 1878 this unremarkable school[69] appointed John Thornton (a former CMS missionary to India) as headmaster.[70] Thornton's first major decision was to model Te Aute on the English grammar school archetype[71] and, within this structure, to place the main emphasis on students achieving academic excellence, rather than merely preparing his Māori graduates to be future agricultural workers (the common objective of most other native schools and Māori boarding schools).[72] Te Aute was unashamedly assimilationist;[73] the implication was that success in the European world was the only success worth striving for, as Thornton later explained when reviewing his time as headmaster:

> I tried from the very first to raise the standard of the school, and a few years later I conceived the idea of preparing Maori boys for the matriculation examination of the New Zealand University. What led me to this idea was that I felt that the Maoris should not be shut out from any chance of competing with English boys in the matter of higher education. I saw that the time would come when the Maoris would wish to have their own doctors, their own lawyers, and their own clergymen, and I felt it was only just to the race to provide facilities for them doing so.[74]

Thornton's attitude to Māori was sympathetic, progressive for the period, but nonetheless founded on the conviction that the traditional Māori way of life was an encumbrance to progress, and therefore had to be overcome;

and te reo Māori fell into this category. When he was giving evidence before a royal commission in 1906, Thornton's responses to questions divulged something of his views on the matter:

> Do you think the presence of the English boy with the Maori boy is elevating and improving? – Yes, to a certain extent.

> And is the teaching of the English language, which is really the paramount thing, facilitated? – I would not say the Maori boys improve much in English from the English boys. They talk English amongst themselves – in fact, so much so of late that we have had to give them leave to talk Maori.

> Is that desirable? – It is desirable in this way: that we do not want them to go back to their own people to be told, 'You have learned English and forgotten your own tongue.'

> I do not think the Maori will lose his mother tongue very easily in New Zealand? – They are losing it.[75]

This testimony gives us valuable insight into how effective the school system was in this period in discouraging the use of te reo among Maori pupils. The insufficient emphasis Thornton placed on te reo in the syllabus, the widespread use of English among the pupils, and the belief that the transition among young Māori to speaking English conversationally ought not to be impeded, were collectively the embodiment of the programme for the 'improvement' of Māori pupils that Pope had been pontificating about in his various reports to the minister. It was all done with the best of intentions, but its effects on te reo – especially casting it as a language with little value in the modern world – were devastating. Even though te reo was not quickly displaced as the mother tongue of Māori – this would not happen in large numbers until after World War II – the way the language was persistently positioned as something primitive and worthless was a fundamental part of the preconditioning for this subsequent development.[76]

The experience of Reweti Kohere, a Māori former student at Te Aute, suggests that, at least for him, the environment in the school that was prejudiced against te reo Māori was less important than the sense of opportunity the school afforded: 'The knowledge that I was actually on my way to Te Aute College, that seat of learning, inspired me. I had fully made up my mind to seek knowledge – the knowledge of the white man.' He had arrived at the school knowing 'very little English', and could not even recite the alphabet,[77] but he was prepared to set aside his use of te reo for a chance at success in the European world. It was these prospects for social mobility, advanced education and improved employment opportunities that made the prominence of English – and the corresponding devaluing of te reo – in native schools and Māori boarding schools not only acceptable but desirable to many Māori.

It was not as though there was no room in Thornton's curriculum for a language other than English. Latin was introduced to Te Aute and was 'thoroughly taught' because it was essential for entry to some university courses. And, as Thornton acknowledged, there was another purpose:

> I find that the teaching of Latin in the case of Maori boys is a very valuable tool in teaching English. We try in every case to make the Latin help the English, and the English the Latin ... the two things materially assist each other. A Latin sentence has to be translated into good English, and so the study of Latin involves the building-up of English sentences; and when it is remembered that to the Maori the English is a foreign language, this is no inconsiderable point.[78]

So although Latin – a dead language – was experiencing something of a renaissance in New Zealand schools, there was no adjustment to the school curriculum anywhere in the country to strengthen the use of te reo Māori; on the contrary, its increasing marginalisation left it marooned as the language mainly of the kāinga (village). Yes, it was still the mother tongue of most Māori, but the geographical areas where it could be spoken were – like Māori land tenure itself – continually shrinking. So too were its applications contracting. It remained the language of conversation, ritual and inter-hapū and iwi politics; but in commerce, education and employment, even within regions with majority Māori populations, English was being used more often – a progressive trend influenced enormously by the state's strongly assimilationist education regime.

FAITH IN TE REO

Assimilationist intent did not always work to the detriment of te reo; it appears that the effects of the process depended more on who was in control of the assimilation. In the sphere of education, state direction led to te reo being excluded from most schools and its value being denigrated.

In the case of religion, the picture was quite different. Towards the end of the nineteenth century, some denominations persisted in ensuring that te reo remained a fixture in parts of their organisation. Meanwhile, increasing numbers of indigenous sects that were a hybrid of Christianity and traditional Māori beliefs became faiths in which te reo could be spoken, and drew on the sanctity that the language possessed.

The Anglicans had the longest tradition of using te reo, dating from the arrival of their church in 1814, after which, for at least two decades, services were conducted, hymns sung and scriptures read exclusively in the language of the Māori. In the 1860s, though, the Anglican Church lost a great deal of its Māori membership, partly because it was seen as siding with the Crown during the campaigns against 'rebel' Māori, and was perceived to be too sympathetic to the settlers.[79] Some of this lost support was subsequently clawed back, but the percentage of Māori who were Anglicans never again reached the high levels of the pre-1860s.

Towards the end of the century Anglican Māori schools were leading the way with the displacement of te reo for English, but within the church itself te reo still held a position of some prominence. An example of this took place in February 1884 in Parnell, the centre of Anglicanism in Auckland, at a ceremony for the ordination of two Māori clergymen – a deacon and a priest. Bishops, priests and a large contingent of Māori packed St Mary's Church for the event. A journalist who was present recorded that the ceremony 'was almost altogether conducted in the Maori language' and that it was led by the Bishop of Auckland, the Right Reverend Dr William Cowie, 'who displayed an unexpected proficiency in the Maori language'.[80]

Cowie was an enthusiastic advocate for the use of te reo in the church, which had maintained the language mainly because a de facto Māori branch of the church had emerged[81] in which – depending on the perspective of the viewer – elements of Māori culture and language could be shielded and protected, or isolated and marginalised. Cowie was active in appointing Māori clergy and supporting Māori church boards, which had become a fixture of the Anglican Church by the 1880s.

One example of how te reo had lodged itself in a corner of the church relates to the formation of the Diocese of Waiapu in 1858.[82] The following year William Williams was consecrated by Selwyn as its first bishop,[83] presiding over a region where Māori were a substantial majority of the population.[84] Selwyn was keen on ordaining Māori who could preach in te reo, and by the 1860s a small coterie of Māori preachers had been accepted into the clergy. In the 1870s and 1880s, much of the work of the church in the diocese – both spiritual and temporal – was conducted in te reo as the most effective means of both accomplishing the tasks of the church in the region and engaging local Māori.

At times, the reports of the diocese in the 1870s and 1880s offer a glimpse into the priorities some Māori gave te reo. Williams mentioned at a hui held in Pakowhai in December 1872 that there was Māori resistance to teaching English[85] – an apparent anomaly in the otherwise strengthening support in Māori communities around the country for English to be taught, revealing that there was definitely no uniformity in Māori opinion about the linguistic changes that were occurring. In 1883 a request came from the church's Maori Board in Waiapu for more biblical texts to be printed in te reo, and in 1884 there was a request for a map of the region to be printed in te reo. In 1890 the bishop noted in the minutes of a diocese meeting that most of the Māori in the area were still not fluent in English and, consequently, all the work of the diocese was still carried out in te reo.[86]

These small bastions of te reo in the Anglican Church were not exempt from the pressures English was exerting elsewhere in the colony; and at an Assembly meeting in March 1887 in Parawai, the bishop of Auckland requested that Māori children connected with the church be permitted to learn to speak and write English. Yet in 1897, the archdeacon of Waikato advised Māori not to make the mistake of rejecting their language altogether:

> E hari ana au mo te tokomaha o nga tamariki Maori i akona ki te reo Ingarihi: ma reira hoki ka tuwhera ai nga pukapuka matauranga e kore nei e taea te whakamaori. Otira, kaua e whakaparahakotia to koutou ake reo. Kaua koutou e tango i nga tikanga pohehe a te Pakeha, engari hei nga mea e hua ai te pai, te marama, te ata noho.[87]

> (I am happy that so many Maori children learned the English language as it is through this that the books of knowledge, which are unable to be translated into Maori, are open [or available]. However, do not be dismissive of [or derogatory to] your own language. Do not pursue misguided practices [or customs] of the Pakeha but partake of the things that result in benefit, understanding and peaceful settlement.[88]

The Anglicans were not the only church in which te reo Māori maintained a presence long after it had fallen away in most other areas of the country, outside of Māori communities. The Methodists (formerly the Wesleyans) persisted with their historical commitments to te reo, although their congregation was much smaller than that of the Anglicans[89] and the presence of te reo was accordingly less apparent. Both denominations had a long history, and both had initially operated solely in te reo in New Zealand. The Salvation Army (formed in 1865), however, had no such background in the country, yet in 1888, just five years after the first two Salvation Army officers were sent to New Zealand, it proposed to send a group of missionaries throughout the country who were 'versed in the Maori language to carry on the work amongst the Natives of New Zealand'.[90] In these Christian denominations at least – and among the Catholics notably in parts of Northland – te reo was still the language of Māori Christian faith.

One of the more vigorous and in some ways ambitious responses by some Māori communities to the challenges of colonisation was to form new religious movements. These infant sects were in the category of innovation that Edward Gibbon referred to in 1776 as concoctions of corruption and error. In some ways they offered a doctrinal compromise to a people whose traditional religious and spiritual precepts were in a state of turmoil as they collided with one of the world's most formidable and potent civilisations. Traditional Māori beliefs – derided by the missionaries as primitive prejudices – had gradually fallen into decline; but not all Māori found the transition to the new religion an easy process: the associations with their cherished 'old ways' could not always be severed as simply as some missionaries and colonial officials might have hoped. The result was a series of attempts by some Māori at an indigenous interpretation of Christianity, in which elements from both the traditional and introduced beliefs were combined. In the series of 'fusion faiths' that emerged from this process, the strictures of each doctrine were loosened, and new dogmas were fabricated to accommodate the ambivalent requirements of their members.

These experiments in theological fusion, which were most common in regions where Māori had come into some contact with Christian missionaries, tended to be shortlived. The majority did not survive the century, and those few that did managed to do so by further processes of adapting and reinterpreting tenets of their faiths. What all these sects had in common, however, was a steadfast dependence on te reo as the language of their religiosity, despite borrowing or reinterpreting doctrines, rituals and structures from the churches of the coloniser. In matters of sacredness, the adherents of these sects almost instinctively believed that English could not hold a candle to te reo Māori, on the basis that te reo had a much longer history in the country as a language used for sacred purposes.

Around 50 of these hybrid sects flowered in the nineteenth century.[91] The major ones were Ringatū, Paimārire[92] and Nākahi.[93] Each was, in its own way, a faith of defiance against what its members saw as various forms of European intrusion. Settlers tended to view some of these religious movements as a retrograde step. John Logan Campbell, one of the early Auckland settlers, for example, interpreted the wars of the 1860s as proof of 'the utter failure of all missionary labour when the newly-converted tribes fell away from the Christian faith – faith indeed! – and invented new faiths of their own and ran riot in them'.[94] Others were equally cynical about the motives of some of these recently formed sects: some argued that the object of certain 'Maori religions' was 'to detach the Maori people from Christianity and so relieve them from any scruples which the profession of Christianity might cause them to entertain with reference to some of the measures which their leaders might think fit to adopt in the prosecution of War against the Pakeha'.[95]

The urge to 'detach' from European society was certainly an influence and a point of appeal for many of these sects – and it resulted in a linguistic demarcation of sorts. Te reo became, to an extent, a language of defiance that was used by these sects in their rites and rituals in one way as a sign of protest against the spread of English (among much else). More importantly, with the doctrines of these sects in a way codified in te reo, this gave them a more traditional linguistic resonance. And because they were new creations, tradition was otherwise in short supply in these religious movements.

The religious language of these recently conceived sects borrowed heavily from the language of the Māori Bible.[96] In this way, the currents of language became convoluted: the Māori language of Christianity, as introduced by the missionaries, was appropriated by these sects to varying degrees, and merged with the language of pre-European Māori beliefs. The result was an amalgam that combined indigenous and colonial traditions to produce something that was theologically new (albeit compromised), and linguistically ambiguous. Aspects of the Ringatū sect, for example, show just how embroiled these two traditions of language were with each other. Ringatū came from the mind of Te Kooti Arikirangi Te Turuki – a soldier, accused spy and religious leader who experienced visions while he was imprisoned by the Crown in 1866 on the Chatham Islands.[97] The story of Te Kooti's escape from imprisonment, the years he spent on the run from the Crown and the nearly 20 years he and his followers were exiled from their homelands became part of the sect's religious myth-narrative, which simultaneously used the structures of traditional Māori oral culture for its transmission while explicitly appropriating the biblical accounts (in Māori) of the exile of the Israelites, with Te Kooti casting himself as a Māori Moses wandering through the wilderness (of the King Country) to a promised Canaan. In the 1870s, Te Kooti introduced and standardised the sect's rituals, and disseminated its doctrines and his prophesies through meetings at various marae[98] where – again – the traditional Māori oral culture was used for a culturally hybrid religious enterprise, with all aspects of this faith based entirely in te reo.

This tilt to the traditional was offset by Te Kooti's acts of writing down in his diary details of some of his visions and, later, having three secretaries transcribe his statements and predictions. But just at the point where te reo was being used in a written form to consolidate the sect's tenets, these written records were put into storage in a secret location and were initially kept out of reach of all but a select few Ringatū members. Consequently, the sect as a whole reverted to its oral form, although – somewhat paradoxically – with a text at its doctrinal core.[99] This suited the more traditional approach Māori had to religious topics; but at the same time, the direct links that Te Kooti drew with the fate of the Israelites in the Old Testament effectively grafted Ringatū with an oral tradition from the Middle East,[100] bringing about for Te Kooti's followers a change[101] to the interpretation of the Bible and, to a lesser extent, in te reo itself as a spoken language.

Te Kooti's near contemporary, Te Whiti o Rongomai, developed a religious movement that was similar in many respects to Te Kooti's[102] but that accentuated even more the resemblance between the Old Testament narratives and the experiences of Māori in the mid-nineteenth century. Te Whiti's preaching, prognoses and prophesies were delivered entirely in te reo,[103] which, as with Ringatū, gave his sect an air of traditional indigenous authority, notwithstanding the foreign origins and comparatively recent arrival in New Zealand of some of the ideas and histories from which it was assembled.

What these and other nineteenth-century Māori religious movements clearly demonstrated was that the lexicon of te reo Māori had grown to accommodate new concepts, cultures, and even new ways of contextualising the past. This made the language more robust, not only because it had an expanding vocabulary but because it was expanding in an organic way, as needs determined, rather than as the result of some contrived effort at relexification. This constituted a threat to Māori culture – whether because it was a sign of assimilation,[104] or because it enabled the culture to draw on other sources and forms of knowledge, thereby making the culture more robust, adaptable and relevant. Te reo's capacity for expression continued to increase, aided by developments such as the formation of these sects. And the fact that this lexical expansion was being driven by Māori, as opposed to the missionaries, clearly showed that Māori had retaken control over the development of their own language.

MATTERS OF INTERPRETATION

From 1868, when the first Māori-speaking policians were elected to the House of Representatives, te reo held on to its place in New Zealand's parliament, but its presence remained slight. Part of the reason for this, especially before the 1890s, was a shortage of Māori politicians who were fluent in English.[105] Metekingi Paetahi, who was the inaugural member for the Western Māori seat, lamented in 1870 (in te reo, with his words translated) the extent to which the House was alien to Māori culture, politics and language:

> I have been here for four weeks in the House and have said nothing.
> Tareha and I have been in this Parliament for three years. Although,
> perhaps, we may not understand all the matters which you discuss,
> still, my opinion is that we may be allowed to say a few words on Maori
> matters. We are not familiar with your language, and therefore cannot
> follow all the points which are adduced in respect of the laws. It is
> through our not having any knowledge of your language that we have
> been silent during the time the Assembly has been sitting.[106]

It is a measure of the lack of priority given to the language that Māori had to wait until 1872 before the first bill (the Native Councils Bill) was translated and printed in te reo Māori.[107] The translation of this bill demonstrated what a difference it made to Māori engagement in the political system: at hui around the country, Māori debated its contents and decided whether to endorse or reject the bill.[108] Had it appeared only in English, such discussions would not have been possible, and those communities would probably have been none the wiser about the planned legislation that would affect them. The Native Councils Bill was designed to allow Māori in parts of the country to settle disputes in proposed Māori councils, rather than having to resort to the colonial court system;[109] and informing Māori, in te reo, of this planned initiative was a measure aimed to improve the chances of the success of these planned councils.[110]

The arguments about the need for translations into te reo of some aspects of parliamentary business ran both ways. In 1875, an exchange between some of the Māori members of the House of Representatives about the difficulties of following parliamentary proceedings in English led McLean, the native minister, to note before the House that this was 'a reason for inducing the Native youth of the country to attend the English schools and to acquire a knowledge of the English language'. He hoped that within a few years there would be a new generation of Māori in parliament who would not only be able to speak English, but would 'adopt English customs'.[111]

The issue of whether to keep on translating parliamentary business into te reo continued to bubble under the surface, and intermittently burst through. One member, John Sheehan, spoke in favour of translating more bills into te reo on the basis that there was no alternative if the government was serious about protecting Māori interests in the House.[112] McLean offered a concession of sorts by agreeing to continue to provide translations where necessary, but still there was no commitment to extending the provision of translation services beyond the present bare minimum.

From the 1880s there were three interpreters serving in parliament;[113] and from 1881, extracts from *Hansard* were produced in te reo – a practice that was maintained until 1906.[114] Some European members resented the expenditure associated with having interpreters – meagre though it was – but their opposition was likely based on motives other than frugality.[115] As an indication of the relative cost, one newspaper editor informed his readers in 1899: 'While it only costs £50 to wash the towels for the House of Representatives, it costs £25 a year to interpret the Acts in the Maori language.'[116]

There was one problem with the interpreters, though, that was far more important than the cost of providing them, and that was the quality of their work. Such were the concerns about the variable standards across all affected government departments that, in 1888, the Native Land Court Amendment Act stipulated that henceforth, 'All existing licenses to interpreters shall terminate on the thirty-first of December next, and new licenses terminable at any time on revocation shall be issued only to persons of approved moral character and proved knowledge of the Maori language.'[117] There had been innumerable problems with transactions relating to Māori land – both among Māori and between Māori and the Crown – as a result of details on conveyancing documentation being translated by 'incompetent' (and possibly corrupt) interpreters;[118] it was this latter defect that had prompted the clause about the moral character of translators.

Doubts were raised in the Legislative Council in 1886 about the quality of translations being produced by government departments, with Walter Mantell drawing attention to the translation of technical legal material into te reo. He noted, for example, that words such as 'tenata' and 'kamana' were appearing in translations, 'which he had never before seen in Maori and which he knew were not English'. The intended meaning, as 'a skilled Maori scholar' told Mantell, was 'tenants in common'.

The rate of neologisms being created in te reo, particularly in the area of law, was a significant issue in terms of who could comprehend the language. Mantell claimed that when he read official publications in te reo, 'in almost every line he would meet some word which was neither Maori nor English'. This could have severe consequences. As long as Māori could be 'induced to accept gibberish' (his word for these new terms), the legal fraternity would 'be able to prey upon their ignorance'.[119] Mantell's solution was to ask for an agreed list of neologisms in te reo Māori to be drawn up. The challenge was how to translate words from English, especially highly technical ones for which there was no close equivalent in te reo. The matter was referred to officials, for whom lethargy had become a form of strategy, and consequently nothing further was done on this issue for the remainder of the century.[120]

LAND, POLITICS AND THE LANGUAGE OF POWER

It has become almost de rigueur in studies of colonial New Zealand to condemn the nation's colonial governments, especially from the 1870s onwards, as being almost fixated on land grabbing and on eradicating vestiges of Māori authority and civilisation, of which the language was an obvious casualty.[121] There are undoubtedly abundant examples of huge swathes of Māori land being deliberately targeted by officials and sometimes unethically (albeit 'legally') acquired with the assistance of politicians. Likewise, many legislators shared a distaste for aspects of Māori culture, and the conviction that te reo was a redundant language. Equally, however, a handful of politicians and officials were convinced that overall the government ought to do its best to protect Māori interests rather than trample over them. These dissonant motives – apparently at once avaricious and philanthropic – have a bearing on how the state's attitude towards te reo can be assessed as the century's end approached. The issue was not always clear cut: at times, the state might be both opposed to and in favour of the Māori language and culture. This makes it difficult to draw any general, all-embracing conclusions about the views of successive governments towards te reo, other than to observe that the consequences of their policies in this period contributed to the further marginalisation of the language.

The case of a grievance aired by some Māori politicians in 1883 illustrates the ambiguity of the state's approach to Māori issues. On 12 October that year, the secretary of the Aborigines Protection Society in London forwarded to the Secretary of State for Colonies a copy of a letter the society had received from the four Māori members of the House of Representatives – Wi Te Wheoro, Hone Mohi Tawhai, Henare Tomoana and Hori Kerei Taiaroa.[122] The letter, signed by these four Māori politicians and said to have been written on behalf of their tribes (that is, all Māori in the country), sought to have the wrongs committed against them by the Crown addressed in the hope thereby 'to preserve our race from a decay that has already made rapid advance among us, and which now threatens to sweep us entirely from the land of our fathers'. The specific subject of their complaint was the operation of the Native Land Court, which the writers accused – with some merit – of often being 'very unjust'. In addition, the authors of the letter claimed – again with some justification: 'Every year laws are made taking the control of land more out of our hands, and vesting it in the Minister for Native Affairs, and our voices being but four are powerless against eighty-seven representing the European portion of the population in the New Zealand Parliament.'[123] The governor responded: 'In cases in which it is possible, great care is taken by the existing law to respect Maori customs and feelings.' To illustrate this, he pointed out that

> the succession to property is according to Native custom, not English
> law; in criminal cases where both prosecutor and prisoner are Maoris,
> the prisoner may claim to be tried by a Maori jury; and in civil cases,
> where both parties are Maoris, either may claim a Maori jury, or if only
> one is a Maori, he may claim a mixed jury. Special arrangements are also
> made with reference to the representation of Maoris in Parliament and
> on the Licensing benches.[124]

These were areas where the state had indeed made concessions to Māori (irrespective of the underlying motives).

The native minister, John Bryce, was less circumspect: he blasted the letter from the Aborigines Protection Society. He pointed out that it could not have been agreed on fully by the four members because of its obvious partiality towards Kīngitanga (to which some of the signatories of the letter were opposed), and he noted that the Native Land Court[125] could determine native title 'by the best ways and means, irrespective of legal technicalities, being guided in its decisions by Native custom'. Bryce followed up this statement with assurances about the formation of native committees to work with the court, and other measures to ensure that the Māori voice was heard during proceedings. From this, it looked as though some degree of protection was already in place for the country's indigenous people and culture as the state continued with its programme of individualising the title to Māori land.[126]

In particular, te reo was used in testimony before the Native Land Court. This represented a major intersection between the country's judicial system and its indigenous population, mediated through two languages instead of only that of the coloniser. The purpose of the Native Land Court was to 'provide for the ascertainment of the persons who according to such [Māori proprietary] customs are the owners', and to establish rules for the transfer of land which partly accorded with Māori custom.[127] But as with every other encounter of te reo with the state, the Native Land Court was hardly a neutral place for the language to be spoken. Thomas Lewis, an official in the Native Department in 1891, testified in a surprisingly candid way about the ideological basis of the court; concluding that

> the whole object of appointing a Court for the ascertainment of Native title was to enable alienation for settlement. Unless this object is attained the Court serves no good purpose, and the Natives would be better without it, as, in my opinion, fairer Native occupation would be had under the Maoris' own customs and usages without any intervention whatever from outside.[128]

The reduction of the Māori population that had been evident in New Zealand since the 1820s was continuing unabated at the close of the century, and this gave the settler society a very firm upper hand. 'There are between thirty thousand and forty thousand Maoris scattered over the whole of the North Island: the European population of the colony exceeds half a million, and is rapidly increasing,' Bryce informed the governor in 1884. 'It is self-evident that the Maoris must cast in their lot with the Europeans, accepting their institutions and laws. Any other course would assuredly result in disaster to the Native race.'[129]

Developing a clear impression of whether Māori were being sanctioned or shunned by the state depends on which voice you listen to. Many Māori felt they were being politically and economically subjugated by successive colonial governments. This feeling manifested itself in the various attempts made at self-government, all of which failed to realise the over-ambitious aim of achieving autonomy by somehow wriggling loose from European rule.

So while some politicians in parliament proclaimed that they were acting in the interests of the nation's indigenous people, many Māori saw little reason to be thankful for such 'assistance' and were instead looking within for solutions to the grave problems their society was facing. Supporters of the various Māori autonomy movements that flowered around this time saw these as the last best hope in countering the state's usurpation of the final vestiges of Māori authority in the country. From a linguistic point of view, these movements were places where te reo was, almost without exception, the sole language of communication and, therefore, of Māori political power.[130] As a consequence, that power extended only as far as the use of te reo did – as was evident in the case of the Kīngitanga delegation to London in 1884.

The Kīngitanga movement, although its political influence was much diminished by a rapid fall-off in adherents since the 1870s, refused to concede defeat and persisted with its structures, which operated in te reo only. In 1884, in an effort to reclaim some political momentum, King Tawhiao, the leader of Kīngitanga, led a group of supporters to London to plead their case before the Queen for Māori land rights to be restored. They got as far as Lord Derby, the Secretary of State for Colonies, before whom Tawhiao stated, 'I am called a king, not for the purpose of separation, but in order that the natives might be united under one race, ever acknowledging the supremacy of the Queen, and claiming her protection.'[131] It was a noticeable retreat from the extensive sovereignty that Kīngitanga had sought in the 1860s, and importantly, from a linguistic perspective, 'The chiefs spoke in the Maori language, and the Rev. F.H. Spencer, of New Zealand, interpreted during pauses made to enable him to do so.'[132] This was a tacit acknowledgement that English was the language of political authority and that, at the centre of the British Empire, te reo had very little standing.

As Kīngitanga's influence receded from the 1870s, and its prospects of leading Māori resistance to Crown rule were all but extinguished by the 1890s, other attempts were made to fill the void. One of the leading autonomy movements that had effectively displaced Kīngitanga by the early 1890s was Te Kotahitanga – a pantribal body[133] whose principal aim was for Māori to be able to legislate in their own parliament, for themselves, in order to resolve land grievances with the Crown, to regain rights to fisheries that had been taken by the state, and to be able to decide on future policies affecting Māori without the interference of the colonial government.[134] It established a Māori parliament and various other paraphernalia of a state-in-waiting, although its achievements existed more in the minds of its supporters than in any authority it was able to exercise.

By 1893, Te Kotahitanga was involved in petitioning the government to grant it the right for Māori to manage their own property and to govern Māori 'so that peace and happiness may reign throughout these islands'.[135] At the same time, some of Te Kotahitanga's leaders produced petitions urging the government to stop passing certain legislation,[136] on the basis that Māori had had little input into these statutes that affected them. These were just the latest efforts in a long line of letters, speeches, petitions and pleas from Māori that had landed on the deaf ears of government. This ongoing lack of official response prompted a change of tactics by Te Kotahitanga: its leaders realised that more direct action was needed if their concerns were to be given any consideration by the state. That action would need to take the form of a Te Kotahitanga leader being elected to parliament – the core of the European system of power. Te Kotahitanga secured this foothold in 1893 when Hone Heke Ngapua was elected member for Northern Māori. There was now a confluence of the two tributaries of Māori political expression: Te Kotahitanga and the House of Representatives.

Ngapua, who had worked as a law clerk and was an official translator in the Native Land Court before he entered parliament,[137] was a rangatira through his whakapapa connections on both his mother's and father's side, and he had been one of the leaders, organisers and main speakers for Te Kotahitanga.[138] His initial purpose in entering the House of Representatives was to spearhead Te Kotahitanga's programme, and his first priority there was to present the Native Rights Bill. This proposed legislation had been drafted mainly by Ngapua, and he had refined it as he travelled around much of the North Island in the previous three years, building support for its cause.

The Native Rights Bill sought to abolish the Native Land Court, which was regarded as an instrument of land appropriation; to assert the right of Māori to make their own laws in some areas; and to ensure Māori control of reserved lands and land development. All the hui held in its planning stages, as well as the resolutions that emerged regarding the bill, were in te reo, but when it came to introducing the planned legislation in the House to give effect to these revolutionary political aspirations, the language used had to be English. This was in itself a symbolic concession (just as the translation of Tawhiao's words in London had been): language was the instrument of political power. In the case of the Native Rights Bill, the fact that it had to be presented in English symbolically signalled its inevitable fate: at its first reading, all non-Māori members walked out of the debating chamber, thus denying the bill a quorum.[139]

Supporters of the bill did not see its translation into English as in any way detrimental, though. English was slowly becoming the language of national Māori politics in the House of Representatives, with a new generation of Māori members who were fluent in English as well as te reo displacing the first echelon, who spoke just te reo in the House, and tended to do so only very occasionally.[140] By the 1890s, this new crop of Māori politicians were inclined to deliver almost all their speeches before the House in English, and spoke much more frequently.[141] Wi Parata, the member for Southern Māori, saw this knowledge of English as an asset for Māori politicians. According to him, 'The class of Native who should be called to that position is a man who can look at things from the European standpoint … and can identify himself with European ideas and habits of thought, and in that way perhaps do some good to both races of the people.'[142]

Clearly there was a tension emerging between English and te reo as the preferred language Māori politicians were using to pursue their political aspirations. Those movements where te reo was the sole or predominant language were the ones that had failed to make any real headway for close to half a century, and would survive into the 1900s as only a shadow of their former selves. On the other hand, Māori politicians in the House of Representatives were achieving small victories around this time, in areas such as the establishment of Māori councils and improved health provision to Māori communities. These minor triumphs had been reached through the politicians conducting their business and arguing their case in English. Forsaking te reo in the seat of the nation's power was the price extracted by the coloniser for such advances.

From the 1890s onwards it was Māori politicians who were giving ground linguistically, polishing their English skills to better their chances of achieving gains for their causes. Te reo was appparently not one of those causes, and as it gradually disappeared from debates and documentation in parliament, it was being progressively eliminated from the centre of power and cast further to the political margins of the country. And although it may not have been intentional, in this case, te reo was being marginalised in part through the actions of Māori themselves in the House.

CHAPTER 7

Te reo Māori in 1899

The survival of te reo Māori into the twentieth century was one of New Zealand's great escape acts. By 1899 the language and its indigenous speakers looked to just about everyone to be doomed. The colony's self-proclaimed literati, sensing they were witnessing something fateful yet vaguely majestic, were quick to churn out elegiac prose and verse on the subject. '[T]he blood of the Maori and the pakeha will not mix. Where the one plants his foot, the other fades into nothingness'[1] was novelist Jessie Weston's summation of the respective fate of Māori and Europeans in the 1890s. In one of Weston's books, a female Māori character decides to return to her community; she explains her decision with the melodramatic line: 'The night that has fallen upon my race has fallen upon me, and it is well that I should share the darkness with my own people.'[2] Arthur Adams – Alfred Hill's lyricist – conveyed in verse the pathos of a race and culture that was about to end:

Land where all winds whisper one word
'Death!' – though skies are fair above her.
Newer nations white press onward:
Her brown warriors' fight is over –
One by one they yield their place,
Peace-slain chieftains of her race.[3]

It was all suitably sentimental, yet devoid of empathy. For some Europeans in New Zealand at the end of the nineteenth century just about everything to do with Māori – the art, culture, language and even the people themselves – had been reduced to a sort of abstraction. These Europeans had a concept of Māori, but that was as far as their knowledge went. As a *New Zealand Herald* report put it in 1899 – obviously for its overwhelmingly European readership – Māori and Europeans had lived together 'for nearly two generations, but, as yet, no one will call them our people'; and, later, 'The people in Auckland city have no conception of the Maoris of the North.'[4] Assimilation evidently had a long way yet to go.

For Māori, the prospect of not surviving as a people for much longer was not easy to contend with: there was no precedent to draw from and no notion of how to grapple with imminent disappearance. What did matter – if a hui held at Papawai in February 1899 is anything to go by – was the hope that, even if Māori themselves did not last that much longer, at least their culture and language might be preserved in perpetuity through text. At this hui, Tamahau Mahupuku reminded those in attendance of the advice that James Carroll, the nation's first Māori Cabinet minister, had given recently. Carroll had recommended that the histories, whakapapa and all the other talk that had been handed down orally in Māori communities be collected while there were still elders around to pass on this information and explain its significance. The hui duly formed a committee to manage this process, and books were filled with the handwritten transcriptions of this detailed and precious kōrero, almost without exception in te reo.[5] For some Māori, there was an encroaching sense that their history, culture, and only to a slightly lesser extent language, were being memorialised. This was one of the inevitable consequences of this drive to 'preserve' what might otherwise be lost.[6] The fear that an entire culture was on the brink of disappearing served to focus people's minds on the value of that culture, but more as an endangered object in need of protection than as the culture and language of a thriving society.

Elsewhere the prognosis was more hopeful. In September 1899 the Auckland branch of the British and Foreign Bible Society authorised the printing of around 3000 Bibles, New Testaments and portions of the Scriptures, of which about 10 per cent would be in te reo for Māori readers.[7] Three months later, the Southern Maori Mission Committee reported that it was distributing religious materials in Māori through the Otago region and that they were being received by Māori with 'great acceptance'.[8] There were calls for further revisions to the Bible in te reo, too, so that its text more closely resembled the vernacular form of the language. But with the existing stock still only partially distributed, Reverend Fred Spencer, the highly effective agent of the British and Foreign Bible Society in the colony,[9] who was reasonably fluent in Māori, was hesitant about further efforts in this area. 'The Maoris should at least wait,' was his verdict.[10]

On 10 February 1899 one of the country's most prominent missionaries from an earlier age in the colony – William Colenso – died in Napier, with his own major contribution to te reo still incomplete. Six decades earlier, he had begun work on his Māori–English lexicon[11] (some of the content of which was later incorporated into Herbert Williams' *A Dictionary of the Maori Language*),[12] and in 1865 he revived his efforts when the government contracted him to compile a dictionary which – in the ambitious wording of the officials – would contain 'every known word in the Maori tongue, with clear unquestionable examples of pure Maori usage'. In 1870, however, the government cancelled the agreement with Colenso and the project once again lost momentum until the 1890s when Colenso, now retired, revisited it: he managed to publish a portion (words beginning with 'A') of his planned magnum opus in 1898. In his will, Colenso bequeathed his incomplete dictionary and editorial notes to the state 'with the expressed wish that it shall be shortly completed'.[13] The task was handed over to Herbert Williams, a translator, who was openly critical of the work: he argued that despite Colenso's 'intimate acquaintance with the language, the author lacked many of the qualities requisite for success as a lexicographer', and that 'Mr Colenso's personal contributions are meagre and disappointing'.[14] Among much else, this indicates that the standard of scholarship applied to te reo in its printed form had improved compared to that in the mid-1800s – and definitely earlier.

'HE PRONOUNCED SOME MAORI WORDS WRONG'

Issues of standards and authenticity in te reo arose elsewhere, including in the unlikely venue of the theatre circuit, where a Māori raconteur and performer named Rawei was staging shows during 1898 and 1899. Under the title *The Land of the Maori*, Rawei and his wife Hine Taimoa – 'two educated and cultured members of the Maori race' – appeared in 'flax costumes' and displayed large images of scenery and of carved Māori wharenui. Rawei, who was a member of Ngāti Kurawhatia iwi from Pipiriki on the Whanganui River, gave lectures to audiences in towns and cities around the North Island 'in a very interesting, conversational manner, and [with] … amusing anecdotes' about the history of certain locations and their significance to Māori. His lectures were accompanied by songs and duets, 'some of which were loudly encored'.[15] Here was Māori culture, liberally peppered with words and phrases in te reo, put on show largely for European consumption as a form of entertainment. The issue of what constituted 'authentic' te reo and Māori culture, though, trailed Rawei and his show. The most frequent allegation was that neither the language nor the culture that he was presenting was 'pure' Māori; some people regarded it as cultural miscegenation and therefore artificial.

If anything, by the 1890s there was mounting insistence on Māori cultural and linguistic purity. Robert Stout, a former premier and now chief justice, concluded in 1908 that, by the turn of the century, 'Pure Maori was being lost; the natives were speaking a sort of pigeon Maori, and departing from the idioms of their mother tongue.'[16] Concerns such as Stout's were not necessarily a sign that Europeans were rushing to the aid of the indigenous language as soon as they saw it was being adulterated, however, and they did not serve the interests of te reo. Indeed, in the face of the overwhelming pressures of colonisation, te reo had stood its ground partly by admitting elements of linguistic hybridity into the language – based on an enlarged lexicon that was being compiled, mainly by Māori.[17] Rather, the demand by some Europeans that the supposed purity of Māori culture and te reo be upheld reinforced something quite different: it represented an essentialist[18] view of Māori. Concerns among some Europeans that the Māori language and culture might be deviating from their supposedly untainted form suggests that there was a degree of intolerance[19] and even anxiety at the evolutionary prospects of tikanga and te reo. It was acceptable, from the standpoint of some colonists – even if only subconsciously – for English to be endlessly malleable, but not so te reo – perhaps because it was precisely this great flexibility that had given English its strength as a colonising language. It was as though colonial society in New Zealand preferred to cast Māori as the unadulterated, primitive[20] or exotic Other, and insisted on Māori linguistic purity more as a subconscious act of repression[21] than as anything more charitable. The power relationship between te reo and English was still heavily out of balance.

Rawei recoiled in response to the criticism of his show: he said he 'never professed to be a Maori but a halfcaste, a representative of both races'. Reacting to accusations that he did not pronounce Māori 'correctly', he said he 'had endeavoured to give what information he possessed about the Maoris to the best of his ability'. Rawei's defensiveness led him to make an observation that went to the core of the different standards by which te reo and English were judged: he noted that 'No pakeha would like to be condemned because he mispronounced some words in his mother's language.'[22] And that was the point. The demand to straitjacket te reo – even in this small instance

– debilitated the language's ability to grow and evolve, while English was left free to roam and to incorporate terms and concepts at will. For this reason alone, it was not surprising that Māori parents in some regions were leading the call for English to be taught to their children in schools – its capacity for adaptation seemed beyond anything that te reo could match.

It was not just the fossilising of te reo through demands that it remain 'pure' that was gradually deterring Māori from speaking it as their only language. The tiny fraction of legislation and government documentation translated into te reo was a constant reminder that English was the language of political power in the nation, just as the workings of banks and businesses – which conducted their transactions exclusively in English – confirmed it as the language of commerce. Finding out what was happening in the country relied on being able to read newspapers in English. In 1899 there were just three newspapers still being published in te reo – *Te Puke ki Hikurangi, Te Tiupiri* and *He Kupu Whakamarama* – which was meagre compared with the at least 53 newspapers in English that were being issued regularly at the time.

These practical pressures on Māori to learn English in order to get on in the colony were still being gilded with the rhetoric of civilisation. The assertion that Māori needed to be civilised by the settler, which had been perpetuated throughout the century, had still not abated. In February 1899 Reverend William Gittos concluded regretfully that 'the natives are in a worse condition now than they were when they first came in contact with Europeans'. Oblivious to the irony of his explanation for this, he blamed the corrupting influence of some settlers as preventing Māori from assimilating and becoming more civilised. Regardless of where the blame lay, he was convinced that 'now a once vigorous race is content to lounge through life with no object in view but mere existence'.[23] What was needed was for Māori to make even greater efforts to embrace the culture and language of the majority population in the colony.

And by 1899 there were signs that even the more stubborn areas of resistance to European colonisation were yielding to this pressure. A comment that appeared in a government report on Māori education pitched changes taking place as a triumph over indigenous intransigence:

> It is worthy of note that in some districts in which anti-European
> feeling was formerly very strong the desire for education is beginning
> to take hold of the people, and not only are the schools that are already
> established appreciated, but proposals are being made for new schools.

As examples of this promising development might be mentioned … the
school asked for at Parawera, near Kihikihi, formerly King Tawhiao's
settlement.[24]

The specific mention of King Tawhiao here was no incidental detail: it was
a barbed allusion to the eviscerated power of Kīngitanga, and an emphatic
reminder of the ascendency of all things English in the colony.

Given these forces at play, it is little wonder that there was no enthusiasm
for a legislative ban on te reo in the nineteenth century. The conversion of te
reo into a literate language, its attachment to the ideology of an introduced
religion, its declining appearance in the documentation of the state, a settler
culture that condemned it as anti-civilisation, its progressive banishment
from the state school system, and the near terminal decline in its indigenous
speakers were collectively far more effective at marginalising the language
while largely avoiding provoking a backlash from Māori – which could have
been the consequence of a blanket legislative prohibition.

If what's past is prologue,[25] the fate of te reo Māori heading into the
twentieth century must have appeared almost certain. The arenas in which
it could be used – commercially, politically, culturally and socially – were
contracting at an accelerating rate, and geographically the country had gone
from one in which te reo was spoken everywhere inhabited by people at the
beginning of the century to one where it was confined to small, isolated,
generally impoverished pockets of depopulated Māori settlements.

But while the mantra of the 'dying race' was still regularly being trotted out,
small shoots of optimism were sprouting from what looked to just about
everyone to be the dead wood of Māori as a people, culture and language. In
December 1908, Thomas Hocken proposed to the Council of the University
of Otago that the Māori language be introduced as an optional subject for
the university's matriculation examination. He argued that there would be
no difficulty in getting examiners, and that there was already a reasonable
body of Māori literature (albeit – in the form of the Bible and Grey's
collections – written predominantly by Europeans); and that the motion, if
adopted, would go some small way to 'rescue the Maori language from the
woeful condition into which it had fallen'. In addition, it would have 'great
importance from an ethnological and linguistic point of view'.[26]

Māori, too, were becoming more vocal in advocating for the language;
they were no longer satisfied with the supposed superior wisdom of Europeans on this matter. Reweti Kohere, a clergyman, journalist and former

Te Aute student, testifying before a royal commission in 1906, advocated eloquently for the teaching of te reo Māori as a subject in some schools. 'I think if a boy is taught to despise his own mother-tongue,' he suggested with simple, inarguable logic, 'we should not be surprised if he comes to despise his own mother.' He added that, from his own experience 'the more I learn of that language the more I find there is in it. I derive a great deal of pleasure from learning it. Besides, it helps to make a boy love things Maori ... if you take away the racial pride from the Maori heart, and pride in the traditions of his people, you lower his character.'[27]

If te reo did achieve more widespread use, there might also be other benefits. William Bird, a native schools inspector, pointed out in 1908 that 'the genius of the Maori language transforms many topics tabooed by the somewhat irrational European, and allows the Maori to speak sensibly and rationally upon them.'[28] Māori health could be improved, Bird believed, if te reo was used more widely and was unencumbered by European restrictions and prejudices.

There were no more compelling cases than those put by Kohere and Bird for te reo to become a feature in twentieth-century New Zealand; yet, in that same century, the state enacted more strident measures against the language and came close to rendering it little more than a linguistic antiquity – something to be studied rather than spoken, and to be held up as a relic, if not of a dying race, then certainly of a dying culture.

Te reo Māori emerged in the 1890s heavily battered by its encounters with English, besieged by state policies that were depriving the language of the means of survival, and facing the prospect of disappearing altogether in the near future (along with Māori themselves). But perhaps it was precisely because of these dire circumstances that Māori society became more anxious about this approaching loss and started to voice its concerns – not only at hui and in marae but in the arenas of the coloniser – about the fate of te reo. From the 1900s, articulate Māori leaders, educated in the Māori world and increasingly in the European one as well, fluent in te reo Māori and English, and committed to reviving te reo and Māori as a people, served their culture with a devotion and energy that exceeded anything the language's opponents could muster, and spearheaded te reo's uphill battle for survival as a living language.

Notes

INTRODUCTION

1   C.M. Hovey (ed.), *Magazine of Horticulture, Botany, and All Useful Discoveries*, vol. 6, Boston, 1840, 105.

2   *Sydney Gazette and New South Wales Advertiser*, 15 April 1834, 2; C. von Hügel (trans. & ed. **Dymphna Clark**), *New Holland Journal, November 1833 – October 1834*, Melbourne, 1994; W. Yate, *An Account of New Zealand; and of the formation and progress of the Church Missionary Society's mission in the Northern Island*, 2nd edn, London, 1835, 193, 229.

3   See T. Gardiner, *View of the Missionary House, Waimate, New Zealand* [1834 or 1835], ref. A-049-020, ATL.

4   Yate, 229.

5   Ibid.

6   P. Adams, *Fatal Necessity: British intervention in New Zealand, 1830–1847*, Wellington, 1977, 7.

7   J. Clifford, *The Predicament of Culture*, Cambridge, MA, 1998, 11.

8   R.L. Cartwright, 'Some remarks on essentialism', *Journal of Philosophy*, vol. 65, no. 20, 1968, 615–26.

9   Said's construction of the Other is used here: E.W. Said, 'Orientalism reconsidered', *Cultural Critique*, no. 1, Autumn 1985, 89–107.

10 Clifford, *The Predicament of Culture*, 14.

11 J.C. Crawford, *Recollections of Travel in New Zealand and Australia*, Edinburgh, 1880, 335; A.S. Atkinson to W.B.D. Mantell, 22 Jan 1887, in G. Scholefield (ed.), *The Richmond-Atkinson Papers*, vol. II, Wellington, 1961, 538.

12 T. Gilbert, *New Zealand Settlers and Soldiers; or, The war in Taranaki*, London, 1861, 214.

13 K.D. Harrison, *When Languages Die: The extinction of the world's languages and the erosion of human knowledge*, Oxford, 2007, 5.

14 G. Baumgratz, 'Language, culture and global competence: An essay on ambiguity', *European Journal of Education*, vol. 30, no. 4, December 1995, 437–47.

15 This locus classicus of native extinction is found in writings throughout the British Empire in the nineteenth century, often as though it was a foregone conclusion. See D. Arnold, '"An ancient race outworn": Malaria and race in colonial India, 1860–1930', in B. Harris et al. (eds), *Race, Science and Medicine,*

1700-1960, London, 1999, 137–38, cited in T.D. Salesa, '"The power of the physician": Doctors and the "dying Maori" in early colonial New Zealand', *Health and History,* vol. 3, no. 1, 2001, 13.

16   W.H. Pearson, 'Attitudes to the Maori in some Pakeha fiction', *JPS,* vol. 67, no. 3, September 1958, 211–38; R.S. Hill, *State Authority, Indigenous Autonomy: Crown–Maori relations in New Zealand/Aotearoa, 1900–1950,* Wellington, 2004, 43; Salesa, '"The power of the physician"', 13–15.

17   Cited in Waitangi Tribunal, *Report of the Waitangi Tribunal on the Te Reo Maori Claim,* Wai-11, Wellington, 1986, 7.

18   This approach is explicit in A. Moorehead, *The Fatal Impact: An account of the invasion of the South Pacific, 1767–1840,* Harmondsworth, 1968.

19   A. Ballara, 'The pursuit of mana? A re-evaluation of the process of land alienation by Maoris, 1840–1890', *JPS,* vol. 91, no. 4, December 1982, 519; K. Howe, 'The fate of the "savage" in Pacific historiography', *NZJH,* vol. 11, 1977, 146.

20   The survival of traditional Māori society is examined in A. Ballara, 'Settlement patterns in the early European Maori phase of Maori society', *JPS,* vol. 88, 1979, 211.

21   The paradoxical nature of anti-systematic movements was identified by various dependency theorists. See A.G. Frank, 'Transitional ideological modes: feudalism, capitalism, socialism', in A.G. Frank and B.K. Gills (eds), *The World System: Five hundred years or five thousand?,* New York, 1996, 203. Wallerstein, 'The West, capitalism, and the modern world-system', *Review (Fernand Braudel Center),* vol. 15, no. 4, Fall, 1992, 561–619.

22   Shaw, Saville & Co., *The New Zealand Handbook,* 11th edn, London, 1866, 26.

23   J. Henare, Waitangi Tribunal, *Report of the Waitangi Tribunal on the Te Reo Maori Claim,* 9.

24   J. Thornton, *Press,* 5 June 1899, 5.

25   Variants of this include 'Ka puta mai taku ngoi', and 'Ka tūte riri, ka tūnguha ka puta': Graham Rankin, Ngāpuhi.

CHAPTER 1: 'HE TAONGA TUKU IHO NGĀ TŪPUNA': 1800

1   An extended definition of marae is used here. See R. Higgins and J.C. Moorfield, 'Ngā tikanga o te marae – Marae practices', in T.M. Ka`ai, J.C. Moorfield, M.P.J. Reilly and S. Mosely (eds), *Ki te Whaiao: An introduction to Māori culture and society,* Auckland, 2004, 73.

2   R. Higgins & J.C. Moorfield, 'Tangihanga: Death customs', in Ka`ai, Moorfield, Reilly and Mosely (eds), *Ki te Whaiao,* 85–90.

3   J. Sissons, 'The systematisation of tradition: Maori culture as a strategic resource', *Oceania,* vol. 64, no. 2, December 1993, 97–116; M. Silverstein, '"Cultural" concepts and the language–culture nexus', *Current Anthropology,* vol. 45, no. 5, 2004, 621–52; L. Nikora, N. Te Awekotuku and V. Tamanui, 'Home and the spirit in the Maori world', paper presented at *He Manawa Whenua* conference, University of Waikato, Hamilton, 2013, 2.

4   R. Harlow, 'Lexical expansion in Maori', *JPS,* vol. 102, no. 1, March 1993, 99–107. P.J. Keegan, 'The development of Maori vocabulary', in A. Bell, R. Harlow

and D. Starks (eds), *Languages of New Zealand*, Wellington, 2005, 131–48.

5   Although some changes have inevitably occurred; see M. Madagan, R. Harlow, J. King, P. Keegan and C. Watson, 'New Zealand English influence on Māori pronunciation over time', *Te Reo*, vol. 47, 2004, 7–27.

6   This argument is made in a generic sense in K. Risager, *Language and Culture: Global flows and local complexity: From a national to a transnational paradigm*, Clevedon, 2006, 2–4.

7   J. Henare, in Waitangi Tribunal, *Report of the Waitangi Tribunal on the Te Reo Maori Claim*, Wai-11, Wellington, 1986, 34.

8   J. Rangihau, in M.H. Browne, 'Wairua and the relationship it has with learning te reo Māori within Te Ataarangi', report presented in partial fulfilment of the requirements for the degree of Master of Educational Administration at Massey University, 2005, 4. A similar concept is discussed in J.A. Fishman, *In Praise of the Beloved Language: A comparative view of positive ethnolinguistic consciousness*, Berlin, 1996, 13–16.

9   N. Evans and S.C. Levinson, 'The myth of language universals: Language diversity and its importance for cognitive science', *Behavioral and Brain Sciences*, vol. 42, no. 5, 2009, 429–92.

10   B. Haami, *Pūtea Whakairo: Māori and the written word*, Wellington, 2004, 15.

11   M. Henare, 'Nga tikanga me nga ritenga o te ao Maori: Standards and foundations of Maori society', in Report of the Royal Commission on Social Policy, *The April Report: Future Directions Associated Papers*, vol. 3, pt 1, Wellington, 1988.

12   Browne, 'Wairua and the relationship it has', 4.

13   Interview with Hohepa Kereopa, Waimana, January 2003. See also P. Moon, *Tohunga: Hohepa Kereopa*, Auckland, 2003, 90–92, 96; C.T.H. Mika, 'The utterance, the body and the law: Seeking an approach to concretizing the sacredness of Maori language', *Sites: A Journal of Social Anthropology and Cultural Studies*, vol. 4, no. 2, 2007, 186–88.

14   W. Yate, *An Account of New Zealand; and of the formation and progress of the Church Missionary Society's Mission in the Northern Island*, London, 1835, 83.

15   H. Beattie, *Tikau Talks*, Christchurch, 1990, 74.

16   Mika, 'The utterance, the body and the law', 186–88.

17   S.J. Tambiah, 'The magical power of words', *Man*, vol. 3, no 2. June 1968, 186; B. Malinowski, *Coral Gardens and their Magic*, vol. 2, Indiana, 1965, 233.

18   S. Marsden, 2 April 1830, in J.R. Elder (ed.), *The Letters and Journals of Samuel Marsden, 1765–1838*, Dunedin, 1932, 478.

19   T.W. Gudgeon, *The History and Doings of the Maoris, from the Year 1820 to the signing of the Treaty of Waitangi in 1840*, Auckland, 1885, 26.

20   R. Ward, *Life Among the Maories of New Zealand: Being a description of missionary, colonial, and military achievements*, London, 1872, 94.

21   Cited in Haami, *Pūtea Whakairo*, 15.

22   J. Buller, *Forty Years in New Zealand*, London, 1878, 180–81.

23   These are detailed in P. Rewi, '"Ko te waihanga me nga wehewehenga o te whaikorero": The structural system of whaikorero and its components', *Junctures: The Journal for Thematic Dialogue*, vol. 2, June 2004, 16–32. Also see

M. King, *Te Ao Hurihuri*, Wellington, 1975, 23; H. Tauroa and P. Tauroa, *Te Marae: A guide to customs and protocol*, Auckland, 1986, 65–66.

24   L. Pihama, 'Tihei mauri ora – Honouring our voices: Mana wahine as a kaupapa Maori theoretical framework', PhD thesis, University of Auckland, 2001, 117. A variant of this appears in J. McRae, 'Māori oral tradition meets the book', in P. Griffith, P. Hughes and A. Loney (eds), *A Book in the Hand: Essays on the history of the book in New Zealand*, Auckland, 2000, 3.

25   A. Thornton, 'Two features of oral style in Maori narrative', *JPS*, vol. 94, no. 2, 1985, 149.

26   A. Thornton, *Maori Oral Literature as Seen by a Classicist*, Wellington, 1999, 49.

27   L. Melville, cited in N. Gunson, 'Understanding Polynesian traditional history', *Journal of Pacific History*, vol. 28, no. 2, 1993, 149.

28   A. Ngata, 'The Maori and printed matter', in R.A. McKay (ed.), *A History of Printing in New Zealand, 1830–1940*, Wellington, 1940, 48–49, cited in J. McRae, 'Māori oral tradition meets the book', 9.

29   C. Pelachaud and I. Poggi, 'Subtleties of facial expressions in embodied agents', *Journal of Visualization and Computer Animation*, vol. 13, no. 5, 2002, 301–12; L.J. Ausburn and F.B. Ausburn, 'Visual literacy: Background, theory and practice', *Programmed Learning and Educational Technology*, vol. 15, no. 4, 1978, 291–97; S. Goldin-Meadow, 'The role of gesture in communication and thinking', *Trends in Cognitive Sciences*, vol. 3, no. 11, 1999, 419–29.

30   R.C. Harding, 'Unwritten literature', *Transactions and Proceedings of the Royal Society of New Zealand*, vol. 25, 1892, 440–42.

31   McRae, 'Māori oral tradition meets the book', 4.

32   G. Eliot, 'The natural history of German life' (July 1856), in T. Pinney (ed.), *Essays of George Eliot*, Columbia, 1963, 288.

33   This metaphor is used in R. Macfarlane, 'The eeriness of the English countryside', *Guardian*, 10 April 2015.

34   P. Rewi, *Whaikōrero: The world of Māori oratory*, Auckland, 2013, ch. 7.

35   T. Kendall, 11 March 1815, in J.R. Elder (ed.), *Marsden's Lieutenants*, Dunedin, 1934, 78.

36   J.A. Fishman, *In Praise of the Beloved Language*, 11. See also M.P. Shirres, 'Ko tona mea nui he tapu: "His greatest possession is his *tapu*"', *JPS*, vol. 91, no. 1, 1982, 31–33.

37   Interview with Hohepa Kereopa, Waimana, January 2003.

38   M. McLean, 'The music of Maori chant', *Te Ao Hou: The New World*, vol. 47, June 1964, 37.

39   H. Kereopa, in Moon, *Tohunga: Hohepa Kereopa*, 114.

40   Ibid., 114.

41   As examples, see G.F. Angas, *Savage Life and Scenes in Australia and New Zealand*, vol. 2, London, 1847, 102; J.M. Crozet (H. Ling Roth, trans.), *Crozet's Voyage to Tasmania, New Zealand, the Ladrone Islands, and the Philippines*, London, 1891, 25; C.O. Davis, *The Life and Times of Patuone: The celebrated Ngapuhi chief*, Auckland, 1876, 46.

42   J. Gascoigne, *The Enlightenment and the Origins of European Australia*, Cambridge, 148–49; N. Thomas, *Colonialism's Culture: Anthropology, travel*

and government, Princeton, 1994, 14. Sometimes this providence had a divine element attached to it: see S. Marsden, in Elder (ed.), *The Letters and Journals of Samuel Marsden*, 151.

43   B. Buchan, 'The empire of political thought: Civilization, savagery and perceptions of Indigenous government', *History of the Human Sciences*, vol. 18, no. 2, May 2005, 10.

44   B. Bowden, 'The ideal of civilisation: Its origins and socio-political character', *Critical Review of International Social and Political Philosophy*, vol. 7, no. 1, 2004, 44.

45   J.C. Moorfield, 'Te whakahē i ētahi pōhēhētanga mō te reo Māori: Challenging some misconceptions about the Māori language', Inaugural Professorial Lecture: Te Kauhau Tīmatanga a te Ahorangi, University of Otago, Dunedin, 26 September, 2001, 7–11, 16–18.

46   G.L. Craik, *The New Zealanders*, London, 1830, 414–15.

47   W.B. Marshall, *A Personal Narrative of Two Visits to New Zealand*, London, 1836, 232.

48   J.S. Polack, *New Zealand: Being a narrative of travels and adventures during a residence in that country between the years 1831 and 1837*, vol. 2, London, 1838, 341.

49   C. Terry, *New Zealand: Its advantages and prospects as a British colony*, London, 1842, 187–88.

50   E. Shortland, *Maori Religion and Mythology*, London, 1882, 3–5.

51   J.R. Forster, in N. Thomas, H. Guest and M. Dettelbach (eds), *Observations Made During a Voyage Round the World: Johann Reinhold Forster, 1729–1798*, Honolulu, 1996, 151–52.

52   J.L. Nicholas, *Narrative of a Voyage to New Zealand*, vol. 2, London, 1817, 299, 303.

53   W. Williams to D. Coates, 10 February 1834, in *Report from the Select Committee of the House of Lords, appointed to inquire into the present state of the Islands of New Zealand*, London, 3 April 1838, 180. Also see J. Beecham, *Remarks upon the Latest Official Documents Relating to New Zealand*, London, 1838, 15.

54   Normanby to W. Hobson, 14 August 1839, *GBPP*, vol. 238, London, 1840, 38.

55   J. Savage, *Some Account of New Zealand: Particularly the Bay of Islands and surrounding country with a description of the religion, arts, manufactures, manners and customs of the Natives*, London, 1807, 20–21.

56   M. King, *The Penguin History of New Zealand*, Auckland, 2003, 81–82.

57   J. Metge, *Rautahi: The Maori of New Zealand*, London, 2004, 5–6.

58   A. Ballara, *Iwi: The dynamics of tribal organisation from c. 1769 to c. 1945*, Wellington, 1998, 161.

59   T. Gallagher, 'Tikanga Māori pre-1840', *Te Kāhui Kura Māori*, issue 1, n.d., art. 1.

60   R. Bowden, 'Tapu and mana: Ritual authority and political power in traditional Maori society', *Journal of Pacific History*, vol. 14, no. 1, 1979, 50.

61   N.K. Hopa, 'The rangatira: Chieftainship in traditional Maori society', BLitt thesis, University of Oxford, Oxford, 1966, 61, in Bowden, 'Tapu and mana', 50.

62   'Tribe' was often the generic designation used. As examples, see E. Dieffenbach, *Travels in New Zealand*, London, 1843, 72–73; A. Johnston, *A Note on Maori Matters*, Auckland, 1860, 27–30.

63   H.M. Mead, *Ngā Pēpeha a Ngā Tīpuna*, Wellington, 2007, 9; H.W. Williams, *A Dictionary of the Maori Language*, Wellington, 1971, 274.

64   E. Gibbon, *The History of the Decline and Fall of the Roman Empire*, Ware, 1998, 144.

65   J.A. Wilson, *The Story of Te Waharoa: A chapter in early New Xealand history, together with sketches of ancient Maori life and history*, Christchurch, 1907, 227; Bowden, 'Tapu and mana', 50.

66   G.W. Rusden, *History of New Zealand*, vol. 1, London, 1883, 18; E. Shortland, *A Short Sketch of the Maori Races*, Dunedin, 1865, 4–5.

67   E. Gellner, *Words and Things*, London, 1959, 22 (emphasis in the original).

68   M.K. Knapp, A. Horsburgh, S. Prost, J. Stanton, H.R. Buckley, R.K. Walter and E.A. Matisoo-Smith, 'Complete mitochondrial DNA genome sequences from the first New Zealanders', *Proceedings of the National Academy of Sciences*, vol. 109, no. 45, 2012, 18350–54.

69   P. King, 1793, in University of Sydney Library, 'The Journal of Philip Gidley King, Lieutenant, R.N. 1787–1790', parts 3 and 4, ABN: 15 211 513 464. CRICOS number: 00026A.

70   Statistics New Zealand, *2012 New Zealand Official Yearbook*, Wellington, 2013, land area spreadsheet.

71   R. Harlow, *Maori: A linguistic introduction*, Cambridge, 2007, 43–45.

72   J. Goody and I. Watt, 'The consequences of literacy', *Comparative Studies in Society and History*, vol. 5, no. 3, April 1963, 306. See also F.C. Bartlett, *Remembering*, Cambridge, 1932, 265–67; F.C. Bartlett, *Psychology and Primitive Culture*, Cambridge, 1923, 42–43, 62–63, 256.

73   As examples of this reductionist approach, see G.C. Mundy, *Our Antipodes, or Residence and rambles in the Australasian colonies*, vol. 2, London, 1852, 285; W. Swainson, *New Zealand and its Colonization*, London, 1859, 2; J.A. Wilson, *Missionary Life and Work in New Zealand, 1833-1862*, Auckland, 1889, 50.

74   J. Pere, 'Oral tradition and tribal history', in R. Selby and A. Laurie, *Māori and Oral History: A collection*, Wellington, 2005, 50.

75   J-F. Lyotard, *The Postmodern Condition: A report on knowledge*, Manchester, 1983, xxiv–xxv; S.J. Grenz, *A Primer on Postmodernism*, Grand Rapids, 1996, 164; K.L. Klein, 'In search of narrative mastery: Postmodernism and the people without history', *History and Theory*, vol. 34, no. 4, December 1995, 275–98.

76   D. Keenan, 'The past from the paepae: uses of the past in Māori oral history', in Selby and Laurie, *Māori and Oral History*, 56.

77   J. Evans, *Ngā Waka o Neherā: The first voyaging canoes*, Auckland, 2009, 21.

78   V. Sturmey, 'Submission of Nga Rauru', Waitangi Tribunal, Te Ihupuku Marae, Waitotara, 14 October 1991, Wai 143, F1, 7, cited in Keenan, 'The past from the paepae', 56–57.

79   H. Tautahi, W. Taipuhi and S. Percy Smith, 'The "Aotea" Canoe: The migration of Turi to Aotea-Roa (New Zealand)', *JPS*, vol. 9, no. 4 (36), 1900, 214.

80   B. Biggs, 'The oral literature of the Polynesians', *Te Ao Hou: The New World*, no. 49, November 1964, 44–45.

81   I am indebted for this section to the analysis provided by M. Roberts, B. Haami, R.A. Benton, T. Satterfield, M.L. Finucane, M. Henare and M. Henare, 'Whakapapa as a Maori mental construct: Some implications for the debate over genetic modification of organisms', *Contemporary Pacific*, vol. 16, no. 1, Spring 2004, 1.

82   T.W. Pohatu and H. Pohatu, 'Mauri: Rethinking human wellbeing', in *MAI Review*, vol. 3, 2011, 4.

83   H. Kereopa in Moon, *Tohunga*, 133–34.

84   As an example of how innovation took place in certain areas of design, see G. Archey, 'Evolution of certain Maori carving patterns', *JPS*, vol. 42, no. 3, September 1933, 171–90; H.D. Skinner, 'Evolution in Maori art', *Journal of the Anthropological Institute of Great Britain and Ireland*, vol. 46, January–June 1916, 184–96.

85   H.M. and N.K. Chadwick, *The Growth of Literature*, vol. 2, pt. 3, New York, 1940, cited in Biggs, 'Oral literature of the Polynesians', 23.

86   Bishop of Wellington, 'Notes on the Maoris of New Zealand and some Melanesians of the South-west Pacific', *Journal of the Ethnological Society of London*, vol. 1, no. 4, 1869, 364, 368.

87   E. Best, *The Maori School of Learning: Its objects, methods, and ceremonial*, Dominion Museum Monograph no. 6, Wellington, 1959, 11.

88   Ibid., 5.

89   For the accuracy of whakapapa, see P. Te Hurinui Jones, 'Maori genealogies', *JPS*, vol. 67, no. 2, June 1958, 162–65.

90   J.W. Stack, 20 June 1885, in A.H. Reed (ed.), *Early Maoriland Adventures of J.W. Stack*, Dunedin, 1935, 86.

91   M. Beckwith, *Hawaiian Mythology*, New Haven, 1940, 230; L. Fison, *Tales from Old Fiji*, London, 1907, 144; C. Gosden and C. Pavlides, 'Are islands insular? Landscape vs seascape in the case of the Arawe Islands, Papua New Guinea', in *Archaeology in Oceania*, vol. 29, no. 3, 1994, 162; I. Barber, 'Sea, land and fish: Spatial relationships and the archaeology of South Island Maori fishing', *World Archaeology*, vol. 35, no. 3, 2003, 434.

92   E. Hadfield, *Among the Natives of the Loyalty Group*, London, 1920, 225; G. Turner, *Nineteen Years in Polynesia*, London, 1861, cited in P.D. Nunn, 'On the convergence of myth and reality: Examples from the Pacific Islands', *Geographical Journal*, vol. 167, no. 2, June 2001, 129; Nunn cited the following sources: G.T. Barker, 'How a coral reef became an island', *Transactions of the Fiji Society*, 1926, 29–34; E.W. Gifford, *Tongan Myths and Tales*, Honolulu, 1924, 15; M. Beckwith, *Hawaiian Mythology*, New Haven, 1940, 308–09, 372–73; G. Ashby (ed.), *Ever and Always: Micronesian stories of the origins of islands, landmarks, and customs*, Oregon, 1978, 22–23; J. Sanga, 'Remembering', in H. Laracy (ed.), *Ples Blong Iumi: Solomon Islands, the past four thousand years*, Suva, 1989, 17.

93   J.S. Polack, *Manners and Customs of the New Zealanders*, vol. 1, London, 1840, 26.

94   B. Malinowski, *Myth in Primitive Psychology*, London, 1926, 23, 43; J. Goody and I. Watt, 'The consequences of literacy', *Comparative Studies in Society and History*, vol. 5, no. 3, April 1963, 308.

95   For an analysis of the transformation of knowledge in such contexts, see S.H. Hyman, 'The ritual view of myth and the mythic', *Journal of American Folklore*, vol. 68, no. 270 (*Myth: A Symposium*), October–December 1955, 463; J.E. Harrison, *Themis*, Cambridge, 1912, 13.

96   N. Mahuika, 'Kōrero iuku ho': Reconfiguring oral history and oral tradition', PhD thesis, University of Waikato, Hamilton, 2012, 20.

97   J.A. Arlow, 'Ego psychology and the study of mythology', *Journal of the American Psychoanalytic Association*, vol. 9, no. 3, 1961, 371–73.

98   Api Mahuika, in Mahuika, 'Kōrero tuku iho', 128.

99   This analysis of indigenous epistemologies is outlined in B.Y. Burkhart, 'What Coyote and Thales can teach us: An outline of American Indian epistemology', in A. Waters (ed.), *American Indian Thought*, Victoria, 2004, 20; S.B. Merriam and S.K. Young, 'Non-Western perspectives on learning and knowing', *New Directions for Adult and Continuing Education*, no. 119, 2008, 73.

100 A whakataukī referring to this sacredness appears in J. Marshall & M. Peters, 'Te reo o te Tai Tokerau: The assessment of oral Maori', *Journal of Multilingual & Multicultural Development*, vol. 10, no. 6, 1989, 499.

101 Ward, *Life Among the Maories of New Zealand*, 113.

102 J. White, *Maori Customs and Superstitions*, Auckland, 1885, 140.

103 Dieffenbach, *Travels in New Zealand*, vol. 2, 57.

104 R. Te Maire Tau, 'Matauranga Maori as an epistemology', *Te Pouhere Korero: Maori history Maori people*, vol. 1, no. 1, March 1999, 15, cited in Haami, *Pūtea Whakairo*, 15.

105 Interview with Hohepa Kereopa, Waimana, January 2003.

106 M. Heidegger, 'Letter on humanism', *Global Religious Vision*, vol. 1, no. 1, July 2000, 83.

107 Savage, *Some Account of New Zealand*, 93.

CHAPTER 2: 'A STRANGE MEDLEY': TO 1814

1   R. McNab, *Murihiku: A history of the South Island of New Zealand and the islands adjacent and lying to the south from 1642 to 1835*, Wellington, 1909, 1–4.

2   K.A. Simpson, 'Tasman, Abel Janszoon 1602/1603?–1659?', *Dictionary of New Zealand Biography*, updated 22 June 2007, n.p.

3   F.V. Visscher, Map of Nova Zeelandia, Reference: B-K 741–96, National Library of New Zealand.

4   M. Lovell-Smith, 'Early mapping – Early mappers: 1642–1800', *Te Ara: The Encyclopedia of New Zealand*, updated 1 March 2009, n.p. The original of the map was lost, and it is known to history only through a 1666 copy.

5   See M.B. Campbell, *The Witness and the Other World: Exotic European travel writing 400–1600*, Cornell, 1991, 1–11; L. Gossman, 'History as decipherment: Romantic historiography and the discovery of the Other', *New Literary History*, vol. 18, no. 1, Autumn, 1986, 24; T.J. Reiss, *Knowledge, Discovery*

     and Imagination in Early Modern Europe: The rise of aesthetic rationalism, Cambridge, 1997, 5, 12, 13.

6   'All returning masters, merchants and mates of Dutch East-Indiamen were obliged to submit their logs and journals to the official cartographer, paying special attention to new discoveries and providing sketches as appropriate. New charts were then drawn up by the cartographer and his assistants to incorporate any improvements to knowledge, making the maps and charts provided through the Amsterdam chamber by far the most relevant maps to VOC [Dutch East Indies Company] business, and the best charts of the day': A.J. Stallard, 'Navigating Tasman's 1642 voyage of exploration: Cartographic instruments and navigational decisions', *Portolan*, no. 69, Fall 2007, 10; G. Schilder, 'Organization and evolution of the Dutch East India Company's Hydrographic Office in the seventeenth century', *Imago Mundi*, vol. 28, 1976, 62.

7   J. Ogilby, *America: Being the latest, and most accurate description of the New World*, London, 1671. See also J. Narborough et al., *An Account of Several Late Voyages & Discoveries to the South and North ...*, London, 1694, xxviii, 136–38.

8   Cook made specific reference to an English edition of Tasman's journal. See J. Cook, 19 April 1770, in W.J.L. Wharton (ed.), *Captain Cook's Journal During His First Voyage Round the World*, Cambridge, 2014, 238. See also A. Sharp, *The Voyages of Abel Janszoon Tasman*, Oxford, 1968, 341–46.

9   J. Milton, *Areopagitica: A speech to the Parliament of England, for the liberty of unlicensed printing*, London, 1644 (text revised).

10   G.C. Spivak, *The Post-colonial Critic: Interviews, strategies, dialogues*, London, 1990, 1–16.

11   C.W.J. Withers, 'Geography, natural history and the eighteenth-century enlightenment: Putting the world in place', *History Workshop Journal*, no. 39, Spring 1995, 142.

12   J.W. Stack, *South Island Maoris: A sketch of their history and legendary lore*, Christchurch, 1898, 12.

13   T.A. Davis, T. O'Regan and J. Wilson, *Nga Tohu Pumahara – The survey pegs of the past: Understanding Maori place names*, Wellington, 1990, 5, cited in P.L. Barton, 'Māori cartography and the European encounter', in D. Woodward and G. Malcolm (eds), *Cartography in the Traditional African, American, Arctic, Australian, and Pacific societies*, Chicago, 1995, 498.

14   W. Colenso, *Three Literary Papers: Read before the Hawke's Bay Philosophical Institute, during the session of 1882*, Napier, 1883, 1–2.

15   Withers, 'Geography, natural history', 138.

16   'Secret instructions for Captain James Cook, commander of his Majesty's sloop *Resolution*, 6 July 1776', in R. McNab (ed.), *Historical Records of New Zealand*, vol. 1, Wellington, 1908, 27.

17   As an example of Banks's description of Māori as specimens, see J. Banks, in J.C. Beaglehole (ed.), *The Endeavour Journal of Joseph Banks, 1768–1771*, vol. 1, Sydney, 1962, 414–17.

18   J. Banks, in J. Hooker (ed.), *Journal of the Right Hon. Sir Joseph Banks*, London, 1896, 238.

19   K. Rountree, 'Maori bodies in European eyes: Representations of the Maori body on Cook's voyages', *JPS*, vol. 107, no. 1, 1998, 35–38.

20   V. Smith, 'Banks, Tupaia, and Mai: Cross-cultural exchanges and friendship in the Pacific', *Parergon*, vol. 26, no. 2, 2009, 139–60.

21   J. Banks, in J. Hawkesworth (ed.), *An account of the voyages undertaken by the order of His present Majesty for making discoveries in the Southern Hemisphere, and successively performed by Commodore Byron, Captain Wallis, Captain Carteret, and Captain Cook, in the* Dolphin, *the* Swallow, *and the* Endeavour: *drawn up from the journals which were kept by the several commanders, and from the papers of Joseph Banks, esq.*, vol. 3, London, 1773, 70–71.

22   State Library of New South Wales, 'Banks' description of places', transcription of Banks' Journal, vol. 2, Sydney, February 2004, 248–49.

23   S. Parkinson, *A Journal of a Voyage to the South Seas*, London, 1773, 79–94, 170–72, 191–215, 225–49.

24   W. Anderson, 25 February 1777, in J.C. Beaglehole (ed.), *The Journals of Captain James Cook: The voyage of the* Resolution *and* Discovery, *1776–1780*, vol. 3, part 2, Cambridge, 1967, 817–18.

25   P.J. Marshall, 'Empire and authority in the later eighteenth century', *Journal of Imperial and Commonwealth History*, vol. 15, no. 2, 1987, 105. As an example, see R. Lowth, *Sermon Preached before the Incorporated Society for the Propagation of the Gospel in Foreign Parts; At their anniversary meeting in the Parish Church of St. Mary-Le-Bow, on Friday February 15, 1771, by … Robert Lord Bishop of Oxford*, Oxford, 1771, 24. The condescending notion of the 'noble savage' may seem to be the exception, but the premise of a utopia cut off from all the ill effects of civilisation was more fantasy than reality.

26   T. Astle, *The Origin and Progress of Writing*, London, 1784, i, 4–5.

27   Richard Steele's libretto for an opera, written in 1717, embodied this belief in the supremacy of English, and contained the stanza, 'Let Anna's Soil be known for all its Charms;/ As Fam'd for Lib'ral Sciences, as Arms:/ Let those Derision meet, who would Advance/ Manners, or Speech, from Italy or France;/ Let them learn You, you wou'd your Favour find,/ And English be the Language of Mankind', *The Dramatic Works of Sir Richard Steele, Knt.*, London, 1761, 72.

28   P. King, 8 November 1793, in R. McNab, *Historical Records of New Zealand*, vol. 2, Wellington, 1914, 546.

29   P. King, 1793, in University of Sydney Library, 'The Journal of Philip Gidley King, Lieutenant, R.N. 1787–1790', parts 3 and 4, ABN: 15 11 513 464. CRICOS number: 00026A. The figure of 199 words excludes a further five or six for which no Māori equivalents were transcribed.

30   J. Boulton, '"It is extreme necessity that makes me do this"': Some "survival strategies" of pauper households in London's West End during the early eighteenth century', *International Review of Social History*, vol. 45, issue S8, 2000, 50, 53–54.

31   Tom Roa comments on this issue, 'As I understand it, "pani" are those who have been "orphaned", i.e. both parents have died. This is not necessarily just young children. But there is also another term: "kua mātuakoretia" – having become without parents. I wonder why these Māori in 1793 didn't give these

terms? I think it is a fair assumption that the "whānau" would "whāngai" the young ones, and the older ones would have resources of their own', T. Roa to P. Moon, personal communication, 2 February 2015.

32   K.O. McRae and L.W. Nikora, 'Whangai: remembering, understanding and experiencing', *MAI Review, Intern Research Report 7*, vol. 1, 2006, 1–3; S.M. Mead (ed.), *Landmarks, Bridges and Visions: Aspects of Maori culture*, Wellington, 1997, 204–12. Jason King adds the following points on the concept of orphans: '1. "Pani"(tia) I have grown up knowing this word to mean "orphaned" but also can mean bereaved person, orphan – depending on the context of the discussion; 2. Pani also means to smear or spread. "Kua pani(a) e te mate" – smeared by death; 3. Yes they were "whāngai" to other families once they became "pani", especially at a young age as it wasn't good for children to remain "pani" and have no one look after them. They would have had to either fend for themselves or die. Pani is a word put on people for recent deaths with the intention that they would be pani for only a short time, as death wasn't a great thing to carry around with you for the rest of your life; 4. I would use: "Mātua kore" – without parents/parentless if I needed to use a word/s. It would be inappropriate to use "pani" in this sense as it gives the idea that they have just lost a loved one. "Pani" also is a generic term not specific to mother/father/ sis/bro/cuz; 5. Pouaru – widow/widower, rawakore – homeless/everything- less, pōririo – bastard child.' J. King to P. Moon, Personal communication, 25 February 2015.

33   'Chart of New Zealand drawn by Tooka-Titter-anue Wari-Ledo [Tuki Tahua], a priest of that country who resided in Norfolk Island 6 months'. No scale shown. Originally enclosed with Lieutenant-Governor King's despatch of 7 November 1793. 1793, CO 201/9, The National Archives, Kew, London, MPG 1/532.

34   R.R.D. Milligan (ed. by J. Dunmore), *The Map Drawn by the Chief Tuki-Tahua in 1793*, Mangonui, 1964, 1–35.

35   J. Kelly, 'Maori Maps', *Cartographica*, vol. 36, no. 2, 1999, 1–30.

36   J. Binney, 'Tuki's universe', *NZJH*, vol. 38, no. 2, 2004, 215–17.

37   G. Byrnes, *Boundary Markers: Land surveying and the colonisation of New Zealand*, Wellington, 2001, 39–54.

38   B.J. Harley, 'Maps, knowledge, and power', in D. Cosgrove and S. Daniels (eds), *The Iconography of Landscape*, Cambridge, 1988, 277.

39   A sample of such a perspective from the eighteenth century can be seen in J.M. Crozet (trans. H.L. Roth), *Crozet's Voyage to Tasmania, New Zealand, the Ladrone Islands, and the Philippines in the years 1771–1772*, London, 1891, 63.

40   Byrnes, *Boundary Markers*, 77.

41   E.G. Wakefield, *A View of the Art of Colonization, with present reference to the British Empire, in letters between a statesman and a colonist*, London, 1849, 48–49, 118.

42   G.W. Beckett, *A Population History of Colonial New South Wales: The economic growth of a new colony*, Singapore, 2013, 259.

43   I. Wallerstein, *The Capitalist World-Economy*, Cambridge, 1979, 27, 30, 198–99. Wallerstein saw this expansion as being part of the culmination of four centuries of capitalist encroachment and exploitation. See A. Quijano and I.

Wallerstein, 'Americanity as a concept, or the Americas in the modern world', *International Social Science Journal*, 1992, 549–57.

44   N.S. Ndebele, 'The English language and social change in South Africa', *English Academy Review*, vol. 4, 1987, 3–4.

45   P. Palmer, *Language and Conquest in Early Modern Ireland: English renaissance literature and Elizabethan imperial expansion*, Cambridge, 2004, 20.

46   A. Carli, C. Guardiano, M. Kaucic-Baca, E. Sussi, M. Tessarolo and M. Ussai, 'Asserting ethnic identity and power through language', *Journal of Ethnic and Migration Studies*, vol. 29, no. 5, 2003, 868.

47   E. Stokes, 'Maori geography or geography of Maoris', *New Zealand Geographer*, vol. 43, issue 3, December 1987, 118–23; R. Maaka and A. Fleras, 'Engaging with indigeneity: Tino rangatiratanga in Aotearoa', in D. Ivison, P. Patten and W. Sanders (eds), *Political Theory and the Rights of Indigenous Peoples*, Cambridge, 2000, 89–90.

48   J. Boyle, 'Imperialism and the English language in Hong Kong', *Journal of Multilingual and Multicultural Development*, vol. 18, no. 3, 1997, 170–72. The metaphor of cloning is used by James Belich: see J. Belich, *Replenishing the Earth: The settler revolution and the rise of the Angloworld, 1783–1939*, New York, 2009, 165–69.

49   T. DeQuincey, in D. Madden (ed.), *The Collected Writing of Thomas DeQuincey*, vol. 2, London, 1896, 251.

50   F. Nietzsche, in R.C. Holub, 'Nietzsche's colonialist imagination: Nueva Germania, good Europeanism, and great politics', in S. Friedrichsmeyer, S. Lennox and S. Zantop (eds), *The Imperialist Imagination: German colonialism and its legacy*, Michigan, 1999, 36.

51   This argument is used in relation to settler colonialism in P. Wolfe, 'Settler colonialism and the elimination of the native', *Journal of Genocide Research*, vol. 8, no. 4, 2006, 387. The role of this coercion in colonial expansion is detailed in S.L. Morgensen, 'The biopolitics of settler colonialism: Right here, right now', *Settler Colonial Studies*, vol. 1, no. 1, 2011, 52.

52   W. Smith, *Journal of a voyage in the missionary ship* Duff, *to the Pacific Ocean in the years 1796, 7, 8, 9, 1800, 1, 2, &c.*, New York, 1813.

53   Ibid., 227.

54   A. Salmond, *Between Worlds: Early exchanges between Maori and Europeans 1773–1815*, Auckland, 1997, 259.

55   Te Taura Whiri i te Reo Māori, *He Pātaka Kupu: Te kai a te rangatira*, Auckland, 2008, 558.

56   Smith, *Journal of a voyage in the missionary ship* Duff, 228, 234.

57   S. Marsden in J.R. Elder (ed.), *The Letters and Journals of Samuel Marsden, 1765–1838*, Dunedin, 1932, 22.

58   A.K. Pugh, 'A history of English teaching', in N. Mercer and J. Swann (eds), *Learning English: Development and diversity*, Oxford, 1996, 189.

59   D. Crystal, *English as a Global Language*, 2nd edn, Cambridge, 2003, 16.

60   J.A. Fishman, 'Sociology of English as an Additional Language', in B.B. Kachru (ed.), *The Other Tongue: English across cultures*, 2nd edn, Illinois, 1992, 22–23.

61   C. Searle, 'A common language', *Race and Class*, vol. 25, no. 2, 1983, 68;
T. Threadgold, *Feminist Poetics: Poiesis, performance, histories*, London, 1997,

136; A. Pennycook, *English and the Discourses of Colonialism*, London, 1998, 4–5.

62   L. Macquarie to Viscount Castlereagh, Sydney, New South Wales, 12th March, 1810, in McNab (ed.), *Historical Records of New Zealand*, vol. 1, 296–97.

63   L. Macquarie, 'Government and general order: 1st December 1813', in McNab (ed.), *Historical Records of New Zealand*, vol. 1, 316.

64   *Sydney Gazette and New South Wales Advertiser*, 30 March 1811, 3.

65   J.L. Nicholas, *Narrative of a Voyage to New Zealand*, vol. 2, 292–95.

66   This term was used by Marsden on his first visit to New Zealand. See S. Marsden, 20 December 1814, in Elder (ed.), *The Letters and Journals of Samuel Marsden*, 89.

67   P.E. King to Earl Camden, 30 April 1805, in McNab (ed.), *Historical Records of New Zealand*, vol. 1, 255.

68   Savage, *Some Account of New Zealand*, 3–4.

69   Nicholas, *Narrative of a Voyage to New Zealand*, vol. 2, 167.

70   S. Marsden, 12 August 1823, in Elder (ed.), *Letters and Journals of Samuel Marsden*, 347.

71   S. Marsden to J. Pratt, 7 February 1829, in McNab (ed.), *Historical Records of New Zealand*, vol. 1, 478.

72   R. McNab, *From Tasman to Marsden: A history of northern New Zealand from 1642 to 1818*, Dunedin, 1914, 131–32; A. Jones and K. Jenkins, *Words Between Us – He Kōrero: First Māori–Pākehā conversations on paper*, Wellington, 2011, 35–37.

73   'Proclamation by His Excellency Lachlan Macquarie', *Sydney Gazette and New South Wales Advertiser*, 11 December 1813, 1.

74   T. Kendall, 18 May 1814, Marsden Archive, Otago University, MS_0054_066, 6.

75   Jones and Jenkins, *Words Between Us*, 37.

76   This principle is dealt with in U. Kim, 'Indigenous, cultural, and cross-cultural psychology: A theoretical, conceptual, and epistemological analysis', *Asian Journal of Social Psychology*, vol. 3, no. 3, 2000, 265–87.

77   T. Bentley, 'Images of Pakeha-Maori: A study of the representation of Pakeha-Maori by historians of New Zealand from Arthur Thomson (1859) to James Belich (1996)', PhD thesis, Waikato University, Hamilton, 2007, 12.

78   A. Wanhalla, *Matters of the Heart: A history of interracial marriage in New Zealand*, Auckland, 2013, 7.

79   *Missionary Journal of the Royal Admiral from Port Jackson to Tahiti, 13 March – 28 July 1801*, in Salmond, *Between Worlds*, 264–65.

80   *Sydney Gazette and New South Wales Advertiser*, 25 August 1810, 2.

81   R. Richards, *Murihiku Re-Viewed: A revised history of Southern New Zealand from 1804 to 1844*, Wellington, 1995, 23–24.

82   I. Campbell, *'Gone Native' in Polynesia: Captivity narratives and experiences from the South Pacific*, Westport, Conn., 1998, 4, in Bentley, 'Images of Pakeha-Maori', 12.

83   T.A. van Dijk, *Elite Discourse and Racism*, Newbury Park, 1993, 54; P.H. Lauren, *Power and Prejudice: The politics and diplomacy of racial discrimination*, Boulder, 1988, 19.

84   S. Dentith, *Epic and Empire in Nineteenth-century Britain*, Cambridge, 2006, 181.

85   J. Flatt, in *Report from the Select Committee of the House of Lords Appointed to Inquire into the Present State of the Islands of New Zealand, with minutes of evidence taken before the committee*, London, 1838, 51.

86   This is discussed in depth in J. Clifford, *The Predicament of Culture*, Cambridge, MA, 1988.

87   Nicholas, *Narrative of a Voyage to New Zealand*, vol. 1, 2.

88   Bentley, 'Images of Pakeha-Maori', 261, 267, 309; A. Calder (ed.), *Old New Zealand and Other Writings*, London, 2001, 1.

89   The tilt towards a binary interpretation is evident in C. Lévi-Strauss, *The Savage Mind*, Chicago, 1966. See also R. White, *The Middle Ground: Indians, empires and republics in the Great Lakes region 1630–1815*, Cambridge, 1991, xvii.

90   D. Thorp, 'Going native in New Zealand and America: Comparing Pakeha Maori and White Indians', *Journal of Imperial and Commonwealth History*, vol. 31, no. 3, 2003, 8; T. Bentley, *Pakeha Maori: The extraordinary story of the Europeans who lived as Maori in early New Zealand*, Auckland, 1999, 30.

91   White, *The Middle Ground*, xvi.

92   The same argument has been used in the English colonisation of Ireland in the Elizabethan era: see P. Palmer, *Language and Conquest in Early Modern Ireland*, 201.

93   The role of trade is discussed in R. Firth, *The Primitive Economics of the New Zealand Maori*, London, 1929, 444–45.

94   G. Clarke, *Notes on Early Life in New Zealand*, Hobart, 1903, 61.

95   The nature of status languages is surveyed in P.H. Lowenberg, 'Variations in Malaysian English: The pragmatics of languages in contact', in J. Cheshire (ed.), *English Around the World: Sociolinguistic perspectives*, Cambridge, 1996, 364–75.

96   See B.B. Kachru, 'Standards, codification, and sociolinguistic realism: The English language in the outer circle', in K. Boulton and B.B. Kachru (eds), *World Englishes: Critical concepts in linguistics*, Oxford, 2006, 241–69.

97   S. Marsden, in Elder (ed.), *The Letters and Journals of Samuel Marsden*, 59–60.

98   Ibid., 39.

99   J.G. Frazer, *The Golden Bough: A study in magic and religion*, London, 1922, 357.

100   Nicholas provided a roughly contemporary European view of tohunga: see J. L. Nicholas, *Narrative of a Voyage to New Zealand*, vol. 2, 174.

101   This term was used by Sir Stamford Raffles to describe the British Empire in 1819: see S. Raffles to T. Addenbrooke, Singapore, 10 June 1819, in T.S. Raffles, 'The founding of Singapore', *Journal of the Straits Branch of the Royal Asiatic Society*, vol. 2, December 1878, 175.

102   Church Missionary Society, *Proceedings of the Church Missionary Society for Africa and the East*, London, 1819, 196–98.

103   Although Marsden did produce his own Māori vocabulary: see Church Missionary Society, *Proceedings of the Church Missionary Society*, vol. 3, London, 1810, 111–26, in Salmond, *Between Worlds*, 411.

104   S. Marsden, in McNab (ed.), *Historical Records of New Zealand*, vol. 1, 391.

105   M. Lake, 'Samuel Marsden, work and the limits of evangelical humanitarianism', *History Australia*, vol. 7, no. 3, 2010, 57.4.

106   The date is variously quoted. The 4 March date is in *Sydney Gazette and New South Wales Advertiser*, 27 August 1814, 2; however, another edition of the same paper states that it would be at least a few days after 4 March that the ship would depart: see *Sydney Gazette and New South Wales Advertiser*, 4 March 1814, 2. The 14 March date, which is almost certainly the correct one, is in J.R. Elder (ed.), *Marsden's Lieutenants*, Dunedin, 1934, 43.

107   'Mr. King remains at Parramatta, as his going would not have been attended with any advantage till they all go, should Providence open a way for them,' wrote Marsden: in Elder (ed.), *Marsden's Lieutenants*, 47.

108   S. Marsden to Capt. Dillon, 9 March 1814, in Church Missionary Society, *The Missionary Register for the Year 1815*, London, 1815, 104.

109   T. Kendall to J. Pratt, in Elder (ed.), *Marsden's Lieutenants*, 49.

110   T. Kendall, in Elder (ed.), *Marsden's Lieutenants*, 68.

111   Not to be confused with John Eyre (1754–1803), the editor of the London Missionary Society's *Evangelical Magazine*.

112   T. Kendall to J. Pratt, 6 September 1814, Marsden Archive, Otago University, MS_0054_066.

113   T. Kendall to J. Pratt, 15 June 1814, Marsden Archive, Otago University, MS_0054_043. Current translations in L. Paterson, 'Speech to text: Missionary endeavours "to fix the Language of the New Zealanders"', paper delivered at the *Dialogues: Exploring the drama of early missionary encounters* symposium, Hocken Collections, Dunedin, 7–8 November 2014. Thanks to Dr Lachlan Paterson for kind permission to reproduce these.

114   T. Kendall to J. Pratt, 15 June 1814, Marsden Archive, Otago University, MS_0054_043.

115   Ibid.

116   T. Kendall, in Elder (ed.), *Marsden's Lieutenants*, 68.

117   A. Bell, *An Experiment in Education, made at the Male Asylum of Madras*, London, 1797, iii.

118   Whetoi later acquired the name Pomare I.

119   T. Kendall, in Elder (ed.), *Marsden's Lieutenants*, 68.

120   *Sydney Gazette and New South Wales Advertiser*, 12 November 1814, 1.

121   Elder (ed.), *The Letters and Journals of Samuel Marsden*, 62.

122   P. Moon, 'Why historical milestones should matter', *New Zealand Herald*, 2 December 2014, 12.

123   *Sydney Gazette and New South Wales Advertiser*, 8 October 1814, 2.

124   S. Marsden, 20 September 1815, in McNab (ed.), *Historical Records of New Zealand*, vol. 1, 403.

125   S. Marsden, in Elder (ed.), *The Letters and Journals of Samuel Marsden*, 78–79.

126   Nicholas, *Narrative of a Voyage to New Zealand*, vol. 1, 70–71.

127   J.L. Nicholas, *Narrative of a Voyage to New Zealand*, vol. 1, 71. As a side note, Nicholas reported: 'It is somewhat remarkable, that almost all the songs that are sung in New Zealand are composed by some tribes living in one part of the

Island, called by Europeans the East Cape, the inhabitants of which seem alone to have engrossed the favour of the muses, and may be exclusively considered as the bards of their country', ibid., 71–72.

128   S. Marsden, in Church Missionary Society, *The Missionary Register*, London, 1816, 461–62.

129   S. Marsden, in Elder (ed.), *The Letters and Journals of Samuel Marsden*, 93.

130   Ibid., 93–94.

131   J. Morgan, 'Oihi Bay, Christmas Day 1814; Samuel Marsden preaching the first sermon to the Maoris', *Weekly News*, Auckland, 1964, ref. no. B-077-002.

132   H. Taepa, 'He aha oti I te ingoa Maori: What's in a Maori name?', *Te Ao Hou: The New World*, no. 71, 1973, 17.

133   A. Jones and K. Jenkins, 'Indigenous discourse and "the material": A post-interpretivist argument', *International Review of Qualitative Research*, vol. 1, no. 2, 2008, 130.

CHAPTER 3: 'E MATE ANA MATOU I TE PUKAPUKA KORE': 1815 TO MID-1830s

1.   S. Muecke, 'A touching and contagious Captain Cook: Thinking history through things', *Cultural Studies Review*, vol. 14, no. 1, 2008, 33; S. Sivasundaram, 'Redeeming memory: The martyrdoms of Captain James Cook and Reverend John Williams', in G. Williams (ed.), *Captain Cook: Explorations and reassessments*, Suffolk, 2004, 201–29; G. Williams, '"As befits our age, there are no more heroes": Reassessing Captain Cook', in Williams (ed.), *Captain Cook*, 230–45; V. Collingridge, *Captain Cook: The life, death and legacy of history's greatest explorer*, London, 2003, 437–40.

2.   Among the first of these in the 1820s was J. Cook, *Voyages round the world, performed by Captain James Cook, F.R.S.: By royal authority, containing the whole of his discoveries in geography, navigation, astronomy, &c ...* , London, 1820; A. Kippis, *Narrative of the voyages round the world performed by Captain James Cook: with an account of his life during the previous and intervening periods*, London, 1820.

3.   A. Earle, *A Narrative of a Nine Months' Residence in New Zealand, In 1827; Together with a journal of a residence in Tristan D'Acunha, an island situated between South America and the Cape of Good Hope*, London, 1832, 148.

4.   J.S. Polack, *New Zealand: Being a narrative of travels and adventures during a residence in that country*, vol. 1, 14.

5.   J.A. Mackay, *Historic Poverty Bay and the East Coast, N.I., N.Z.*, Gisborne, 1949, 464–67; *Poverty Bay Herald*, 29 September 1888, 3.

6.   Polack, *New Zealand: Being a narrative*, vol. 1, 15.

7.   H. Petrie, *Chiefs of Industry: Māori tribal enterprise in early colonial New Zealand*, Auckland, 2006, 32–35; H. Petrie, 'Colonisation and the involution of the Māori economy', *XIII World Conference of Economic History*, Buenos Aires, 2002.

8.   Polack, *New Zealand: Being a narrative of travels and adventures during a residence in that country, between the years 1831 and 1837*, vol. 2, London, 1838, 128–29.

9. J. Moorfield, 6 September 2011, personal correspondence.

10. P. Moon, *Encounters – The Creation of New Zealand: A history*, Auckland, 2013, 340–41.

11. C. Grant, *Observations on the state of society among the Asiatic subjects of Great Britain, particularly with respect to morals: and on the means of improving it*, London, 1813, 78.

12. The father of John Stuart Mill.

13. J. Mill, Court of Directors of the East India Company to the Committee of Public Instruction of Bengal, 1824, in S. Mahmood, *A History of English Education in India*, Aligarh, 1895, 30. The context for Mill's views are in E.H. Cutts, 'The background of Macaulay's minute', *American Historical Review*, vol. 58, no. 4, July 1953, 825.

14. J. Mill in M. Levin, *J.S. Mill on Civilisation and Barbarism*, London, 2006, 31.

15. W. Bentinck, in K.A. Ballhatchet, 'The Home Government and Bentinck's educational policy', *Cambridge Historical Journal*, vol. 10, no. 2, 1951, 224.

16. T.B. Macaulay, 'Minute recorded in the General Department by Thomas Babington Macaulay, law member of the governor-general's council, date 2 February 1835', in M. Moir and L. Zastouopiul (eds), *The Great Indian Education Debate: Documents relating to the Orientalist-Anglicist controversy, 1781–1843*, Oxford, 2013, 165–66.

17. R. Phillipson, *Linguistic Imperialism*, Oxford, 1992, 110–11.

18. B. Davis, *The Problem of Slavery in Western Culture*, Oxford, 1966, 281.

19. M.T. Hodgen, *Early Anthropology in the Sixteenth and Seventeenth Centuries*, Philadelphia, 1971, 332–33.

20. W.W. Rostow, 'The stages of economic growth', in P. Worsley (ed.), *Modern Sociology*, London, 1988, 141.

21. T. Hobbes (ed. A.R. Waller), *Leviathan or the Matter, Forme and Power of a Commonwealth, ecclesiasticall and civill*, London, 1651 (Cambridge 1904), 84.

22. M.F. Borch, *Conciliation, Compulsion, Conversion: British attitudes towards indigenous peoples, 1763–1814*, New York, 2004, ch. 6.

23. And among the British, there was relatively little appetite for the sentimentalism of Rousseau's Noble Savage; see B. Smith, *European Vision and the South Pacific*, New Haven, 1985, 105–09.

24. Moon, *Encounters*, part 1.

25. J.R. Elder (ed.), *The Letters and Journals of Samuel Marsden, 1765–1838*, Dunedin, 1932, 89.

26. W. Williams, *Christianity among the New Zealanders*, London, 1867, 54.

27. F. Mathew (ed. J. Rutherford), *The Founding of New Zealand: The journals of Felton Mathew, first Surveyor-General of New Zealand, and his wife, 1840–1847*, Dunedin, 1940, 52.

28. J.T. Thomson, *Rambles with a Philosopher*, Dunedin, 1867, 140.

29. J.C. Crawford, *Recollections of Travel in New Zealand and Australia*, Edinburgh, 1880, 26.

30. R. Taylor, *Te Ika a Maui, or, New Zealand and its inhabitants*, London, 1855, 317.

31. J. Webster, *Reminiscences of an Old Settler in Australia and New Zealand*, Christchurch, 1908, 274.

32. S.H. Selwyn, *Reminiscences, 1809–1867*, Auckland, 1961, 28.

33. J.S. Polack, *Manners and Customs of the New Zealanders*, vol. 1, London, 1840, 83.

34. W. Gladstone, in M.E. Chamberlain, *'Pax Britannica'? British foreign policy 1789–1914*, Oxford, 1999, 132.

35. Marsden noted: 'We could not ascertain the exact quantity for want of proper measuring instruments, but as it is situated between some natural boundaries expressed in the grant I considered that of no moment; at least I apprehended it to contain more than 200 acres – one side bounded by the harbour,' in Elder (ed.), *The Letters and Journal of Samuel Marsden*, 123.

36. Ibid.

37. A. Jones and K. Jenkins, *Words Between Us – He Kōrero: First Māori-Pākehā conversations on paper*, 92

38. Church Missionary Society, *The Missionary Register 1816*, London, 1816, August, 328.

39. J.L. Nicholas, *Narrative of a Voyage to New Zealand*, vol. 2, 192–93.

40. S. Marsden, in Elder (ed.), *The Letters and Journal of Samuel Marsden*, 123.

41. A. Gaur, *A History of Writing*, London, 1992, 7.

42. N. Te Awekotuku, *'Moko Māori: An understanding of pain'*, in J. Hendry and L. Fitznor (eds), *Anthropologists, Indigenous Scholars and the Research Endeavour: Seeking bridges towards mutual respect*, New York, 2012, 208–25.

43. J. Pratt, in J. Pratt and J.J. Pratt, *Memoir of the Rev. Josiah Pratt, B.D., late Vicar of St. Stephen's, Coleman Street, and for twenty-one years Secretary of the Church Missionary Society*, London, 1849, 109, 211.

44. J. Pratt to T. Kendall, 16 August 1815, Marsden Archive, Otago University, MS_0055_019.

45. B. Stanley, *The Bible and the Flag: Protestant missions and British Imperialism in the nineteenth and twentieth centuries*, Leicester, 1992, 78.

46. T. Kendall to S. Marsden, 27 May 1815, Marsden Archive, Otago University, MS_0055_012.

47. His letter to Marsden emphasised that living in New Zealand incurred very little expense. T. Kendall to S. Marsden, 27 May 1815, Marsden Archive, Otago University, MS_0055_012.

48. T. Kendall, *A Korao no New Zealand, or, The New Zealander's first book: being an attempt to compose some lessons for the instruction of the natives*, Sydney, 1815, in Auckland Museum Library, ref. EMI0001.

49. J. Binney, *The Legacy of Guilt: A life of Thomas Kendall*, Wellington, 2005, 175.

50. L. Paterson, 'Speech to text: Missionary endeavours "to fix the Language of the New Zealanders"', paper delivered at the *Dialogues: Exploring the drama of early missionary encounters* symposium, Hocken Collections, Dunedin, 7–8 November 2014.

51. Binney, *The Legacy of Guilt*, 63.

52. P. Smyth, *Maori Pronunciation and the Evolution of Written Maori*, Christchurch, 1946, 13.

53. W. Brown, *New Zealand and its Aborigines*, 2nd edn, London, 1851, 100.

54. T. Kendall to J. Pratt, 19 October 1815, Marsden Archive, Otago University, MS_0055_022.

55. W. Hall to J. Pratt 22 August 1816, in Elder (ed.), *The Letters and Journals of Samuel Marsden*, 222.

56. J. Venn and J.A. Venn, *Alumni Cantabrigienses from the Earliest Times to 1900*, vol. 4, Cambridge, 1927, pt 2, 133; N. Green, 'The Madrasas of Oxford: Iranian interactions with the English universities in the early nineteenth century', *Iranian Studies*, vol. 44, no. 6, 2011, 814.

57. A.M. Lee, *A Scholar of a Past Generation: A brief memoir of Samuel Lee, D.D.*, London, 1896, 22.

58. As an example, see T. Tooi [sic] to J. Pratt, 17 September 1818, Marsden Archive, Otago University, MS_0056_096.

59. Church Missionary Society, *The Missionary Register 1819*, London, 1819, 465.

60. These would include material such as the Anglican Book of Common Prayer, the Apostles' Creed, the sacraments, and so on.

61. J. Pratt and E. Bickersteth to T. Kendall, 12 March 1818, Marsden Archive, Otago University, MS_0056_076.

62. P. Muhlhausler, '"Reducing" Pacific languages to writings', in J.E. Joseph and T.E. Taylor (eds), *Ideologies of Language*, Oxford, 2014, 198–99.

63. J. Rule, 'Vernacular literacy in the western and lower Southern Highlands provinces: A case study of a mission's involvement', in S.A. Wurm (ed.), *New Guinea Area Languages and Language Study*, vol. 3, Department of Linguistics, Research School of Pacific Studies, Australian National University, Canberra, 1977, 390.

64. W.J. Ong, *Orality and Literacy: The technologization of the word*, London, 1982, 52; P.M. Greenfield, 'Oral or written language: The consequences for cognitive development in Africa, the United States and England', *Language and Speech*, vol. 15, no. 2, 1972, 169–78.

65. P.A. Roberts, *From Oral to Literate Culture: Colonial experience in the English West Indies*, Kingston, 1997, 132.

66. W. Colenso, *Three Literary Papers: Read Before the Hawke's Bay Philosophical Institute, during the session of 1882*, Napier, 1883, 21.

67. M. Tomalin, '" … to this rule there are many exceptions": Robert Maunsell and the Grammar of Maori', *Historiographia Linguistica*, vol. 33, no. 3, 2006, 309.

68. R. Maunsell, *Grammar of the New Zealand Language*, Auckland, 1842, x.

69. Tomalin, '" … to this rule there are many exceptions"', 310–11.

70. A. Hastings, *The Construction of Nationhood: Ethnicity, religion, and nationalism*, Cambridge, 1997, 152, in Tomalin, '"… to this rule there are many exceptions"', 311. There were pronunciation variations even within the Bay of Islands, such as the use of wēnei, wēna, wēra instead of ēnei, ēna, ēra in Rawhiti: M. Howard to P. Moon, personal communication, 3 March 2015.

71. T.A. Pybus, *Maori and Missionary: Early Christian missions in the South Island of New Zealand*, Wellington, 1954, 1.

72. B. Biggs, 'The Maori language past and present', in E. Schwimmer (ed.), *The Maori People in the Nineteen-sixties*, Auckland, 1972, 65.

73. J. Watkins, in Pybus, *Maori and Missionary*, 8.

74. J. Watkins, *He Puka Ako i te Korero Maori*, Mangungu, 1841, ATL, Ref. BIM 99. Also see R. Harlow, *A Word-list of South Island Maori*, Auckland, 1985.

75. R. Harlow, 'Regional variation in Maori', *New Zealand Journal of Archaeology*, vol. 1, 1979, 130–31; J. McRae, 'From Māori oral traditions to print', in P. Griffith, R. Harvey and K. Maslen (eds), *Book & Print in New Zealand: A guide to print culture in Aotearoa*, Wellington, 1997, 19.

76. D.P. Resnick and L.B. Resnick, 'The nature of literacy: An historical exploration', *Harvard Educational Review*, vol. 47, no. 3, 1977, 370–85; J.T. Guthrie, 'Equilibrium of literacy', *Journal of Reading*, vol. 26, no. 7, 1983, 668–70.

77. L. Hallewell, *Books in Brazil: A history of the publishing trade*, New Jersey, 1982, in P.A. Roberts, *From Oral to Literate Culture*, 133.

78. S.H. Steinberg, *Five Hundred Years of Printing*, Bristol, 1961, 11; E.L. Eisenstein, *The Printing Revolution in Early Modern Europe*, 2nd edn, Cambridge, 2005, 5–6.

79. S. Lee, in A.M. Lee, *A Scholar of a Past Generation*, 36–37.

80. J.R. Elder (ed.), *Marsden's Lieutenants*, 144.

81. Church Missionary Society, *The Missionary Register 1820*, 327.

82. S. Lee and T. Kendall, *A Grammar and Vocabulary of the Language of New Zealand*, London, 1820, preface.

83. Ibid.

84. Church Missionary Society, *The Missionary Register 1820*, 499.

85. The first copies of *A Grammar and Vocabulary of the Language of New Zealand* arrived in Hawai`i on 1 January 1822. See A.J. Schutz, *The Voices of Eden: A history of Hawaiian language studies*, Honolulu, 1994, 107; C.M. Wise and W. Hervey, 'The evolution of the Hawaiian orthography', *Quarterly Journal of Speech*, vol. 38, no. 3, 1952, 313.

86. Even in the late twentieth century, orthographic conventions for te reo Māori had still not been standardised.

87. Schutz, *The Voices of Eden*, 251.

88. S. Marsden, in Elder (ed.), *The Letters and Journals of Samuel Marsden*, 373–74.

89. H. Williams to E.G. Marsh, 4 February 1824, in H. Carleton, *The Life of Henry Williams, Archdeacon of Waimate*, vol. 1, Auckland, 1874, 37.

90. T. Kendall to S. Lee, 7 January 1825, in Elder (ed.), *Marsden's Lieutenants*, 215.

91. C. Terry, *New Zealand: Its advantages and prospects as a British colony*, London, 1843, 180–81.

92. And as editor of the *New Zealand Herald and Auckland Gazette*, Terry's readership was particularly wide.

93. An especially thick paper was used to make the books last longer. Details on the quality of paper are included in T.M. Hocken, 'Some account of the beginnings of literature in New Zealand', *Transactions and Proceedings of the New Zealand Institute*, 1900, 474–75.

94. C. Hill, *The English Bible and the Seventeenth-Century Revolution*, London, 1994, 10.

95. S. Marsden, in Elder (ed.), *The Letters and Journals of Samuel Marsden*, 375–76.

96. R.J.C. Young, *Colonial Desire: Hybridity in theory, culture and race*, London, 1994, 21.

97. H.K. Bhabha, *The Location of Culture*, Oxford, 1994, 162; A. Pennycook, *The Cultural Politics of English as an International Language*, Harlow, 1994, introduction.

98. V.B. Lunga, 'Mapping African postcoloniality: Linguistic and cultural spaces of hybridity', *Perspectives on Global Development and Technology*, vol. 3, no. 3, 2004, 291.

99. S. Marsden, in Elder (ed.), *The Letters and Journals of Samuel Marsden*, 375–76.

100. Ibid.

101. T. Kendall, in Binney, *The Legacy of Guilt*, 106.

102. T. Kendall to Church Missionary Society, 10 October 1827, in Elder (ed.), *The Letters and Journals of Samuel Marsden*, 418.

103. Ibid.

104. Lee, *A Scholar of a Past Generation*, 250.

105. T. Kendall to Church Missionary Society, 10 October 1827, in Elder (ed.), *The Letters and Journals of Samuel Marsden*, 418.

106. Mark 16: 14–16, Bible, New International Version.

107. A.S. Thomson, *The Story of New Zealand: Past and present, savage and civilized*, vol. 1, London, 1859, 310.

108. Ibid., 312.

109. P. Lineham, 'Tampering with the sacred text: The second edition of the *Maori Bible*', in P. Griffith, P. Hughes and A. Loney (eds), *A Book in the Hand: Essays on the history of the book in New Zealand*, Auckland, 2000, 30–31, 39.

110. W. Colenso, cited in Lineham, 'Tampering with the sacred text', 31.

111. This issue of church and state is addressed in W. Hobhouse, *The Church and the World in Idea and History*, London, 1910, 312–27; A. Porter, 'Introduction', in A. Porter (ed.), *The Imperial Horizons of British Protestant Missions 1880–1914*, Michigan, 2003, 4.

112. One of the more overt cases made for the missionaries in New Zealand being cultural imperialists appears in R. Walker, *Ka Whawhai Tonu Matou: Struggle without end*, Auckland, 1990, 81ff.

113. A. Porter, '"Cultural imperialism" and the Protestant missionary enterprise, 1780–1914', *Journal of Imperial and Commonwealth History*, vol. 25, no. 3, September 1997, 373.

114. D.L. Robert, 'Introduction', in D.L. Robert (ed.), *Converting Colonialism: Visions and realities in mission history, 1706–1914*, Michigan, 2008, 3.

115. E. Stock, *The History of the Church Missionary Society in New Zealand*, Wellington, 1935, foreword.

116. W. Knight, *Memoir of Henry Venn, B.D.: Prebendary of St. Paul's, and honorary secretary of the Church Missionary Society*, London, 1882, 287.

117. C.P. Williams, 'The Church Missionary Society and the indigenous church in the second half of the nineteenth century: The defense and destruction of the Venn ideals', in Robert (ed.), *Converting Colonialism*, 86.

118. H. Venn to H. Townsend, 4 February 1862, in CMS Letter-book, 24 December 1860 – 23 September 1867, CMS/B/OMS/C A2 L3, Cadbury Research Library, Special Collections, University of Birmingham; H. Venn to G.L.C. Cotton, 26 December 1864, in CMS Letter-book, 25 January 1862 – 30 April 1866, CMS/B/OMS/C I1 L6, Cadbury Research Library, Special Collections, University of Birmingham.

119. J.G. Turner, *The Pioneer Missionary: Life of the Rev. Nathaniel Turner, missionary in New Zealand, Tonga, and Australia*, Melbourne, 1872, 167.

120. As an example involving French loanwords, see F. Mossé, 'On the chronology of French loan-words in English', *English Studies*, vol. 25, issue 1–6, 1943, 33–40.

121. S. Marsden, in Elder (ed.), *The Letters and Journals of Samuel Marsden*, 329.

122. W. Williams (ed. F. Porter), *The Turanga Journals, 1840–1850*, Wellington, 1974, 43; R. Davis to J.N. Coleman, 28 December 1824, in J.N. Coleman, *A Memoir of the Rev. Richard Davis*, London, 1865, 61.

123. J. Shepherd to S. Marsden, 12 February 1822, and J. Shepherd to Church Missionary Society, 2 December 1822, in CMS Mission Book: documents received 29 May 1822 – 3 July 1824, CMS/B/OMS/C N M2, Cadbury Research Library, Special Collections, University of Birmingham.

124. Church Missionary Society, *The Missionary Register 1824*, London, 1824, 78.

125. Williams, *The Turanga Journals, 1840–1850*, 43.

126. R. Davis to J.N. Coleman, 28 December 1824, in Coleman, *A Memoir of the Rev. Richard Davis*, 61.

127. Church Missionary Society, *The Missionary Register 1814*, London, 1814, 29–30.

128. J. Philip to S. Wilderspin, 29 July 1831, in S. Wilderspin, *Early Discipline Illustrated; or, The infant system prospering and successful*, London, 1832, 16–17, cited in L. Prochner, H. May and B. Kaur, '"The blessings of civilisation": Nineteenth-century missionary infant schools for young native children in three colonial settings – India, Canada and New Zealand 1820s–1840s', *Paedagogica Historica: International Journal of the History of Education*, vol. 45, nos. 1–2, 2009, 87.

129. W. Brown, *New Zealand and Its Aborigines*, 2nd edn, London, 1851, 97–98.

130. Henry Williams established a school in Paihia in December 1827: L.M. Rogers (ed.), *The Early Journals of Henry Williams*, Christchurch, 1961, 90. However, in some cases, the age range was still considerable: Rogers (ed.), *The Early Journals of Henry Williams*, 362, 367, 378; T. Kendall, in Elder (ed.), *Marsden's Lieutenants*, 133–34.

131. T. Kendall, in Elder (ed.), *Marsden's Lieutenants*, 134.

132. J. Shepherd to S. Marsden, 12 February 1822, Marsden Archive, Otago University, MS_0057_070.

133. R. Davis to S. Marsden, 23 October 1826, in Coleman, *A Memoir of the Rev. Richard Davis*, 83.

134. R. Davis, 11 September 1827, in Coleman, *A Memoir of the Rev. Richard Davis*, 96; Church Missionary Society, *The Church Missionary Register 1828*, London, 1828, 214.

135. Church Missionary Society, *The Church Missionary Register 1831*, London, 1831, 67–68.

136. Paterson, 'Speech to text'.

137. W. Yate, *An Account of New Zealand; and of the formation and progress of the Church Missionary Society's mission in the Northern Island*, 2nd edn, London, 1835, 231.

138. Ibid., 232.

139. Ibid., 239.

140. The term 'slave', although it is widely used, is a bit of a misnomer: many of these 'slaves' eventually integrated into the community that had captured them

and occasionally even assumed important roles there, and their offspring were usually not considered slaves or captives in any sense.

141. Yate, *An Account of New Zealand*, 240.

142. E. Shortland, *Traditions and Superstitions of the New Zealanders: With illustrations of their manners and customs*, 2nd edn, London, 1856, 85.

143. J.S. Polack, *New Zealand, Being a Narrative of Travels and Adventures during a Residence in that Country Between the Years 1831 and 1837*, vol. 2, London, 1838, 253.

144. Ibid., 253.

145. As examples, see T. Fitzgerald, 'Jumping the fences: Maori women's resistance to missionary schooling in northern New Zealand 1823–1835', *Paedagogica Historica*, vol. 37, no. 1, 2001, 177–80; B.J. Hokowhitu, 'Te mana Maori : Te tatari i nga korero parau', PhD thesis, University of Otago, Dunedin, 2002, ii, 3, 37, 45; R. Whaitiri, 'A sovereign mission: Maori maids, maidens and mothers', in G. Stilz (ed.), *Missions of Interdependence: A literary directory*, New York, 2002, 380.

146. C.J. Parr, 'A missionary library: Printed attempts to instruct the Maori, 1815–1845', *Journal of the Polynesian Society*, vol. 70, no. 4, 1961, 429–36; S. May, 'Language and education rights for indigenous peoples', *Language, Culture and Curriculum*, vol. 11, no. 3, 1998, 284; B. Spolsky, 'Reassessing Māori regeneration', *Language in Society*, vol. 32, no. 4, October 2003, 556.

147. W. Wade, *A Journey in the Northern Island of New Zealand*, Hobart, 1842, 123.

148. *The Colonist*, 17 September 1835, 303.

149. A. Jones and K. Jenkins, 'Invitation and refusal: A reading of the beginnings of schooling in Aotearoa New Zealand', *History of Education*, vol. 37, no. 2, March 2008, 187.

150. D. Cannadine, *Ornamentalism: How the British saw their empire*, Oxford, 2001, xvi; P.B. Rich, *Race and Empire in British Politics*, Cambridge, 1990, 12, 77; R. Strong, *Anglicanism and the British Empire, c. 1700–1850*, Oxford, 2007, ch. 1.

151. Jones and Jenkins, 'Invitation and refusal', 191.

152. Church Missionary Society, *The Missionary Register 1827*, London, 1827, 341; *Sydney Gazette and New South Wales Advertiser*, 10 February 1827, 2; S. Marsden to D. Coates, 24 February 1827, in McNab (ed.), *Historical Records of New Zealand*, vol. 1, 669.

153. B.S. Cohn, *Colonisation and Its Forms of Knowledge: The British in India*, Princeton, 1996, 41–42; J.A. Mangan, 'Images for confident control: Stereotyoes in imperial discourse', in J.A. Mangan (ed.), *The Imperial Curriculum: Racial images and education in the British colonial experience*, Oxford, 2012, 9, 10; C. McGeorge, 'Race, empire and the Maori in the New Zealand primary school curriculum, 1880–1940', in Mangan (ed.), *The Imperial Curriculum*, 76.

154. M.C. Hawkins, '"Disrupted" historical trajectories and indigenous agency: Rethinking imperial impact in Southeast Asian history', *Sojourn: Journal of Social Issues in Southeast Asia*, vol. 22, no. 2, 2007, 274.

155. H. Petrie, *Chiefs of Industry*, chs 4 and 5.

156. The revolution in the Māori economy at this time is detailed in Petrie, *Chiefs of Industry*, 67–73.

157. D.R. Olson, *The World on Paper: The conceptual and cognitive implications of writing and reading*, Cambridge, 1998, 2–7.
158. Earle cites such an example in *A Narrative of Nine Months' Residence in New Zealand in 1827*, 154–55.
159. Ruatara was an example of a chief who offered his patronage to the Anglican mission in the Bay of Islands but held back from embracing Christianity personally, even though he was apparently happy to let members of his hapū convert to the new religion.
160. Jones and Jenkins, 'Invitation and refusal', 201.
161. Petrie, 'Colonisation and the involution of the Māori economy'; A. Middleton, *Te Puna: A New Zealand mission station*, New York, 2008, 84–117.
162. L.M. Rogers (ed.), *The Early Journals of Henry Williams*, 480–81.
163. Nicholas, *Narrative of a Voyage to New Zealand*, vol. 2, 324. These difficulties in hearing the details of vowels and consonant sounds in te reo Māori account for a huge range of spellings attempted by some Europeans. Interview with Robert Pouwhare, 19 January 2005.
164. Lawrence Rogers, the editor of Henry Williams' early journals, explains this trend to greater uniformity, citing Maunsell's *Grammar*: 'By 1827 more of the difficulties had been solved. The phonetic symbol *d* had been dropped as an initial consonant, although it was still used medially. There were indeed two sounds represented by *r*, but *d* as a symbol did not represent the difference. In Henry Williams' journal there is evidence of the development of the conviction that *r* was the best symbol. For example, at first he spells *Kedi kedi*, later it becomes *Keri Kedi*, and later still *Keri Keri*; at first he spells *Waikadi*, and later it becomes *Waikari*. He never uses the *wh* symbol, but uses *w* in all cases, e.g., *wakawa* for *whakawa*; *wakaaro* for *whakaaro*. There was, in fact, some considerable discussion over the use of the symbol *wh,* and finality did not come until much later. Maunsell, in his *Grammar of the New Zealand Language*, published in 1842, treats *wh* as merely a variant of *w,* "which has two sounds, one simple, as that in *wind, &c; wai,* water, *waka,* a canoe, *ware,* a plebeian. 2. An aspirated *w,* as in *when, where, &c.: whai,* follow, *whare,* a house, &c." But this does not satisfy him, for he adds a footnote: "The reader will observe that the author has deviated from the established usage, and occasionally introduced the *wh* into his pages. The fact is, he had not proceeded far when he found the simple *w* very inconvenient. There are multitudes of words in the language very diverse in meaning, spelt in the same way, and yet distinguished in speaking by the aspirated *w.* In some of the Polynesian islands to the northward, this sound is denoted by *f,* and such a practice is well worthy of attention. As for the remark that the simple *w* is desirable for simplicity, the author would observe, that, if by simplicity, be meant jumbling together things that are totally different, then Maori has to acknowledge its obligations to such a plan, for not only *poverty,* but *simplicity.* In a language so contracted in the range of its consonants as Maori, our object should not, the author conceives, be to abridge, but enlarge. Indeed, as the organs of speech, as well as knowledge, of the aborigines improve, there is little doubt but that an addition to our present characters will be necessary."' Rogers (ed.), *The Early Journals of Henry Williams*, 482.

165. E. Markham (ed. by E.H. McCormick), *New Zealand or Recollections of it*, Wellington, 1963, 62.

166. Church Missionary Society, *The Church Missionary Record*, London, 1831, 21.

167. Ibid., 22.

168. A voiceless palato-alveolar sibilant.

169. Paterson, 'Speech to text'.

170. Polack, *New Zealand*, vol. 2, 280.

171. A. Earle, 'The residence of Shulitea chief of Kororadika [Kororareka], Bay of Islands, New Zealand', watercolour; 21.9 x 36.2 cm, Rex Nan Kivell Collection; NK12/71, nla.pic-an2820827, National Library of Australia.

172. A. Earle, *A Narrative of a Nine Months' Residence in New Zealand*, 53.

173. Ibid., 62.

174. S. Marsden to J. Pratt, 12 February 1820, in Marsden Archive, Otago University, MS_0057_024.

175. T. Kendall to J. Pratt, 16 October 1820, in Marsden Archive, Otago University, MS_0498_096.

176. R.J. Barton (ed.), *Earliest New Zealand: The journals and correspondence of the Rev. John Butler*, Masterton, 1927, 403.

177. G. Craik, *The New Zealanders*, London, 1830, 115. Craik most probably copied the spelling from another source.

178. Barton (ed.), *Earliest New Zealand*, 395.

179. J. Shepherd to S. Marsden, 12 February 1822, in Marsden Archive, Otago University, MS_0057_070.

180. McNab, *Historical Records of New Zealand*, vol. 1, 482.

181. Ibid., 602.

182. H. Piripi, 'Te Tiriti o Waitangi and the New Zealand public sector', in V.M.H. Tawhai and K. Grey-Sharp (eds), *"Always Speaking": The Treaty of Waitangi and public policy*, Wellington, 2011, 229–44.

183. Māori letter from Eruera Hongi to CMS missionaries, 1825: Webster collection and papers of Kenneth Athol Webster, MS-Papers-1009-2/71-01, ATL.

184. R.J. Barton (ed.), *Earliest New Zealand*, 103.

185. F.R. Chapman (ed.), A. McCrae, *Journal Kept in New Zealand in 1820 by Ensign Alexander McCrae*, Wellington, 1928, 5.

186. S. Marsden, in Elder (ed.), *The Letters and Journals of Samuel Marsden*, 431.

187. Ibid., 124.

188. T. Kendall to J. Pratt, 15 June 1814, in in Marsden Archive, Otago University, MS_0054_043.

189. S. Lee and T. Kendall, *A Grammar and Vocabulary*, ii.

190. R. Maunsell, *Grammar of the New Zealand Language* (1842), 2nd edn, Auckland, 1862, 7.

191. M. Mutu to P. Moon, personal communication, 8 April 2015.

192. 'Ishu Karaiti' was spoken by some members of Ngāti Hine in church services, rather than the commonly used Ihu Karaiti (for 'Jesus Christ'). E. Henare to P. Moon, personal communication, 8 April 2015.

193. K. Kelly to P. Moon, personal communication, 3 March 2015; M. Howard to P. Moon, personal communication, 3 March 2015.

194. The effect of standardisation on other languages is surveyed in S. Hadebe, *The Standardisation of the Ndebele Language through Dictionary-making*, Allex Project, University of Zimbabwe, Harere, 2002, 29–30; G. Ansre, 'Language standardisation in sub-Saharan Africa', in J. Fishman (ed.), *Advances in Language Planning*, The Hague, 1974, 369–90; N.C. England, 'Linguistics and indigenous American languages: Mayan examples', *Journal of Latin American Anthropology*, vol. 1, no. 1, 1995, 122–49; K.A. King, 'Language ideologies and heritage language education', *International Journal of Bilingual Education and Bilingualism*, vol. 3, no. 3, 2000, 167–84.

195. Rogers (ed.), *The Early Journals of Henry Williams*, 482.

196. Coleman, *A Memoir of the Rev. Richard Davis*, 62; Rogers (ed.), *The Early Journals of Henry Williams*, 107.

197. Rogers (ed.), *The Early Journals of Henry Williams*, 494.

198. Ibid., 482.

199. This figure is an extrapolation of Thomson's statistic of two thirds by 1838: Thomson, *The Story of New Zealand*, vol. 1, 312.

200. Ibid.

201. H. Williams in Carleton, *The Life of Henry Williams*, 96.

202. E. Ramsden, *Marsden and the Missions*. Sydney, 1936, 125.

203. Church Missionary Society, *The Missionary Register 1833*, London, 1833, 550.

204. F. Porter (ed.), *The Turanga Journals, 1840–1850: The letters and journals of William and Jane Williams*, Wellington, 1974, 53.

205. D.F. McKenzie, *Oral Culture, Literacy and Print in Early New Zealand: The Treaty of Waitangi*, Wellington, 1985, 32.

206. Ibid., 31.

207. The same perception of books has existed in other cultures too, at times: see D. Cressy, 'Books as totems in seventeenth-century England and New England', *Journal of Library History*, vol. 21, no. 1, Winter 1986, 92–93.

208. R. Davis, 21 November 1832, in Church Missionary Society, *The Missionary Register 1833*, 548.

209. H. Williams, 8 November 1833, in Rogers (ed.), *The Early Journals of Henry Williams*, 342–43.

210. G. Clarke, *Notes on Early Life in New Zealand*, Hobart, 1903, 31–32.

211. N.J. Smelser and S.M. Lipset, 'Social structure, mobility and development', in N.J. Smelser and S.M. Lipset (eds), *Social Structure and Mobility in Economic Development*, New Brunswick, 2005, 12.

212. J.P. Greene, *The Intellectual Construction of America*, Chapel Hill, 1993, 55; H.M. Beckles, 'The "Hub of empire": The Caribbean and Britain in the seventeenth century', in N. Canny (ed.), *The Oxford History of the British Empire*, vol. 1, Oxford, 2001, 222; D. Armitage, *The Ideological Origins of the British Empire*, Cambridge, 2001, 53; E.D. Smith, *Globalisation, Utopia, and Post-colonial Science Fiction*, London, 2012, 48.

213. T.R. Metcalf, *Ideologies of the Raj*, Cambridge, 1995, 32–34; D. Heath, *Purifying Empire: Obscenity and the politics of moral regulation in Britain, India, and Australia*, Cambridge, 2010, 154.

214. W. Jacob, 13 March 1833, Church Missionary Society, *Church Missionary*

Record: Detailing the Proceedings of the Church Missionary Society, vol. 3, London, 1834, 9.

215. For the sense in which this term is used, see D.C. Tipps, 'Modernization theory and the comparative study of national societies: A critical perspective', *Comparative Studies in Society and History*, vol. 15, no. 2, 1973, 199–226.

216. The Society for Promoting Christian Knowledge, *Domestic Scenes in New Zealand*, 2nd edn, London (1845) 1857, 77–78.

217. Their irreducibility meant they could not be modified in any way to make them more acceptable to the coloniser. This issue is identified in N. Thomas, 'Colonial conversations: Difference, hierarchy and history in early twentieth-century evangelical propaganda', in C. Hall (ed.), *Cultures of Empire: A reader*, Manchester, 2000, 299.

218. This issue is raised in J. Buller, *Forty Years in New Zealand: Including a personal narrative, an account of Maoridom, and of the Christianization and colonization of the country*, London, 1878, 181.

219. J.B.F. Pompallier, *Early History of the Catholic Church in Oceania*, Auckland, 1888, 49–50.

220. J.M.R. Owens, 'Christianity and the Maoris to 1840', *NZJH*, vol. 2, no. 1, 1968, 20–21; M.H. Wright, *New Zealand 1769–1840*, 142–57; K. Sinclair, *A History of New Zealand*, Auckland, 1988, 46. Poia Rewi has rightly identified this as a complex issue, fed by a number of factors, including the influence of proximity to settler communities on the perception of te reo by Māori: P. Rewi to P. Moon, personal communication, 27 January 2015. In a similar vein, Te Haumihiata Mason suggests that 'a sudden influx of a great number of new terms, whether they be loanwords or neologisms, might cause a divide between the old and the new both linguistically and culturally. The translation of the Bible is certainly an example from the 1800s and the coining of a considerable number of new words to enable the curriculum to be taught in Māori might be a more modern example'. T.H.H. Mason to P. Moon, personal communication, 27 January 2015.

221. Richard Benton's comments on the issue of linguistic destabilisation are instructive: 'The Māori belief system was undoubtedly challenged both by missionary ideas and also the contact with capitalism, post-Enlightenment science, and the new social and political order which arrived together with and after the missionaries. But the missionaries worked through the Māori language, and I think that much of the new vocabulary constituted the addition of new ideas, which was probably semantically helpful – simply because they were new ideas, it was sensible to encode them in a different vocabulary. The new coinages respected the sound system of Māori as far as phonemes and syllable structure were concerned, with only a few minor violations of Māori phonotactics (the first syllable wuru, "wool", contains a sound combination not found in indigenous Māori words, but such aberrations are rare exceptions).

CHAPTER 4: 'A MERE LANGUAGE OF TRADITION': MID-1830s TO c. 1850

1.   R.A. Huttenback, 'The British Empire as a "white man's country": Racial attitudes and immigration legislation in the colonies of white settlement', *Journal of British Studies*, vol. 13, no. 1, November 1973, 108–37; for the nineteenth-century perspective on the benefits of these 'white colonies', see D.A. Wells, 'Great Britain and the United States: Their true relations', *North American Review*, vol. 162, April 1896, 394–403.

2.   F. Nietzsche, *On the Genealogy of Morals* (1887), New York, 1923, 10, 43.

3.   S. Raffles to Somerset, 12 June 1821, in S. Raffles, *Memoir of the Life and Public Services of Sir Thomas Stamford Raffles*, London, 1830, 498.

4.   P. Brantlinger, 'Victorians and Africans: The genealogy of the myth of the dark continent', *Critical Inquiry*, vol. 12, no. 1, Autumn, 1985, 166.

5.   A. Pennycook, *The Cultural Politics of English as an International Language*, Harlow, 1994, 76–77.

6.   Ibid., 77.

7.   G. Viswanathan, *Masks of Conquest: Literary study and British rule in India*, New York, 1989, 167, in A. Pennycook, *The Cultural Politics of English as an International Language*, 79–80.

8.   E. Guest, *A History of English Rhythms*, vol. 2, London, 1838, 429.

9.   Bentham's comprehensive utilitarian philosophy, which dealt with areas such as colonial government and the administration of laws in nations with both 'civilised' and 'uncivilised' populations, served to provide an ideology of empire where none before had existed to anywhere near the same extent. See E.M. O'Brien, *The Foundation of Australia: 1786–1800*, London, 1937, 235; J.S. Mill, *Autobiography* (1873), London, 1995, 77; J.S. Mill, *Utilitarianism*, London, 1863, in M. Warnock (ed.), *Utilitarianism: On Liberty: Essay on Bentham*, Glasgow, 1986, 257; L.C. Boralevi, *Bentham and the Oppressed*, Berlin, 1984, 131.

10.   J.S. Polack, *New Zealand, being a narrative of travels and adventures during a residence in that country between the years 1831 and 1837*, vol. 2, London, 1838, 280.

11.   C. Terry, *New Zealand: Its advantages and prospects as a British colony*, London, 1843, 188.

12.   W.J. Cameron, 'A printing press for the Maori people', *JPS*, vol. 67, no. 3, September 1958, 204.

13.   W. Colenso, *Fifty Years Ago in New Zealand*, Napier, 1888, 4.

14.   N. Turner in J.G. Turner, *The Pioneer Missionary: Life of the Rev. Nathaniel Turner, missionary in New Zealand, Tonga, and Australia*, Melbourne, 1872, 205.

15.   C.J. Parr, 'A missionary library: Printed attempts to instruct the Maori, 1815–1845', *JPS*, vol. 70, no. 4, 1961, 436–37.

16.   H.M. Wright, *New Zealand, 1769–1840: Early years of Western contact*, Princeton, 1959, 53.

17.   S.M.D. Martin, *New Zealand: In a series of letters*, London, 1845, 312.

18.   *Report of the Formation and Establishment of the New Zealand Temperance Society*, Paihia, 1836.

19.   Colenso, *Fifty Years Ago in New Zealand*, 12.

20.   Wright, *New Zealand, 1769–1840: Early years of Western contact*, 162.

21.   Church Missionary Society, *The Missionary Register 1840*, London, 1840, 55.

22.   V.M. Mojela, 'Borrowing and loan words: The lemmatizing of newly acquired lexical items in Sesotho sa Leboa', *Lexikos*, vol. 20, no. 1, 2010, 700–07; N. Alembong, 'On the interface of orality and literacy: the case of Jacques Fame Ndongo's "Espaces de lumière"', *Institute of African Studies Research Review*, vol. 26, no. 2, 2010, 37–54; I. Klajn, 'Neologisms in present-day Serbian', *International Journal of the Sociology of Language*, no. 151, September 2001, 89–110.

23.   This distinction is discussed in R. Fischer, *Lexical Change in Present-Day English*, Tubingen, 1998, 1–5, 17–19.

24.   Although phrases that were bastardised forms of te reo Māori, such as 'up the buhai' or 'pakaru', were later adopted by Europeans.

25.   The nature of such destabilisation is dealt with in J. Millward, *Dystopian Wor(l)ds: Language within and beyond experience*, dissertation, University of Sheffield, Sheffield, 2007, 112; L. Pfeffer, 'Challenging tongues: The "irreducible hybridity" of language in contemporary bilingual poetry', *Synthesis*, vol. 4, 2012, 154.

26.   M. Foucault (ed. C. Gordon), *Power/Knowledge: Selected interviews and other writings, 1972–1977*, Harlow, 1980, 133; P. López-Rúa, 'The manipulative power of word-formation devices in Margaret Atwood's *Oryx and Crake*', *Revista alicantina de estudios ingleses*, no. 18, November 2005, 150–51.

27.   G. Orwell, *1984*, London, 1949, 28–29.

28.   *Southern Cross*, 23 December 1843, 3.

29.   Ibid., 3.

30.   W. Brown, *New Zealand and Its Aborigines*. 2nd edn, London, 1851, 98–99.

31.   R.G. Jameson, *New Zealand, South Australia, and New South Wales: A record of recent travels in these colonies with especial reference to emigration and the advantageous employment of labour and capital*, London, 1842, 261–62.

32.   Ibid.

33.   T. Karetu, 'Māori print culture: The newspapers', in J. Curnow, N. Hopa and J. McRae (eds), *Rere Atu, Taku Manu: Discovering history, language and politics in the Māori-language newspapers*, Auckland, 2002, 2. See also I.L. Sutherland, 'Nineteenth-century Māori letters of emotion: Orality, literacy and context', PhD thesis, University of Auckland, Auckland, 2007, i.

34.   Among the hundreds of examples, see Te Otene Pauanui to Colenso, 11 December 1841, ref. MS-Papers-0032-0668-02. Object #1032895, ATL; Hoani Ropiha to McLean, 1844, ref. no: MS-Papers-0032-0668-07, Object #1030005, ATL; Epiha to McLean, 1844, ref. no: MS-Papers-0032-0668-03, Object #1030723, ATL; Wanganui chiefs to Fitzroy, 12 September 1844, ref. no: MS-Papers-0032-0668-10, Object #1031097, ATL; Wi Kingi and others to Governor, 14 Dec 1844, ref. no: MS-Papers-0032-0668-14, Object #1030992, ATL.

35. Jameson, *New Zealand, South Australia, and New South Wales*, 261–62.

36. Maori Language Act 1987.

37. Waitangi Tribunal, *Report of the Waitangi Tribunal on the Te Reo Maori Claim*, Wai-11, Wellington, 1986, 10.

38. 'He Wakaputanga o te Rangatiratanga o Nu Tirene' (A Declaration of the Independence of New Zealand), Paihia, 1836, Archives New Zealand Te Whare Tohu Tuhituhinga o Aotearoa, ref. no: IA 9/1.

39. As an example, see R. Bourke to J. Busby, 24 April 1834, in N. Bayly, 'James Busby, British Resident in New Zealand 1833–1840', MA thesis, University of Auckland, Auckland, 1949, 49.

40. The declaration and the subsequent events were described by Sir George Gipps, governor of New South Wales, as 'a silly and unauthorised act, a paper pellet fired off at Baron de Thierry'. Cited in A.S. Thomson, *The Story of New Zealand: Past and present, savage and civilized*, vol. 1, 1859, 278.

41. Lord Glenelg responded diplomatically, noting that 'His Majesty will not fail to avail himself of any opportunity of shewing his good will, and of affording to the chiefs such support and protection, as may be consistent with a due regard to the just rights of others, and to the interests of His Majesty's subjects.' Cited in Terry, *New Zealand: Its advantages and prospects*, 81.

42. M. Mutu, 'The Humpty Dumpty principle at work', in S. Fenton (ed.), *For Better or Worse: Translation as a tool for change in the South Pacific*, Oxford, 2004, 11–29.

43. Waitangi Tribunal, *He Whakaputanga me te Tiriti – The Declaration and the Treaty: The report on Stage 1 of the Te Paparahi o Te Raki Inquiry*, Wai-1040, Wellington, 2014, s. 4.3.3.

44. Ibid.

45. M. Heller, 'Repositioning the multilingual periphery: Class, language, and transnational markets in Francophone Canada', in S. Pietikainen and H. Kelly-Holmes (eds), *Multilingualism and the Periphery*, Oxford, 2013, 23; J. Irvine and S. Gal, 'Language, ideology and linguistic differentiation', in P. Kroskrity (ed.), *Regimes of Languages: Ideologies, polities, and identities*, Santa Fe, 2000, 35–81.

46. These dynamics of indigenous languages in a colonial state are described in B. Spolsky, *Language Management*, Cambridge, 2009, 152, 166.

47. This population shift is detailed in D.I. Pool, *The Maori Population of New Zealand: 1769–1971*, Auckland, 1977, 55ff.

48. A period that coincided with the apointment Sir James Stephen as head of the Colonial Office (1836–1847). Stephen's evangelical Christianity and leading role in the Abolitionist movement reflected in his policies that aimed to promote a more humanitarian approach to British imperial policy.

49. The influence of (Protestant) missionaries was pronounced at the select committee. 'In reality, the Select Committee was a contingent intervention by a particular lobby group in ongoing transnational debates. It was the product of transnational evangelical networks, and of Fowell Buxton's family and religious networks in Britain': E. Elbourne, 'The sin of the settler: The 1835–36 Select Committee on Aborigines and debates over virtue and conquest in the

early nineteenth-century British white settler empire', *Journal of Colonialism and Colonial History*, vol. 4, no. 3, 2004, 9; A. Lester, 'British settler discourse and the circuits of empire', *History Workshop Journal*, vol. 54, no. 1, Autumn 2002, 24–48.

50. *Report of the Parliamentary Select Committee on Aboriginal Tribes (British Settlements)*, London, 1837, v–vi.

51. Ibid.

52. Ibid., 121.

53. Ibid., 126.

54. An additional British Resident, Thomas McDonnell, was appointed in 1835, but resigned the following year.

55. As an example of this, neither of Busby's successors – Governors William Hobson (1840–42) and Robert FitzRoy (1843–45) – learned to speak te reo.

56. B. Semmel, 'The philosophic radicals and colonialism', *Journal of Economic History*, vol. 21, no. 4, 1961, 513–25.

57. E.G. Wakefield, *A View of the Art of Colonization, with present reference to the British Empire: In letters between a statesman and a colonist*, London, 1849, 153–54.

58. E.J. Wakefield, *Adventure in New Zealand from 1839–1844*, vol. 1, 42; vol. 2, 450.

59. A. Ward, 'Alienation rights in traditional Maori society: A comment', *JPS*, vol. 95, no. 2, June 1986, 259–65.

60. A. Caughey, *The Interpreter: The biography of Richard 'Dicky' Barrett*, Auckland, 1998, 17.

61. Ibid., 18.

62. The deed goes to over 1200 words. 'Copy of the New Zealand Company's Third Deed of Purchase from the Natives, dated 8th November, 1839', in A. Mackay, *A Compendium of Official Documents Relative to Native Affairs in the South Island*, vol. 1, Wellington, 1873, 65–67; Caughey, *The Interpreter*, 118.

63. Busby had similarly attempted to make the text of the Treaty of Waitangi sound more legalistic.

64. 'There was no writing to show the boundarys or any quantity of land but a certain hill or point so the natives did not know what land they sold,' is how James Heberley described the translation, cited in A. Caughey, *The Interpreter*, 119.

65. G. Clarke, *Notes on Early Life in New Zealand*, Hobart, 1903, 49.

66. D. McLean, 21 July 1854, evidence before the Committee on the New Zealand Company's Debt, Votes and Proceedings of the House of Representatives, 1854, Session I-II, in *AJHR*, 1854, 17.

67. E.J. Wakefield, *Adventure in New Zealand from 1839–1844*, London, 1845, 38.

68. *Report from the Select Committee of the House of Lords appointed to inquire into the present state of the Islands of New Zealand and the expediency of regulating the settlement of British subjects therein: with the minutes of evidence taken before the Committee and an index thereto, brought from the Lords 7th August 1838*, London, 1838.

69. J. Watkins, in *Report from the Select Committee*, 18, 24.

70. J. Flatt, in *Report from the Select Committee*, 34.
71. A. Ballara, 'The pursuit of mana? A re-evaluation of the process of land alienation by Maoris, 1840–1890', *JPS*, vol. 91, no. 4, December 1982, 519–41.
72. J. Flatt, in *Report from the Select Committee*, 40–41.
73. D.L. Petersen, 'The Bible in public view', in F.R. Ames and C.W. Miller (eds), *Foster Biblical Scholarship: Essays in honor of Kent Harold Richards*, Atlanta, 2010, 124.
74. The original was written in te reo Māori. See J.R. Elder (ed.), *The Letters and Journals of Samuel Marsden, 1765–1838*, Dunedin, 1932, 532, n. 24.
75. Cited in D. Coates, in *Report from the Select Committee*, 272.
76. J. Jennings, *New Zealand Colonization*, London, 1843, 5, 11.
77. The extent of European travel through the country is outlined in W. Wakefield, 10 October 1839, in J. Ward, *Supplementary Information Relative to New Zealand*, London, 1840, 27–60. See also P. Moon, *The Voyagers: Remarkable European explorations of New Zealand*, Auckland, 2014.
78. A. Anderson, 'Old ways and new means, AD 1810–1830', in A. Anderson, J. Binney and A. Harris (eds), *Tangata Whenua: An illustrated history*, Wellington, 2014, 186; E. Bohan, *Climates of War*, Christchurch, 2005, 32.
79. Waitangi Tribunal, *Ngai Tahu Report*, Wai-27, Wellington, 1991, s. 3.2.
80. R. McGregor, 'The doomed race: A scientific axiom of the late nineteenth century', *Australian Journal of Politics & History*, vol. 39, no. 1, 1993, 14–22; N. Finzsch, '"It is scarcely possible to conceive that human beings could be so hideous and loathsome": Discourses of genocide in eighteenth- and nineteenth-century America and Australia', *Patterns of Prejudice*, vol. 39, no. 2, 2005, 97–115.
81. J. Busby to Colonial Secretary, New South Wales, 16 June 1837, *Correspondence with the Secretary of State Relative to New Zealand*, London, 1840, 13.
82. Beecham's involvement in matters of colonial policy is discussed in A. Porter, *Religion Versus Empire? British Protestant missionaries and overseas expansion, 1700–1914*, Manchester, 2004, 141.
83. J. Beecham, *Remarks upon the Latest Official Documents Relating to New Zealand*, London, 1838, 8–9; R. Astridge, *Waikato Wesleyan Missions: A brief insight into the work of the early Wesleyan missionaries in the Waikato of New Zealand*, n.p., 2013, 7.
84. The various processes of this reversal are dealt with in K. McSweeney and S. Arps, '"A demographic turnaround": The rapid growth of the indigenous populations in Lowland Latin America', *Latin American Research Review*, vol. 40, no. 1, 2005, 3–29; T. Alfred and J. Corntassel, 'Being indigenous: Resurgences against contemporary colonialism', *Government and Opposition*, vol. 40, no. 4, 2005, 597–614; M.P.K. Sorrenson, 'Land purchase methods and their effect on Maori population, 1865–1901', *JPS*, vol. 65, no. 3, September 1956, 183–99.
85. The basis and demographics of this change are detailed in Pool, *The Maori Population of New Zealand*.
86. M. Hawtrey, *Justice to New Zealand, Honour to England*, London, 1861, 9; D.I.

Salesa, *Racial Crossings: Race, intermarriage, and the Victorian British Empire*, Oxford, 2011, 32.

87. M.J.G. Hawtrey, *An Earnest Address to New Zealand Colonists, with reference to their intercourse with the native inhabitants*, London, 1840, 10. So much for the motto with which he commenced his book: an extract from 1 Peter 2:17: 'Honour all men'.

88. Ibid., 4.

89. P. Burns, *Fatal Success: A history of the New Zealand Company*, Auckland, 1989, 81–82; T. Williams, 'James Stephen and British intervention in New Zealand, 1838–40', *Journal of Modern History*, vol. 13, no. 1, 1941, 25, 32–33.

90. These are normally known as Normanby's Instructions, although Stephen's first draft of the instructions had appeared in January 1836 and the wording is almost identical in places to Normanby's instructions.

91. T.J. Barron, 'James Stephen, the 'Black Race' and British Colonial Administration, 1813–47', *Journal of Imperial and Commonwealth History*, vol. 5, no. 2, 1977, 131–50.

92. Normanby to W. Hobson, 14 August 1839, *GBPP*, vol. 23, London, 1840, 38. The issues arising from the translation, particularly constitutional, are complex. See M. Goldsmith, 'Translated identities: 'Pakeha' as subjects of the Treaty of Waitangi', *Sites: A Journal of Social Anthropology and Cultural Studies*, vol. 2, no. 2, 2005, 64–82; M. Mutu, 'Constitutional intentions: The Treaty texts', in M. Mulholland and V.M.H. Tawhai (eds), *Weeping Waters: The Treaty of Waitangi and constitutional change*, Wellington, 2010, 13–40.

93. Normanby to W. Hobson, 14 August 1839, 38.

94. C. Orange, *The Treaty of Waitangi*, Wellington, 2011, 68ff.

95. The details of the translation process are explored in R. Ross, 'Te Tiriti o Waitangi: Texts and translations', *New Zealand Journal of History*, vol. 6, no. 2, 1972, 129–57.

96. B. Reay, 'The context and meaning of popular literacy: Some evidence from nineteenth-century rural England', *Past and Present*, no. 131, May 1991, 89–91, 96; L. Stone, 'Literacy and education in England, 1640–1900', *Past and Present*, no. 42, February 1969, 69–139; R.S. Schofield, 'Dimensions of illiteracy, 1750–1850', *Explorations in Economic History*, vol. 10, 1973, 437–54; R.E. Gallman, 'Two problems in the measurement of American colonial signature-mark literacy', *Historical Methods: A Journal of Quantitative and Interdisciplinary History*, vol. 20, no. 4, 1987, 137–41.

97. C.F. Kaestle, 'The history of literacy and the history of readers', *Review of Research in Education*, vol. 12, no. 1, January 1985, 11–53; Schofield, 'Dimensions of illiteracy', 473–54.

98. D.F. McKenzie, *Oral Culture, Literacy and Print in Early New Zealand: The Treaty of Waitangi*, Wellington, 1985, 35.

99. Ibid., 35.

100. An example of committing information to memory around this time is cited in P. Lineham, 'This is my weapon: Maori Response to the Maori Bible', in R. Glen (ed.), *Mission and Moko: Aspects of the work of the Church Missionary Society in New Zealand, 1814–1882*, Christchurch, 1992, 170–71.

101. Waitangi Tribunal, *He Whakaputanga me te Tiriti – The Declaration and the Treaty: The report on stage 1 of the Te Paparahi o Te Raki Inquiry*, Wai-1040, Wellington, 2014. See also D. Keenan, 'Aversion to print? Māori resistance to the written word', in P. Griffith, P. Hughes and A. Loney (eds), *A Book in the Hand: Essays on the history of the book in New Zealand*, Auckland, 2000, 19.

102. The Catholic Church was slightly less successful during this period than its Protestant counterparts. See J. Thomson, 'Some reasons for the failure of the Roman Catholic Mission to the Maoris, 1838–1860', *NZJH*, vol. 3, no. 2, 1969, 166–74.

103. As an example, the Bishop of Australia wrote during a tour of New Zealand: 'At every station which I visited the converts were so numerous as to bear a very visible and considerable proportion to the entire population; and I had sufficient testimony to convince me that the same state of things prevailed at other places, which it was not in my power to reach. In most of the native villages … The chief and the slave stood side by side, with the same holy volume in their hands, and exerted their endeavours each to surpass the other, in returning proper answers to the questions put to them concerning what they had been reading. A very great work has been accomplished in providing them with a translation of the whole New Testament, which will ever remain a monument of laborious and well-directed piety', cited in G. Selwyn, *Annals of the Diocese of New Zealand*, London, 1847, 25–26.

104. Although this was a matter of some debate. As an example, see *Daily Southern Cross*, 22 June 1844, 2.

105. W. Williams (ed. F. Porter), *The Turanga Journals, 1840–1850*, 383–84.

106. Church Missionary Society, *The Missionary Register 1848*, London, 1848, 320, 322.

107. *An Ordinance for Promoting the Education of Youth in the Colony of New Zealand*, Auckland, 7 October 1847, s. 3.

108. G.A. Wood, 'Church and State in New Zealand in the 1850s', *Journal of Religious History*, vol. 8, no. 3, June 1975, 266–68.

109. R. Ka`ai-Mahuta, 'He kupu tuku iho mō tēnei reanga: A critical analysis of waiata and haka as commentaries and archives of Māori political history', PhD thesis, Auckland University of Technology, Auckland, 2010, 138; A. Darder, *Culture and Power in the Classroom: A critical foundation for bicultural education*, Westport, Connecticut, 1991, 3.

110. *An Ordinance for Appointing a Board of Trustees for the Management of Property to be Set Apart for the Education and Advancement of the Native Race*, Auckland, 1844, preamble.

111. St John's Native Teachers' School, later St John's College, was the idea of Bishop George Selwyn; it closed in 1853 because of financial and administrative difficulties.

112. 'Rules for St. John's Native Teachers' School', *Calendar of St John's College New Zealand*, Auckland 1846. The rules appeared in 1844; see F. Porter (ed.), *The Turanga Journals, 1840–1850: Letters and Journals of William and Jane Williams*, Wellington, 1974, 305, n. 82. The rules were reported on favourably in the *Sydney Morning Herald*, 24 March 1845, 2.

113. W. Morley, *The History of Methodism in New Zealand*, Wellington, 1900, 111.

114. Cited in M. Barrington and T.H. Beaglehole, '"A part of Pakeha society": Europeanising the Maori child', in J.A. Mangan (ed.), *Making Imperial Mentalities: Socialisation and British imperialism*, Manchester, 1990, 170.

115. 'Appendix', in G. Grey to Grey, 24 December 1850, *GBPP 1851*, London, 1851, 95.

116. *An Ordinance for Appointing a Board of Trustees*, preamble. This is discussed in a broader historical context in S. May, 'Māori-medium education in Aotearoa/New Zealand', in J.W. Tollefson and A.B.M. Tsui (eds), *Medium of Instruction Policies: Which agenda? Whose agenda?*, New Jersey, 2008, 25–26.

117. *An Ordinance for Appointing a Board of Trustees*, s. 5; J.M. Barrington and T.H. Beaglehole, *Maori Schools in a Changing Society: An historical review*, Wellington, 1974, 45–50.

118. S. Makoni and A. Pennycook, 'Disinventing and reconstituting languages', in S. Makoni and A. Pennycook (eds), *Disinventing and Reconstituting Languages*, Cleveland, 2007, 27–28.

119. This concept is examined in the case of Nigeria in R. Phillipson, 'Linguistic imperialism: African perspectives', *ELT Journal*, vol. 50, no. 2, 1996, 162. In similar vein, William Williams demonstrated language's potential to affect communities, by hoping that literacy would lead to moral change among Māori. See W. Williams in Church Missionary Society, *The Missionary Register 1834* (November), London, 1834, 513, in McKenzie, *Oral Culture, Literacy and Print*, 13.

120. G. Grey, in R. McGregor, *Imagined Destinies: Aboriginal Australians and the doomed race theory, 1880 –1939*, Melbourne, 1997, 10; A. Ward, *A Show of Justice: Racial 'amalgamation' in nineteenth century New Zealand*, Toronto, 1973, 36; A.G.L. Shaw, 'British policy towards the Australian Aborigines, 1830–1850', *Australian Historical Studies*, vol. 25, no. 99, 1992, 265–85.

121. 'The Sir George Grey Grants, Three Kings', 15 October 1850, in R. Hobbs, *Wesleyan Native Institution, Established in 1844 by Rev. W. Lawry ... and Rev Thos. Buddle: Grafton Road and 192 Acres at Three Kings*, Auckland, 1906, 9–10.

122. Statistics New Zealand, *New Zealand Long Term Data Series, Population*, 5 March 2008, Table A1.1.

123. W. Swainson, *New Zealand and Its Colonization*, London, 1859, 8.

124. S. Blackburn, *The Oxford Dictionary of Philosophy*, 2nd edn, Oxford, 2008; J. Friedman, 'Marxism, structuralism and vulgar materialism', *Man*, vol. 9, no. 3, September 1974, 451; B.H. Mayhew, 'Structuralism versus individualism: Part 1, Shadowboxing in the dark', *Social Forces*, vol. 59, no. 2, 1980, 335–75.

125. A.S. Thomson, *The Story of New Zealand*, vol. 2, 292.

126. M. Daunton and R. Halpern (eds), *Empire and Others: British encounters with indigenous peoples, 1600–1850*, Pennsylvania, 1999; R. Phillipson, 'English language spread policy', *International Journal of the Sociology of Language*, vol. 107, no. 1, 1994, 7–24; T. Niranjana, 'Translation, colonialism and rise of English', *Economic and Political Weekly*, vol. 25, no. 15, April 1990, 773–79.

127. J.B Thompson, 'Editor's Introduction', in Paul Ricoeur (ed. and trans. by J.B.

Thompson), *Hermeneutics and the Human Sciences: Essays on language, action and interpretation*, Cambridge, 1998, 8–9.

128. De Saussure argued for a distinction between *langue* (an idealised abstraction of language) and *parole* (language as actually used in daily life). See F. de Saussure, *Cours de Linguistique Generale* (Paris, 1916), W. Baskin (trans.), New York, 1959, 120.

129. This was especially the case with religious activity.

130. This is broadly along the lines of Heidegger's observation that all knowledge is relative to what is already known. P. Ricoeur, 'Hermeneutics and structuralism', in E. Kurzweil (ed.), *The Age of Structuralism: From Lévi-Strauss to Foucault*, New Brunswick, 1996, 87–88.

131. This process is described in R. Inglehart and W.E. Baker, 'Modernization, cultural change, and the persistence of traditional values', *American Sociological Review*, vol. 65, no. 1, 2000, 21–22.

132. S. Martin, *The Taranaki Question*, 3rd edn, London, 1861, 92–93.

133. G.A. Selwyn, *Annals of the Diocese of New Zealand*, London, 1847, 153–54.

134. R. Maunsell in Selwyn, *Annals of the Diocese of New Zealand*, 153–54.

135. Cited in D.F. McKenzie, *Oral Culture, Literacy and Print*, 31.

136. This concept is addressed in R. Negrine, *Politics and the Mass Media in Britain*, London, 1994, 1–2.

137. E.S. Herman and N. Chomsky, *Manufacturing Consent: The political economy of the mass media*, London, 2008, xi–xiv.

138. S.N. Eisenstadt, 'Post-traditional societies and the continuity and reconstruction of tradition', *Daedalus*, vol. 102, no. 1, Winter 1973, 3.

139. A.E. Vercoe, *Educating Jake: Pathways to empowerment*, Auckland, 1998, 68, in L. Paterson, 'Kiri mā, Kiri mangu: The terminology of race and civilisation in the mid-nineteenth-century Māori-language newspapers', in Curnow, Hopa and McRae (eds), *Rere Atu, Taku Manu*, 81.

140. He was related to the filmstar of the same name.

141. W.T. Power, *Sketches in New Zealand*, London, 1849, 184.

142. *Te Karere o Niu Tireni* (trans.), 1 January 1842, 1, in Alexander Turnbull Library, 'Niupepa: Maori newspapers', commentary, n.d.

143. *New Zealand Gazette and Wellington Spectator*, 17 July 1844, 2.

144. G. Clarke, *Extracts from the Final Report of the Chief Protector of Aborigines in New Zealand*, Auckland, 1846, 1–15.

145. T.M. Hocken, *Otago Daily Times*, 20 July 1910, 8.

146. *New Zealand Gazette and Wellington Spectator*, 21 October 1843, 3.

147. Cited in *Daily Southern Cross*, 25 September 1847, 2.

148. D.J. Lowe, 'Polynesian settlement of New Zealand and the impacts of volcanism on early Maori society: An update', in D.J. Lowe (ed.), 'Guidebook for Pre-conference North Island Field Trip A1 "Ashes and Issues"', 28–30 November 2008, in New Zealand Society of Soil Science, *Australian and New Zealand 4th Joint Soils Conference*, Massey University, Palmerston North, 1–5 December 2008, 142–47; J.A. Trejaut, T. Kivisild, J.H. Loo, C.L. Lee, C.L. He, C.J. Hsu and M. Lin, 'Traces of archaic mitochondrial lineages persist in Austronesian-speaking Formosan populations', *PLoS Biology*, vol. 3, no. 8, 2005, e247; S.J.

Greenhill, Q.D. Atkinson, A. Meade and R.D. Gray, 'The shape and tempo of language evolution', *Proceedings of the Royal Society B: Biological Sciences*, vol. 277, 2010, 2443–50; S.J. Greenhill and R.D. Gray, 'Austronesian language phylogenies: Myths and misconceptions about Bayesian computational methods', *Austronesian Historical Linguistics and Culture History: A festschrift for Robert Blust*, 2009, 375–97.

149. R. Green, 'Linguistic subgrouping within Polynesia: The implications for prehistoric settlement', *JPS*, vol. 75, no. 1, 1966, 6–38; A. Pawley, 'Polynesian languages: A subgrouping based on shared innovations in morphology', *JPS*, vol. 75, no. 1, 1966, 39–64; P.W. Hohepa, 'The accusative-to-ergative drift in Polynesian languages', *JPS*, vol. 78. no. 3, 1969, 295–329.

150. It was typically defined, as a starting point, as a 'primitive language'. F. von Hochstetter, *New Zealand: Its physical geography, geology and natural history*, Stuttgart, 1867, 209n.

151. B.S. Cohn, *Colonialism and its Forms of Knowledge: The British in India*, Princeton, 1996, 4–5.

152. L. Rosier, 'Crawford, James Coutts', *Dictionary of New Zealand Biography*, Wellington, June 2013, n.p.

153. J.C. Crawford, *Recollections of Travel in New Zealand and Australia*, Edinburgh, 1880, 347.

154. Ibid., 348.

155. Ibid.

156. S. Marsden, in Elder (ed.), *The Letters and Journals of Samuel Marsden*, 219–20.

157. R. Maunsell, *Grammar of the New Zealand Language*, Auckland, 1842.

158. Ibid., iii.

159. M. Tomalin, '"… to this rule there are many exceptions": Robert Maunsell and the Grammar of Maori', 303–34; T. Ballantyne, *Orientalism and Race: Aryanism in the British Empire*, Basingstoke, 2002.

160. Crawford, *Recollections of Travel*, 349.

161. W.S.W. Vaux, 'On the probable origin of the Maori races', *Transactions and Proceedings of the Royal Society of New Zealand*, vol. 8, 1875, 18–19.

162. Crawford, *Recollections of Travel*, 349–50.

163. von Hochstetter, *New Zealand*, 209.

164. A.C. Haddon and S.H. Ray, *Reports of the Cambridge Anthropological Expedition to Torres Straits*, vol. 3, *Linguistics*, Cambridge, 1907, 504.

165. W. Ellis, *Polynesian Researches during a Residence of Nearly Eight Years in the Society and Sandwich Islands*, vol. 1, London, 1853, 121.

166. C. Phillips, 'Civilization of the Pacific', *Transactions and Proceedings of the Royal Society of New Zealand*, vol. 9. 1876, 65.

167. F.W. Christian, 'On the outlying islands', *Transactions and Proceedings of the Royal Society of New Zealand*, vol. 30. 1897, 96.

168. R. Taylor, *Te Ika a Maui, or, New Zealand and its inhabitants*, London, 1855, 179.

169. Ibid., 180.

170. Ibid.

171. Ibid., 184.

172. von Hochstetter, *New Zealand*, 209–10.

173. This topic is dealt with comprehensively in Ballantyne, *Orientalism and Race*.

174. The context for this is discussed in T. McKenzie, 'Edward Robert Tregear, 1846 – 1931', *Kōtare 7*, no. 3, 2008, 32–33.

175. F.M. Müller, *A History of Ancient Sanskrit Literature*, London, 1860.

176. *Poverty Bay Herald*, 11 September 1885, 2; *Hawkes Bay Herald*, 22 October 1885, 4. There was also strong criticism of the work, however: see *Auckland Star*, 19 September 1885, 4.

177. E. Tregear, *The Aryan Maori*, Wellington, 1885.

178. Ibid., 5–6.

179. A.S. Atkinson, 'The Aryo-Semitic Maori', *Transactions of the New Zealand Institute*, vol. 19, 1886, 552–76.

180. As an example, see J.F.H. Wohlers, *Memoirs of the Life of J.F.H. Wohlers, Missionary at Ruapuke, New Zealand*, Dunedin, 1895, 139.

181. *New Zealand Herald*, 18 August 1885, 4.

182. B.J. Harley, 'Maps, knowledge, and power', in G. Henderson and M. Waterstone (eds), *Geographic Thought: A praxis perspective*, Oxford, 2009, 130; W.J.T. Mitchell, *Iconology: Image, text, ideology*, Chicago, 1987, 38.

183. G. Selwyn, in H.W. Tucker, *Memoir of the Life and Episcopate of George Augustus Selwyn*, vol. 1, London, 1879, 165.

184. E. Dieffenbach, *Travels in New Zealand, With contributions to the geography, botany, and natural history of that country*, vol. 2, London, 1843, 152–53 (emphasis added).

185. The European population in 1840 was around 2000, while the number of Maori was perhaps 90,000–100,000.

186. *New Zealand Gazette and Wellington Spectator*, 21 October 1843, 3.

187. *New Zealand Spectator and Cook's Strait Guardian*, 1 November 1845, 2.

188. G.C. Mundy, *Our Antipodes, or Residence and rambles in the Australasian colonies*, vol. 2, London, 1852, 97.

189. H. Browne, in O. Hadfield, *The New Zealand War: The second year of one of England's little wars*, London, 1861, 33. Harold Browne, a professor of divinity at Cambridge, was the brother of the governor of New Zealand, Colonel Gore Browne.

190. T. Gilbert, *New Zealand Settlers and Soldiers, or, The war in Taranaki*, London, 1861, 214.

191. Normanby to W. Hobson, 14 August 1839, *GBPP*, London, 1840, 39–41.

192. Ibid., 40.

193. A. Marjoribanks, *Travels in New Zealand*, London, 1846, 115.

194. Terry, *New Zealand: Its advantages and prospects*, 187.

195. T. Reedy, 'Te reo Māori: The past 20 years and looking forward', *Oceanic Linguistics*, vol. 39, no. 1, June 2000, 157–69.

196. R. Hill, 'Keats, Antiquarianism, and the picturesque', *Essays in Criticism*, vol. 64, no. 2, 2014, 119–37; E. Alexander, 'Enduring fictions', *Wilson Quarterly*, vol. 21, no. 2, Spring 1997, 40–47.

197. G.W. Rusden, *History of New Zealand*, vol. 1, London, 1883, 6; J.S. Polack, *Manners and Customs of the New Zealanders*, vol. 1, London, 1840, 261.

198. Some of the risks of romanticising culture are surveyed in J.C. Walker, 'Romanticising resistance, romanticising culture: Problems in Willis's theory of cultural production', *British Journal of Sociology of Education*, vol. 7, no. 1, 1986, 59–80.

199. Mundy, *Our Antipodes*, 97.

200. G.F. Angas, *Savage Life and Scenes in Australia and New Zealand*, vol. 2, London, 1847, 77.

201. W.B. Marshall, *A Personal Narrative of Two Visits to New Zealand*, London, 1836, 78.

202. J. Buller, *Forty Years in New Zealand: Including a personal narrative, an account of Maoridom, and of the Christianization and colonization of the country*, London, 1878, 254–55.

203. M. Reilly, 'John White: The making of a nineteenth-century writer and collector of Maori tradition', *NZJH*, vol. 23, no. 2, 1989, 159–60.

204. In 1879 the government commissioned White to compile the work. Six volumes were published between 1887 and 1890. White died the following year and the remaining volumes were compiled from his handwritten manuscripts.

205. Reilly, 'John White', 164.

206. Ballantyne, *Orientalism and Race*, 154.

207. As typical examples, see *The New Zealander*, 15 August 1846, 2 and 12 December 1849, 3; *Nelson Examiner and New Zealand Chronicle*, 5 October 1844, 2; *Wellington Independent*, 10 October 1846, 2; *Daily Southern Cross*, 1 February 1845, 2.

208. *Wellington Independent*, 4 March 1848, 2.

209. S. May, *Language and Minority Rights: Nationalism and the politics of language*, 2nd edn, New York, 2012, 1–2.

210. These themes are addressed in the American context in J. Crawford (ed.), *Language Loyalties: A source book on the Official English controversy*, Chicago, 1992.

211. For details on this, see '"An alphabet on her coffin": Infant schools for Māori children in New Zealand', in H. May, B. Kaur and L. Prochner, *Empire, Education, and Indigenous Childhoods: Nineteenth-century missionary infant schools in three British colonies*, Farnham, Surrey, 2014, 206ff.

212. 'Report of Turanga, Wairoa, and Ahuriri, from July 1, 1843, to Dec. 31, 1844', Church Missionary Society, *The Missionary Register 1846*, London, 1846, 370.

213. Ibid.

214. Parr, 'A missionary library', 448–49.

215. Brown, *New Zealand and Its Aborigines*, 100.

216. Martin, *New Zealand: In a series of letters*, 313.

217. Morley, *The History of Methodism in New Zealand*, 193.

218. Barrington and Beaglehole, '"A part of Pakeha society"', 167.

219. This process, which applies in several other examples around the world, is described in May, *Language and Minority Rights*, 2–4.

220. M.P. Cowen and R.W. Shenton, *Doctrines of Development*, London, 2005, 171–74.

CHAPTER 5: 'FORGE A WAY FORWARD': 1850s TO 1860s

1. L. Bastings, 'History of the New Zealand Society, 1851–1868: A Wellington scientific centenary', *Transactions and Proceedings of the Royal Society of New Zealand*, vol. 80, 1952, 359.

2. D. Kerr, 'Sir George Grey and his book-collecting activities in New Zealand', in P. Griffith, P. Hughes and A. Loney (eds), *A Book in the Hand: Essays on the history of the book in New Zealand*, Auckland, 2000, 48–49.

3. G. Grey, 26 September 1851, *The New Zealander*, 12 November 1851, 2.

4. Ibid.

5. Even though Māori were not included in the legislation for the census, see Census Act 1858, s. 17.

6. Statistics New Zealand, 'Principal results for 1858 Census, Aboriginal native population – Appendix H', Wellington, n.d.

7. As examples, see A. Baker, 'New Zealand compared with Great Britain in its physical and social aspects: A lecture delivered in the hall of the Athenaeum, Wellington, on Thursday, July 23, 1857, by the Rev. A. Baker , M.A.', Wellington, 1857, 4; C. Hursthouse, *New Zealand, or Zealandia, the Britain of the South*, vol. 1, London, 1857, 190; Lay Association of the Free Church of Scotland, *Scheme of the Colony of the free Church, Otago, in New Zealand*, Glasgow, 1845, 15.

8. This dynamic is discussed in C. Chase-Dunn and R. Rubinson, 'Toward a structural perspective on the world-system', *Politics & Society*, vol. 7, no. 4, 1977, 453–76.

9. A. Lester, 'British settler discourse and the circuits of empire', *History Workshop Journal*, vol. 54, 2002, 27–50; A. McDonald, 'Wallerstein's world-economy: How seriously should we take it', *Journal of Asian Studies,* vol. 38, no. 3, May 1979, 535–40; I. Wallerstein, 'Dependence in an interdependent world: The limited possibilities of transformation within the capitalist world economy', *African Studies Review*, vol. 17, no. 1, April 1974, 1–26; I. Wallerstein, 'Globalization or the age of transition?: A long-term view of the trajectory of the world-system', *International Sociology*, vol. 15, 2000, 249; I. Wallerstein, 'World system versus world-systems: A critique', *Critique of Anthropology*, vol. 11, 1990, 190.

10. G.S. Cooper, *Journal of an Expedition Overland from Auckland to Taranaki*, Auckland, 1851.

11. Ibid., 3.

12. G. Grey, 26 September 1851, *The New Zealander*, 12 November 1851, 2.

13. C. Phillips and H. Allen, 'Archaeology at Opita: Three hundred years of continuity and change', *Research in Anthropology and Linguistics*, no. 5, 2013, 1, 3.

14. Cooper, *Journal of an Expedition Overland*, 18, 102, 180.

15. Ibid., 66–68.

16. Ibid., 68–70.

17. M.P.K. Sorrenson, *Maori Origins and Migrations: The genesis of some Pakeha myths and legends*, Auckland, 1993, 37.

18. G. Grey, *Polynesian Mythology and Ancient Traditional History of the New Zealand Race*, London, 1855.

19. Ibid., iii–iv.

20. Ibid., vi.
21. One of the more detailed illustrations of these features is contained in A. Ngata (trans. P. Te Hurinui Jones), *Ngā Mōteatea: The songs*, Auckland, 2004.
22. Grey, *Polynesian Mythology*, viii.
23. Ibid., xi–xii. A similar argument was made in G. Grey, 'Ancient inhabitants of New Zealand', address delivered to the Museum of Practical Geology, London, 8 May 1869, 333–36.
24. This was his baptismal name. His father, also called Te Rangikaheke, was from the Ngāti Kererū hapū of Ngāti Rangiwewehi of Te Arawa, and had ties with Ngāti Rangitihi. His mother, Kaihau, was descended from Tamahou, Pupu and Hinepo. He worked for Grey from 1849 (and possibly earlier) to 1856, and was paid with money, goods and accommodation; see J. McRae, 'Māori oral tradition meets the book', in P. Griffith, P. Hughes and A. Loney (eds), *A Book in the Hand: Essays on the history of the book in New Zealand*, Auckland, 2000, 3.
25. J. Curnow, 'Wiremu Maihi Te Rangikaheke: His life and work', *JPS*, vol. 94, no. 2, 1985, 97, 102.
26. M. Reilly, 'John White: Seeking the elusive mohio: White and his Maori informants', *NZJH*, vol. 24, 1990, 45–55.
27. M. Reilly, 'John White: The making of a nineteenth-century writer and collector of Maori tradition', 167. See also D. Simmons, 'The sources of Sir George Grey's *Nga Mahi a Nga Tupuna*', *JPS*, vol. 75, no. 2, 1966, 177–88; K. Smithyman, 'Making history: John White and S. Percy Smith at work', *JPS*, vol. 88, no. 4, 1979, 375–413.
28. Curnow, 'Wiremu Maihi Te Rangikaheke'; McRae, 'Māori oral tradition meets the book', 7.
29. M.A.K. Halliday and R. Hasan, *Language, Context, and Text: Aspects of language in a social-semiotic perspective*, Geelong, 1985, 4; K.L. O'Halloran, 'Multimodal discourse analysis', in K. Hyland and B. Paltridge (eds), *Continuum Companion to Discourse Analysis*, London, 2011, ch. 8.
30. M. Cronin, *Translating Ireland: Translation, languages, cultures*, Cork, 1996, 92, in McRae, 'Māori oral tradition meets the book', 8.
31. M. Tennent, 'Introduction', in M. Tennent (ed.), *Training for the New Millennium: Pedagogies for translation and interpreting*, Amsterdam, 2005, xvi.
32. The term 'modernisation' is used here in the sense that it is applied by modernisation theorists such as Walt Rostow and Neil Smelser. See W.W. Rostow, 'The stages of economic growth', *Economic History Review*, vol. 12, no. 1, 1959, 1–16; N.J. Smelser, 'The modernization of social relations', in M. Weiner (ed.), *Modernization: The dynamics of growth*, New York, 1966, 110–21.
33. J. Morgan in Encl. 2 in 91, in G. Grey to Newcastle, 10 June 1853, *GBPP 1854*, London, 1854, 253.
34. R. Maunsell, in Encl. 2 in 91, in G. Grey to Newcastle, 10 June 1853, *GBPP 1854*, London, 1854, 253.
35. G.A. Kissling, in Encl. 2 in 91, in G. Grey to Newcastle, 10 June 1853, *GBPP 1854*, London, 1854, 257.
36. O. Hadfield, 'Report on the Otaki Industrial School, 1855', 13 January 1856, *AJHR*, 1858, Session I, E-01, 33–34.
37. 'Reports on native schools, 1858', *AJHR*, 1858, Session I, E-01, 1–77.

38. O. Hadfield, in 'Reports on native schools, 1858', 35; J. Nathan, 'An analysis of an industrial boarding school 1847–1860: A phase in Maori education', *NZJH*, vol. 7, no. 1, 1973, 49.

39. 'Reports on native schools, 1858', 12, 45.

40. W.H. Russell, 'Report on schools in the province of Auckland', 16 February 1858, *AJHR*, 1858, Session I, E-01, 60.

41. W. Fitzherbert, in 'Reports on native schools, 1858', 55.

42. H. Carleton, 'Further report on schools in the province of Auckland', in 'Reports on native schools, 1858', 77.

43. The Act set aside £7000 annually for the next seven years for the provision of education to 'natives' and 'half-castes'. Native Schools Act 1858, s. 1.

44. Native Schools Act 1858, s. 9.

45. T.G. Browne, 'Address of His Excellency the Governor to Maori chiefs assembled at Waitemata on the 10th of June 1860', in 'Further papers relative to Native Affairs', *AJHR*, 1860, Session I, E-01, 34.

46. G.W. Rusden, *History of New Zealand*, vol. 1, London, 1883, 637.

47. J.E. Gorst, 'Report of J.E. Gorst, Esq., Inspector of Schools', *AJHR*, 1862, Session I, E-04, 6–8.

48. J. Morgan, in B. Wells, *The History of Taranaki*, New Plymouth, 1878, 167–68.

49. G.H. Scholefield (ed.), *The Richmond-Atkinson Papers*, vol. 1, Wellington, 1960, 333. Fenton was later the first chief judge of the Native Land Court.

50. 'Native report of the meeting at Paetai', *AJHR 1860*, Session I, F-03, Appendix B, No. 7, 143–45.

51. D. Mahuta, 'Raupatu: A Waikato perspective', *Te Kaharoa* vol. 1, 2008, 174–82; N.K. Hopa, 'Land and re-empowerment: The Waikato case', in A. Cheater (ed.), *The Anthropology of Power*, London, 2005, 101; D. McCan, *Whatiwhatihoe: The Waikato Raupatu Claim*, Wellington 2001, 25–130.

52. F.D. Fenton, *The Laws of England, Compiled and Translated into the Maori Language*, Auckland, 1858, i.

53. Ibid.

54. Ibid.

55. When it ceased publication, *Te Karere Maori* was personified and eulogised: 'Then that *Karere* died. No more will we see him or hear his voice.' Cited in J. Curnow, N. Hopa and J. McRae (eds), *He Pitopito Kōrero nō te perehi Māori: Readings from the Māori-language press,* Auckland, 2006, 11.

56. *Te Karere Maori: The Maori Messenger*, 30 April 1860, 1.

57. J.E. Gorst, 'General report, by J.E. Gorst, Esq., on the state of Upper Waikato June 1862', in 'Further papers relative to the Governor Sir George Grey's plan of Native Government. Report of officers', *AJHR*, 1862, Session I, E-09, 11.

58. Ibid.

59. The geologist Ferdinand von Hochstetter was dropped off by the *Novara* on this stopover to take up exploratory work for the New Zealand Government, investigating Auckland coal deposits.

60. W. Brookes, 'Austria and the Maori people', *Te Ao Hou: The New World*, no. 24, October 1958, 38; K. Scherzer, *Narrative of the Circumnavigation of the Globe by the Austrian Frigate Novara, 1857–59*, vol. 3, London, 1863, 175–76.

61. The printing press is now in the Te Awamutu Museum. In April 1935, the Te Awamutu Historical Society travelled to the banks of the Waipa River to recover a printing press that had been abandoned.

62. Patara Te Tuhi became the editor and principal writer of the newspaper: W.J. Cameron, 'A printing press for the Maori people', *JPS*, vol. 67, no. 3, September, 1958, 204–9. The paper was named after a mythical bird that was flying to spread the news.

63. J. Curnow, 'A brief history of Maori-language newspapers', in J. Curnow, N. Hopa, J. McRae (eds), *Rere Atu, Taku Manu: Discovering history, language and politics in the Māori-language newspapers*, Auckland, 2002, 21.

64. L. Paterson, *Colonial Discourses: Niupepa Maori 1855–1863*, Dunedin, 2006, 27.

65. Ibid.

66. Cameron, 'A printing press for the Maori People', 209.

67. G.S. Cooper, 'Report from G.S. Cooper, Esq., Resident Magistrate, Napier', in 'Reports on the social and political state of the natives in various districts at the time of the arrival of Sir G.F. Bowen', *AJHR*, 1868, Session I, A-04, 13.

68. Appointed 11 February 1865. B.D. Gilling, *The Nineteenth-century Native Land Court Judges: An introductory report commissioned by the Waitangi Tribunal*, Wellington, 1994.

69. 'Report from W.B. White, Esq., Resident Magistrate, Mangonui', in 'Reports on the social and political state of the natives in various districts at the time of the arrival of Sir G.F. Bowen', *AJHR*, 1868, Session I, A-04, 37.

70. M. Barrington and T.H. Beaglehole, '"A part of Pakeha society": Europeanising the Maori child', in J.A. Mangan (ed.), *Making Imperial Mentalities: Socialisation and British imperialism*, Manchester, 1990, 174.

71. G.A. Wood, 'Church and State in New Zealand in the 1850s', *Journal of Religious History*, vol. 8, no. 3, 1975, 269–70.

72. A. Durie, 'Emancipatory Maori education: Speaking from the heart', *Language Culture and Curriculum*, vol. 11, no. 3, 1998, 300.

73. J.C. Richmond, *NZPD*, 1867, 862–63.

74. T.K.M. Dewes, 'The case for oral arts', in M. King (ed.), *The World Moves On*, Wellington, 1975, 56.

75. The legislation was amended in 1871, which alleviated the financial commitment Māori communities were expected to make towards schools in their regions.

76. Native Schools Act 1867, ss. 3, 4, 5, 15, 18, 19.

77. Ibid., s. 21.

78. *Daily Southern Cross*, 29 July 1868, 4.

79. A. Ward, *A Show of Justice: Racial 'amalgamation' in nineteenth century New Zealand*, Toronto, 1973, 211.

80. *Wellington Independent*, 20 April 1867, 6.

81. S. Bannister, *British Colonization and Coloured Tribes*, London, 1838, 76–85, 95–96; M.I. Murphy, 'The peaceable kingdom of nineteenth century humanitarianism: The Aborigines Protection Society and New Zealand', MA thesis, University of Canterbury, Christchurch, 2002, 107; T. Hodgkin, *On the Importance of Studying and Preserving the Languages Spoken by Uncivilized*

Nations, with a view of elucidating the physical history of mankind, London, 1835, 24.

82. *Lyttelton Times*, 31 July 1868, 2.

83. W. Rolleston, 'Papers relative to Native Schools', *AJHR*, 1867, Session I, A-03, 4.

84. Ibid., 1–3. The purported benefits of the secularism in the 1867 Act were lauded by some in the press. See *Lyttelton Times*, 31 July 1868, 2.

85. 'Statement of operations under the "Native Schools Act 1867"', *AJHR*, 1868, Session I, A-06a, 1–2.

86. R.O. Stewart, 'Extract from the report of R.O. Stewart, Esq., R.M., Raglan', in 'Further papers relative to Native Schools', *AJHR*, 1868, Session I, A-06, 9.

87. M. Soutar, 'Ngāti Porou leadership: Rāpata Wahawaha and the politics of conflict: "Kei te ora nei hoki tātou, me tō tātou whenua"', PhD thesis, Massey University, Palmerston North, 2000, ch. 1; A.T. Ngata, *The Price of Citizenship: Ngarimu V.C.*, Wellington, 1943; N. Mahuika, '"Kōrero tuku iho": Reconfiguring oral history and oral tradition', 147; K. Sinclair, *A Destiny Apart: New Zealand's search for national identity*, Wellington, 1986, 205, 207.

88. I. Featherston, cited in T.R. Hiroa, 'The passing of the Maori', *Transactions and Proceedings of the Royal Society of New Zealand*, vol. 55, 1924, 362.

89. P. Parkinson, *'Strangers in the House': The Maori Language in Government and the Maori language in parliament 1865–1900*, Wellington, 2001, 3.

90. The legislation passed in the 1850s and 1860s that directly affected Māori included New Zealand Native Reserves Act 1856; Native District Regulations Act 1858; Native Circuit Courts Act 1858; Resident Magistrates Court Act 1858; New Zealand Native Reserves Amendment Act 1858; Native Schools Act 1858; Native Territorial Rights Act 1858; Half-caste Disability Act 1860; Native Council Act 1860; Intestate Native Succession Act 1861; Native Reserves Amendment Act 1862; Native Purposes Appropriation Act 1862; Native Districts Regulation Act Amendment Act 1862; Native Circuit Courts Act Amendment Act 1862; Native Lands Act 1862; New Zealand Settlements Act 1863; Native Purposes Appropriation Act Amendment Act 1863; New Zealand Settlement Act Amendment Act 1864; Public Works Lands Act 1864; Native Lands Act Amendment Act 1864; Native Rights Act 1865; Maori Funds Investment Act 1865; New Zealand Settlements Act and Continuance, 1865; Outlying Districts Police Act 1865; Native Commission Act 1865; Native Lands Act 1865; Friendly Native Contracts Confirmation Act 1866; East Coast Land Titles Investigation Act 1866; New Zealand Settlements Act Amendment Act 1866; Native Lands Act Amendment Act 1866; Auckland and Onehunga Native Hostelries Act 1867; Resident Magistrates Act 1867; Maori Real Estate Management Act 1867; Native Schools Act 1867; Native Lands Act 1867; Confiscated Lands Act 1867; East Coast Land Titles Investigation Act 1867; Tauranga District Lands Act 1867; Native Representation Act 1867; Ngaitatui Reference Validation Act 1868; Tauranga District Lands Act Amendment Act 1868; Gold-fields Act Amendment Act (Native Lands), 1868; Native Lands Act Amendment Act 1868; Native Lands (East Coast), 1868; Native Lands Amendment Act 1869. See A. Mackay, *A Compendium of Official Documents Relative to Native Affairs in the South Island*, vol. 2, Nelson, 1872, 348.

91. The first Act passed by the New Zealand House of Representatives was in 1854: the English Acts Act 1854.

92. Including the New Zealand Native Reserves Act 1856, the Land Claims Settlement Act 1856; the Land Orders and Script Act 1856, the Marriage Act 1854, the Public Offences Act 1856, the Waste Lands Act 1856 and the Public Reserves Act 1854.

93. Two Acts passed by the General Assembly of New Zealand, 1858, relating to native affairs: the Native Districts Regulation Act, and the Native Circuit Courts Act: He Ture hou, erua, i whakatakotoria e te Runanga Nui o Niu Tirani 1858. Ara; Ko te Ture whakakoto Ture-iti ki nga Takiwa Maori, ko te Ture whakarite Kooti Maori, Auckland, 1859, 1.

94. Fighting started on 17 March 1860 with a Crown attack on Te Kohia pā in Taranaki.

95. The role of the Treaty of Waitangi in the context of the conference is addressed in L. Paterson, 'The Kohimarama Conference of 1860: A contextual reading', *Journal of New Zealand Studies*, no. 12, November 2011, 29–46.

96. T.G. Browne, *Proceedings of the Kohimarama Conference, comprising nos. 13 to 18 of the* Maori Messenger, Auckland, 1860, 2.

97. Ibid.

98. J.C. Richmond, *The Colonist*, 10 October 1862, 1.

99. W. Colenso, *The Colonist*, 10 October 1862, 1.

100. By 1868, parliament had resolved that a 'simple text-book' of parliamentary practice be published in Māori; that tabled papers be translated and relevant sessional papers also be translated and printed in Māori; and that an interpreter be appointed.

101. Parkinson, *'Strangers in the House'*, 10–14. This provision survived with little change until the end of the century. See 'Standing Orders of the House of Representatives', *AJHR*, 1894, Session I, H-11, 17.

102. Te Rangikaheke, cited in *GBPP*, 1860, London, 1860, 181.

103. Ibid.

104. B. Wells, *The History of Taranaki: A standard work on the history of the province*, New Plymouth, 1878, 167–68.

105. *AJHR*, 1860, Session I, E-07, 7–8.

106. S. McClelland, 'Maori electoral representation: Challenge to orthodoxy', *New Zealand Universities Law Review*, vol. 17, June 1997, 272–91. A contrary view has been proposed by T. Dahlberg, 'Maori representation in Parliament and Tino Rangatiratanga', *He Pukenga Kōrero*, vol. 2, no. 1, 1996, 63. See also New Zealand Parliamentary Library, *The Origins of the Maori Seats*, Wellington, May 2009, 7.

107. A. Fleras, 'From social control towards political self-determination? Maori seats and the politics of separate Maori representation in New Zealand', *Canadian Journal of Political Science*, vol. 18, no. 3, September 1985, 555; Ward, *A Show of Justice*, 209.

108. P. Tukairangi, 30 November 1864, in 'Letters from Native Chiefs to Mr. Fitzgerald M.H.R. relative to their admission into the General Assembly', *AJHR*, 1864, Session I, E-15, 3.

109. Fleras, 'From social control towards political self-determination?', 555. Ironically, the first candidate to stand for the Northern Maori electorate was F.N. Russell, a half-caste. M.P.K. Sorrenson, 'A history of Maori representation in Parliament', *Report on the Royal Commission on the Electoral System*, Wellington, 1986, B-20.

110. *AJHR*, 1868, Session I, A-04, 15; Fleras, 'From social control towards political self-determination?', 559; P. Moon, '"A proud thing to have recorded": The origins and commencement of national indigenous political representation in New Zealand through the 1867 Maori Representation Act', *Journal of New Zealand Studies*, vol. 16, 2013, 52–65.

111. T. McDowell, 'Te Ana o te Raiona: Māori political movements and the Māori seats in Parliament, 1867–2008', PhD thesis, University of Auckland, Auckland 2013, 101.

112. Ibid., 102.

113. *NZPD*, 1868, vol. 2, 466; *NZPD*, 1872, vol. 12, 454; *NZPD*, 1888, vol. 60, 331–32; and *NZPD*, 1881, vol. 38, 289, cited in McDowell, 'Te Ana o te Raiona', 102.

114. *NZPD*, 1868, vol. 2, 271, cited in McDowell, 'Te Ana o te Raiona', 102.

115. J. Patterson, *NZPD*, 1868, vol. 2, 372.

116. *Taranaki Herald*, 5 September 1868, 3.

117. *Evening Post*, 15 August 1868, 2.

118. Parkinson, *'Strangers in the House'*, 17–18.

119. As an example, see H.K. Taiaroa, *NZPD*, 6 October 1871, vol. 11, 158.

120. Parkinson, *'Strangers in the House'*, 18–21.

121. As an example, see 'Further papers relative to the Manawatu Block', *AJHR*, 1866, Session I, A-04, 1–35.

122. D. Keenan, 'Aversion to print? Māori resistance to the written word', 27; D. Keenan, 'Haere whakamua, hoki whakauri, Going forward, thinking back: Tribal and hapu perspectives of the past in 19th century Taranaki', PhD thesis, Massey University, Palmerston North, 1994, 177.

123. W. Colenso, *Three Literary Papers: Read before the Hawke's Bay Philosophical Institute, during the session of 1882*, Napier, 1883, 22.

124. Ibid., 22–23.

125. This was an estimate contained in *NZPD*, 1867, vol. 1, 336, 458. Cf. Statistics New Zealand, 'Statistics of New Zealand, 1867', in *Census Results and General Statistics of New Zealand for 1867, Report to the Honourable Edward William Stafford, Colonial Secretary*, Wellington, 1867, Appendix B; *Hawke's Bay Weekly Times*, vol. 2, issue 82, 27 July 1868, 182.

126. H. Carleton, *NZPD*, 1867, 862–63.

127. W.T.L. Travers, 'On the changes effected in the natural features of a new country by the introduction of civilized races', *Transactions and Proceedings of the Royal Society of New Zealand*, vol. 2, 1869, 299–330.

128. This environment is examined in E. Henry and H. Pene, 'Kaupapa Maori: Locating indigenous ontology, epistemology and methodology in the academy', *Organization*, vol. 8, no. 2, 2001, 234–42.

129. The dynamics of language use in a multilinguistic environment are dealt with in S. Canagarajah, 'Lingua franca English, multilingual communities, and

language acquisition', *Modern Language Journal*, vol. 91, no. 1, 2007, 923–39. See also E. Haugen, 'The ecology of language', in A. Dil (ed.), *The Ecology of Language: Essays by Einar Haugen*, Stanford, 1972, 325; R.S. Hill, *State Authority, Indigenous Autonomy: Crown–Maori relations in New Zealand/Aotearoa, 1900–1950*, Wellington, 2004, 26–28.

130. R. Walker, 'Quality assurance in tertiary education from a Māori (indigenous) perspective', in J.S. Te Rito, B. Duffin, P. Fletcher and J. Sinclair (eds), *Tihei Oreore*, vol. 1, no. 1, December 2005, 152ff.

131. The author has been present on a number of occasions when whakapapa books have been copied and added to.

132. For an alternative perspective of this process, see K.F. Lian, 'Tribe, class and colonisation: The political organisation of Maori society in the 19th century', *JPS*, vol. 101, no. 4, December 1992, 387–408.

133. The first hui was convened in 1860. See M. Carter, 'The preservation of the Maori oral tradition', in R. Selby and A. Laurie, *Maori and Oral History: A collection*, Wellington, 2005, 43–44.

134. P.J. Mataira, 'Mana and tapu: Sacred knowledge, sacred boundaries', in G. Harvey, *Indigenous Religions*, London, 2000, 99–111; T.G. Hammond, 'The tohunga Maori', *JPS*, vol. 17, no. 3, 1908, 162–65; A. Fletcher, 'Sanctity, power, and the "impure sacred": Analyzing Maori concepts of tapu and noa in early documentary sources', *History of Religions*, vol. 47, no. 1, 2007, 51–74.

135. D.R. Simmons, 'The words of Te Matorohanga', *JPS*, vol. 103, no. 2, 1994, 116.

136. Ibid., 137.

137. Even if it was acknowledged that the authors were transcribers, they also became part of the history. See T.A.C. Royal, 'Te Whare Tapere: Towards a model for Māori and/or tribal theatre', lecture delivered at the Stout Centre, Victoria University of Wellington, 14 May 1997, 5. Also see M.J. Stevens, 'Kai Tahu writing and cross-cultural communication', *Journal of New Zealand Literature*, vol. 28, no. 2, 2010, 130–57.

138. As just one example, the material in T.M. Tau (ed.), *'I whānau au ki Kaiapoi': The story of Natanahira Waruwarutu as recorded by Thomas Green*, Dunedin, 2011, offers a narrative that may not have survived to the present day had it not been transcribed.

139. See M. Clyne, 'Can the shift from immigrant languages be reversed in Australia?', in J.A. Fishman (ed.), *Can Threatened Languages Be Saved?*, Cleveland, 2001, 366–69.

140. This process is detailed in W.W. Rostow, *The Stages of Economic Growth: A non-communist manifesto*, Cambridge, 1960, 4–16.

CHAPTER 6: NGĀ ĀTETE: 1870s TO 1890s

1. C.F. Goldie, *Memories. The Last of her Tribe*, Auckland, 1913, Aigantighe Art Gallery, Timaru, object no. 1956.017.

2. H.P. Sealy, 'In the studio, Mr Goldie's work', *New Zealand Illustrated Magazine*, vol. 5, no. 2, November 1901, 147.

3. A.K. Newman, 'A study of the causes leading to the extinction of the Maori',

Transactions and Proceedings of the Royal Society of New Zealand, vol. 14, 1882, 459.

4.   Ibid., 477.

5.   The influence of utilitarian thinking in colonial activity is discussed in P. Moon, 'The influence of "Benthamite" philosophies on British colonial policy in New Zealand in the era of the Treaty of Waitangi', *Journal of Imperial and Commonwealth History*, vol. 43, no. 3, 2015, 1–20.

6.   J. Stenhouse, '"A disappearing race before we came here": Doctor Alfred Kingcome Newman, the dying Maori, and Victorian scientific racism', *NZJH*, vol. 30, no. 2, 1996, 124–33.

7.   W. Buller, 'The decrease of the Maori race', *New Zealand Journal of Science*, vol. 2, 1884, 55; *Te Aroha News*, 5 April 1884, 5.

8.   R. Weikart, 'The origins of social Darwinism in Germany, 1859–1895', *Journal of the History of Ideas*, vol. 54, no. 3, 1993, 469.

9.   Ibid., 470; S. Weaver, 'Nietzsche's Antichrist: 19th-century Christian Jews and the real big lie', *Modern Judaism*, vol. 17, no. 2, 1997, 163–77.

10. H-G. Zmarzlik, 'Social Darwinism in Germany: An example of the sociopolitical abuse of scientific knowledge', in G. Altner (ed.), *Human Creature*, Garden City, 1974, 355.

11. O. Schmidt, *The Doctrine of Descent and Darwinism*, London, 1875, 140.

12. F. Nietzsche, *Daybreak: Thoughts on the prejudices of morality*, Cambridge, 1997, 126.

13. F. Nietzsche, *Beyond Good and Evil*, Cambridge, 2002, 133.

14. W.E. Gladstone, 'England's mission', in A. Burton (ed.), *Politics and Empire in Victorian Britain: A reader*, New York, 2001, 135.

15. *Manawatu Standard*, 3 March 1884, 2.

16. *Auckland Star*, 3 August 1889, 2.

17. *New Zealand Illustrated Magazine*, vol. 1, no. 1, 1 October 1899, 37.

18. S. Shieff, 'Alfred Hill's "Hinemoa" and musical marginality', *Turnbull Library Record*, vol. 28, 1995, 61–78.

19. *Otago Daily Times*, 22 April 1899, 6.

20. M. Cross, 'The forgotten soundtrack of Maoriland: Imagining the nation through Alfred Hill's songs for *Rewi's Last Stand*', MMus thesis, Massey University and Victoria University, Wellington, 2015, 17.

21. *New Zealand Herald*, 6 September 1892, 5.

22. These categories are derived from R.A. Rogers, 'From cultural exchange to transculturation: A review and reconceptualization of cultural appropriation', *Communication Theory*, vol. 16, no. 4, 2006, 474–503.

23. B. Ziff and P.V. Rao, 'Introduction to cultural appropriation: A framework for analysis', in B. Ziff and P.V. Rao (eds), *Borrowed Power: Essays on cultural appropriation*, New Brunswick, NJ, 1997, 9.

24. The fashion of giving houses Māori names was reasonably widespread until the end of the 1930s; it tailed off after that time.

25. M.P.K. Sorrenson, 'Land purchase methods and their effect on Maori population, 1865–1901', *JPS*, vol. 65, no. 3, September 1956, 183.

26. This sentiment is conveyed in R.A. Loughnan, *Royalty in New Zealand: The visit*

of Their Royal Highnesses the Duke and Duchess of Cornwall and York to New Zealand, 10th–27th June 1901: A descriptive narrative, Wellington, 1902, 74.

27. E. Keenan, 'Māori urban migrations and identities "Ko ngā iwi nuku whenua": A study of urbanisation in the Wellington region during the twentieth century', PhD thesis, Victoria University of Wellington, 2014, 77–78; A. Wanhalla, 'In/ Visible sight: Māori–European families in urban New Zealand, 1890–1940', *Visual Anthropology*, vol. 21, no. 1, 2008, 39.

28. J. Stafford and M. Williams, *Maoriland: New Zealand literature, 1872–1914*, Wellington, 2006, 10.

29. Some examples from the turn of the century include 'Scenes in Maoriland' [postcard], Ref: Eph-B-POSTCARD-Vol-2-17, ATL; 'A little nonsense now and then' [postcard], Ref: Eph-POSTCARD-Stephens-02, ATL; 'F.T. Series No. 2322. Maori salutation. New Zealand post-card' [postcard], Ref: Eph-POSTCARDS-Robertson-04; '"Tenakoe" 22983' [postcard], Ref: Eph-B-POSTCARD-Vol-10-024-3, ATL; 'The Maoris; Living races of the world' [postcard], Ref: Eph-F-POSTCARD-Vol-1-09-1, ATL; 'Maoris cooking, Whakarewarewa, N.Z.' [postcard], Ref: Eph-POSTCARD-Stephens-01, ATL.

30. As examples, see A.H. Adams, *Maoriland and Other Verses*, Sydney, 1899; T. Bracken, *Musing in Maoriland*, Dunedin, 1890; A.A. Grace, *Maoriland Stories*, Nelson, 1895; J. Mackay, *The Spirit of Rangatiratanga and Other Ballads*, Melbourne, 1889.

31. For a discussion of this term, see J.O.C. Phillips, 'Musings in Maoriland, or Was there a *Bulletin* school in New Zealand?' in *Historical Studies*, vol. 20, no. 81, 1983, 520–35.

32. Stafford and Williams, *Maoriland*, 11–22.

33. H. Talbot-Tubbs, *New Zealand Illustrated Magazine*, vol. 1, issue 1, 1 October 1899, 5.

34. Ibid.

35. Native Schools Amendment Act 1871, ss. 5, 6, 7.

36. F.E. Maning to D. McLean, 1 November 1873, in Inward letters: F.E. Maning, Reference Number MS-Papers-0032-0445, Series 1, ATL.

37. C.B. Paulston and K. Heidemann, 'Language policies and the education of linguistic minorities', in T. Ricento (ed.), *An Introduction to Language Policy: Theory and method*, Oxford, 2006, 296.

38. S. Lieberson, G. Dalto and M.E. Johnston, 'The course of mother-tongue diversity in nations', *American Journal of Sociology*, vol. 81, no. 1, 1975, 53.

39. 'Reports from officers in native districts', *AJHR*, 1872, Session I, F-03, 4.

40. 'Petition of Wi Te Hakiro and 336 others', *AJHR*, 1876, Session I, J-04, 1–3.

41. Ibid. See also J. Ewing and J. Shallcrass, *Introduction to Maori Education*, Wellington, 1970, 30, cited in A. Durie, 'Emancipatory Maori education: Speaking from the heart', *Language Culture and Curriculum*, vol. 11, no. 3, 1998, 297–308.

42. *Te Paki o Matariki*, 25 July 1893, in J.A. Williams, *Politics of the New Zealand Maori: Protest and cooperation, 1891–1909*, Auckland, 1969, 41.

43. 'One is to be at Kopua, near Alexandra, one at Waotu, near Cambridge, and one at Tapapa, near Oxford', in 'Reports from officers in native districts', *AJHR*, 1886, Session I, G-01, 8.

44. Ibid.
45. Arthur Ormsby, Arekatera te Wera and Karanama te Whakaheke, among others, were named as being responsible.
46. Education Act 1877, s. 10.
47. Ibid., s. 89.
48. A. Ward, *A Show of Justice: Racial 'amalgamation' in nineteenth century New Zealand*, Toronto, 1973, 308.
49. Education Act 1877, s. 84 (1), (2).
50. The title Inspector of Native Schools was created in 1885, but Pope took up the position in 1880 under its earlier designation. For biographical details, see The Cyclopedia Company, *The Cyclopedia of New Zealand: Industrial, descriptive, historical, biographical, facts, figures, illustrations*, Wellington, 1897, 169.
51. Minister of Education, 'Report to the General Assembly', *AJHR*, 1880, Session I, H-01a, 21.
52. Interestingly, the code was not gazetted. For a discussion of this, see J. Holdom, 'Schooling for "lesser beings" Part One: The political culture, and historiography, of schooling for Maori. Part Two: Te Kopua Native/Maori School: A biography ', MEd thesis, University of Waikato, Hamilton, 1998, 42.
53. It was also in line with the government's longer-term intention of assimilating native schools into the mainstream education system. See J.D.S. McKenzie, 'More than a show of justice? The enrolment of Maoris in European schools prior to 1900', *New Zealand Journal of Educational Studies*, vol. 17, no. 1, 1982, 1–20.
54. 'Education: Native Schools', *AJHR*, 1880, Session I, H-01f, 1.
55. Cited in W.W. Bird, 'The education of the Maori' in I. Davey (ed.), *Fifty Years of National Education in New Zealand 1878–1928*, Christchurch, 1928, 64.
56. As examples, see W. Colenso, *Willie's First English Book: Written by Order of the Government*, Wellington, 1872; L. Williams, *Lessons in the English Language for Maori Schools*, Wellington, 1875. These are referenced in C. McGeorge, 'James Pope's textbooks for New Zealand Native Schools', *Paradigm 2/3*, 2–3.
57. Three of his books were still in print and in use in the early twentieth century. Some of his works for adults were also widely read by Māori, including W.T. Ratana, who was said to have been influenced by one of them: J.M. Henderson, *Ratana: The man, the church, the political movement*, Wellington, 1972, 24, 35.
58. McGeorge, 'James Pope's textbooks', 2.
59. J.H. Pope, *Lessons in Reading and Spelling for Use in Native Schools*, Wellington, 1884, 5, 20.
60. 'Education: Native Schools' [In continuation of E-2, 1887], *AJHR*, 1888, Session I, E-02, 1.
61. Ibid., 9.
62. Ibid.
63. J.H. Pope, in 'Education: Native Schools', *AJHR*, 1881, Session I, E-07, 6–7.
64. 'Education: Native Schools', *AJHR*, 1885, Session I, E-02, 1-22.
65. 'Native Schools' [In Continuation of E-2, 1892], *AJHR*, 1893, Session I, E-02, 1–18.
66. J.H. Pope, in 'Education: Native Schools', *AJHR*, 1898, Session I, E-02, 14.

67. 'The interest taken by the Maori people in the school education of their children is constantly growing. In 1896 the number of village schools rose from 69 to 74 the number of children on the roll in December, from 2675 to 2862 the mean of the weekly returns of pupils on the roll, from 2656 to 2874; and the strict average attendance for the year, from 2084 to 2220. On the average the daily attendance was equal to 77 per cent, of the roll-number for the time being. About 9 per cent, of the children are half-castes, about 14 per cent are European (or inclining to European), and nearly 77 per cent, are Maori (or inclining to Maori)', 'Education: Native Schools' [In continuation of E-2, 1896], *AJHR* 1897, Session II, E-02, 1.

68. W.L. Williams, *East Coast (N.Z.) Historical Records*, Gisborne, 1932, 75.

69. Its modest role and finances are detailed in H.B. Morton, *Recollections of Early New Zealand*, Auckland, 1925, 54–56.

70. J.P.H. Graham, 'Whakatangata kia kaha: Toitū te whakapapa, toitū te tuakiri, toitū te mana: An examination of the contribution of Te Aute College to Māori advancement', PhD thesis, Massey University, Palmerston North, 2009, ch. 3.

71. F. McDonald, *The Game of Our Lives*, Auckland, 1996, 13–14.

72. J. Barrington, 'Learning the "dignity of labour": Secondary education policy for Maoris', *New Zealand Journal of Educational Studies*, vol. 23, 1988, 49; B. Hokowhitu, 'The death of Koro Paka: "Traditional" Māori patriarchy', *Contemporary Pacific*, vol. 20, no. 1, 2008, 121–24.

73. R. Walker, *Ka Whawhai Tonu Matou: Struggle without end*, Auckland, 1990, 173.

74. J. Thornton, *AJHR*, 1906, Session II, G-05, 32.

75. Ibid., 41.

76. This preconditioning phase, as part of the modernisation process, is detailed in W. Rostow, *The Five Stages of Economic Growth: A non-communist manifesto*, London, 1960.

77. R.T. Kohere, *The Autobiography of a Maori*, Wellington, 1951, 65–66.

78. J. Thornton, *AJHR*, 1906, Session II, G-05, 35.

79. A.K. Davidson, *Christianity in Aotearoa: A history of Church and society in New Zealand*, Wellington, 1991, 44.

80. *New Zealand Herald*, 2 February 1886, 5.

81. The Bicultural Commission of the Anglican Church on the Treaty of Waitangi/ Te Ripoata a te Komihana mo te Kaupapa Tikanga Rua mo te Tiriti o Waitangi, *The Report of the Bicultural Commission of the Anglican Church on the Treaty of Waitangi*, Christchurch, 1986, 1–4. Technically speaking, until 1857 the Anglican Church in New Zealand was a Māori Church formed by the Mission to the Maori People of the Church Missionary Society. See M. Stephens, 'The Anglican Constitution: A model for New Zealand?', Honours research seminar, 2 October 2000, 3. For the origins of Māori clergy in the Church, see R. Lange, 'Ordained ministry in Maori Christianity, 1853–1900', *Journal of Religious History*, vol. 27, no. 1, February 2003, 47–53. W.R. Nicholson, 'Hei timatanga korero: Maori language regenesis and mihinare clergy', MA thesis, University of Canterbury, Christchurch, 2000, 53–60.

82. Formed by Letters Patent, dated 27 September 1858.

83. W. Rosevear, *Waiapu: The story of a diocese*, Hamilton, 1960, 48–50.

84. So overwhelming was the Māori population that Selwyn saw it as a missionary diocese. Nicholson, 'Hei timatanga korero', 53; S.H. Selwyn, *Reminiscences, 1809–1867*, Auckland, 1961, 62.

85. Nicholson, 'Hei timatanga korero', 56.

86. As samples of the records in te reo Māori, see *Te Maramataka, Me Te Tau*, Kihipane, 1894; Church of England, Diocese of Auckland, *Reports of Meetings on Maori Church Matters, 1872–1888*, Auckland, 1888. See also Nicholson, 'Hei timatanga korero', 57.

87. Church of England, Diocese of Auckland, *Reports of Meetings on Maori Church Matters, 1897*, Auckland, 1897, 22.

88. Translation by Robert Pouwhare. Personal communication to P. Moon, 30 March 2015.

89. The Wesleyan Church membership was around 22 per cent the size of the Anglican membership in the 1890s in New Zealand.

90. *Press* (Sydney), 27 January 1888, 5.

91. J. Belich, *Making Peoples: A history of New Zealand from Polynesian settlement to the end of the nineteenth century*, Auckland, 1996, 220.

92. J. Binney, 'Ancestral voices: Maori prophet leaders', in K. Sinclair (ed.), *The Oxford Illustrated History of New Zealand*, Auckland, 1990, 1.

93. P. Moon, 'Nākahi: The Matarahurahu Cult of the Snake', *Te Kaharoa*, vol. 4, no. 1, 2011, 119–37.

94. J.L. Campbell, *Poenamo: Sketches of the early days of New Zealand romance and reality of Antipodean life in the infancy of a new colony*, book IV, London, 1881, 265.

95. W.L. Williams, in F.W. Williams, *Through Ninety Years, 1826–1916: Life and work among the Maoris in New Zealand: Notes of the lives of William and William Leonard Williams, First and Third Bishops of Waiapu*, Auckland, 1939, 197.

96. H. Pieter, 'The contribution of Maori religious movements', *Exchange*, vol. 8, no. 1, 1979, 1–36.

97. O. Wilson, *War in the Tussock: Te Kooti and the battle at Te Porere*, Wellington, 1961; W. Greenwood, *The Upraised Hand, or The spiritual significance of the rise of the Ringatu faith*, Wellington, 1980; J. Binney and G. Chaplin, *Nga Morehu: The survivors*, Auckland, 1986.

98. J. Binney, 'The Ringatu traditions of predictive history', *Journal of Pacific History*, vol. 23, no. 2, October 1988, 167–68.

99. As an example, see 'Ko te maroma tenei i nui ai toku mate 21 o nga ra ka hemo au', in Te Kooti Arikirangi, MS Notebook 1867–8, ATL, contemporary translation in G.H. Davies, Maori Manuscripts 3, ATL, in Binney, 'The Ringatu traditions of predictive history', 169–73. Also see J. Binney, 'Myth and explanation in the Ringatu tradition: Some aspects of the leadership of Te Kooti Arikirangi Te Turuki and Rua Kenana Hepetipa', *JPS*, vol. 93, no. 4, December 1984, 348.

100. W.J. Ong, *Orality and Literacy: The technologizing of the word*, London, 1982, 75.

101. This is discussed in F. Kermode, *The Genesis of Secrecy: On the interpretation of narrative*, Cambridge, Massachusetts, 1979, 107, in Binney, 'Myth and

explanation in the Ringatu tradition', 349; J. Friedman, 'Oral history, hermeneutics, and embodiment', *Oral History Review*, vol. 41, no. 2, Summer/ Fall 2014, 290–93.

102. B. Gadd, 'The teachings of Te Whiti o Rongomai, 1831–1907', *JPS*, vol. 75, no. 4, December 1966, 445–57.

103. As examples, see J. Cowan, *The Maoris Yesterday and Today*, Wellington, 1930, 230–31; D. Scott, *The Parihaka Story*, Auckland, 1954, 155.

104. M. McCarthy, 'Raising a Māori child under a New Right state', in P. Te Whaiti, M. McCarthy and A. Durie (eds), *Mai i Rangiātea: Māori wellbeing and development*, Auckland, 1997, 30.

105. M. Stephens, 'A house with many rooms: Rediscovering Māori as a civic language in the wake of the Maori Language Act (1987)', in R. Higgins, P. Rewi and V. Olsen-Reeder (eds), *The Value of the Māori Language: Te hua o te reo Māori*, Wellington, 2014, 64.

106. M. Paetahi, 19 July 1870, *NZPD*, 1870, 513. This lack of understanding of some of the processes of parliament was not indicative of a lack of interest in representation in the House of Representatives. See J. Waymouth, 'Parliamentary representation for Maori: Debate and ideology in *Te Wananga* and *Te Waka Maori o Niu Tirani*, 1874–8', in J. Curnow, N. Hopa and J. McRae (eds), *Rere Atu, Taku Manu: Discovering history, language and politics in the Māori-language newspapers,* Auckland, 2002, 153–55.

107. 'Kaunihera Maori (Native Councils): he ture i huaina: he ture hei whakatakoto tikanga mo nga kaunihera i nga takiwa Maori, a hei whakatakoto tikanga hoki mo te mahi o aua kaunihera', acc. 269960, ATL. McLean later withdrew the bill.

108. J. Binney, *Encircled Lands: Te Urewera, 1820–1921*, Wellington, 2009, 240.

109. A version of the bill was published in *Te Waka Maori o Niu Tireni*, vol. 8, no. 21, 30 October 1872.

110. Demands that bills be translated into te reo also came from the Legislative Council (parliament's upper house) where, for example, one of its Māori members, Wi Tako Ngatata, formally requested in 1872 that a bill be produced in te reo so that he could understand it. Even if it did so grudgingly, Parliament could occasionally yield to the need to have some planned legislation translated into te reo, if only to avoid accusations that by not doing so there could be some prejudicial effect on Māori. W.T. Ngatata, *NZPD*, vol. 13, 15 October 1872, 651–52.

111. D. McLean, *NZPD*, vol. 28, 15 September 1875, 348.

112. J. Sheehan, *NZPD*, vol. 21, 11 August 1876, 257.

113. Although as two historians claimed, 'Ignorant of European customs and political traditions, clustered together with an interpreter, Maori Members of parliament appeared all too amenable to influence by those who spoke their tongue, and their votes could determine the fate of a government.' W.K. Jackson and G.A. Wood, 'The New Zealand parliament and Maori representation', *Historical Studies: Australia and New Zealand*, vol. 11, no. 43, 1964, 389. Legislature Expenditure, *AJHR*, 1887, Session I, A-14, 1–2.

114. M. Stephens and P. Monk, 'A language for buying biscuits: Māori as a civic language in the modern New Zealand Parliament', *Victoria University of*

Wellington Legal Research Papers, Paper No. 14, vol. 2, no. 3, 2012, 6; M. Stephens, '"Tame Kaka" still? Maori members and the use of Maori language in the New Zealand Houses of Representatives', *Law, Culture, Text*, vol. 14, no. 1, 2010, 223.

115. Legislative Expenditure Committee, *AJHR*, 1886, Session I, I-10, 7.
116. *Mataura Ensign* , 24 August 1899, 2.
117. Native Land Court Amendment Act 1888, s. 29.
118. *Auckland Star*, 7 January 1889, 4.
119. W. Mantell, in P. Parkinson, *'Strangers in the House': The Maori language in Government and the Maori language in Parliament 1865–1900*, Wellington, 2001, 42.
120. Parkinson, *'Strangers in the House'*, 42–43.
121. J.A. Simon, 'Anthropology, "native schooling" and Maori: The politics of "cultural adaptation" policies', *Oceania*, vol. 69, no. 1, 1998, 67; E. Henry and H. Pene, 'Kaupapa Maori: Locating indigenous ontology, epistemology and methodology in the academy', *Organization*, vol. 8, no. 2, 2001, 234–42; L. Pihama, P. Reynolds, C. Smith, J. Reid, L.T. Smith and R. Te Nana, 'Positioning historical trauma theory within Aotearoa New Zealand', *AlterNative: An International Journal of Indigenous Peoples*, vol. 10, no. 3, 2014, 248–62; M. Mutu, 'Māori issues', *Contemporary Pacific*, vol. 21, no. 1, 2009, 162–69. G.R. Hook and L.P. Raumati, 'Does the New Zealand government owe Māori an apology', *MAI Review*, vol. 3, no. 11, 2008, 1–11.
122. The Aborigines Protection Society to the Earl of Derby, 12 October 1883, and Sub-enclosure, 16 July 1883, *AJHR*, 1884, Session I, A-02, 13–14.
123. Sub-enclosure, 16 July 1883, *AJHR*, 1884, Session I, A-02, 14.
124. Governor to the Secretary of State for Colonies, 1 March 1884, *AJHR*, 1884, Session I, A-01, 10–11. Also see V. O'Malley, *Agents of Autonomy: Maori committees in the nineteenth century*, Wellington, 1997, 146–47.
125. Created by the Native Land Act 1862 and the Native Lands Act 1865. B.D. Gilling, 'Engine of destruction: An introduction to the history of the Maori Land Court', Victoria University of Wellington, 1994, 122–23.
126. J. Bryce, Memorandum for His Excellency, 11 January 1884, *AJHR*, 1884, Session I, A-01, 11–12.
127. Native Lands Act 1865.
128. T. Lewis, *AJHR*, 1891, Session II, G-01, 145.
129. J. Bryce, Memorandum for His Excellency, 11 January 1884, *AJHR*, 1884, Session I, A-01, 11–12.
130. As examples, see H.H. Ngapua to W. Katene, 15 August 1894 (David Rankin Private Collection); T.N. MacKenzie, 'Illuminated presentation letter to Thomas MacKenzie by his Rangatira friends', 1894, Ref: fMS-Papers-8994, ATL.
131. Tawhiao to Derby, 1884, in G.W. Rusden, *History of New Zealand*, vol. 3, 2nd edn, Melbourne, 1895, 355.
132. Rusden, *History of New Zealand*, vol. 3, 356.
133. Although it failed to win the support of Kīngitanga or Te Whiti. M.P.K. Sorrenson, *Ko Te Whenua Te Utu, Land Is the Price: Essays on Maori history, land and politics*, Auckland, 2014, ch. 8.

134. R.J. Walker, 'The genesis of Maori activism', *JPS*, vol. 93, no. 3, 1984, 273.

135. Petition of the Federated Maori Assembly of New Zealand, *AJHR*, 1893, Session I, J-01, 2.

136. Petition of Hone Heke, *AJHR*, 1893, Session I, I-03, 11.

137. H.H. Ngapua to Native Minister (A. Cadman), 7 September 1891, Archives New Zealand, MA 1 1892/815; Telegram from Native Office, 7 April 1892, ANZ, MA 1 1892/815; M. Morpeth to A. Cadman, 26 May 1892, ANZ, MA 1 1892/828.

138. P. Moon, *Ngapua: The political life of Hone Heke Ngapua MHR*, Auckland, 2006, 21–24; D. Rankin, 'Hone Heke Ngapua, He Manatunga o Ngapuhi, 1869–1909: A voice silenced by prejudice', unpublished paper, 2006, 2.

139. Wi Pere, cited in Walker, 'The genesis of Maori activism', 273.

140. P. Buck, 'He Poroporoaki, A farewell message', *JPS*, vol. 60, no. 1, 1951, 22–31; R.J. Walker, *He Tipua: The life and times of Sir Apirana Ngata*, Auckland, 2002, 107–8; Belich, *Making Peoples*, 266.

141. T. McDowell, 'Te Ana o te Raiona: Māori political movements and the Māori seats in Parliament, 1867–2008', PhD thesis, University of Auckland, Auckland 2013, 75.

142. W. Parata, *NZPD*, 1903, vol. 123, 187. Also see G. Butterworth, 'The politics of adaptation: The career of Sir Apirana Ngata, 1874–1928', MA thesis, Victoria University of Wellington, 1969, 6.

CHAPTER 7: TE REO MĀORI IN 1899

1. J. Weston, *Ko Meri, or, Cycle of Cathay: A story of New Zealand life*, London, 1890, 390.

2. J. Weston, in J. Stevens, *The New Zealand Novel, 1860–1965*, Wellington, 1966, 25.

3. A.H. Adams, *Maoriland and Other Verses*, Sydney, 1899, 3.

4. *New Zealand Herald*, 8 April 1899, 1.

5. D.R. Simmons, 'The words of Te Matorohanga', *JPS*, vol. 103, no. 4, 1994, 117. Also see P. Cleave, 'Said, heard, written, read', *Te Kaharoa*, vol. 2, 2009, 89–95.

6. T. van Meijl, 'Historicising Maoritanga colonial ethnography and the reification of Maori traditions', *JPS*, vol. 105, no. 3, 1996, 312.

7. *Auckland Star*, 28 September 1899, 6.

8. *Otago Witness*, 28 December 1899, 8.

9. *Wanganui Chronicle*, 11 November 1902, 2.

10. F.H. Spencer, in P. Lineham, 'Tampering with the sacred text: The second edition of the *Māori Bible*', in P. Griffith, P. Hughes and A. Loney (eds), *A Book in the Hand: Essays on the history of the book in New Zealand*, Auckland, 2000, 41.

11. An incomplete version was published in 1889. W. Colenso, *A Maori–English Lexicon: Being a comprehensive dictionary of the New Zealand tongue*, Wellington, 1889.

12. 'The chronology of its editions and reprints: [1844, 1852, 1871, 1892, 1915, 1917, 1921, 1932, 1957, 1971, 1975, 1985, 1988, 1989, 1991, 1992, 1995, 1997, 2000], serves as a reminder of its continued authority. The 1852, 1871 and 1892 editions all contained an English–Maori section, these editions being basically

amended reprints of the 1844 (first) edition.' See T. Duval and K. Kuiper, 'Maori dictionaries and Maori loan words', *International Journal of Lexicography*, vol. 14, no. 4, 2001, 258.

13. *New Zealand Herald*, 16 February 1899, 5.

14. H.W. Williams, *A Dictionary of the Maori Language*, Wellington (1917), 1957, ix–x.

15. *Auckland Star*, 27 December 1898, 2.

16. This view was expressed in the early twentieth century. R. Stout, *Waihi Daily Telegraph*, 8 August 1908, 2.

17. The importance of indigenous agency in this process is identified in R. Henze and K. A. Davis, 'Authenticity and identity: Lessons from indigenous language education', *Anthropology and Education*, vol. 30. no. 1, March 1999, 3–4.

18. R.L. Cartwright, 'Some remarks on essentialism', *Journal of Philosophy*, vol. 65, no. 20, 1968, 615–26.

19. R. Duschinsky and S. Lampitt, 'Managing the tensions of essentialism: Purity and impurity', *Sociology*, vol. 46, no. 6, 2012, 1194–97; A. Bell, 'Relating Maori and Pakeha: The politics of indigenous and settler identities', PhD thesis, Massey University, Palmerston North, 2004, 29–65.

20. J. Clifford, *The Predicament of Culture*, 14.

21. The origins of this repression are covered in P. Bourdieu, 'Genesis and structure of the religious field' in *Comparative Social Research*, vol. 13, no. 1, 1991, 1–44.

22. *The Colonist*, 16 May 1899, 2.

23. *New Zealand Herald*, 15 February 1899, 3.

24. 'Education: Native Schools', *AJHR*, 1899, Session I, E-02, 1–2.

25. W. Shakespeare, *The Tempest*, Act 2, scene 1.

26. *New Zealand Herald*, 9 December 1908, 8.

27. R. Kohere, in 'Te Aute and Wanganui School Trusts (Report and Evidence of the Royal Commission on the)', *AJHR*, 1906, Session II, G-05, 73.

28. W. Bird, in Annual Report of the Public Health Department, *AJHR* 1908, Session I, H-31, 131.

Glossary

ahikā	the burning fires of occupation. Entitlement to land through continuous occupation by a group
ātete	resistance
atua	god, deity, supernatural being, object of veneration, ancestor with a supernatural presence
haka	choreographed dance, used for ceremonial purposes or as a prelude to engagement in battle
hapū	subtribe, clan, extended kinship group
hui	meeting, gathering
iwi	tribe, nation, people
kāinga	village, settlement, place of residence for a community
karakia	prayer, incantation, chant
karanga	ceremonial welcome call performed on marae
kaumātua	elder, person of status
kōrero	(v.) to talk, speak, orate; (n.) speech, conversation
kuia	grandmother, elderly mother, female elder
mana	respect, prestige, power, control, authority
manuhiri	guest, visitor
Māori	indigenous New Zealanders; ordinary, normal
marae	courtyard area in front of wharenui; the communal buildings of a Māori community
marae ātea	courtyard area in front of wharenui where certain rituals of welcome take place
mauri	life force, vital essence, the essential element of a being or object
noa	free from restrictions of tapu, ordinary, safe from tapu
pepeha	tribal saying, a saying used to identify tribal members
pounamu	greenstone, jade
rākau	stick, baton

rangatira	chief, highly ranked person
rangatiratanga	sovereignty, chieftainship
raranga	weaving, plaiting
reo	language, voice, dialect
tā moko	tattoo
tangata whenua	people of the land, indigenous people
tangi	funeral rite, rites for the dead, shortened version of tangihanga; (v.) to cry or weep
tangihanga	funeral rite, rites for the dead
taonga	treasure, possession, something valued
tapu	sacred; prohibited, forbidden
tauparapara	incantation commencing a speech, oration, formal speech
tikanga	procedure, custom, protocol, correct way of doing something
tīpuna	ancestors, grandparents; variant of tūpuna
tohunga	wise person, priest, expert, shaman
Tūhoe	an iwi or tribe in the Urewera
tūpāpaku	dead person, corpse
tūpuna	ancestors, grandparents; variant of tīpuna
tūrangawaewae	a location or place to which an individual belongs and where they have a right to stand
waiata	song, chant
waka	canoe, vessel
whaikōrero	formal speech, oratory
whakapapa	ancestry, genealogy, history; layers
whakataukī	proverb, saying, aphorism
whānau	family, kinship
whare	house, building
whare rūnanga	meeting house
whare wānanga	house of learning, school, place where important knowledge is imparted
wharekura	school, school house, house of learning
wharenui	large house, meeting house, part of marae

Bibliography

ABBREVIATIONS

AJHR	Appendices to the Journals of the House of Representatives
ANZ	Archives New Zealand
ATL	Alexander Turnbull Library
AWMM	Auckland War Memorial Museum
CMS	Church Missionary Society
GBPP	*Great Britain Parliamentary Papers*
JPS	*Journal of the Polynesian Society*
NZJH	*New Zealand Journal of History*
NZPD	*New Zealand Parliamentary Debates*

NEWSPAPERS AND PERIODICALS

Auckland Star
Daily Southern Cross
Evening Post
Hawke's Bay Weekly Times
Hawkes Bay Herald
Manawatu Standard
Mataura Ensign
Nelson Examiner and New Zealand Chronicle
New Zealand Gazette and Wellington Spectator
New Zealand Herald
New Zealand Herald and Auckland Gazette
New Zealand Illustrated Magazine
New Zealand Spectator and Cook's Strait Guardian
Otago Daily Times
Otago Witness
Poverty Bay Herald
Press (Christchurch)
Press (Sydney)
Sydney Gazette and New South Wales Advertiser
Sydney Morning Herald
Taranaki Herald
Te Aroha News
Te Karere Maori: The Maori Messenger
Te Karere o Nui Tireni
Te Paki o Matariki

Te Waka Māori o Niu Tireni
The Anglo Maori Warder
The Colonist
The Guardian [Britain]
The Lyttelton Times
The Native Gazette
The New Zealander
The New Zealand Messenger
The Southern Cross
The Wellington Independent
Waihi Daily Telegraph
Wanganui Chronicle
Weekly News
Wellington Independent

LEGISLATION

An Ordinance for Appointing a Board of Trustees for the Management of Property to be
    Set Apart for the Education and Advancement of the Native Race, Auckland, 1844
An Ordinance for promoting the Education of Youth in the Colony of New Zealand,
    Auckland, 7 October, 1847
Auckland and Onehunga Native Hostelries Act 1867
Census Act 1858.
Confiscated Lands Act 1867
East Coast Land Titles Investigation Act 1866
East Coast Land Titles Investigation Act 1867
Education Act 1877
English Acts Act 1854.
Friendly Native Contracts Confirmation Act 1866
Gold-fields Act Amendment Act (Native Lands), 1868
Half-caste Disability Act 1860
Intestate Native Succession Act 1861
Land Claims Settlement Act 1856
Maori Funds Investment Act 1865
Maori Language Act 1987
Maori Real Estate Management Act 1867
Marriage Act 1854
Native Circuit Courts Act Amendment Act 1862
Native Circuit Courts Act 1858
Native Commission Act 1865
Native Council Act 1860
Native District Regulations Act 1858
Native Districts Regulation Act Amendment Act 1862
Native Land Court Amendment Act 1888
Native Lands (East Coast) Act 1868

Native Lands Act Amendment Act 1864

Native Lands Act Amendment Act 1866

Native Lands Act Amendment Act 1868

Native Lands Act 1862

Native Lands Act 1865

Native Lands Act 1867

Native Lands Amendment Act 1869

Native Purposes Appropriation Act Amendment Act 1863

Native Purposes Appropriation Act 1862

Native Representation Act 1867

Native Reserves Amendment Act 1862

Native Rights Act 1865

Native Schools Act 1867

Native Schools Act 1858

Native Schools Amendment Act 1871

Native Territorial Rights Act 1858

New Zealand Native Reserves Act 1856

New Zealand Native Reserves Amendment Act 1858

New Zealand Settlements Act Amendment Act 1864

New Zealand Settlements Act Amendment Act 1866

New Zealand Settlements Act and Continuance, 1865

New Zealand Settlements Act 1863

Ngaitatui Reference Validation Act 1868

Outlying Districts Police Act 1865

Public Offences Act 1856

Public Reserves Act 1854

Public Works Lands Act 1864

Resident Magistrates Act 1867

Resident Magistrates Court Act 1858

Tauranga District Lands Act Amendment Act 1868

Tauranga District Lands Act 1867

The Land Orders and Script Act 1856

Waste Lands Act 1856

PERSONAL COMMUNICATIONS

Benton, R. to P. Moon, personal communication, 29 January 2015.

Kereopa, H. interview, Waimana, January 2003.

Henare, E. to P. Moon, personal communication, 8 April 2015.

Howard, M. to P. Moon, personal communication, 3 March 2015.

Kelly, K. to P. Moon, personal communication, 3 March 2015.

King, J. to P. Moon, personal communication, 25 February 2015.

Mason, T.H.H.H. to P. Moon, personal communication, 27 January 2015.

Moorfield, J. to P. Moon, personal communication, 6 September 2011.

Mutu, M. to P. Moon, personal communication, 8 April 2015.

Pouwhare, R. interview, Auckland, 19 January 2005.

Pouwhare, R. to P. Moon, personal communication, 30 March 2015.

Rewi, P. to P. Moon, personal communication, 27 January 2015.

Roa, T. to P. Moon, personal communication, 2 February 2015.

IMAGES

'A little nonsense now and then' [postcard], Ref: Eph-POSTCARD-Stephens-02, ATL.

Earle, A., 'The residence of Shulitea chief of Kororadika [i.e. Kororareka] Bay of Islands, New Zealand', watercolour; 21.9 x 36.2 cm, Rex Nan Kivell Collection; NK12/71, nla. pic-an2820827, National Library of Australia.

F.T. Series No. 2322. Māori salutation. New Zealand post-card [postcard], Ref: Eph-POSTCARDS-Robertson-04, ATL.

Gardiner, T., *View of the Missionary House, Waimate, New Zealand* [1834 or 1835], ref. A-049-020, ATL.

Goldie, C. F., *Memories. The Last of her Tribe*, Auckland, 1913, Aigantighe Art Gallery, Timaru, object no. 1956.017.

'Maoris cooking, Whakarewarewa, N.Z.' [postcard], Ref: Eph-POSTCARD-Stephens-01, ATL.

Morgan, J., 'Oihi Bay, Christmas Day 1814; Samuel Marsden preaching the first sermon to the Maoris', in *Weekly News*, Auckland, 1964, Reference Number B-077-002.

'Scenes in Maoriland' [postcard], Ref: Eph-B-POSTCARD-Vol-2-17, ATL.

Tenakoe 22983 [postcard], Ref: Eph-B-POSTCARD-Vol-10-024-3, ATL.

'The Maoris; Living races of the world' [postcard], Ref: Eph-F-POSTCARD-Vol-1-09-1, ATL.

UNPUBLISHED MATERIAL

Chart of New Zealand drawn by Tooka-Titter-anue Wari-Ledo [Tuki Tahua], a priest of that country who resided in Norfolk Island for 6 months. No scale shown. Originally enclosed with Lieutenant-Governor King's despatch of 7 November 1793.1793, in CO 201/9, The National Archives, Kew, London, MPG 1/532.

Epiha to McLean, 1844, MS-Papers-0032-0668-03. Object #1030723, ATL.

He Wakaputanga o te Rangatiratanga o Nu Tirene (A Declaration of the Independence of New Zealand), Paihia, 1836, ANZ, Te Whare Tohu Tuhituhinga o Aotearoa, IA 9/1.

Hoani Ropiha to McLean, 1844, ref. no. MS-Papers-0032-0668-07. Object #1030005, ATL.

Kaunihera Maori (Native Councils): he ture i huaina: he ture hei whakatakoto tikanga mo nga kaunihera i nga takiwa Māori, a hei whakatakoto tikanga hoki mo te mahi o aua kaunihera, acc. 269960, ATL.

Kendall, T. to Marsden, S., 27 May 1815, Marsden Archive, Otago University, MS_0055_012.

Kendall, T. to Pratt, J., 15 June 1814, Marsden Archive, Otago University, MS_0054_043.

Kendall, T. to Pratt, J., 16 October 1820, Marsden Archive, Otago University, MS_0498_096.

Kendall, T. to Pratt, J., 19 October 1815, Marsden Archive, Otago University, MS_0055_022.

Kendall, T. to Pratt, J., 6 September 1814, Marsden Archive, Otago University, MS_0054_066.

Kendall, T., 18 May 1814, Marsden Archive, Otago University, MS_0054_066.

King, P., 1793, in University of Sydney Library, 'The Journal of Philip Gidley King, Lieutenant, R.N. 1787-1790', parts 3 and 4, ABN: 15 211 513 464. CRICOS number: 00026A.

Maning, F. E. to McLean, D., 1 November 1873, in Inward letters – Maning, F.E., MS-Papers-0032-0445, Series 1, ATL.

Maori letter from Eruera Hongi to Church Missionary Society missionaries, 1825, the Webster collection and papers of Kenneth Athol Webster, MS-Papers-1009-2/71-01, ATL.

Marsden, S. to Pratt, J., 12 February 1820, in Marsden Archive, Otago University, MS_0057_024.

MacKenzie, T.N., 'Illuminated presentation letter to Thomas MacKenzie by his Rangatira friends', 1894, fMS-Papers-8994, ATL.

Morpeth, M. to Cadman, A. 26 May 1892, ANZ, MA 1 1892/828. Te Kooti Arikirangi, MS Notebook 1867-8, ATL, contemporary translation in Davies, G.H., Maori Manuscripts 3, ATL.

Ngapua, H.H. to Katene, W., 15 August 1894 (David Rankin Private Collection).

Ngapua, H.H. to Native Minister (A. Cadman), 7 September 1891, ANZ, MA 1 1892/815.

Pratt, J. and Bickersteth, E. to Kendall, T., 12 March 1818, Marsden Archive, Otago University, MS_0056_076.

Pratt, J. to Kendall, T., 16 August 1815, Marsden Archive, Otago University, MS_0055_019.

Rankin, D., 'Hone Heke Ngapua, He Manatunga o Ngapuhi, 1869–1909, a voice silenced by prejudice', unpublished paper, Auckland, 2006.

Shepherd, J. to Marsden, S., 12 February 1822, and Shepherd, J. to Church Missionary Society, 2 December 1822, in CMS Mission Book: documents received 29 May 1822 – 3 July 1824, CMS/B/OMS/C N M2, Cadbury Research Library, Special Collections, University of Birmingham.

Shepherd, J. to Marsden, S., 12 February 1822, in Marsden Archive, Otago University, MS_0057_070.

State Library of New South Wales, 'Banks' Description of Places', transcription of Banks' Journal, vol. 2, Sydney, February 2004.

Te Otene Pauanui to Colenso, 11 December 1841, MS-Papers-0032-0668-02. Object #1032895, ATL.

Telegram from Native Office, 7 April 1892, ANZ, MA 1 1892/815.

Tooi [sic], T. to Pratt, J., 17 September 1818, Marsden Archive, Otago University, MS_0056_096.

University of Sydney Library, 'The Journal of Philip Gidley King, Lieutenant, R.N. 1787-1790', parts 3 and 4, ABN: 15 11 513 464. CRICOS number: 00026A.

Venn, H. to Cotton, G.L.C., 26 December 1864, in CMS Letter-book, 25 January 1862 – 30 April 1866, CMS/B/OMS/C I1 L6, Cadbury Research Library, Special Collections, University of Birmingham.

Venn, H. to Townsend, H., 4 February 1862, in CMS Letter-book, 24 December 1860
    – 23 September 1867, CMS/B/OMS/C A2 L3, Cadbury Research Library, Special
    Collections, University of Birmingham.
Visscher, F.V., Map of Nova Zeelandia, B-K 741-96, National Library of New Zealand.
Wanganui chiefs to FitzRoy, 12 September 1844, MS-Papers-0032-0668-10. Object
    #1031097, ATL.
Wi Kingi and others to Governor, 14 Dec 1844, MS-Papers-0032-0668-14. Object
    #1030992, ATL.

Reports

'Annual Report of the Public Health Department', in *AJHR*, 1908, Session I, H-31.
Clarke, G., *Extracts from the final report of the Chief Protector of Aborigines in New
    Zealand*, Auckland, 1846.
Cooper, G.S., 'Report from G.S. Cooper, Esq., Resident Magistrate, Napier', in 'Reports
    on the Social and Political State of the Natives in Various Districts at the Time of the
    Arrival of Sir G.F. Bowen', in *AJHR*, 1868, Session I, A-04.
Education, Native Schools, in *AJHR*, 1880, Session I, H-01f, 1.
——, in *AJHR*, 1885, Session I, E-02.
——, in *AJHR*, 1881, Session I, E-07.
——, in *AJHR*, 1898, Session I, E-02.
——, [In continuation of E.-2, 1887], in *AJHR*, 1888, Session I, E-02.
——, [In continuation of E.-2, 1896], in *AJHR*, 1897, Session II, E-02.
Education, 'Native Schools', *AJHR*, 1899, Session I, E-02.
Further Papers Relative to the Manawatu Block, in *AJHR*, 1866, Session I, A-04.
Gorst, J.E., 'General Report, by J.E. Gorst, Esq., on the State of Upper Waikato June
    1862', in 'Further Papers Relative to the Governor Sir George Grey's Plan of Native
    Government. Report of Officers', in *AJHR*, 1862, Session I, E-09.
——, 'Report of J.E. Gorst, Esq., Inspector of Schools', in *AJHR*, 1862, Session I, E-04.
Governor to the Secretary of State for Colonies, 1 March 1884, in *AJHR*, 1884, Session I,
    A-01.
Haddon, A.C. and S.H. Ray, *Reports of the Cambridge Anthropological Expedition to Torres
    Straits*, vol. 3, *Linguistics*, Cambridge, 1907.
Hadfield, O., 'Report on the Otaki Industrial School, 1855', 13 January 13, 1856, in *AJHR*,
    1858, Session I, E-01.
Henare, M., 'Nga tikanga me nga ritenga o te ao Maori: Standards and foundations of
    Maori society', in *Report of the Royal Commission on Social Policy. The April Report:
    Future Directions Associated Papers*, vol. 3, pt 1, Wellington, 1988.
Lay Association of the Free Church of Scotland, *Scheme of the Colony of the Free Church,
    Otago, in New Zealand*, Glasgow, 1845.
Legislative Expenditure Committee, AJHR, 1886, Session I, I-10.
Legislature Expenditure, in *AJHR*, 1887, Session I, A-14.
Lewis, T., in *AJHR*, 1891, Session II, G-01, 145.
Minister of Education, 'Report to the General Assembly', in *AJHR*, 1880, Session I, H-01a.

Native Report of the Meeting at Paetai, in *AJHR*, 1860, Session I, F-03, Appendix B, No. 7.

'Report from the Select Committee of the House of Lords appointed to inquire into the present state of the Islands of New Zealand and the expediency of regulating the settlement of British subjects therein: with the minutes of evidence taken before the Committee and an index thereto, brought from the Lords 7th August 1838', London, 1838.

'Report from W.B. White, Esq., Resident Magistrate, Mangonui', in 'Reports on the Social and Political State of the Natives in Various Districts at the Time of the Arrival of Sir G.F. Bowen', in *AJHR*, 1868, Session I, A-04.

Report of the Formation and Establishment of the New Zealand Temperance Society, Paihia, 1836.

Report of the Parliamentary Select Committee on Aboriginal Tribes (British Settlements), London, 1837.

'Reports from Officers in Native Districts', in *AJHR*, 1872, Session I, F-03.

'Reports from Officers in Native Districts', in *AJHR*, 1886, Session I, G-01.

'Reports on Native Schools, 1858', in *AJHR*, 1858, Session I, E-01, 1–77.

Russell, W.H., 'Report on Schools in the Province of Auckland', 16 February 1858, in *AJHR*, 1858, Session I, E-01.

Standing Orders of the House of Representatives, in *AJHR*, 1894, Session I, H-11, 17.

Stewart, R.O., 'Extract from the Report of R.O. Stewart, Esq., R.M., Raglan', in 'Further Papers Relative to Native Schools', in *AJHR*, 1868, Session I, A-06.

Sturmey, V., 'Submission of Nga Rauru', Waitangi Tribunal, Te Ihupuku Marae, Waitotara, 14 October 1991, Wai 143, F1.

Sub-Enclosure, 16 July 1883, in *AJHR*, 1884, Session I, A-02.

Te Aute and Wanganui School Trusts (Report and Evidence of the Royal Commission on the), in *AJHR*, 1906, Session II, G-05.

Waitangi Tribunal, *He Whakaputanga me te Tiriti The Declaration and the Treaty: The Report on Stage 1 of the Te Paparahi o Te Raki Inquiry*, Wai 1040, Wellington, 2014, s. 4.3.3.

Waitangi Tribunal, *Ngai Tahu Report*, Wai 27, Wellington, 1991, s. 3.2.

Waitangi Tribunal, *Report of the Waitangi Tribunal on the te reo Māori Claim*, Wai-11, Wellington, 1986.

Theses and dissertations

Bayly, N., 'James Busby, British Resident in New Zealand 1833–1840', MA thesis, University of Auckland, Auckland, 1949.

Bell, A., 'Relating Māori and Pākehā: The politics of indigenous and settler identities', PhD thesis, Massey University, Palmerston North, 2004.

Bentley, T., 'Images of Pākehā-Māori: A study of the representation of Pākehā-Māori by historians of New Zealand from Arthur Thomson (1859) to James Belich (1996)', PhD thesis, Waikato University, Hamilton, 2007.

Browne, M.H., 'Wairua and the relationship it has with learning te reo Māori within Te Ataarangi', a report presented in partial fulfilment of the requirements for the degree of Master of Educational Administration at Massey University, 2005.

Butterworth, G., 'The politics of adaptation: The career of Sir Apirana Ngata, 1874–1928', MA thesis, Victoria University of Wellington, 1969.

Cross, M., 'The forgotten soundtrack of Maoriland: Imagining the nation through Alfred Hill's songs for *Rewi's Last Stand*', MMus thesis, Massey University and Victoria University, Wellington, 2015.

Graham, J.P.H., 'Whakatangata kia kaha: Toitū te whakapapa, toitū te tuakiri, toitū te mana: An examination of the contribution of Te Aute College to Māori advancement', PhD thesis, Massey University, Palmerston North, 2009.

Hokowhitu, B.J., 'Te mana Māori: Te tātari i ngā kōrero parau', PhD thesis, University of Otago, Dunedin, 2002.

Holdom, J., 'Schooling for "lesser beings". Part One: The political culture, and historiography, of schooling for Māori. Part Two: Te Kopua Native/Māori School: A biography', MEd thesis, University of Waikato, Hamilton, 1998.

Hopa, N.K., 'The rangatira: Chieftainship in traditional Māori society', BLitt thesis, University of Oxford, Oxford, 1966.

Ka`ai-Mahuta, R., 'He kupu tuku iho mō tēnei reanga: A critical analysis of waiata and haka as commentaries and archives of Māori political history', PhD thesis, Auckland University of Technology, Auckland, 2010.

Keenan, D., 'Haere whakamua, hoki whakauri. Going forward, thinking back: Tribal and hapū perspectives of the past in 19th century Taranaki', PhD thesis, Massey University, Palmerston North, 1994.

Keenan, E., 'Māori urban migrations and identities "Ko ngā iwi nuku whenua": A study of urbanisation in the Wellington region during the twentieth century', PhD thesis, Victoria University of Wellington, 2014.

Mahuika, N., '"Kōrero tuku iho": Reconfiguring oral history and oral tradition', PhD thesis, University of Waikato, Hamilton, 2012.

McDowell, T., 'Te Ana o te Raiona: Māori political movements and the Māori seats in parliament, 1867–2008', PhD thesis, University of Auckland, Auckland 2013.

Millward, J., 'Dystopian wor(l)ds: Language within and beyond experience', dissertation, University of Sheffield, Sheffield, 2007.

Murphy, M.I., 'The peaceable kingdom of nineteenth century humanitarianism: The Aborigines Protection Society and New Zealand', MA thesis, University of Canterbury, Christchurch, 2002.

Nicholson, W.R., 'Hei tīmatanga kōrero: Māori language regenesis and mihinare clergy', MA thesis, University of Canterbury, Christchurch, 2000.

Pihama, L., 'Tihei mauri ora: Honouring our voices. Mana wahine as a kaupapa Māori theoretical framework', PhD thesis, University of Auckland, Auckland 2001.

Soutar, M., 'Ngāti Porou leadership: Rāpata Wahawaha and the politics of conflict: "Kei te ora nei hoki tātou, me tō tātou whenua"', PhD thesis, Massey University, Palmerston North, 2000.

Stephens, M., 'The Anglican Constitution: A model for New Zealand?', Honours research seminar, 2 October 2000.

Sutherland, I.L., 'Nineteenth-century Māori letters of emotion: Orality, literacy and context', PhD thesis, University of Auckland, Auckland, 2007.

JOURNAL ARTICLES AND CONFERENCE PAPERS

Alembong, N., 'On the interface of orality and literacy: The case of Jacques Fame Ndongo's "Espaces de lumière"', *Institute of African Studies Research Review*, vol. 26, no. 2, 2010.

Alexander, E., 'Enduring fictions', *Wilson Quarterly*, vol. 21, no. 2, Spring 1997.

Alfred, T. and J. Corntassel, 'Being indigenous: Resurgences against contemporary colonialism', *Government and Opposition*, vol. 40, no. 4, 2005.

Archey, G., 'Evolution of certain Maori carving patterns', *JPS*, vol. 42, no. 3, September 1933.

Arlow, J.A., 'Ego psychology and the study of mythology', *Journal of the American Psychoanalytic Association*, vol. 9, no. 3, 1961.

Atkinson, A.S., 'The Aryo-Semitic Maori', *Transactions of the New Zealand Institute*, vol. 19, 1886.

Ausburn, L.J. and F.B. Ausburn, 'Visual literacy: Background, theory and practice', *Programmed Learning and Educational Technology*, vol. 15, no. 4, 1978.

Baker, A., 'New Zealand compared with Great Britain in its physical and social aspects: A lecture delivered in the hall of the Athenaeum, Wellington, on Thursday, July 23, 1857, by the Rev. A. Baker, M.A.' Wellington, 1857.

Ballara, A., 'Settlement patterns in the early European Maori phase of Maori society', *JPS*, vol. 88, 1979.

——, 'The pursuit of mana? A re-evaluation of the process of land alienation by Māoris, 1840–1890', *JPS*, vol. 91, no. 4, December 1982.

Ballhatchet, K.A., 'The Home Government and Bentinck's educational policy', *Cambridge Historical Journal*, vol. 10, no. 2, 1951.

Barber, I., 'Sea, land and fish: Spatial relationships and the archaeology of South Island Māori fishing', *World Archaeology*, vol. 35, no. 3, 2003.

Barker, G.T., 'How a coral reef became an island', *Transactions of the Fiji Society*, 1926.

Barrington, J., 'Learning the "dignity of labour": Secondary education policy for Maoris', *New Zealand Journal of Educational Studies*, vol. 23, 1988.

Barron, T.J., 'James Stephen, the 'Black Race' and British Colonial Administration, 1813–47', *The Journal of Imperial and Commonwealth History*, vol. 5, no. 2, 1977.

Bastings, L., 'History of the New Zealand Society, 1851–1868: A Wellington scientific centenary', *Transactions and Proceedings of the Royal Society of New Zealand*, vol. 80, 1952.

Baumgratz, G., 'Language, culture and global competence: An essay on ambiguity', *European Journal of Education*, vol. 30, no. 4, December 1995.

Biggs, B., 'The oral literature of the Polynesians', *Te Ao Hou: The New World*, no. 49, November 1964.

Binney, J., 'Myth and explanation in the Ringatu tradition: Some aspects of the leadership of Te Kooti Arikirangi Te Turuki and Rua Kenana Hepetipa', *JPS*, vol. 93, no. 4, December 1984.

——, 'The Ringatu traditions of predictive history', *Journal of Pacific History*, vol. 23, no. 2, October 1988.

——, 'Tuki's universe', *NZJH*, vol. 38, no. 2, 2004, 215–17.

Bishop of Wellington, 'Notes on the Maoris of New Zealand and some Melanesians of the South-west Pacific', *Journal of the Ethnological Society of London*, vol. 1, no. 4, 1869.

Boulton, J., '"It is extreme necessity that makes me do this": Some "survival strategies" of pauper households in London's West End during the early eighteenth century', *International Review of Social History*, vol. 45, issue S8, 2000.

Bourdieu, P., 'Genesis and structure of the religious field', *Comparative Social Research*, vol. 13, no. 1, 1991.

Bowden, B., 'The ideal of civilisation: Its origins and socio-political character', *Critical Review of International Social and Political Philosophy*, vol. 7, no. 1, 2004.

Bowden, R., 'Tapu and mana: Ritual authority and political power in traditional Maori society', *Journal of Pacific History*, vol. 14, no. 1, 1979.

Boyle, J., 'Imperialism and the English language in Hong Kong', *Journal of Multilingual and Multicultural Development*, vol. 18, no. 3, 1997.

Brantlinger, P., 'Victorians and Africans: The genealogy of the myth of the dark continent', *Critical Inquiry*, vol. 12, no. 1, Autumn 1985.

Brookes, W., 'Austria and the Māori people', *Te Ao Hou: The New World*, no. 24, October 1958.

Buchan, B., 'The empire of political thought: Civilization, savagery and perceptions of indigenous government', *History of the Human Sciences*, vol. 18, no. 2, May 2005.

Buck, P., 'He Poroporoaki: A farewell message', *JPS*, vol. 60, no. 1, 1951.

Buller, W., 'The decrease of the Maori race', *New Zealand Journal of Science*, vol. 2, 1884.

Cameron, W.J., 'A printing press for the Maori people', *JPS*, vol. 67, no. 3, September 1958.

Canagarajah, S., 'Lingua franca English, multilingual communities, and language acquisition', *Modern Language Journal*, vol. 91, no. 1, 2007.

Carli, A., C. Guardiano, M. Kaucic-Baca, E. Sussi, M. Tessarolo and M. Ussai, 'Asserting ethnic identity and power through language', *Journal of Ethnic and Migration Studies*, vol. 29, no. 5, 2003.

Cartwright, R.L., 'Some remarks on essentialism', *Journal of Philosophy*, vol. 65, no. 20, 1968.

Chase-Dunn, C. and R. Rubinson, 'Toward a structural perspective on the world-system', *Politics & Society*, vol. 7, no. 4, 1977.

Christian, F.W., 'On the outlying islands', *Transactions and Proceedings of the Royal Society of New Zealand*, vol. 30, 1897.

Cleave, P., 'Said, heard, written, read', *Te Kaharoa*, vol. 2, 2009.

Colenso, W., *Three literary papers: Read before the Hawke's Bay Philosophical Institute, during the session of 1882*, Napier, 1883.

Cressy, D., 'Books as totems in seventeenth-century England and New England', *Journal of Library History*, vol. 21, no. 1, Winter 1986.

Curnow, J., 'Wiremu Maihi Te Rangikaheke: His life and work', *JPS*, vol. 94, no. 2, 1985.

Cutts, E.H., 'The background of Macaulay's Minute', *American Historical Review*, vol. 58, no. 4, July 1953.

Dahlberg, T., 'Māori representation in parliament and Tino Rangatiratanga', *He Pukenga Korero*, vol. 2, no. 1, 1996

Durie, A., 'Emancipatory Māori education: Speaking from the heart', *Language Culture and Curriculum*, vol. 11, no. 3, 1998.

Duschinsky, R. and S. Lampitt, 'Managing the tensions of essentialism: Purity and impurity', *Sociology*, vol. 46, no. 6, 2012.

Duval, T. and K. Kuiper, 'Māori dictionaries and Māori loan words', *International Journal of Lexicography*, vol. 14, no. 4, 2001.

Eisenstadt, S.N., 'Post-traditional societies and the continuity and reconstruction of tradition', *Daedalus*, vol. 102, no. 1, Winter 1973.

Elbourne, E., 'The sin of the settler: The 1835–36 Select Committee on Aborigines and debates over virtue and conquest in the early nineteenth-century British white settler empire', *Journal of Colonialism and Colonial History*, vol. 4, no. 3, 2004.

England, N.C., 'Linguistics and indigenous American languages: Mayan examples', *Journal of Latin American Anthropology*, vol. 1, no. 1, 1995.

Evans, N. and S.C. Levinson, 'The myth of language universals: Language diversity and its importance for cognitive science', *Behavioral and Brain Sciences*, vol. 42, no. 5, 2009.

Finzsch, N., '"It is scarcely possible to conceive that human beings could be so hideous and loathsome": Discourses of genocide in eighteenth- and nineteenth-century America and Australia', *Patterns of Prejudice*, vol. 39, no. 2, 2005.

Fitzgerald, T., 'Jumping the fences: Māori women's resistance to missionary schooling in northern New Zealand 1823–1835', *Paedagogica Historica* , vol. 37, no. 1, 2001.

Fleras, A., 'From social control towards political self-determination? Māori seats and the politics of separate Māori representation in New Zealand', *Canadian Journal of Political Science*, vol. 18, no. 3, September 1985.

Fletcher, A., 'Sanctity, power, and the "impure sacred": Analyzing Māori concepts of tapu and noa in early documentary sources', *History of Religions*, vol. 47, no. 1, 2007.

Friedman, J., 'Marxism, structuralism and vulgar materialism', *Man*, vol. 9, no. 3, September 1974.

Friedman, J., 'Oral history, hermeneutics, and embodiment', *Oral History Review*, vol. 41, no. 2, Summer/Fall 2014.

Gadd, B., 'The teachings of Te Whiti o Rongomai, 1831–1907', *JPS*, vol. 75, no. 4, December 1966.

Gallagher, T., 'Tikanga Māori pre-1840', *Te Kāhui Kura Māori*, issue 1, n.d., art. 1.

Gallman, R.E. 'Two problems in the measurement of American colonial signature-mark literacy', *Historical Methods: A Journal of Quantitative and Interdisciplinary History*, vol. 20, no. 4, 1987.

Gilling, B.D., 'Engine of destruction: An introduction to the history of the Maori Land Court', Victoria University of Wellington Law Review, vol. 24, no. 2, 1994.

Gosden, C. and C. Pavlides, 'Are islands insular? Landscape vs. seascape in the case of the Arawe Islands, Papua New Guinea', *Archaeology of Oceania*, vol. 29, 1994.

Goldin-Meadow, S., 'The role of gesture in communication and thinking', *Trends in Cognitive Sciences*, vol. 3, no. 11, 1999.

Goldsmith, M., 'Translated identities: "Pakeha" as subjects of the Treaty of Waitangi', *Sites: A Journal of Social Anthropology and Cultural Studies*, vol. 2, no. 2, 2005, 64–82.

Goody, J. and I. Watt, 'The consequences of literacy', *Comparative Studies in Society and History*, vol. 5, no. 3, April 1963.

Gossman, L., 'History as decipherment: Romantic historiography and the discovery of the other', *New Literary History*, vol. 18, no. 1, Autumn 1986.

Green, N., 'The Madrasas of Oxford: Iranian interactions with the English universities in the early nineteenth century', *Iranian Studies*, vol. 44, no. 6, 2011.

Green, R., 'Linguistic subgrouping within Polynesia: The implications for prehistoric settlement', *JPS*, vol. 75, no. 1, 1966.

Greenfield, P.M., 'Oral or written language: The consequences for cognitive development in Africa, the United States and England', *Language and Speech*, vol. 15, no. 2, 1972.

Greenhill, S.J. and Gray, R.D., 'Austronesian language phylogenies: Myths and misconceptions about Bayesian computational methods', *Austronesian Historical Linguistics and Culture History: A Festschrift for Robert Blust*, 2009.

Greenhill, S.J., Q.D. Atkinson, A. Meade and R.D. Gray, 'The shape and tempo of language evolution', *Proceedings of the Royal Society B: Biological Sciences*, vol. 277, 2010.

Grey, G., 'Ancient inhabitants of New Zealand', address delivered to Museum of Practical Geology, London, 8 May 1869.

Gunson, N., 'Understanding Polynesian traditional history', *The Journal of Pacific History*, vol. 28, no. 2, 1993.

Guthrie, J.T., 'Equilibrium of literacy', *Journal of Reading*, vol. 26, no. 7, 1983.

Hammond, T.G., 'The tohunga Maori', *JPS*, vol. 17, no. 3, 1908.

Harding, R.C., 'Unwritten literature', *Transactions and Proceedings of the Royal Society of New Zealand*, vol. 25, 1892.

Harlow, R., 'Regional variation in Maori', *New Zealand Journal of Archaeology*, vol. 1, 1979.

Harlow, R., 'Lexical expansion in Māori', *JPS*, vol. 102, no. 1, March 1993.

Hawkins, M.C., '"Disrupted" historical trajectories and indigenous agency: Rethinking imperial impact in Southeast Asian history', *Sojourn: Journal of Social Issues in Southeast Asia*, vol. 22, no. 2, 2007.

Heidegger, M., 'Letter on humanism', *Global Religious Vision*, vol. 1, no. 1, July 2000.

Henry, E. and Pene, H., 'Kaupapa Māori: Locating indigenous ontology, epistemology and methodology in the academy', *Organization*, vol. 8, no. 2, 2001.

Henze, R. and Davis, K.A., 'Authenticity and identity: Lessons from indigenous language education', *Anthropology and Education*, vol. 30. no. 1, March 1999.

Hill, R., 'Keats, antiquarianism, and the picturesque', *Essays in Criticism*, vol. 64, no. 2, 2014.

Hiroa, T.R., 'The passing of the Maori', *Transactions and Proceedings of the Royal Society of New Zealand*, vol. 55, 1924.

Hocken, T.M., 'Some account of the beginnings of literature in New Zealand', *Transactions and Proceedings of the New Zealand Institute*, 1900.

Hohepa, P.W., 'The accusative-to-ergative drift in Polynesian languages', *JPS*, vol. 78, no. 3, 1969.

Hokowhitu, B., 'The death of Koro Paka: "Traditional" Māori patriarchy', *Contemporary Pacific*, vol. 20, no. 1, 2008.

Hook, G.R. and L.P. Raumati, 'Does the New Zealand government owe Māori an apology', *MAI Review*, vol. 3, no. 11, 2008.

Howe, K., 'The fate of the "savage" in Pacific historiography', *NZJH*, vol. 11, 1977.

Huttenback, R.A., 'The British Empire as a "white man's country": Racial attitudes and immigration legislation in the colonies of white settlement', *Journal of British Studies*, vol. 13, no. 1, November 1973.

Hyman, S.H., 'The ritual view of myth and the mythic', *Journal of American Folklore*, vol. 68, no. 270, *Myth: A Symposium*, October–December 1955.

Inglehart, R. and W.E. Baker, 'Modernization, cultural change, and the persistence of traditional values', *American Sociological Review*, vol. 65, no. 1, 2000.

Jackson, W.K. and G.A. Wood, 'The New Zealand parliament and Maori representation', *Historical Studies: Australia and New Zealand*, vol. 11, no. 43, 1964.

Jones, A. and K. Jenkins, 'Indigenous discourse and "the material": A post-interpretivist argument', *International Review of Qualitative Research*, vol. 1, no. 2, 2008.

——, 'Invitation and refusal: A reading of the beginnings of schooling in Aotearoa New Zealand', *History of Education*, vol. 37, no. 2, March 2008.

Jones, P.T.H., 'Maori genealogies', *Journal of the Polynesian Society*, vol. 67, no. 2, June 1958.

Kaestle, C.F., 'The history of literacy and the history of readers', *Review of Research in Education*, vol. 12, no. 1, January 1985.

Kelly, J., 'Māori maps', *Cartographica*, vol. 36, no. 2, 1999.

Kim, U., 'Indigenous, cultural, and cross-cultural psychology: A theoretical, conceptual, and epistemological analysis', *Asian Journal of Social Psychology*, vol. 3, no. 3, 2000.

King, K.A., 'Language ideologies and heritage language education', *International Journal of Bilingual Education and Bilingualism*, vol. 3, no. 3, 2000.

Klajn, I., 'Neologisms in present-day Serbian', *International Journal of the Sociology of Language*, no. 151, September 2001.

Klein, K.L., 'In search of narrative mastery: Postmodernism and the people without history', *History and Theory*, vol. 34, no. 4, December 1995.

Knapp, M.K., A. Horsburgh, S. Prost, J. Stanton, H.R. Buckley, R.K. Walter and E.A. Matisoo-Smith, 'Complete mitochondrial DNA genome sequences from the first New Zealanders', *Proceedings of the National Academy of Sciences* , vol. 109, no. 45, 2012.

Lake, M., 'Samuel Marsden, work and the limits of evangelical humanitarianism', *History Australia*, vol. 7, no. 3, 2010.

Lange, R., 'Ordained ministry in Maori Christianity, 1853–1900', *Journal of Religious History*, vol. 27, no. 1, February 2003.

Lester, A., 'British settler discourse and the circuits of empire', *History Workshop Journal*, vol. 54, issue 1, Autumn 2002.

Lian, K.F., 'Tribe, class and colonisation: The political organisation of Maori society in the 19th century', *JPS*, vol. 101, no. 4, December 1992.

Lieberson, S., Dalto, G. and Johnston, M.E., 'The course of mother-tongue diversity in nations', *American Journal of Sociology*, vol. 81, no. 1, 1975.

López Rúa, P., 'The manipulative power of word-formation devices in Margaret Atwood's *Oryx and Crake*', *Revista alicantina de estudios ingleses*, no. 18, November 2005.

Lowe, D.J. (ed.), 'Guidebook for pre-conference North Island Field Trip A1 "Ashes and Issues"', 28–30 November 2008, New Zealand Society of Soil Science, *Australian and New Zealand 4th Joint Soils Conference*, Massey University, Palmerston North, 1–5 December 2008.

Lunga, V.B., 'Mapping African postcoloniality: Linguistic and cultural spaces of hybridity', *Perspectives on Global Development & Technology*, vol. 3, no. 3, 2004.

Madagan, M., R. Harlow, J. King, P. Keegan and C. Watson, 'New Zealand English influence on Māori pronunciation over time', *Te Reo*, vol. 47, 2004.

Mahuta, D., 'Raupatu: A Waikato perspective', *Te Kaharoa*, vol. 1, 2008.

Marshall, J. and M. Peters, 'Te reo o te Tai Tokerau: The assessment of oral Maori', *Journal of Multilingual & Multicultural Development*, vol. 10, no. 6, 1989.

Marshall, P.J., 'Empire and authority in the later eighteenth century', *Journal of Imperial and Commonwealth History*, vol. 15, no. 2, 1987.

May, S., 'Language and education rights for indigenous peoples', *Language, Culture and Curriculum*, vol. 11, no. 3, 1998.

Mayhew, B.H., 'Structuralism versus individualism: Part 1, Shadowboxing in the dark', *Social Forces*, vol. 59, no. 2, 1980.

McClelland, S., 'Maori electoral representation: Challenge to orthodoxy', *New Zealand Universities Law Review*, vol. 17, June 1997.

McDonald, A., 'Wallerstein's world-economy: How seriously should we take it?', *Journal of Asian Studies*, vol. 38, no. 3, May 1979.

McGeorge, C., 'James Pope's textbooks for New Zealand Native Schools', *Paradigm 2/3*, July 2001.

McGregor, R., 'The doomed race: A scientific axiom of the late nineteenth century', *Australian Journal of Politics & History*, vol. 39, no. 1, 1993.

McKenzie, J.D.S., 'More than a show of justice? The enrolment of Maoris in European schools prior to 1900', *New Zealand Journal of Educational Studies*, vol. 17, no. 1, 1982.

McKenzie, T., 'Edward Robert Tregear, 1846–1931', *Kōtare 7*, no. 3, 2008.

McLean, M., 'The music of Maori chant', *Te Ao Hou: The New World*, vol. 47, June 1964.

McRae, K.O. and L.W. Nikora, 'Whāngai: Remembering, understanding and experiencing', *MAI Review, Intern Research Report 7*, vol. 1, 2006.

McSweeney, K. and S. Arps, '"A demographic turnaround": The rapid growth of the indigenous populations in Lowland Latin America', *Latin American Research Review*, vol. 40, no. 1, 2005.

Merriam, S.B. and S.K. Young, 'Non-Western perspectives on learning and knowing', *New Directions for Adult and Continuing Education*, no. 119, 2008.

Mika, C.T.H., 'The utterance, the body and the law: Seeking an approach to concretizing the sacredness of Māori language', *Sites: A Journal of Social Anthropology and Cultural Studies*, vol. 4, no. 2, 2007.

Mojela, V.M., 'Borrowing and loan words: The lemmatizing of newly acquired lexical items in Sesotho sa Leboa', *Lexikos*, vol. 20, no.1, 2010.

Moon, P., '"A proud thing to have recorded": The origins and commencement of national indigenous political representation in New Zealand through the 1867 Maori Representation Act', *Journal of New Zealand Studies*, vol. 16, 2013.

Moon, P., 'Nākahi: The Matarahurahu Cult of the Snake', *Te Kaharoa*, vol. 4, no. 1, 2011.

Moon, P., 'The influence of "Benthamite" philosophies on British colonial policy on New Zealand in the era of the Treaty of Waitangi', *Journal of Imperial and Commonwealth History*, 2015.

Moorfield, J.C., 'Te whakahē i ētahi pōhēhētanga mō te reo Māori: Challenging some misconceptions about the Māori language', Inaugural Professorial Lecture – Te Kauhau Tīmatanga a te Ahorangi, University of Otago, Dunedin, 26 September 2001.

Morgensen, S.L., 'The biopolitics of settler colonialism: Right here, right now', *Settler Colonial Studies*, vol. 1, no. 1, 2011.

Mossé, F., 'On the chronology of French loan-words in English', *English Studies*, vol. 25, issue 1–6, 1943.

Muecke, S., 'A touching and contagious Captain Cook: Thinking history through things', *Cultural Studies Review*, vol. 14, no. 1, 2008.

Mutu, M., 'Māori issues', *The Contemporary Pacific*, vol. 21, no. 1, 2009.

Nathan, J., 'An analysis of an industrial boarding school, 1847–1860: A phase in Māori education', *NZJH*, vol. 7, no. 1, 1973.

Ndebele, N.S., 'The English language and social change in South Africa', *English Academy Review*, vol. 4, 1987.

Newman, A.K., 'A study of the causes leading to the extinction of the Maori', *Transactions and Proceedings of the Royal Society of New Zealand*, vol. 14, 1882.

Nikora, L., N. Te Awekotuku and V. Tamanui, 'Home and the spirit in the Māori world', Paper presented at the He Manawa Whenua Conference, University of Waikato, Hamilton, 2013.

Niranjana, T., 'Translation, colonialism and rise of English', *Economic and Political Weekly*, vol. 25, no. 15, April 1990.

Nunn, P.D., 'On the convergence of myth and reality: Examples from the Pacific Islands', *Geographical Journal*, vol. 167, no. 2, June 2001.

Owens, J.M.R., 'Christianity and the Maoris to 1840', *NZJH*, vol. 2, no. 1, 1968.

Parr, C.J., 'A missionary library: Printed attempts to instruct the Maori, 1815–1845', *JPS*, vol. 70, no. 4, 1961.

Paterson, L., 'Speech to text: Missionary endeavours "to fix the language of the New Zealanders"', paper delivered at the *Dialogues: Exploring the Drama of Early Missionary Encounters* symposium, Hocken Collections, Dunedin, 7–8 November, 2014. Thanks to Lachlan Paterson for kind permission to reproduce extracts.

Paterson, L., 'The Kohimarama Conference of 1860: A contextual reading', *Journal of New Zealand Studies*, no. 12, November 2011.

Pawley, A., 'Polynesian languages: A subgrouping based on shared innovations in morphology', *JPS*, vol. 75, no. 1, 1966.

Pearson, W.H., 'Attitudes to the Maori in some Pakeha fiction', *JPS*, vol. 67, no. 3, September 1958.

Pelachaud, C. and I. Poggi, 'Subtleties of facial expressions in embodied agents', *Journal of Visualization and Computer Animation*, vol. 13, no. 5, 2002.

Petrie, H., 'Colonisation and the involution of the Māori economy', *XIII World Conference of Economic History*, Buenos Aires, 2002.

Pfeffer, L., 'Challenging tongues: The "irreducible hybridity" of language in contemporary bilingual poetry', *Synthesis*, vol. 4, 2012.

Phillips, C. and H. Allen, 'Archaeology at Opita: Three hundred years of continuity and change', *Research in Anthropology and Linguistics*, no. 5, 2013.

Phillips, C., 'Civilization of the Pacific', *Transactions and Proceedings of the Royal Society of New Zealand*, vol. 9. 1876.

Phillips, J.O.C., 'Musings in Maoriland, or, Was there a *Bulletin* school in New Zealand?' in *Historical Studies*, vol. 20, no. 81, 1983.

Phillipson, R., 'English language spread policy', *International Journal of the Sociology of Language*, vol. 107, no. 1, 1994.

Phillipson, T.R., 'Linguistic imperialism: African perspectives', *ELT Journal*, vol. 50, no. 2, 1996.

Pieter, H., 'The contribution of Maori religious movements', *Exchange*, vol. 8, no. 1, 1979.

Pihama, L., P. Reynolds, C. Smith, J. Reid, L.T. Smith and R. Te Nana, 'Positioning historical trauma theory within Aotearoa New Zealand', *AlterNative: An International Journal of Indigenous Peoples*, vol. 10, no. 3, 2014.

Pohatu, T.W. and H. Pohatu, 'Mauri: Rethinking human wellbeing', *MAI Review*, vol. 3, 2011.

Porter, A., '"Cultural Imperialism" and the Protestant missionary enterprise, 1780–1914', *Journal of Imperial and Commonwealth History*, vol. 25, no. 3, September 1997.

Prochner, L.H. May, H. and B. Kaur, '"The blessings of civilisation": Nineteenth-century missionary infant schools for young native children in three colonial settings – India, Canada and New Zealand, 1820s–1840s', *Paedagogica Historica: International Journal of the History of Education*, vol. 45, nos 1–2, 2009.

Quijano, A. and I. Wallerstein, 'Americanity as a concept, or the Americas in the modern world', *International Social Science Journal*, 1992.

Raffles, T.S., 'The founding of Singapore', *Journal of the Straits Branch of the Royal Asiatic Society*, vol. 2, December 1878.

Reay, B., 'The context and meaning of popular literacy: Some evidence from nineteenth-century rural England', *Past and Present*, no. 131, May 1991.

Reedy, T., 'Te Reo Māori: The past 20 years and looking forward', *Oceanic Linguistics*, vol. 39, no. 1, June 2000.

Reilly, M., 'John White: Seeking the elusive mohio: White and his Maori informants', *NZJH*, vol. 24, 1990.

Reilly, M., 'John White: The making of a nineteenth-century writer and collector of Maori tradition', *NZJH*, vol. 23, no. 2, 1989.

Resnick, D.P. and L.B. Resnick, 'The nature of literacy: An historical exploration', *Harvard Educational Review*, vol. 47, no. 3, 1977.

Rewi, P., '"Ko te waihanga me nga wehewehenga o te whaikorero": The structural system of whaikorero and its components', *Junctures: The Journal for Thematic Dialogue*, vol. 2, June 2004.

Roberts, M., B. Haami, R.A. Benton, T. Satterfield, M.L. Finucane, M. Henare and M. Henare, 'Whakapapa as a Māori mental construct: Some implications for the debate over genetic modification of organisms', *The Contemporary Pacific*, vol. 16, no. 1, Spring 2004.

Rogers, R.A., 'From cultural exchange to transculturation: A review and reconceptualization of cultural appropriation', *Communication Theory*, vol. 16, no. 4, 2006.

Ross, R., 'Te Tiriti o Waitangi: Texts and translations', *NZJH*, vol. 6, no. 2, 1972.

Rostow, W.W., 'The stages of economic growth', *Economic History Review*, vol. 12, no. 1, 1959.

Rountree, K., 'Māori bodies in European eyes: Representations of the Māori body on Cook's voyages', *JPS*, vol. 107, no. 1, 1998.

Royal, T.A.C., 'Te Whare Tapere: Towards a model for Māori and/or tribal theatre', lecture delivered at the Stout Centre, Victoria University of Wellington, 14 May 1997.

Said, E.W., 'Orientalism reconsidered', *Cultural Critique*, no. 1, Autumn 1985.

Salesa, T.D., '"The power of the physician": Doctors and the 'dying Māori' in early colonial New Zealand', *Health and History*, vol. 3, no. 1, 2001.

Schilder, G., 'Organization and evolution of the Dutch East India Company's Hydrographic Office in the seventeenth century', *Imago Mundi*, vol. 28, 1976.

Schofield, R.S., 'Dimensions of illiteracy, 1750–1850', *Explorations in Economic History*, vol. 10, no. 4, Summer 1973.

Sealy, H.P., 'In the studio, Mr Goldie's work', *The New Zealand Illustrated Magazine*, vol. 5, no. 2, November 1901.

Searle, C., 'A common language', *Race and Class*, vol. 25, no. 2, 1983.

Semmel, B., 'The philosophic radicals and colonialism', *Journal of Economic History*, vol. 21, no. 4, 1961.

Shaw, A.G.L., 'British policy towards the Australian Aborigines, 1830–1850', *Australian Historical Studies*, vol. 25, no. 99, 1992.

Shieff, S., 'Alfred Hill's "Hinemoa" and musical marginality', *Turnbull Library Record*, vol. 28, 1995.

Shirres, M.P., '*Ko tona mea nui he tapu*: "His greatest possession is his *tapu*"', *JPS*, vol. 91, no. 1, 1982.

Silverstein, M. '"Cultural" concepts and the language-culture nexus', *Current Anthropology*, vol. 45, no. 5, 2004.

Simmons, D.R., 'The words of Te Matorohanga', *JPS*, vol. 103, no. 4, 1994.

——, 'The sources of Sir George Grey's *Nga Mahi a Nga Tupuna*', *JPS*, vol. 75, no. 2, 1966.

Simon, J.A., 'Anthropology, "native schooling" and Māori: The politics of "cultural adaptation" policies', *Oceania*, vol. 69, no. 1, 1998.

Sissons, J., 'The systematisation of tradition: Māori culture as a strategic resource', *Oceania*, vol. 64, no. 2, December 1993.

Skinner, H.D., 'Evolution in Maori art', *Journal of the Anthropological Institute of Great Britain and Ireland*, vol. 46, January–June 1916.

Smith, V., 'Banks, Tupaia, and Mai: Cross-cultural exchanges and friendship in the Pacific', *Parergon*, vol. 26, no. 2, 2009.

Smithyman, K., 'Making history: John White and S. Percy Smith at work', *JPS*, vol. 88, no. 4, 1979.

Sorrenson, M.P.K., 'Land purchase methods and their effect on Maori population, 1865–1901', *JPS*, vol. 65, no. 3, September 1956.

Spolsky, B., 'Reassessing Māori regeneration', *Language in Society*, vol. 32, no. 4, October 2003.

Stallard, A.J., 'Navigating Tasman's 1642 voyage of exploration: Cartographic instruments and navigational decisions', *Portolan*, no. 69, Fall 2007.

Stenhouse, J., '"A disappearing race before we came here": Doctor Alfred Kingcome Newman, the dying Maori, and Victorian scientific racism', *NZJH*, vol. 30, no. 2, 1996.

Stephens, M., '"Tame Kaka" still? Māori members and the use of Māori language in the New Zealand Houses of Representatives', *Law, Culture, Text*, vol. 14, no. 1, 2010.

Stephens, M. and P. Monk 'A language for buying biscuits: Māori as a civic language in the modern New Zealand parliament', *Victoria University of Wellington Legal Research Papers*, Paper No 14, vol. 2, no. 3, 2012.

Stevens, M.J., 'Kai Tahu writing and cross-cultural communication', Journal of New Zealand Literature, vol. 28, no. 2, 2010.

Stokes, E., 'Maori geography or geography of Maoris', *New Zealand Geographer*, vol. 43, issue 3, December 1987.

Stone, L., 'Literacy and education in England, 1640–1900', *Past and Present*, no. 42, February 1969.

Taepa, H., 'He aha oti i te ingoa Maori/ What's in a Maori name?', *Te Ao Hou: The New World*, no. 71, 1973.

Tambiah, S.J., 'The magical power of words', *Man*, vol. 3, no 2. June 1968.

Tau, R.T.M., 'Matauranga Māori as an epistemology', *Te Pouhere Korero: Māori History Māori People*, vol. 1, no. 1, March 1999.

Tautahi, H., W. Taipuhi and S. Percy Smith, 'The *Aotea* canoe: The migration of Turi to Aotea-Roa (New Zealand)', *JPS*, vol. 9, no. 4 (36), 1900.

Thomson, J., 'Some reasons for the failure of the Roman Catholic mission to the Maoris, 1838–1860', *NZJH*, vol. 3, no. 2, 1969.

Thornton, A., 'Two features of oral style in Maori narrative', *JPS*, vol. 94, no. 2, 1985.

Thorp, D., 'Going native in New Zealand and America: Comparing Pakeha Maori and white Indians', *Journal of Imperial and Commonwealth History*, vol. 31, no. 3, 2003.

Tipps, D.C., 'Modernization theory and the comparative study of national societies: A critical perspective', *Comparative Studies in Society and History*, vol. 15, no. 2, 1973.

Tomalin, M., '"… to this rule there are many exceptions": Robert Maunsell and the *Grammar of Maori*', *Historiographia Linguistica*, vol. 33, no. 3, 2006.

Travers, W.T.L., 'On the changes effected in the natural features of a new country by the introduction of civilized races', *Transactions and Proceedings of the Royal Society of New Zealand*, vol. 2, 1869.

Trejaut, J.A., T. Kivisild, J.H. Loo, C.L. Lee, C.L. He, C.J. Hsu and M. Lin, 'Traces of archaic mitochondrial lineages persist in Austronesian-speaking Formosan populations', *PLoS Biology*, vol. 3, no. 8, 2005.

van Meijl, T., 'Historicising Maoritanga: Colonial ethnography and the reification of Maori traditions', *JPS*, vol. 105, no. 3, 1996.

Vaux, W.S.W., 'On the probable origin of the Maori races', *Transactions and Proceedings of the Royal Society of New Zealand*, vol. 8, 1875.

Walker, J.C., 'Romanticising resistance, romanticising culture: Problems in Willis's theory of cultural production', *British Journal of Sociology of Education*, vol. 7, no. 1, 1986.

Walker, R.J., 'The genesis of Maori activism', *JPS*, vol. 93, no. 3, 1984.

Wallerstein, I., 'Dependence in an interdependent world: The limited possibilities of transformation within the capitalist world economy', *African Studies Review*, vol. 17, no. 1, April 1974.

Wallerstein, I., 'Globalization or the age of transition?: A long-term view of the trajectory of the world-system', *International Sociology*, vol. 15, 2000.

Wallerstein, I., 'The West, capitalism, and the modern world-system', *Review (Fernand Braudel Center)*, vol. 15, no. 4, Fall 1992.

Wallerstein, I., 'World system versus world-systems: A critique', *Critique of Anthropology*, vol. 11, 1990.

Wanhalla, A., 'In/Visible sight: Māori–European families in urban New Zealand, 1890–1940', *Visual Anthropology*, vol. 21, no. 1, 2008.

Ward, A., 'Alienation rights in traditional Maori society: A comment', *JPS*, vol. 95, no. 2, June 1986.

Weaver, S., 'Nietzsche's Antichrist: 19th-century Christian Jews and the Real Big Lie', *Modern Judaism*, vol. 17, no. 2, 1997.

Weikart, R., 'The origins of social Darwinism in Germany, 1859–1895', *Journal of the History of Ideas*, vol. 54, no. 3, 1993.

Wells, D.A., 'Great Britain and the United States: Their true relations', *North American Review*, vol. 162, April 1896.

Williams, T., 'James Stephen and British intervention in New Zealand, 1838–40', *Journal of Modern History*, vol. 13, no. 1, 1941.

Wise, C.M. and Hervey, W., 'The evolution of the Hawaiian orthography', *Quarterly Journal of Speech*, vol. 38, no. 3, 1952.

Withers, C.W.J., 'Geography, natural history and the eighteenth-century Enlightenment: Putting the world in place', *History Workshop Journal*, no. 39, Spring 1995.

Wolfe, P., 'Settler colonialism and the elimination of the native', *Journal of Genocide Research*, vol. 8, no. 4, 2006.

Wood, G.A., 'Church and State in New Zealand in the 1850s', *Journal of Religious History*, vol. 8, no. 3, June 1975.

BOOKS AND OFFICIAL PUBLICATIONS

Adams, A.H., *Maoriland and Other Verses*, Sydney, 1899.

Adams, P., *Fatal Necessity: British Intervention in New Zealand, 1830–1847*, Wellington, 1977.

Altner, G. (ed.), *Human Creature*, Garden City, 1974.

Ames, F. R. and Miller, C.W. (eds), *Foster Biblical Scholarship: Essays in honor of Kent Harold Richards*, Atlanta, 2010.

Angas, G.F., *Savage Life and Scenes in Australia and New Zealand*, vol. 2, London, 1847.

Anderson, A., Binney, J., Harris, A. (eds), *Tangata Whenua: An illustrated history*, Wellington, 2014.

Ansre, G., 'Language standardisation in sub-Saharan Africa', in J. Fishman (ed.), *Advances in Language Planning*, The Hague, 1974.

Appendix, in G. Grey to Grey, 24 December 1850, in *GBPP 1851*, London, 1851.

Armitage, D., *The Ideological Origins of the British Empire*, Cambridge, 2001.

Arnold, D., '"An ancient race outworn": Malaria and race in colonial India, 1860–1930', in B. Harris et al. (eds), *Race, Science and Medicine, 1700–1960*, London, 1999.

Ashby, G. (ed.), *Ever and Always: Micronesian stories of the origins of islands, landmarks, and customs*, Oregon, 1978.

Astle, T., *The Origin and Progress of Writing*, London, 1784.

Astridge, R., *Waikato Wesleyan Missions: A brief insight into the work of the early Wesleyan missionaries in the Waikato of New Zealand*, n.p., 2013.

Ballantyne, T., *Orientalism and Race: Aryanism in the British Empire*, Basingstoke, 2002.

Ballara, A., *Iwi: The dynamics of tribal organisation from c. 1769 to c. 1945*, Wellington, 1998.

Bannister, S., *British Colonization and Coloured Tribes*, London, 1838.

Barrington M. and T.H. Beaglehole, '"A part of Pakeha society": Europeanising the Maori child', in J.A. Mangan (ed.), *Making Imperial Mentalities: Socialisation and British imperialism*, Manchester, 1990.

——, *Maori Schools in a Changing Society: An historical review*, Wellington, 1974.

Bartlett, F.C., *Psychology and Primitive Culture*, Cambridge, 1923.

——, *Remembering*, Cambridge, 1932.

Barton, P.L., 'Maori cartography and the European encounter', in D. Woodward and G. Malcolm (eds), *Cartography in the Traditional African, American, Arctic, Australian, and Pacific Societies*, Chicago, 1995.

Barton, R.J. (ed.), *Earliest New Zealand: The journals and correspondence of the Rev. John Butler*, Masterton, 1927.

Beaglehole, J.C., *The Endeavour Journal of Joseph Banks, 1768–1771*, vol. 1, Sydney, 1962.

Beaglehole, J.C. (ed.), *The Journals of Captain James Cook: The voyage of the Resolution and Discovery, 1776–1780*, vol. 3, pt. 2, Cambridge, 1967.

Beattie, H., *Tikao Talks*, Christchurch, 1990.

Beckett, G.W., *A Population History of Colonial New South Wales: The economic growth of a new colony*, Singapore, 2013.

Beckles, H.M., 'The "hub of empire": The Caribbean and Britain in the seventeenth century', in N. Canny (ed.), *The Oxford History of the British Empire*, vol. 1, Oxford, 2001.

Beckwith, M., *Hawaiian Mythology*, New Haven, 1940.

Beecham, J., *Remarks upon the Latest Official Documents Relating to New Zealand*, London, 1838.

Belich, J., *Making Peoples: A history of New Zealand from Polynesian settlement to the end of the nineteenth century*, Auckland 1996.

Belich, J., *Replenishing the Earth: The settler revolution and the rise of the Angloworld, 1783–1939*, New York, 2009.

Bell, A., *An Experiment in Education, Made at the Male Asylum of Madras*, London, 1797.

Bell, A., R. Harlow and D. Starks (eds), *Languages of New Zealand*, Wellington, 2005.

Bentley, T., *Pakeha Māori: The extraordinary story of the Europeans who lived as Māori in early New Zealand*, Auckland, 1999.

Best, E., *The Maori School of Learning: Its objects, methods, and ceremonial*, Dominion Museum Monograph no. 6, Wellington, 1959.

Bhabha, H.K., *The Location of Culture*, Oxford, 1994.

Biggs, B., 'The Maori language past and present', in E. Schwimmer (ed.), *The Maori People in the Nineteen-sixties*, Auckland, 1972.

Binney, J. and G. Chaplin, *Nga Morehu: The survivors*, Auckland, 1986.

Binney, J., 'Ancestral voices: Maori prophet leaders', in K. Sinclair (ed.), *The Oxford Illustrated History of New Zealand*, Auckland, 1990.

Binney, J., *Encircled Lands: Te Urewera, 1820–1921*, Wellington, 2009.

Binney, J., *The Legacy of Guilt: A life of Thomas Kendall*, Wellington, 2005.

Bird, W.W., 'The education of the Maori' in I. Davey (ed.), *Fifty Years of National Education in New Zealand 1878–1928*, Christchurch, 1928.

Blackburn, S., *The Oxford Dictionary of Philosophy*, 2nd edn, Oxford, 2008.

Bohan, E., *Climates of War*, Christchurch, 2005.

Boralevi, L.C., *Bentham and the Oppressed*, Berlin, 1984.

Borch, M.F., *Conciliation, Compulsion, Conversion: British attitudes towards indigenous peoples, 1763–1814*, New York, 2004.

Boultion, K. and B.B. Kachru (eds), *World Englishes: Critical concepts in linguistics*, Oxford, 2006.

Bracken, T., *Musing in Maoriland*, Dunedin, 1890.

Brown, W., *New Zealand and its Aborigines*, 2nd edn, London, 1851.

Browne, T.G., 'Address of His Excellency the Governor to Maori Chiefs assembled at Waitemata on the 10th of June 1860', in 'Further Papers Relative to Native Affairs', in *AJHR*, 1860, Session I, E-01, 1860.

Browne, T.G., in *Proceedings of the Kohimarama Conference, Comprising Nos 13 to 18 of the* Maori Messenger, Auckland, 1860.

Bryce, J., Memorandum for His Excellency, 11 January 1884, in *AJHR*, 1884, Session I, A-01.

Buller, J., *Forty Years in New Zealand: Including a personal narrative, an account of Maoridom, and of the Christianization and colonization of the country*, London, 1878.

Burkhart, B.Y., 'What Coyote and Thales can teach us: An outline of American Indian epistemology', in A. Waters,(ed.), *American Indian Thought*, Victoria, 2004.

Burns, P., *Fatal Success: A history of the New Zealand Company*, Auckland, 1989.

Burton, A. (ed.), *Politics and Empire in Victorian Britain: A reader*, New York, 2001.

Byrnes, G., *Boundary Markers: Land surveying and the colonisation of New Zealand*, Wellington, 2001.

Calder, A. (ed.), *Old New Zealand and Other Writings*, London, 2001.

Campbell, I., *"Gone Native" in Polynesia: Captivity narratives and experiences from the South Pacific*, Westport, Conn., 1998.

Campbell, J.L., *Poenamo: Sketches of the early days of New Zealand romance and reality of Antipodean life in the infancy of a new colony*, book IV, London, 1881.

Campbell, M.B., *The Witness and the Other World: Exotic European travel writing 400–1600*, Cornell, 1991.

Cannadine, D., *Ornamentalism: How the British saw their empire*, Oxford, 2001.

Canny, N. (ed.), *The Oxford History of the British Empire*, vol. 1, Oxford, 2001.

Carleton, H., *The Life of Henry Williams: Archdeacon of Waimate*, vol. 1, Auckland, 1874.

Carter, M., 'The preservation of the Māori oral tradition', in R. Selby and A. Laurie, *Māori and Oral History: A collection*, Wellington, 2005.

Caughey, A., *The Interpreter: The biography of Richard 'Dicky' Barrett*, Auckland, 1998.

Chadwick, H.M. and N.K. Chadwick, *The Growth of Literature*, vol. 2, pt. 3, New York, 1940.

Chamberlain, M.E., *'Pax Britannica'? British foreign policy 1789–1914*, Oxford, 1999.

Chapman, F.R. (ed.), *A. McCrae: Journal kept in New Zealand in 1820*, Wellington, 1928.

Cheater, A. (ed.), *The Anthropology of Power*, London, 2005.

Cheshire, J. (ed.), *English around the World: Sociolinguistic perspectives*, Cambridge, 1996.

Church Missionary Society, *Church Missionary Record: Detailing the Proceedings of the Church Missionary Society*, vol. 3, London, 1834.

—— *Proceedings of the Church Missionary Society for Africa and the East*, London, 1810, 1819.

——, *The Missionary Register for the Year 1815*, London, 1815; *The Missionary Register for the Year 1816*, London, 1816; *The Missionary Register for the Year 1819*, London, 1819; *The Missionary Register for the Year 1820*, London, 1820; *The Missionary Register for the Year 1824*, London, 1824; *The Missionary Register 1827*, London, 1827; *The Missionary Register for the Year 1828*, London, 1828; *The Missionary Register for the Year 1831*, London, 1831; *The Missionary Register 1833*, London, 1833; *The Missionary Register, November 1834*, London, 1834; *The Missionary Register 1840*, London, 1840; *The Missionary Register 1846*, London, 1846; *The Missionary Register 1848*, London, 1848.

Church of England, Diocese of Auckland, *Reports of Meetings on Maori Church Matters, 1872–1888*, Auckland, 1888.

——, *Reports of Meetings on Maori Church Matters, 1897*, Auckland, 1897.

Clarke, G., *Notes on Early Life in New Zealand*, Hobart,1903.

Clifford, J., *The Predicament of Culture*, Cambridge, MA, 1988.

Clyne, M., 'Can the shift from immigrant languages be reversed in Australia?', in J.A. Fishman (ed.), *Can Threatened Languages Be Saved?*, Cleveland, 2001.

Cohn, B.S., *Colonisation and its Forms of Knowledge: The British in India*, Princeton, 1996.

Coleman, J.N., *A Memoir of the Rev. Richard Davis*, London, 1865.

Colenso, W., *A Maori–English Lexicon: Being a comprehensive dictionary of the New Zealand tongue*, Wellington, 1889.

——, *Fifty Years Ago in New Zealand*, Napier, 1888.

——, *Willie's First English Book: Written by Order of the Government*, Wellington, 1872

Collingridge, V., *Captain Cook: The life, death and legacy of history's greatest explorer*, London, 2003.

Cook, J., *Voyages round the World, Performed by Captain James Cook, F.R.S.: By Royal authority, containing the whole of his discoveries in geography, navigation, astronomy, &c ...*, London, 1820.

Cooper, G.S., *Journal of an Expedition Overland from Auckland to Taranaki*, Auckland, 1851.

'Copy of the New Zealand Company's Third Deed of Purchase from the Natives, Dated 8th November, 1839', in A. Mackay, *A Compendium of Official Documents Relative to Native Affairs in the South Island*, vol. 1, Wellington, 1873.

Correspondence with the Secretary of State Relative to New Zealand, London, 1840.

Cosgrove, D. and S. Daniels (eds), *The Iconography of Landscape*, Cambridge, 1988.

Cowan, J., *The Maoris Yesterday and Today*, Wellington, 1930.

Cowen, M.P. and R.W. Shenton, *Doctrines of Development*, London, 2005.

Craik, G.L., *The New Zealanders*, London, 1830.

Crawford, J. (ed.), *Language Loyalties: A source book on the Official English controversy*, Chicago, 1992,

Crawford, J.C., *Recollections of Travel in New Zealand and Australia*, Edinburgh, 1880.

Cronin, M., *Translating Ireland: Translation, languages, cultures*, Cork, 1996.

Crozet, J.M. (trans. H. Ling Roth), *Crozet's Voyage to Tasmania, New Zealand, the Ladrone Islands, and the Philippines*, London, 1891.

Crystal, D., *English as a Global Language*, 2nd edn, Cambridge, 2003.

Curnow, J., 'A brief history of Māori-language newspapers', in J. Curnow, N. Hopa and J. McRae (eds), *Rere Atu, Taku Manu: Discovering history, language and politics in the Māori-language newspapers*, Auckland, 2002.

Curnow, J., N. Hopa and J. McRae (eds), *He Pitopito Kōrero nō te Perehi Māori: Readings from the Māori-language press*, Auckland, 2006.

——, *Rere Atu, Taku Manu: Discovering history, language and politics in the Māori-language newspapers*, Auckland, 2002.

Darder, A., *Culture and Power in the Classroom: A critical foundation for bicultural education*, Westport, Connecticut, 1991.

Daunton, M. and R. Halpern (eds), *Empire and Others: British encounters with indigenous peoples, 1600–1850*, Pennsylvania, 1999.

Davey, I. (ed.), *Fifty Years of National Education in New Zealand 1878–1928*, Christchurch, 1928.

Davidson, A.K., *Christianity in Aotearoa: A history of church and society in New Zealand*, Wellington, 1991.

Davis, B., *The Problem of Slavery in Western Culture*, Oxford, 1966.

Davis, C.O., *The Life and Times of Patuone: The celebrated Ngapuhi chief*, Auckland, 1876.

Davis, T.A., T. O'Regan and J. Wilson, *Nga Tohu Pumahara – The Survey Pegs of the Past: Understanding Maori place names*, Wellington, 1990.

de Saussure, F., *Cours de linguistique générale* (Paris, 1916), W. Baskin (trans.), New York, 1959.

Dentith, S., *Epic and Empire in Nineteenth-century Britain*, Cambridge, 2006.

Dewes, T.K.M., 'The case for oral arts', in M. King (ed.), *The World Moves On*, Wellington, 1975.

Dieffenbach, E., *Travels in New Zealand, With contributions to the geography, botany, and natural history of that country*, vols. 1 & 2, London, 1843.

Dil, A. (ed.), *The Ecology of Language: Essays by Einar Haugen*, Stanford, 1972.

Earle, A., *A Narrative of a Nine Months' Residence in New Zealand, in 1827; together with a journal of a residence in Tristan D'Acunha, an island situated between South America and the Cape of Good Hope*, London, 1832.

Eisenstein, E.L., *The Printing Revolution in Early Modern Europe*, 2nd edn, Cambridge, 2005.

Elder, J.R. (ed.), *Marsden's Lieutenants*, Dunedin, 1934.

——, *The Letters and Journals of Samuel Marsden, 1765–1838*, Dunedin, 1932.

Eliot, G., 'The natural history of German life' (1856), in T. Pinney (ed.), *Essays of George Eliot*, Columbia, 1963.

Ellis, W., *Polynesian Researches during a Residence of Nearly Eight Years in the Society and Sandwich Islands*, vol. 1, London, 1853.

Evans, J., *Ngā Waka o Neherā: The first voyaging canoes*, Auckland, 2009.

Ewing, J. and J. Shallcrass, *Introduction to Maori Education*, Wellington, 1970.

Fenton, F.D., *The Laws of England, Compiled and Translated into the Maori Language*, Auckland, 1858.

Fenton, S. (ed.), *For Better or Worse: Translation as a tool for change in the South Pacific*, Oxford, 2004.

Firth, R., *The Primitive Economics of the New Zealand Maori*, London, 1929.

Fischer, R., *Lexical Change in Present-day English*, Tübingen, 1998.

Fishman, J.A., 'Sociology of English as an additional language', in B.B. Kachru (ed.), *The Other Tongue: English across cultures*, 2nd edn, Illinois, 1992.

——, *In Praise of the Beloved Language: A comparative view of positive ethnolinguistic consciousness*, Berlin, 1996.

Fishman, J. (ed.), *Advances in Language Planning*, The Hague, 1974.

——, *Can Threatened Languages Be Saved?*, Cleveland, 2001.

Fison, L., *Tales from Old Fiji*, London, 1907.

Foucault, M. (ed. C. Gordon), *Power/Knowledge: Selected interviews and other writings, 1972–1977*, Harlow, 1980.

Frank A.G. and B.K. Gills (eds), *The World System: Five hundred years or five thousand?* New York, 1996.

Frazer, J.G., *The Golden Bough: A study in magic and religion*, London, 1922.

Friedrichsmeyer, S., S. Lennox and S. Zantop (eds), *The Imperialist Imagination: German colonialism and its legacy*, Michigan, 1999.

Gascoigne, J., *The Enlightenment and the Origins of European Australia*, Cambridge, 2002.

Gaur, A., *A History of Writing*, London, 1992.

Gellner, E., *Words and Things*, London, 1959.

Gibbon, E., *History of the Decline and Fall of the Roman Empire*, Ware, 1998.

Gifford, E.W., *Tongan Myths and Tales*, Honolulu, 1924.

Gilbert, T., *New Zealand Settlers and Soldiers, or, The war in Taranaki*, London, 1861.

Gilling, B.D., *The Nineteenth-century Native Land Court Judges: An introductory report: A report commissioned by the Waitangi Tribunal*, Wellington, 1994.

Gladstone, W.E., 'England's mission', in A. Burton (ed.), *Politics and Empire in Victorian Britain: A reader*, New York, 2001.

Glen, R. (ed.), *Mission and Moko: Aspects of the work of the Church Missionary Society in New Zealand, 1814–1882*, Christchurch, 1992.

Grace, A.A., *Maoriland Stories*, Nelson, 1895.

Grant, C., *Observations on the State of Society Among the Asiatic Subjects of Great Britain: Particularly with Respect to Morals: and on the means of improving it*, London, 1813.

Greene, J.P., *The Intellectual Construction of America*, Chapel Hill, 1993.

Greenwood, W., *The Upraised Hand, or the spiritual significance of the rise of the Ringatu faith*, Wellington, 1980.

Grenz, S.J., *A Primer on Postmodernism*, Grand Rapids, 1996.

Grey, G., *Polynesian Mythology and Ancient Traditional History of the New Zealand Race*, London, 1855.

Griffith, P., R. Harvey and K. Maslen (eds), *Book & Print in New Zealand: A guide to print culture in Aotearoa*, Wellington, 1997.

Griffith, P., P. Hughes and A. Loney (eds), *A Book in the Hand: Essays on the history of the book in New Zealand*, Auckland, 2000.

Gudgeon, T.W., *The History and Doings of the Maoris, from the year 1820 to the signing of the Treaty of Waitangi in 1840*, Auckland, 1885.

Guest, E., *A History of English Rhythms*, vol. 2, London, 1838.

Haami, B., *Pūtea Whakairo: Māori and the written word*, Wellington, 2004.

Hadebe, S., *The Standardisation of the Ndebele Language through Dictionary-making*, Allex Project, University of Zimbabwe, Harere, 2002.

Hadfield, E., *Among the Natives of the Loyalty Group*, London, 1920.

Hadfield, O., *The New Zealand War: The second year of one of England's little wars*, London, 1861.

Hall, C. (ed.), *Cultures of Empire: A reader*, Manchester, 2000.

Hallewell, L., *Books in Brazil: A history of the publishing trade*, New Jersey, 1982.

Halliday, M.A.K. and R. Hasan, *Language, Context, and Text: Aspects of language in a social-semiotic perspective*, Geelong, Victoria, 1985.

Harley, B.J., 'Maps, knowledge, and power', in D. Cosgrove and S. Daniels (eds), *The Iconography of Landscape*, Cambridge, 1988.

——, 'Maps, knowledge, and power', in G. Henderson and M. Waterstone (eds), *Geographic Thought: A praxis perspective*, Oxford, 2009.

Harlow, R., *A Word-list of South Island Maori*, Auckland, 1985.

——, *Māori: A linguistic introduction*, Cambridge, 2007.

Harris, B. et al (eds), *Race, Science and Medicine, 1700–1960*, London, 1999.

Harrison, J.E. *Themis*, Cambridge, 1912.

Harrison, K.D., *When Languages Die: The extinction of the world's languages and the erosion of human knowledge*, Oxford, 2007.

Harvey, G., *Indigenous Religions*, London, 2000.

Hastings, A., *The Construction of Nationhood: Ethnicity, religion, and nationalism*, Cambridge, 1997.

Haugen, E., 'The ecology of language', in A. Dil (ed.), *The Ecology of Language: Essays by Einar Haugen*, Stanford, 1972.

Hawkesworth, J. (ed.), *An Account of the Voyages Undertaken by the Order of His Present Majesty for Making Discoveries in the Southern Hemisphere, and successively performed by Commodore Byron, Captain Wallis, Captain Carteret, and Captain Cook, in the* Dolphin, *the* Swallow, *and the* Endeavour: *Drawn up from the journals which were kept by the several commanders, and from the papers of Joseph Banks, Esq.*, vol. 3, London, 1773.

Hawtrey, M., *An Earnest Address to New Zealand Colonists, with reference to their intercourse with the native inhabitants*, London, 1840.

——, *Justice to New Zealand, Honour to England*, London, 1861.

Heath, D., *Purifying Empire: Obscenity and the politics of moral regulation in Britain, India, and Australia*, Cambridge, 2010.

Heller, M., 'Repositioning the multilingual periphery: Class, language, and transnational markets in Francophone Canada', in S. Pietikainen and H. Kelly-Holmes (eds), *Multilingualism and the Periphery*, Oxford, 2013.

Henderson, G. and M. Waterstone (eds), *Geographic Thought: A praxis perspective*, Oxford, 2009.

Henderson, J.M., *Ratana: The man, the church, the political movement*, Wellington, 1972.

Hendry, J. and L. Fitznor (eds), *Anthropologists, Indigenous Scholars and the Research Endeavour: Seeking bridges towards mutual respect*, New York, 2012.

Herman, E.S.N. and Chomsky, *Manufacturing Consent: The political economy of the mass media*, London, 2008.

Higgins, R., P. Rewi. and V. Olsen-Reeder (eds), *The Value of the Māori Language: Te hua o te reo Māori*, Wellington, 2014.

Higgins, R. and J.C. Moorfield, 'Ngā tikanga o te marae: Marae practices', in T.M. Ka`ai, J.C. Moorfield, M.P.J. Reilly and S. Mosley (eds), *Ki te Whaiao: An introduction to Māori culture and society*, Auckland, 2004.

——, 'Tangihanga: Death customs', in T.M. Ka`ai, J.C. Moorfield, M.P.J. Reilly and S. Mosley (eds), *Ki te Whaiao: An introduction to Māori culture and society*, Auckland, 2004.

Hill, R.S., *State Authority, Indigenous Autonomy: Crown–Māori relations in New Zealand/Aotearoa, 1900–1950*, Wellington, 2004.

Hobbes, T. (ed. A.R. Waller), *Leviathan, or The matter, forme & power of a commonwealth, ecclesiasticall and civill* (1651), Cambridge, 1904.

Hobbs, R., *Wesleyan Native Institution, Established in 1844 by Rev. W. Lawry ... and Rev Thos. Buddle: Grafton Road and 192 acres at Three Kings*, Auckland, 1906.

Hobhouse, W., *The Church and the World in Idea and History*, London, 1910.

Hodgen, M.T., *Early Anthropology in the Sixteenth and Seventeenth Centuries*, Philadelphia, 1971.

Hodgkin, T., *On the Importance of Studying and Preserving the Languages Spoken by Uncivilized Nations, with a view of elucidating the physical history of mankind*, London, 1835.

Holub, R.C., 'Nietzsche's colonialist imagination: Nueva Germania, good Europeanism, and great politics', in Friedrichsmeyer, S., S. Lennox and S. Zantop (eds), *The Imperialist Imagination: German colonialism and its legacy*, Michigan, 1999.

Hooker, J. (ed.), *Journal of the Right Hon. Sir Joseph Banks*, London, 1896.

Hopa N.K., 'Land and re-empowerment: The Waikato case', in Cheater, A. (ed.), *The Anthropology of Power*, London, 2005.

Hover, C.M. (ed.), *Magazine of Horticulture, Botany, and All Useful Discoveries*, vol. 6, Boston, 1840.

Hursthouse, C., *New Zealand, or Zealandia, the Britain of the South*, vol. 1, London, 1857.

Hyland, K. and B. Paltridge (eds), *Continuum Companion to Discourse Analysis*, London, 2011.

Irvine, J. and S. Gal, 'Language, ideology and linguistic differentiation', in P. Kroskrity (ed.), *Regimes of Languages: Ideologies, polities, and identities*, Santa Fe, 2000.

Ivison, D., P. Patten and W. Sanders (eds), *Political Theory and the Rights of Indigenous Peoples*, Cambridge, 2000.

Jameson, R.G., *New Zealand, South Australia, and New South Wales: A record of recent travels in these colonies with especial reference to emigration and the advantageous employment of labour and capital*, London, 1842.

Jennings, J., *New Zealand Colonization*, London, 1843.

Johnston, A., *A Note on Maori Matters*, Auckland, 1860.

Jones, A. and K. Jenkins, *Words Between Us – He Kōrero: First Māori-Pākehā conversations on paper*, Wellington, 2011.

Joseph, J.E. and T.E. Taylor (eds), *Ideologies of Language*, Oxford, 2014.

Ka'ai, T.M., J.C. Moorfield, M.P.J. Reilly and S. Mosley (eds), *Ki te Whaiao: An introduction to Māori culture and society*, Auckland, 2004.

Kachru, B.B. (ed.), *The Other Tongue: English across cultures*, 2nd edn, Illinois, 1992.

——, 'Standards, codification, and sociolinguistic realism: The English language in the outer circle', in , K. Boultion and B.B. Kachru (eds), *World Englishes: Critical concepts in linguistics*, Oxford, 2006.

Karetu, T., 'Māori print culture: The newspapers', in J. Curnow, N. Hopa and J. McRae (eds), *Rere Atu, Taku Manu: Discovering history, language and politics in the Māori-language newspapers*, Auckland, 2002.

Keegan, P.J., 'The development of Māori vocabulary', in A. Bell, R. Harlow and D. Starks (eds), *Languages of New Zealand*, Wellington, 2005.

Keenan, D., 'The past from the paepae – uses of the past in Māori oral history', in R. Selby and A. Laurie, *Māori and Oral History: A collection*, Wellington, 2005.

Kendall, T., *A Korao no New Zealand, or, The New Zealander's first book: being an attempt to compose some lessons for the instruction of the natives*, Sydney, 1815, in AWMM, EMI0001.

Kermode, F., *The Genesis of Secrecy: On the interpretation of narrative*, Cambridge, Massachusetts, 1979.

Kerr, D., 'Sir George Grey and his book-collecting activities in New Zealand', in P. Griffith, P. Hughes and A. Loney (eds), *A Book in the Hand: Essays on the history of the book in New Zealand*, Auckland, 2000.

King, M. (ed.), *Te Ao Hurihuri*, Wellington, 1975.

——, *The World Moves On*, Wellington, 1975.

——, *The Penguin History of New Zealand*, Auckland, 2003.

Kippis, A., *Narrative of the voyages round the world performed by Captain James Cook, with an account of his life during the previous and intervening periods*, London, 1820.

Kissling, G.A., in Encl. 2 in 91, in G. Grey to Newcastle, 10 June 1853, in *GBPP 1854*, London, 1854.

Knight, W., *Memoir of Henry Venn, B.D.: Prebendary of St. Paul's, and Honorary Secretary of the Church Missionary Society*, London, 1882.

Kohere, R.T., *The Autobiography of a Maori*, Wellington, 1951.

Kroskrity, P. (ed.), *Regimes of Languages: Ideologies, polities, and identities*, Santa Fe, 2000.

Kurzweil, E. (ed.), *The Age of Structuralism: From Lévi-Strauss to Foucault*, New Brunswick, 1996.

Laracy, H. (ed.), *Ples Blong Iumi: Solomon Islands, the past four thousand years*, Suva, 1989.

Lauren, P.H., *Power and Prejudice: The politics and diplomacy of racial discrimination*, Boulder, 1988.

Lee, A.M., *A Scholar of a Past Generation: A brief memoir of Samuel Lee, D.D.*, London, 1896.

Lee, S. and T. Kendall, *A Grammar and Vocabulary of the Language of New Zealand*, London, 1820.

Levin, M., *J.S. Mill on Civilisation and Barbarism*, London, 2006.

Lévi-Strauss, C., *The Savage Mind*, Chicago, 1966.

Lineham, P., 'Tampering with the sacred text: The second edition of the Maori Bible', in P. Griffith, P. Hughes and A. Loney (eds), *A Book in the Hand: Essays on the history of the book in New Zealand*, Auckland 2000.

——, 'This is my weapon: Maori response to the Maori Bible', in R. Glen (ed.), *Mission and Moko: Aspects of the work of the Church Missionary Society in New Zealand, 1814–1882*, Christchurch, 1992.

Loughnan, R.A., *Royalty in New Zealand: The visit of Their Royal Highnesses the Duke and Duchess of Cornwall and York to New Zealand, 10th–27th June 1901: A descriptive narrative*, Wellington, 1902.

Lovell-Smith, M., 'Early mapping – Early mappers: 1642–1800', in *Te Ara: The Encyclopedia of New Zealand*, updated 1 March 2009, n.p.

Lowenberg, P.H., 'Variations in Malaysian English: The pragmatics of languages in contact', in J. Cheshire (ed.), *English Around the World: Sociolinguistic perspectives*, Cambridge, 1996.

Lowth, R., *Sermon Preached Before the Incorporated Society for the Propagation of the Gospel in Foreign Parts; At their anniversary meeting in the Parish Church of St Mary-Le-Bow, on Friday February 15, 1771. by ... Robert Lord Bishop of Oxford*, Oxford, 1771.

Lyotard, J-F., *The Postmodern Condition: A report on knowledge*, Manchester, 1983.

Maaka, R. and A. Fleras, 'Engaging with indigeneity: Tino rangatiratanga in Aotearoa', in D. Ivison, P. Patten, and W. Sanders (eds), *Political Theory and the Rights of Indigenous Peoples*, Cambridge, 2000.

Mackay, A., *A Compendium of Official Documents Relative to Native Affairs in the South Island*, vol. 1, Wellington, 1873.

Mackay, J., *The Spirit of Rangatiratanga and Other Ballads*, Melbourne, 1889.

Mackay, J.A., *Historic Poverty Bay and the East Coast, N.I., N.Z.*, Gisborne, 1949.

Macaulay to H.S. Randall, 23 May 1857, in T. Pinney (ed.), *The Letters of Thomas Babington Macaulay*, vol. 6, Cambridge, 1981.

Macaulay, T.B., 'Minute recorded in the General Department by Thomas Babington Macaulay, law member of the governor-general's council, date 2 February 1835', in M. Moir and L. Zastoupil (eds), *The Great Indian Education Debate: Documents relating to the Orientalist–Anglicist controversy, 1781–1843*, Oxford, 2013.

McDonald, F., *The Game of Our Lives*, Auckland, 1996.

Madden, D. (ed.), *The Collected Writing of Thomas DeQuincey*, vol. 2, London, 1896.

Mahmood, S., *A History of English Education in India*, Aligarh, 1895.

Makoni, S. and A. Pennycook (eds), *Disinventing and Reconstituting Languages*, Cleveland, 2007.

Malinowski, B., *Coral Gardens and Their Magic*, vol. 2, Indiana, 1965.

Malinowski, B., *Myth in Primitive Psychology*, London, 1926

Mangan J.A. (ed.), *Making Imperial Mentalities: Socialisation and British imperialism*, Manchester, 1990.

——, *The Imperial Curriculum: Racial images and education in the British colonial experience*, Oxford, 2012.

Marjoribanks, A., *Travels in New Zealand*, London, 1846.

Markham, E. (ed. E.H. McCormick), *New Zealand or Recollections of It*, Wellington, 1963.

Marshall, W.B., *A Personal Narrative of Two Visits to New Zealand*, London, 1836.

Martin, S.M.D., *New Zealand: In a series of letters*, London, 1845.

Martin, S., *The Taranaki Question*, 3rd edn, London, 1861.

Mataira, P.J., 'Mana and tapu: Sacred knowledge, sacred boundaries', in G. Harvey, *Indigenous Religions*, London, 2000.

Mathew, F. (ed. J. Rutherford), *The Founding of New Zealand: The journals of Felton Mathew, First Surveyor-General of New Zealand, and his wife, 1840–1847*, Dunedin, 1940.

Maunsell, R., *Grammar of the New Zealand Language*, Auckland, 1842.

Maunsell, R., in Encl. 2 in 91, in Grey, G. to Newcastle, 10 June 1853, in *GBPP 1854*, London, 1854.

May, H., B. Kaur and L. Prochner, *Empire, Education, and Indigenous Childhoods: Nineteenth-century missionary infant schools in three British colonies*, Farnham, Surrey, 2014.

May, S., 'Māori-medium education in Aotearoa/New Zealand', in J.W. Tollefson and A.B.M. Tsui (eds), *Medium of Instruction Policies: Which agenda? Whose agenda?*, New Jersey, 2008.

May, S., *Language and Minority Rights: Nationalism and the politics of language*, 2nd edn, New York, 2012.

McCan, D., *Whatiwhatihoe: The Waikato Raupatu Claim*, Wellington 2001.

McCarthy, M., 'Raising a Māori child under a New Right state', in P. Te Whaiti, M. McCarthy and A. Durie (eds), *Mai i Rangiātea: Māori wellbeing and development*, Auckland, 1997.

McGeorge, C., 'Race, empire and the Māori in the New Zealand primary school curriculum, 1880–1940', in J.A. Mangan (ed.), *The Imperial Curriculum: Racial images and education in the British colonial experience*, Oxford, 2012.

McGregor, R., *Imagined Destinies: Aboriginal Australians and the doomed race theory, 1880 –1939*, Melbourne, 1997.

McKay, R.A. (ed.), *A History of Printing in New Zealand, 1830–1940*, Wellington, 1940.

McKenzie, D.F., *Oral Culture, Literacy and Print in Early New Zealand: The Treaty of Waitangi*, Wellington, 1985.

McLean, D., 21 July 1854, evidence before the Committee on the New Zealand Company's Debt, Votes and Proceedings of the House of Representatives, in *AJHR*, 1854, Session I-II.

——, in *NZPD*, vol. 28, 15 September 1875.

McNab, R., *From Tasman to Marsden: A history of Northern New Zealand from 1642 to 1818*, Dunedin, 1914.

——, *Murihiku: A history of the South Island of New Zealand and the islands adjacent and lying to the south from 1642 to 1835*, Wellington, 1909.

McNab, R. (ed.), *Historical Records of New Zealand*, vol. 1, Wellington, 1908.

McRae, J., 'From Māori oral traditions to print', in P. Griffith, R. Harvey and K. Maslen (eds), *Book & Print in New Zealand: A guide to print culture in Aotearoa*, Wellington, 1997.

McRae, J., 'Māori oral tradition meets the book', in P. Griffith, P. Hughes and A. Loney (eds), *A Book in the Hand: Essays on the history of the book in New Zealand*, Auckland, 2000.

Mead, H.M., *Ngā Pēpeha a Ngā Tīpuna*, Wellington, 2007.

Mead, S.M. (ed.), *Landmarks, Bridges and Visions: Aspects of Māori culture*, Wellington, 1997.

Mercer, N. and J. Swann, (eds), *Learning English: Development and diversity*, Oxford, 1996.

Metcalf, T.R., *Ideologies of the Raj*, Cambridge, 1995.

Metge, J., *Rautahi: The Māori of New Zealand*, London, 2004.

Middleton, A., *Te Puna: A New Zealand mission station*, New York, 2008.

Mill, J.S., *Autobiography*, London, 1873 (London, 1995).

——, *Utilitarianism*, London, 1863, in M. Warnock (ed.), *Utilitarianism, On Liberty, Essay on Bentham*, Glasgow, 1986.

Milligan, R.R.D. (ed. J. Dunmore), *The Map Drawn by the Chief Tuki-Tahua in 1793*, Mangonui, 1964.

Milton, J., *Areopagitica: A Speech to the Parliament of England, for the Liberty of Unlicensed Printing*, London, 1644.

Mitchell, W.J.T., *Iconology: Image, text, ideology*, Chicago, 1987.

Moir, M. and L. Zastoupil (eds), *The Great Indian Education Debate: Documents relating to the Orientalist–Anglicist controversy, 1781–1843*, Oxford, 2013.

Moon, P., *A Savage Country: The untold story of New Zealand in the 1820s*, Auckland, 2012.

——, *Encounters: The creation of New Zealand: A history*, Auckland, 2013.

——, *Ngapua: The political life of Hone Heke Ngapua MHR*, Auckland, 2006.

——, *The Voyagers: Remarkable European explorations of New Zealand*, Auckland, 2014.

——, *Tohunga: Hohepa Kereopa*, Auckland, 2003.

Moorehead, A., *The Fatal Impact: An account of the invasion of the South Pacific, 1767–1840*, Harmondsworth, 1968.

Morgan J. in Encl. 2 in 91, in Grey, G. to Newcastle, 10 June 1853, in *GBPP 1854*, London, 1854.

Morley, W., *The History of Methodism in New Zealand*, Wellington, 1900.

Morton, H.B., *Recollections of Early New Zealand*, Auckland, 1925.

Muhlhausler, P., '"Reducing" Pacific languages to writings', in J.E. Joseph and T.T. Taylor (eds), *Ideologies of Language*, Oxford, 2014.

Mulholland, M. and V.M.H. Tawhai (eds), *Weeping Waters: The Treaty of Waitangi and constitutional change*, Wellington, 2010.

Müller, F.M., *A History of Ancient Sanskrit Literature*, London, 1860.

Mundy, G.C., *Our Antipodes, or, Residence and rambles in the Australasian colonies*, vol. 2, London, 1852.

Mutu, M., 'Constitutional intentions: The Treaty texts', in M. Mulholland and V.M.H. Tawhai (eds), *Weeping Waters: The Treaty of Waitangi and constitutional change*, Wellington, 2010.

Mutu, M., 'The Humpty Dumpty principle at work', in S. Fenton (ed.), *For Better or Worse: Translation as a tool for change in the South Pacific*, Oxford, 2004.

Narborough J. et al., *An Account of Several Late Voyages & Discoveries to the South and North ...*, London, 1694.

Native Schools [In Continuation of E.-2, 1892.], in *AJHR*, 1893, Session I, E-02.

Negrine, R., *Politics and the Mass Media in Britain*, London, 1994.

New Zealand Parliamentary Library, *The Origins of the Māori Seats*, Wellington, May 2009.

Ngata, A., *The Price of Citizenship: Ngarimu V.C.*, Wellington, 1943.

——, 'The Maori and printed matter', in R.A. McKay (ed.), *A History of Printing in New Zealand, 1830-1940*, Wellington, 1940.

Ngata A. (trans. P.T.H. Jones), *Ngā Mōteatea: The songs*, Auckland, 2004.

Ngatata, W.T., *NZPD*, vol. 13, 15 October 1872.

Nicholas, J.L., *Narrative of a Voyage to New Zealand*, vol. 2, London, 1817.

Nietzsche, F., *Beyond Good and Evil*, Cambridge, 2002.

——, *Daybreak: Thoughts on the prejudices of morality*, Cambridge, 1997.

Nietzsche, F., *On the Genealogy of Morals*, New York (1887), 1923.

Normanby to W. Hobson, 14 August 1839, in *GBPP 1840*, vol. 238, London, 1840.

O'Brien, E.M., *The Foundation of Australia, 1786-1800*, London, 1937.

O'Halloran, K.L., 'Multimodal discourse analysis', in K. Hyland and B. Paltridge (eds), *Continuum Companion to Discourse Analysis*, London, 2011.

O'Malley, V., *Agents of Autonomy: Māori committees in the nineteenth century*, Wellington, 1997.

Ogilby, J., *America: Being the latest, and most accurate description of the New World*, London, 1671.

Olson, D.R., *The World on Paper: The conceptual and cognitive implications of writing and reading*, Cambridge, 1998.

Ong, W.J., *Orality and Literacy: The technologizing of the word*, London, 1982.

Orange, C., *The Treaty of Waitangi*, Wellington, 2011.

Orwell, G., *1984*, London, 1949.

Paetahi, M., 19 July 1870, in *NZPD*, 1870.

Palmer, P., *Language and Conquest in Early Modern Ireland: English Renaissance literature and Elizabethan imperial expansion*, Cambridge, 2004.

Parata, W., *NZPD*, 1903.

Parkinson, P., 'Strangers in the House': The Māori language in government and the Māori language in parliament 1865-1900*, Wellington, 2001.

Parkinson, S., *A Journal of a Voyage to the South Seas*, London, 1773.

Paterson, L., 'Kiri mā, kiri mangu: The terminology of race and civilisation in the mid-nineteenth-century Māori-language newspapers', in J. Curnow, N. Hopa and J. McRae (eds), *Rere Atu, Taku Manu: Discovering history, language and politics in the Māori-language newspapers*, Auckland, 2002.

Paterson, L., *Colonial Discourses: Niupepa Māori 1855-1863*, Dunedin, 2006.

Patterson, J., in *NZPD*, 1868, vol. 2.

Paulston, C.B. and K. Heidemann, 'Language policies and the education of linguistic minorities', in Ricento T. (ed.), *An Introduction to Language Policy: Theory and method*, Oxford, 2006.

Pennycook, A., *English and the Discourses of Colonialism*, London, 1998.

——, *The Cultural Politics of English as an International Language*, Harlow, 1994.

Pere, J., 'Oral tradition and tribal history', in R. Selby and A. Laurie, *Māori and Oral History: A collection*, Wellington, 2005.

Petersen, D.L., 'The Bible in public view', in F.R. Ames and C.W. Miller (eds), *Foster Biblical Scholarship: Essays in honor of Kent Harold Richards*, Atlanta, 2010.

Petition of Hone Heke, in *AJHR*, 1893, Session I, I-03.

Petition of the Federated Maori Assembly of New Zealand, in *AJHR*, 1893, Session I, J-01.

Petition of Wi Te Hakiro and 336 others, in *AJHR*, 1876, Session I, J-04.

Petrie, H., *Chiefs of Industry: Māori tribal enterprise in early colonial New Zealand*, Auckland, 2006.

Phillipson, R., *Linguistic Imperialism*, Oxford, 1992.

Pietikainen, S. and H. Kelly-Holmes (eds), *Multilingualism and the Periphery*, Oxford, 2013.

Pinney, T. (ed.), *Essays of George Eliot*, Columbia, 1963.

——, *The Letters of Thomas Babington Macaulay*, vol. 6, Cambridge, 1981.

Piripi, H., 'Te Tiriti o Waitangi and the New Zealand public sector', in V.M.H. Tawhai and K. Grey-Sharp (eds), *'Always Speaking': The Treaty of Waitangi and public policy*, Wellington, 2011.

Polack, J.S., *Manners and Customs of the New Zealanders*, vol. 1, London, 1840.

——, *New Zealand: Being a narrative of travels and adventures during a residence in that country between the years 1831 and 1837*, vol. 2, London, 1838.

Pompallier, J.B.F., *Early History of the Catholic Church in Oceania*, Auckland, 1888.

Pool, D.I., *The Maori Population of New Zealand: 1769–1971*, Auckland, 1977.

Pope, J.H., *Lessons in Reading and Spelling for Use in Native Schools*, Wellington, 1884.

Porter F. (ed.), *The Turanga Journals, 1840–1850: The letters and journals of William and Jane Williams*, Wellington, 1974.

Porter, A. (ed.), *The Imperial Horizons of British Protestant Missions 1880–1914*, Michigan, 2003.

Porter, A., *Religion Versus Empire? British Protestant missionaries and overseas expansion, 1700–1914*, Manchester, 2004.

Power, W.T., *Sketches in New Zealand*, London, 1849.

Pratt, J. and J.J. Pratt, *Memoir of the Rev. Josiah Pratt, B.D., late Vicar of St. Stephen's, Coleman Street, and for twenty-one years Secretary of the Church Missionary Society*, London, 1849.

Pugh, A.K., 'A history of English teaching', in N. Mercer and J. Swann (eds), *Learning English: Development and diversity*, Oxford, 1996.

Pybus, T.A., *Maori and Missionary: Early Christian missions in the South Island of New Zealand*, Wellington, 1954.

Raffles, S., *Memoir of the Life and Public Services of Sir Thomas Stamford Raffles*, London, 1830.

Ramsden, E., *Marsden and the Missions*, Sydney, 1936.

Reed, A.H. (ed.), *Early Maoriland Adventures of J.W. Stack*, Dunedin, 1935.

Reiss, T.J., *Knowledge, Discovery and Imagination in Early Modern Europe: The rise of aesthetic rationalism*, Cambridge, 1997.

Rewi, P., *Whaikōrero: The world of Māori oratory*, Auckland, 2013.

Ricento, T. (ed.), *An Introduction to Language Policy: Theory and method*, Oxford, 2006.

Rich, P.B., *Race and Empire in British Politics*, Cambridge, 1990.

Richards, R., *Murihiku Re-Viewed: A revised history of Southern New Zealand from 1804 to 1844*, Wellington, 1995.

Richmond, J.C., in *NZPD*, 1867.

Ricoeur, P., 'Hermeneutics and structuralism', in E. Kurzweil (ed.), *The Age of Structuralism: From Lévi-Strauss to Foucault*, New Brunswick, 1996.

Risager, K., *Language and Culture: Global flows and local complexity*, Clevedon, 2006.

Robert, D.L. (ed.), *Converting Colonialism: Visions and realities in mission history, 1706–1914*, Michigan, 2008.

Roberts, P.A., *From Oral to Literate Culture: Colonial Experience in the English West Indies*, Kingston, 1997.

Rogers, L.M. (ed.), *The Early Journals of Henry Williams*, Christchurch, 1961.

Rolleston, W., 'Papers relative to Native Schools', in *AJHR*, 1867, Session I, A-03.

Rosevear, W., *Waiapu: The story of a diocese*, Hamilton, 1960.

Rosier, L. 'Crawford, James Coutts', in *Dictionary of New Zealand Biography*, Wellington, June 2013.

Rostow, W.W., 'The stages of economic growth', in P. Worsley (ed.), *Modern Sociology*, London, 1988.

Rostow, W.W., *The Stages of Economic Growth: A non-communist manifesto*, Cambridge, 1960.

Rule, J., 'Vernacular literacy in the Western and Lower Southern Highlands provinces: A case study of a mission's involvement', in S.A. Wurm (ed.), *New Guinea Area Languages and Language Study*, vol. 3, Department of Linguistics, Research School of Pacific Studies, Australian National University, Canberra, 1977.

Rusden, G.W., *History of New Zealand*, vol. 1, London, 1883.

Salesa, D.I., *Racial Crossings: Race, intermarriage, and the Victorian British Empire*, Oxford, 2011.

Salmond, A., *Between Worlds: Early exchanges between Māori and Europeans 1773–1815*, Auckland, 1997.

Sanga, J., 'Remembering', in H. Laracy (ed.), *Ples Blong Iumi: Solomon Islands, the past four thousand years*, Suva, 1989.

Savage, J., *Some Account of New Zealand Particularly the Bay of Islands and Surrounding Country with a description of the religion, arts, manufactures, manners and customs of the natives*, London, 1807.

Scherzer, K., *Narrative of the Circumnavigation of the Globe by the Austrian Frigate Novara, 1857–59*, vol. 3, London, 1863.

Schmidt, O., *The Doctrine of Descent and Darwinism*, London, 1875.

Scholefield, G.H. (ed.), *The Richmond-Atkinson Papers*, vol. 1, Wellington, 1960.

——, *The Richmond-Atkinson Papers*, vol. 2, Wellington, 1961.

Schutz, A.J., *The Voices of Eden: A history of Hawaiian language studies*, Honolulu, 1994.

Schwimmer, E. (ed.), *The Maori People in the Nineteen-sixties*, Auckland, 1972.

Scott, D., *The Parihaka Story*, Auckland, 1954.

Selby, R. and A. Laurie, *Māori and Oral History: A collection*, Wellington, 2005.

Selwyn, G., *Annals of the Diocese of New Zealand*, London, 1847.

Selwyn, S.H., *Reminiscences, 1809–1867*, Auckland, 1961.

Sharp, A., *The Voyages of Abel Janszoon Tasman*, Oxford, 1968.

Shaw, Saville & Co., *The New Zealand Handbook*, 11th edn, London, 1866.

Sheehan, J., in *NZPD*, vol. 21, 11 August 1876.

Shortland, E., *A Short Sketch of the Maori Races*, Dunedin, 1865.

——, *Maori Religion and Mythology*, London, 1882.

——, *Traditions and Superstitions of the New Zealanders: With illustrations of their manners and customs*, 2nd edn, London, 1856.

Simpson, K.A., 'Tasman, Abel Janszoon 1602/1603? – 1659?', in *Dictionary of New Zealand Biography*, n.p.

Sinclair, K., *A Destiny Apart: New Zealand's search for national identity*, Wellington, 1986.

——, *A History of New Zealand*, Auckland, 1988.

Sinclair, K. (ed.), *The Oxford Illustrated History of New Zealand*, Auckland, 1990.

Sivasundaram, S., 'Redeeming memory: The martyrdoms of Captain James Cook and Reverend John Williams', in G. Williams (ed.), *Captain Cook: Explorations and reassessments*, Suffolk, 2004.

Smelser, N.J., 'The modernization of social relations', in M. Weiner (ed.), *Modernization: The dynamics of growth*, New York, 1966.

Smelser, N.J. and S.M. Lipset (eds), *Social Structure and Mobility in Economic Development*, New Brunswick, 2005.

Smith, B., *European Vision and the South Pacific*, New Haven, 1985.

Smith, E.D., *Globalisation, Utopia, and Post-Colonial Science Fiction*, London, 2012.

Smith, W., *Journal of a Voyage in the Missionary Ship* Duff, *to the Pacific Ocean in the years 1796, 7, 8, 9, 1800, 1, 2, &c.*, New York, 1813.

Smyth, P., *Maori Pronunciation and the Evolution of Written Maori*, Christchurch, 1946.

Sorrenson, M.P.K., 'A history of Maori representation in parliament', in *Report on the Royal Commission on the Electoral System*, Wellington, 1986.

——, *Ko Te Whenua Te Utu, Land is the Price: Essays on Maori history, land and politics*, Auckland, 2014.

——, *Maori Origins and Migrations: The genesis of some Pakeha myths and legends*, Auckland, 1993.

Spivak, G.C., *The Post-Colonial Critic: Interviews, strategies, dialogues*, London, 1990.

Spolsky, B., *Language Management*, Cambridge, 2009.

St. John's College, 'Rules for St John's Native Teachers' School', *The Calendar of St John's College New Zealand*, Auckland 1846.

Stack, J.W., *South Island Maoris: A sketch of their history and legendary lore*, Christchurch, 1898.

Stafford, J. and M. Williams, *Maoriland: New Zealand literature, 1872–1914*, Wellington, 2006.

Stanley, B., *The Bible and the Flag: Protestant missions and British imperialism in the nineteenth and twentieth centuries*, Leicester, 1992.

Statement of Operations Under the 'Native Schools Act 1867', in *AJHR*, 1868, Session I, A-06a.

Statistics New Zealand, 'Principal Results for 1858 Census, Aboriginal Native Population – Appendix H', Wellington, n.d.

——, 'Statistics of New Zealand, 1867', in *Census Results and General Statistics of New Zealand for 1867, Report to the Honourable Edward William Stafford, Colonial Secretary*, Wellington, 1867.

——, *New Zealand Long Term Data Series, Population*, 5 March 2008.

——, *2012 New Zealand Official Yearbook*, Wellington, 2013.

Steele, R., *The Dramatic Works of Sir Richard Steele, Knt*, London, 1761.

Steinberg, S.H., *Five Hundred Years of Printing*, Bristol, 1961.

Stephens, M., 'A house with many rooms: Rediscovering Māori as a civic language in the wake of the Maori Language Act (1987)', in R. Higgins, P. Rewi and V. Olsen-Reeder (eds), *The Value of the Māori Language: Te Hua o te Reo Māori*, Wellington, 2014.

Stevens, J., *The New Zealand Novel, 1860–1965*, Wellington, 1966.

Stilz, G. (ed.), *Missions of Interdependence: A literary directory*, New York, 2002.

Stock, E., *The History of the Church Missionary Society in New Zealand*, Wellington, 1935.

Strong, R., *Anglicanism and the British Empire, c. 1700–1850*, Oxford, 2007.

Swainson, W., *New Zealand and Its Colonization*, London, 1859.

Taiaroa, H.K., in *NZPD*, 6 October 1871.

Tau, T.M. (ed.), *I whānau au ki Kaiapoi: The story of Natanahira Waruwarutu as recorded by Thomas Green*, Dunedin, 2011.

Tauroa H., and P. Tauroa, *Te Marae: A guide to customs and protocol*, Auckland, 1986.

Tawhai, V.M.H. and K. Grey-Sharp (eds), *'Always Speaking': The Treaty of Waitangi and public policy*, Wellington, 2011.

Taylor, R., *Te Ika a Maui, or New Zealand and its inhabitants*, London, 1855.

Te Awekotuku, N., 'Moko Māori: An understanding of pain', in J. Hendry and L. Fitznor (eds), *Anthropologists, Indigenous Scholars and the Research Endeavour: Seeking bridges towards mutual respect*, New York, 2012.

Te Rito, J.S., B. Duffin, P. Fletcher and J. Sinclair (eds), *Tihei Oreore*, vol. 1, no. 1, December 2005.

Te Taura Whiri i te Reo Māori, *He Pātaka Kupu: Te Kai a te Rangatira*, Auckland, 2008.

Te Whāiti, P., M. McCarthy and A. Durie (eds), *Mai i Rangiātea: Māori wellbeing and development*, Auckland, 1997.

Tennent, M. (ed.), *Training for the New Millennium: Pedagogies for translation and interpreting*, Amsterdam, 2005.

Terry, C., *New Zealand: Its advantages and prospects as a British colony*, London, 1843.

The Aborigines Protection Society to the Earl of Derby, 12 October 1883, and sub-enclosure, 16 July 1883, in *AJHR*, 1884, Session I, A-02.

The Bicultural Commission of the Anglican Church on the Treaty of Waitangi/Te Ripoata a te Komihana mo te Kaupapa Tikanga Rua mo te Tiriti o Waitangi, *The Report of the Bicultural Commission of the Anglican Church on the Treaty of Waitangi*, Christchurch, 1986.

The Cyclopedia Company, *The Cyclopedia of New Zealand: Industrial, descriptive, historical, biographical, facts, figures, illustrations*, Wellington, 1897.

The Society for Promoting Christian Knowledge, *Domestic Scenes in New Zealand*, 2nd edn, London (1845) 1857.

Thomas, N., 'Colonial conversations: Difference, hierarchy and history in early twentieth-century evangelical propaganda', in C. Hall (ed.), *Cultures of Empire: A reader*, Manchester, 2000.

——, *Colonialism's Culture: Anthropology, travel and government*, Princeton, 1994.

Thomas, N., H. Guest and M. Dettelbach (eds), *Observations Made during a Voyage round the World: Johann Reinhold Forster, 1729–1798*, Honolulu, 1996.

Thompson, J.B. (ed.), *Paul Ricoeur: Hermeneutics and the Human Sciences: Essays on Language, Action and Interpretation*, Cambridge, 1998.

Thomson, A.S., *The Story of New Zealand: Past and present, savage and civilized*, vol. 1, London, 1859.

Thomson, J.T., *Rambles with a Philosopher*, Dunedin, 1867.

Thornton, A., *Māori Oral Literature as Seen by a Classicist*, Wellington, 1999.

Thornton, J., in *AJHR*, 1906, Session II, G-05.

Threadgold, T., *Feminist Poetics: Poiesis, performance, histories*, London, 1997.

Tollefson, J.W. and A.B.M. Tsui (eds), *Medium of Instruction Policies: Which agenda? Whose agenda?*, New Jersey, 2008.

Tregear, E., *The Aryan Maori*, Wellington, 1885.

Tucker, H.W., *Memoir of the Life and Episcopate of George Augustus Selwyn*, vol. 1, London, 1879.

Tukairangi, P., 30 November 1864, in 'Letters from Native Chiefs to Mr. Fitzgerald M.H.R. Relative to their Admission into the General Assembly', in *AJHR*, 1864, I, E-15.

Turner, G., *Nineteen Years in Polynesia*, London, 1861.

Turner, J.G., *The Pioneer Missionary: Life of the Rev. Nathaniel Turner, Missionary in New Zealand, Tonga, and Australia*, Melbourne, 1872.

Two Acts passed by the General Assembly of New Zealand, 1858, relating to native affairs, namely: the Native Districts Regulation Act; and the Native Circuit Courts Act. He Ture hou, erua, i whakatakotoria e te Runanga Nui o Niu Tirani, 1858. Ara; Ko te Ture whakakoto Ture-iti ki nga Takiwa Māori, ko te Ture whakarite Kooti Maori, Auckland, 1859.

van Dijk, T.A., *Elite Discourse and Racism*, Newbury Park, 1993.

Venn, J. and J.A. Venn, *Alumni Cantabrigienses from the Earliest Times to 1900*, vol. 4, Cambridge, 1927.

Vercoe, A.E., *Educating Jake: Pathways to empowerment*, Auckland, 1998.

Viswanathan, G., *Masks of Conquest: Literary study and British rule in India*, New York, 1989.

von Hochstetter, F., *New Zealand: Its physical geography, geology and natural history*, Stuttgart, 1867.

von Hügel, C. (trans. and ed. Dymphna Clark), *New Holland Journal, November 1833–October 1834*, Melbourne, 1994.

Wade, W., *A Journey in the Northern Island of New Zealand*, Hobart, 1842.

Wakefield, E.G., *A View of the Art of Colonization, with Present Reference to the British Empire: In letters between a statesman and a colonist*, London, 1849.

Wakefield, E.J., *Adventure in New Zealand from 1839 to 1844*, vol. 1, London, 1845.

Walker, R.J., *He Tipua: The life and times of Sir Apirana Ngata*, Auckland, 2002.

Walker, R., 'Quality assurance in tertiary education from a Māori (indigenous) perspective', in J.S. Te Rito, B. Duffin, P. Fletcher and J. Sinclair (eds), *Tihei Oreore*, vol. 1, no. 1, December 2005.

Walker, R., *Ka Whawhai Tonu Matou: Struggle without end*, Auckland, 1990.

Wallerstein, I., *The Capitalist World-Economy*, Cambridge, 1979.

Wanhalla, A., *Matters of the Heart: A history of interracial marriage in New Zealand*, Auckland, 2013.

Ward, A., *A Show of Justice: Racial 'amalgamation' in nineteenth century New Zealand*, Toronto, 1973.

Ward, J., *Supplementary Information Relative to New Zealand*, London, 1840.

Ward, R., *Life Among the Maories of New Zealand*, London, 1872.

Warnock, M. (ed.), *Utilitarianism, On Liberty, Essay on Bentham*, Glasgow, 1986.

Waters, A. (ed.), *American Indian Thought*, Victoria, 2004.

Watkins, J., *He Puka Ako i te Korero Maori*, Mangungu, 1841, ATL, BIM 99.

Waymouth, J., 'Parliamentary representation for Māori: Debate and ideology in *Te Wananga* and *Te Waka Maori o Niu Tirani*, 1874–78', in J. Curnow, N. Hopa and J. McRae (eds), *Rere Atu, Taku Manu: Discovering history, language and politics in the Māori-language newspapers*, Auckland, 2002.

Webster, J., *Reminiscences of an Old Settler in Australia and New Zealand*, Christchurch, 1908.

Weiner, M. (ed.), *Modernization: The dynamics of growth*, New York, 1966.

Wells, B., *The History of Taranaki: A standard work on the history of the province*, New Plymouth, 1878.

Weston, J., *Ko Meri, or, Cycle of Cathay: A story of New Zealand life*, London, 1890.

Whaitiri, R., 'A sovereign mission: Māori maids, maidens and mothers', in G. Stilz (ed.), *Missions of Interdependence: A literary directory*, New York, 2002.

Wharton, W.J.L. (ed.), *Captain Cook's Journal during His First Voyage Round the World*, Cambridge, 2014.

White, J., *Maori Customs and Superstitions*, Auckland, 1885.

White, R., *The Middle Ground: Indians, empires and republics in the Great Lakes region 1630–1815*, Cambridge, 1991.

Wilderspin, S., *Early Discipline Illustrated; or, The infant system prospering and successful*, London, 1832.

Williams, C.P., 'The Church Missionary Society and the indigenous church in the second half of the nineteenth century: The defense and destruction of the Venn ideals', in D.L. Robert (ed.), *Converting Colonialism: Visions and realities in mission history, 1706–1914*, Michigan, 2008.

Williams, F.W., *Through Ninety Years, 1826–1916, Life and Work Among the Maoris in New Zealand: Notes of the lives of William and William Leonard Williams, First and Third Bishops of Waiapu*, Auckland, 1939.

Williams, G. (ed.), *Captain Cook: Explorations and reassessments*, Suffolk, 2004.

Williams, G., '"As befits our age, there are no more heroes": Reassessing Captain Cook', in G. Williams (ed.), *Captain Cook: Explorations and reassessments*, Suffolk, 2004.

Williams, H.W., *A Dictionary of the Maori Language*, Wellington (1917), 1957.

Williams, J.A., *Politics of the New Zealand Maori: Protest and cooperation, 1891–1909*, Auckland, 1969.

Williams, L., *Lessons in the English Language for Maori Schools*, Wellington, 1875.

Williams, W., *Christianity among the New Zealanders*, London, 1867.

Williams, W. (ed. F. Porter), *The Turanga Journals, 1840–1850*, Wellington, 1974.

Williams, W.L., *East Coast (N.Z.) Historical Records*, Gisborne, 1932.

Wilson, J.A., *Missionary Life and Work in New Zealand, 1833–1862*, Auckland, 1889.

——, *The Story of Te Waharoa: A chapter in early New Zealand history, together with sketches of ancient Maori life and history*, Christchurch, 1907.

Wilson, O., *War in the Tussock: Te Kooti and the Battle at Te Porere*, Wellington, 1961.

Wohlers, J.F.H., *Memoirs of the Life of J.F.H. Wohlers, Missionary at Ruapuke, New Zealand*, Dunedin, 1895.

Woodward D. and G. Malcolm (eds), *Cartography in the Traditional African, American, Arctic, Australian, and Pacific Societies*, Chicago, 1995.

Worsley, P. (ed.), *Modern Sociology*, London, 1988.

Wright, M.H., *New Zealand 1769–1840: Early years of Western contact*, Cambridge, Mass., 1959.

Wurm, S.A. (ed.), *New Guinea Area Languages and Language Study*, vol. 3, Department of Linguistics, Research School of Pacific Studies, Australian National University, Canberra, 1977.

Yate, W., *An Account of New Zealand; and of the Formation and Progress of the Church Missionary Society's Mission in the Northern Island*, 2nd edn, London, 1835.

Young, R.J.C., *Colonial Desire: Hybridity in theory, culture and race*, London, 1994.

Ziff, B. and P.V. Rao (eds), *Borrowed Power: Essays on cultural appropriation*, New Brunswick, 1997.

Zmarzlik, H-G., 'Social Darwinism in Germany: An example of the sociopolitical abuse of scientific knowledge', in G. Altner (ed.), *Human Creature*, Garden City, 1974.

Index